Macroeconomic Policies for EU Accession

Published in Association with the Central Bank of the Republic of Turkey

Macroeconomic Policies for EU Accession

Edited by

Erdem Başçı

Vice Governor of the Central Bank of the Republic of Turkey

Sübidey Togan

Professor of Economics, Director of the Centre for International Economics, Bilkent University, Turkey

Jürgen von Hagen

Professor of Economics, University of Bonn, Germany, Indiana University, USA and CEPR

Edward Elgar

Cheltenham, UK • Northampton, MA, USA

Published by
Edward Elgar Publishing Limited
Glensanda House
Montpellier Parade
Cheltenham
Glos GL50 1UA
UK

Edward Elgar Publishing, Inc.
William Pratt House
9 Dewey Court
Northampton
Massachusetts 01060
USA

A catalogue record for this book
is available from the British Library

Library of Congress Control Number: 2006048159

ISBN 978 1 84720 000 6

Printed and bound in Great Britain by MPG Books Ltd, Bodmin, Cornwall

Contents

Contributors

Erdem Başçı, Vice Governor, Central Bank of the Republic of Turkey

Hakan Berument, Associate Professor, Department of Economics, Bilkent University, Turkey

Marco Buti, Director, Directorate-General for Economic and Financial Affairs, European Commission

Fabio Canova, ICREA Research Professor, UPF, Italy, CREI, AMeN and CEPR

Omar Choudhry, Graduate Student, Department of Economics, University of California, Berkeley, USA

Barry Eichengreen, Professor, Department of Economics, University of California, Berkeley, USA

Hasan Ersel, Associate Professor, Graduate School of Management, Sabancı University, Turkey

Carlo Favero, Professor, Department of Economics, Bocconi University and CEPR, Italy

Paul De Grauwe, Professor, Faculty of Economics and Applied Economics, Catholic University Leuven, Belgium

Ricardo Hausmann, Professor, Kennedy School of Government, Harvard University, USA

Ali Hakan Kara, Deputy Director General, Research Department, Central Bank of the Republic of Turkey

Anne O. Krueger, Special Advisor to the Managing Director, International Monetary Fund, former First Deputy Managing Director, IMF

Ali M. Kutan, Professor, Department of Economics and Finance, Southern Illinois University, Edwardsville, USA

Manfred J.M. Neumann, Professor, Director, IIW – University of Bonn, Germany

Lucjan T. Orlowski, Chairman, Department of Economics and Finance, Sacred Heart University, USA

Fatih Özatay, Dean, Faculty of Economics and Administrative Sciences, TOBB University of Economics and Technology, Turkey, former Vice Governor, Central Bank of the Republic of Turkey

Graham C. Scott, Principal, Graham Scott (NZ) Ltd, former Secretary to the Treasury in New Zealand

Süreyya Serdengeçti, Director, Stability Institute, TOBB University of Economics and Technology and Economic Policy Research Institute, Turkey, former Governor, Central Bank of the Republic of Turkey

Fatma Taşkın, Associate Professor, Department of Economics, Bilkent University, Turkey

Sübidey Togan, Professor of Economics, Director, Centre for International Economics, Bilkent University, Turkey

Pierre van der Haegen, Director General, International and European Relations – ECB

Jürgen von Hagen, Professor of Economics, University of Bonn, Germany, Indiana University, USA and CEPR

Max Watson, Economic Adviser (Eastern Europe) in Directorate-General for Economic and Financial Affairs, European Commission

Taner M. Yiğit, Assistant Professor, Department of Economics, Bilkent University, Turkey

Preface and acknowledgements

Aiming at reviewing the macroeconomic aspects and challenges of EU accession for the Turkish economy, this book is the product of the compilation of eight papers and the panel discussion presented in the Macroeconomic Policies for EU Accession conference held in Ankara, Turkey on 6–7 May 2005. The conference was organized jointly by Bilkent University, Ankara, the Central Bank of the Republic of Turkey and the Centre for European Integration Studies at the University of Bonn, with the participation of leading experts from Turkey, several EU member states, the European Commission, the European Central Bank and the International Monetary Fund.

Key policy issues related to fiscal policy, monetary policy, euro adoption and the management of capital inflows constitute the bases of the studies. Moreover, the comments following each main paper reflect the discussions held during the conference.

We hope that this volume will contribute to the discussion on the challenges and opportunities of the EU accession process for Turkey as well as other prospective EU candidate countries.

The preparation of this volume owes much to the support, assistance and advice of many contributors. The contributions represent the views of the authors and do not necessarily reflect those of other conference participants or the organizing institutions.

We would like to express our special thanks to the authors and other contributors for their excellent work included in this volume. In addition to the authors, we are indebted to the three institutions, the Central Bank of the Republic of Turkey, Bilkent University and CEIS-University of Bonn, for support in the organization of the conference. We are grateful to Süreyya Serdengeçti, former Governor of the Central Bank of the Republic of Turkey, for his valuable guidance and contributions to the conference as well as Professor Manfred Neumann; Şükrü Binay, columnist and former Vice Governor of the Central Bank of the Republic of Turkey; Professor Bilsay Kuruç, former Member of the Board, Central Bank of the Republic of Turkey; Hansjörg Kretschmer, Head of the European Commission Representation to Turkey; Ahmet Tıktık, Undersecretary of State Planning Organization and Hugh Bredenkamp, IMF Resident Representative to Turkey for chairing the conference sessions. We also would like to thank the staff of the Central Bank of the Republic of Turkey, in particular the Protocol Division of the Foreign Relations Department for their essential efforts in the editing and preparation of this manuscript.

Erdem Başçı
Sübidey Togan
Jürgen von Hagen

Introduction

Erdem Başçı, Sübidey Togan and Jürgen von Hagen

After 50 years of inward-oriented development strategies, Turkey switched to outward-oriented policies in 1980. A new policy of opening up the economy has been pursued with the aim of integrating Turkey into the European Union (EU). At the Association Council Meeting in Brussels on 6 March 1995, Turkey and the EU agreed to form a customs union starting on 1 January 1996. Turkey's recognition as a candidate country for EU membership at the Helsinki European Council in December 1999 ushered in a new era in the relations between Turkey and the EU. After the approval of the Accession Partnership by the Council and the adoption of the Framework Regulation on 26 February 2001, the Turkish Government announced its own National Programme for the adoption of the *Acquis Communautaire* on 19 March 2001. In late 2004, another milestone was reached with the European Commission's recommendation that the European Council endorse the opening of formal accession negotiations and establish a timetable. The Copenhagen European Council, in December 2002, concluded that 'if the European Council in December 2004, on the basis of a report and a recommendation from the Commission, decides that Turkey fulfils the Copenhagen political criteria, the European Union will open accession negotiations with Turkey without delay'. The December 2004 Council decided to start membership talks with Turkey on 3 October 2005.

Although the process has been launched, significant uncertainties continue to prevail as to whether Turkey will be able to achieve its goal of accession to the EU. The ultimate outcome will only be revealed in the long term. What matters in the short to medium term is the impact that continued progress towards meeting the conditions for membership will have on Turkey. The EU is the focal point for reforms in a large number of policy areas, and the pre-accession process, which has been ongoing for several years, is a unique experiment in using international harmonization as a tool for implementing a comprehensive reform strategy.

The purpose of this volume is to highlight the macroeconomic aspects and challenges of EU accession for the Turkish economy. After being hit by the most severe crisis of its recent history in 2000–01, Turkey has shown a remarkable recovery. Inflation fell from 68.5 per cent in 2001 to 9.3 per cent in 2004, thanks to the maintenance of fiscal and monetary discipline. The fiscal deficit decreased from 20.9 per cent in 2001 to 6.2 per cent in 2004. After contracting by 9.5 per cent in 2001, real GNP expanded by 7.9 per cent in 2002, 5.9 per cent in 2003 and 9.9 per cent in 2004. The unemployment rate, after reaching 12.3 per cent in the first quarter of 2002, fell to 10.3 per cent in 2004 and the average interest rate on government debt declined from 96.2 per cent in 2001 to 25.7 per cent in 2004. The ratio of gross public debt to GDP is still high, but it fell from 102.6 per cent of GDP in 2001 to 80.2 per cent in 2003, and further to 78.4 per cent in 2004 as a result of significant income growth, the attainment of sizeable primary surpluses over the last three years, and an appreciation of the real exchange rate. At the same time, the net public debt to GNP ratio decreased from 90.5 per cent in 2001 to 63.5 per cent in 2004.

Turkey realizes that, in the long run, price stability and fiscal discipline create the best conditions for sustained and robust economic growth. As of 2005, the challenge Turkey faces is how to move from the current state of affairs to the one in which the Maastricht criteria are satisfied. The main issues are reducing the inflation rate to about 3 per cent, the public debt to GDP ratio to below 60 per cent and decreasing the unemployment rate while preserving the sustainability of public finances as well as the external account.

The chapters constituting this volume were presented at a conference on Macroeconomic Policies for EU Accession held in Ankara, Turkey, on 6–7 May 2005. The conference focused on four main issues: fiscal policy, monetary policy, euro adoption and the management of capital inflows. Below, we give a brief summary of the chapters which are grouped under the same headings.

In Chapter 2, Jürgen von Hagen analyses fiscal policies and the sustainability of public finances in the EU. The author first evaluates the strength and weaknesses of the fiscal institutions of the EU. These institutions, though not perfect, were put in place as essential supporting elements of the European Monetary Union. He then criticizes the recent modifications to the Excessive Deficit Procedure, which has been put in place as a mechanism to enforce the Stability and Growth Pact.

EU countries experienced strong fiscal consolidations between 1998 and 2003. This has widely been attributed to the Stability and Growth Pact. Von Hagen, however, argues that a significant part of the improvements observed in the primary surplus ratios is a result of strong output growth experienced during this period. After filtering out the growth effects, the consolidation efforts are not all that impressive.

Furthermore, von Hagen studies the 'quality' of fiscal adjustments in the EU countries, that is, their contribution to medium-term growth. He argues that, on the revenue side, direct taxes hurt output growth more than indirect taxes do. Likewise, on the expenditure side, higher investment spending and lower amounts of current expenditures and transfers would be better for growth. Empirical data from the past 10 years support this argument. Von Hagen concludes that maintaining a 'high quality' of fiscal policies is an essential precondition for the sustainability of public finances in the European Monetary Union, but one that has been neglected in the policy debate so far.

In Chapter 3, Graham C. Scott considers fiscal policy challenges and the sustainability of public finances in Turkey. He emphasizes that Turkey's fiscal policy rapidly went into crisis in 2000–01 due mainly to real interest rates rising to levels well in excess of the rate of economic growth and because government policies and weak fiscal institutions had rendered the government's financial position very vulnerable to disturbances in the economy and financial markets. In subsequent years, there have been remarkable improvements in this situation. The recovery was based on vigorous fiscal corrections leading to large primary surpluses. The author stresses that sustaining a fiscal framework that promotes growth, stability and social and political cohesion will require the design and implementation of an agenda of change in key fiscal institutions over the medium term, aimed at bringing these up to international standards of performance in supporting strategy, policy, greater efficiency and effectiveness in service provision and greater democratic accountability.

Turkey's past experiences show how difficult it can be to sustain a comprehensive, acceptable and determined initiative to reform fiscal institutions. The prospect of admission to the EU will, in the long term, have a significant influence on Turkey's fiscal policy, but it will not be decisive over the time period in which the authorities' endeavours will be tested with regard to the implementation of the new laws and other initiatives that are under way. Revenue policies, budget institutions, external surveillance, agricultural and regional policies will be influential, although the major influence will be through the growth-enhancing prospects of EU membership. Prosperity within the EU will be best assured by adopting fiscal policies and modern fiscal institutions that match the best anywhere and are better than those found in some EU economies, including some of the developed ones. Turkey should learn lessons from other EU accession countries in order to develop its fiscal policies in ways that ensure the greatest benefits to its prosperity in the transition years ahead.

In Chapter 4, Fabio Canova and Carlo Favero examine monetary policy in the euro area from both theoretical and empirical perspectives. They discuss what theory says about the strategy that central banks should follow and contrast it with the one employed by the European Central Bank. They review the accomplishments (and failures) of monetary policy in the euro area during the first five years and suggest changes that would increase the correlation between words and actions, streamline the understanding that markets have of the policy process, and anchor expectation formation more strongly. They examine the transmission of monetary policy shocks in the euro area and in some potential member countries and try to infer the effects likely to occur when Turkey joins the EU and, later, the euro area. Much of the analysis here warns against having too high expectations of economic gains that membership in the EU and the euro club will produce.

In Chapter 5, Fatih Özatay analyses Turkey's EU accession process from the perspective of monetary policy. He stresses that, while sound macroeconomic policies and structural reforms, such as those Turkey has been implementing since May 2001, are necessary for improving economic fundamentals and creating a positive trend in macroeconomic variables, a considerable amount of time is needed to reduce the vulnerability of an economy that has accumulated problems related to changes in international and domestic risk factors over the years. This points to the fact that challenges to monetary policy over the medium term will not only arise from the EU accession process, but that fiscal dominance and the transition to monetary dominance will also create problems.

Özatay highlights the difficulties inherited from the period of fiscal dominance as the first challenge to the monetary policy authorities. Given that the policy implemented since May 2001 has been successful, this problem will lose importance in the initial phase of the EU accession process. The main challenge to monetary policy will stem from a surge in capital inflows and a reverse dollarization process. Özatay envisages a monetary policy response based on two pillars: a non-aggressive market-friendly reserve accumulation strategy and policy rate cuts, provided that the inflation outlook looks promising. He argues that the third challenge is the need for a radical change in the balance sheet structure of the Central Bank of the Republic of Turkey (CBRT), which is a mirror image of the past macroeconomic imbalances. Finally, the CBRT Law should be amended to comply with the European Treaty.

Lucjan T. Orlowski's study in Chapter 6 revisits the process of macroeconomic stabilization policy in Poland in the course of the preparations for EU accession. It reviews the changes in fiscal policy that brought about compliance with the EU budgetary procedures and evaluates the Polish Government's fiscal consolidation efforts. It further addresses systemic changes in the monetary policy framework, mainly the implementation of a direct inflation targeting strategy, which helped establish a satisfactory degree of financial stability. Suggestions for modification of the current monetary policy framework for the final passage towards the euro adoption are also discussed. A policy framework based on relative inflation forecast targeting is advocated for effective monetary convergence to the euro.

In Chapter 7, Paul De Grauwe discusses the short and long-run conditions that countries must meet to join the European Monetary Union. The long-run conditions are those postulated by the traditional theory of Optimum Currency Areas, that is, the symmetry of the shocks hitting the candidate countries and the incumbent members of the EMU, a high degree of economic integration between them, and a high degree of market flexibility. The short-run conditions are set by the Maastricht Treaty.

De Grauwe reminds the reader that the incumbent members of the EMU are unlikely to represent an optimal currency area today, as numerous empirical studies have pointed out. To be sustainable in the long run, the EMU needs a sufficiently large degree of political integration. De Grauwe defines political integration in two aspects, the possibility of creating a system of taxes and transfers responding to asymmetric shocks across member countries and the absence of possibilities for creating asymmetric shocks by means of national economic policies such as tax or government spending shocks. In both aspects, the current EMU has a low degree of political integration today. De Grauwe argues that the willingness to increase political integration is likely to be even lower in an enlarged monetary union including the new member states of the EU. Furthermore, the enlargement will also aggravate the problem of asymmetric shocks in the EMU, which has already been larger than expected in the incumbent EMU. As a result, enlargement could threaten the sustainability of the EMU.

Turning to the short-run conditions for the adoption of the euro, De Grauwe points out that these are quite arbitrary. Whether or not future candidates for EMU membership meet the short-run conditions successfully has no implications for the sustainability of the monetary union in the long run, as the former concerns successful macroeconomic management in the period before entering the EMU and the latter concerns successful structural reforms. The most important requirement for meeting the short-run conditions is a credible political commitment to joining the EMU. Given that such a commitment exists, the short-run conditions become largely self-fulfilling, as financial market expectations will drive interest rates and exchange rates to their required terminal conditions. The only serious obstacle, which could result from the requirement of a two-year participation in the Exchange Rate Mechanism and a low rate of inflation, could be overcome by granting the candidate countries an exchange rate band of 30 per cent, which would make the exchange rate constraint largely irrelevant.

Barry Eichengreen and Omar Choudhry in Chapter 8 discuss the problems of managing capital inflows in the accession economies of Eastern Europe and the rapidly industrializing economies of East Asia. The authors note that in Emerging Europe, savings are insufficient to finance domestic investments, whereas savings in Emerging Asia are larger than the amount needed for financing the region's investment. The result is, in most years, a current account deficit in Emerging Europe financed by capital inflows and a current account surplus in Emerging Asia requiring private capital inflows to be more than the levels absorbed into foreign reserves if they are not to produce unacceptable inflationary pressure. Hence, discussions in Eastern Europe have centred on the question of whether real exchange rates are overvalued and current account deficits at current levels can be sustained, whereas in Emerging Asia the focus has been on whether real exchange rates are undervalued and there are limits to reserve accumulation.

Analysing the determinants of real exchange rates reveals that real exchange rates are overvalued in the Czech Republic, Hungary, Slovakia, Slovenia and Turkey, and that they are modestly undervalued in most of the East Asian countries. Considering the risks associated with large capital inflows and appreciating real exchange rates, the risks are immediate for the economies of Emerging Europe but less immediate for the economies of Emerging Asia. Turning to the question of what governments and central banks should do when faced with a surge of capital inflows, the authors note that countries can respond by increasing exchange rate flexibility, maintaining capital account restrictions, strengthening prudential supervision, sterilizing inflows, loosening monetary policy, tightening fiscal policy, and negotiating a programme with the IMF. They emphasize that the economies of Emerging Europe have experimented with most of these strategies. However, most of the burden falls on tightening fiscal policy. Since this is problematic as there are political constraints on fiscal adjustment, the authors suggest that the authorities might impose holding-period taxes and/or deposit requirements on portfolio capital inflows in an effort to bias the latter towards longer maturities, like the taxes and deposit requirements used for a time by Chile.

In Chapter 9, Sübidey Togan and Hasan Ersel consider the problems related to current account sustainability in Turkey. The authors start from the notion that under current account sustainability, a country must satisfy its intertemporal budget constraint. The current stance of policies in Turkey can be sustained as long as neither these policies nor private sector behaviour lead to a drastic policy shift or a currency or balance of payments crisis. They clarify this concept by making use of the balance of payments relation. They show that the current account is not sustainable if the discounted value of the debt to GDP ratio at the end of a finite number of years exceeds the debt to GDP ratio at the beginning of the period. Calculations for 2004 reveal that the current account is not sustainable. The sustainability of the current account requires that the sum of non-interest current account to GDP ratio and foreign direct investment to GDP ratio be increased at each period under consideration. Turning to the question of how to increase these ratios, the authors note that the non-interest current account to GDP ratio depends largely on the real exchange rate and on aggregate demand for goods and services in the home country as well as the rest of the world. Since Turkey is following, and has to follow, a tight fiscal policy over the next few years, an alternative solution is to depreciate the real exchange rate. In addition, the authors show that the required rate of depreciation of the real exchange rate in order to attain sustainability in the current account decreases with increases in foreign direct investment to GDP ratio. Finally, they note that the appreciation of the real exchange rate and attainment of sustainability in the current account can be achieved in the case of Turkey by (i) taking measures to increase FDI inflow into Turkey, (ii) changing the exchange rate regime from independent float to crawling bands or managed float and/or by (iii) imposing restrictions on capital account transactions.

The conference on Macroeconomic Policies for EU Accession was organized jointly by Bilkent University, Ankara, the Central Bank of the Republic of Turkey and the Centre for European Integration Studies at the University of Bonn, with participants from Turkey, several EU member states, the European Commission, the European Central Bank, and the International Monetary Fund. We are grateful to the host institutions for their support.

The eight papers collected in this volume cover key policy issues related to fiscal policy, monetary policy, euro adoption and the management of capital inflows. The contributions of the discussants give the reader a glimpse of the lively debates held at the conference. We hope that this volume will provide a basis for and shape the debates about the challenges and exigencies of EU accession among policymakers and academics in Turkey as well as in other candidate and prospective candidate countries for EU membership.

1. Opening remarks

Süreyya Serdengeçti and Anne O. Krueger

SÜREYYA SERDENGEÇTİ

Rector Doğramacı, Director Vorkink, Distinguished Academicians, Bureaucrats, Guests.

I would like to welcome you all to this two-day conference on Macroeconomic Policies for EU Accession. I would also like to thank Bilkent University and the University of Bonn for joining the Central Bank of Turkey in organizing this very important conference.

I would like to just make some brief remarks. I will start by making two important points, which are important at least for me. The first one is about the fact that in this country, as we are all very aware, EU accession has always been a long-term goal. In the accession process, we have to recognize the significance of the 17 December 2004 summit. I will be very short in presenting my view on the significance of that particular date by borrowing the words of Sir Winston Churchill. On 10 November 1942, after the victory at El Alamein that changed the course of the Second World War, he said 'This is not the end. It is not even the beginning of the end. But it is, perhaps, the end of the beginning.' Personally, I think this is exactly how we should envisage the 17 December 2004 summit; it is the end of the beginning.

The second point I want to make is about the whole process leading to the eventual membership of Turkey of the European Union. The eventual membership will depend on a lot of factors, including political ones, and probably there will be referendums, not only in France, but also in other countries and who knows, maybe even in Turkey. Clearly, it is impossible to know in advance what the outcomes of such referendums will be. But I believe that the whole process until these referendums or eventual membership, whatever that is, is more important than being a member; because it will involve serious political, legal and economic reforms that we have to do for ourselves anyway.

In this regard, we all know about the achievements in the last few years. We all appreciate the success of disinflation, which came about not only through the implementation of very tight monetary and fiscal policies, but also, as I constantly underline, with the Central Bank independence that came after 28 years of hesitation. The success of the disinflation process also came through a very transparent communication policy, which has been instrumental in changing the expectations of the public about the economy. Through these achievements, we were able to get the public debt to GNP ratio down and put it on a downward path. We were able to get nominal interest rates down by almost 50 points and expected real interest rates down by more than 20 points in recent years. Furthermore, we were able to ensure high growth rates year after year, thanks to the tight monetary and fiscal policies that have been enforced in the last few years. And these are achievements that we all know about. As a result, real growth in the economy has reached 25.5 per cent since 2001. This is the highest among European Union countries and also the highest among the accession countries. Additionally, such strong growth performance is crucial for catching up with the European Union in the future.

In addition to these very high growth rates, the growth dynamics in the country has also been undergoing transformation. First of all, growth is now taking root from the private sector. Furthermore, it is based very much on the wave of the productivity surge that we have witnessed in the economy. Beside these factors, we see that exports contribute to growth with an increasing share.

Parallel to these developments, another set of changing dynamics concerns the external balances and the opening up of the Turkish economy to the whole world. In fact, Turkish foreign trade volume in the last four years, since 2001, has actually grown by 120 per cent. That is a very significant development; especially bearing in mind that most of our foreign trade is with the European Union.

So, what prompted me to tell you about all these developments, which you are clearly already very well informed of? Because by considering these developments I reached a conclusion and according to this, I do not think that the 17 December 2004 decision, albeit an essentially political decision, would have been possible at all, if we had not made all these achievements in the last few years. We have to be very certain of this point. Now, as I mentioned before, we have single digit inflation and positive growth rates. We have even done the currency reform that nobody believed was possible only two years ago by dropping six zeros from the currency.

However, in our view, all these achievements now belong to the past. Nowadays, as I constantly keep urging the public on various occasions, we have to start viewing developments with a broader perspective. We also have to adopt a longer-term view of developments. In other words, we now have to get out of this narrow short-term triangle, which I describe as the triangle of the stock exchange, interest rates and exchange rates and adopt a longer-term view in the framework of price stability, sustainable growth and sustainable increase in employment. That longer-term view will be vital for eventual EU accession. Especially sustainable growth is a very important area. The more we are able to work on how high and how sustainable a growth rate we can achieve in this country in the coming years, the more chance we will have for eventual membership of the European Union.

We already know that saving and investment ratios have been increasing in the last few years due to tight fiscal policy, better macro indicators and good market sentiment. We know about the favourable population dynamics in this country. The population between 15 to 64 years old is increasing, leading to the expectation of a fall in the dependency ratio. Certainly, all these factors hold important implications for future European Union membership.

All these are important achievements, but we know that they are not sufficient in themselves to maintain a satisfactory level of sustainable growth. That is why the Central Bank attaches great emphasis to banking sector reform. We know that it has been a very painful process, but it has to continue unabated. Another area which we place special emphasis on is that of tax reform, which is not only about modernizing our tax system or increasing our revenues, but also plays a crucial role in transforming the unregistered economy into a registered economy, as well as ensuring the public support for further stabilization of our economy. Of course, the social security reform is very important, not only for the high primary surplus that we are obtaining, but also for the quality of the fiscal adjustment. These issues will continue to be very important in the future. Another area in which there are still some largely misunderstood issues is that related to institutional developments. These developments are not simply related to the independence of the Central Bank; but go beyond it. They have to become understood in the future due to the fact that we have already been able to reap the benefits of institutional reforms in this country.

Distinguished guests, in the past, price stability was an unknown concept in Turkey. But now, despite the fact that we have not yet reached price stability, it is now a more familiar concept with the single digit inflation. Even today, sustainable growth continues to be an unknown concept in this country. However, we are convinced that as we keep mentioning it, its importance will become better understood and we will manage to come closer to maintaining a path of sustainable growth. Another unknown concept is that of good governance. And we believe, as a society, we have to continue our efforts to put the principles of good governance into practice. One other very important area, as you are aware, concerns the need for foreign capital in this country, given the still low saving ratios and need for high growth rates in the future. And we need to work more and more on attracting FDI, which has never come to this country in the past because of macroeconomic instability. Finally, as already mentioned in the EU reports, we have to work on issues related to economic policy coordination, as well.

Up to this point, I have commented briefly on developments in the Turkish economy and the challenges ahead in the process of Turkey's accession to the European Union. I am sure the conference will address all of these issues in detail. So, I would like to thank you very much for listening to me.

ANNE O. KRUEGER

Good afternoon. I am pleased to be in Turkey and that I was able to join you.

It is especially good to be in Turkey at a time of such strong economic performance. Progress here has been striking in recent years. The government's continuing commitment to its economic reform program is impressive. The strength of this commitment has underpinned the government's request for a new $10 billion standby arrangement with the IMF. This is intended to support a three-year economic program that aims to sustain growth, deliver price stability, and move towards convergence with the EU economies. The Fund's Executive Board will consider this program next week. We are confident that the economy will strengthen and continue its progress over the life of the program.

As the government builds on the success achieved so far, so attention is turning to the policy framework that will be needed if the accession negotiations between Turkey and the European Union are successfully concluded: hence this conference.

The economic agenda is a challenging one, as I'm sure your discussions this morning highlighted. But as the experience of recent years has already demonstrated, the potential rewards are great.

I want today to assess what has been achieved in the past few years; and to look ahead to the policy challenges of the future. First, though, let me say something about the context of the economic reform agenda.

The prospect of EU membership has certainly focused thinking on the further progress needed. It is important to remember, though, that the principal reason for pushing ahead with further reforms is that they will bring great benefits for Turkey and its citizens *regardless* of EU membership. Achieving macroeconomic stability has already made possible higher growth rates over a sustained period: this raises real incomes and helps to reduce poverty.

The best reason for undertaking economic reforms anywhere, and at any time, is that they make sense in themselves because they improve the lives of citizens. Turkey's economy has achieved macroeconomic stability. But strengthening the economy further to reduce its vulnerability to risks of external shocks and to permit room for maneuver with countercyclical policy is still needed. The fact that, in Turkey's case, further economic progress will be achieved if the full benefits of prospective EU membership are reaped is an added bonus.

Progress So Far

The recent transformation of the Turkish economy has been remarkable. It is difficult, now, to remember quite how difficult was the situation at the time of the 2000–01 crisis. Inflation was a chronic problem, having been at more than 60 per cent a year from the 1980s onwards, in large part because successive governments had failed to achieve fiscal control. Reforms that had been implemented earlier – such as the trade liberalization of the early 1980s – delivered less than they might otherwise have because of macro instability. The consequence was an economy that lurched from crisis to crisis. Short-lived booms were followed by bust.

The crisis of 2000–01 brought things to a head. Here was a country with enormous potential, a potential that was not being fulfilled. There was a clear appetite for making a break with the past and getting to grips with the country's problems once and for all. The overriding motive for change was to achieve an underlying and sustained improvement in Turkey's economic performance.

Turkish economic policymaking and the Turkish economy have been transformed in a remarkably short period. The numbers speak for themselves. Average real GNP growth over the past three years has been close to 8 per cent: last year it was just short of 10 per cent. That contrasts with average growth of 2.3 per cent between 1995 and 2001. Even more remarkable, that acceleration in growth has been achieved in the context of sharply declining inflation and fiscal consolidation. The inflation rate has fallen from 70 per cent three years ago, to close to 8 per cent now – its lowest level for 35 years. The primary surplus was almost 7 per cent of GNP last year – above the 6.5 per cent target. And the public debt to GNP ratio has fallen by 30 percentage points of GNP since the peak in 2001. As I will discuss further in a moment, however, the debt to GNP ratio is still a source of vulnerability and needs to be brought down further.

Inflation

The success of counter-inflationary policy has been exceptional, and has surpassed expectations. The skilful implementation of monetary policy by the Central Bank has, of course, been crucial. For three consecutive years, the CBT has outperformed its end-year inflation target. This has greatly strengthened the credibility of monetary policy. And this sharp decline in inflation has been achieved in the context of rapid growth.

This is a major achievement that brings widespread economic benefits. Inflation distorts resource allocation in the economy. It hurts the poorest members of society disproportionately. It creates uncertainty and it arbitrarily redistributes income and wealth. It undermines macroeconomic stability and it makes sustained rapid growth impossible to achieve.

Getting to an inflation rate of 8 per cent or thereabouts is, as I say, an impressive turnaround in such a short time. There are significant additional benefits to be had from lowering it still further, say to the 2 per cent–4 per cent range. This would greatly reduce, if not eliminate, the inefficiencies associated with inflation; and Turkish inflation would converge with inflation rates in the main industrial economies, including those in Europe. It is clear that the authorities recognize the gains to be had from pursuing further reductions in inflation: a continuing decline in inflation remains a central objective of policy. The independence of the central bank has certainly been important in maintaining downward pressure on the inflation rate, and will continue to be so. And the move to inflation targeting planned for next year should facilitate a further decline in the inflation rate.

Fiscal Policy

The chronic fiscal imbalances of earlier years were the root cause of persistent inflation. Bringing the fiscal situation under control was therefore essential to the success of counter-inflationary policy and to the macroeconomic stability that Turkey currently enjoys. The fiscal adjustment undertaken thus far has permitted a significant reduction in the debt burden, reduced the risk premium on Turkish debts and helped restore confidence in macroeconomic policy. The government is committed to maintaining the primary surplus so that the debt burden can be reduced further. In spite of the reductions already achieved, external debt is still more than 50 per cent of GNP, and gross public debt is over 75 per cent of GNP. A large part of the public debt is indexed either to foreign currencies or linked to short-term interest rates.

Further debt reductions are important if Turkey's vulnerability to rising worldwide interest rates and exchange rate volatility is to be reduced. Experience in other emerging markets suggests that anything above 30 per cent–40 per cent is in the risky zone.

Of course, a continuing primary surplus of 6.5 per cent, to which the government remains committed, will make possible further reductions in debt vulnerabilities. And the government's objective of gradually moving to something close to overall fiscal balance will help strengthen the macroeconomic policy framework still more, and free resources for essential infrastructure and other programs. It is important to remember that the economy has grown rapidly during the period when the government has been meeting, and even exceeding, its primary surplus targets. Moreover, growth performance has far exceeded expectations in the context of rapidly falling inflation rates.

Structural Reform

The pace of growth is likely to moderate a little in the coming years, as the excess capacity in the economy has largely been absorbed. There is every prospect that growth will continue to be relatively rapid and sustained over a long period, provided the reform momentum is maintained. In the next phase of Turkey's expansion, structural reforms will inevitably come to the fore. Indeed, they will be essential if Turkey's potential growth rate is to be raised and its transformation to a well-functioning and stable market economy is to be accelerated. Such a transformation is in the interests of all Turkey's citizens because it will contribute to the rising living standards we all want to see. Without structural reforms, countries experiencing rapid growth soon run into capacity constraints and, with them, inflationary pressures. If action is not taken to alleviate bottlenecks, with reforms that make the economy more flexible and more efficient, and so raise its growth potential, growth soon starts to slow, or the inflation rate starts to tick up very rapidly.

Reforms have already been introduced in a number of areas. There were trade and banking sector reforms in the early 1980s. Since the crisis of 2000–01, many other reforms have been implemented: in the financial sector, in response to the banking crisis that precipitated the radical shift in economic policy; in the management of the public finances; and in the area of business regulation. But further reforms in these areas are needed if the economy's growth potential is to be raised. As you know, many structural reforms have long time lags. The sooner reforms are introduced, the sooner the results will start to show.

Let me mention briefly a few areas where further structural reforms would improve the economy's growth potential.

First, the financial sector. The banking crisis led to important reforms in this area. The regulatory framework has been brought closer to international standards, and state banks have been restructured and recapitalized. Banks have also begun to restructure their portfolios away from government paper, thus enabling commercial and consumer lending to start growing more normally. But further reforms are essential if the financial sector is to fulfil its role in making the economy more productive. Since the 1990s, we have all recognized just how important a sound financial sector is – not least in a rapidly growing economy. The banking system needs to be sound, and financial intermediation to be increasingly wide and deep. Efficient credit allocation becomes increasingly important as an economy becomes increasingly sophisticated.

The government recognizes this. It has already submitted a new Banking Law to Parliament that, in part, attempts to correct weaknesses in the regulatory system that were identified by the İmar Commission Report, published last August. It also aims to tackle problems with bank intervention and bank resolution encountered during the crisis.

But the reform process cannot stop there. The financial system needs continuously to evolve if it is to continue to meet the needs of the economy as it evolves and expands. Otherwise, the financial sector can act as a brake on growth, because credit is allocated less efficiently than desirable. Inefficient or less than optimal allocation of credit reduces the rate of growth and therefore impedes the growth potential of the economy.

Next let me say something about reforms in management of the public finances.

Reforms to improve budgetary transparency are under way, as are improvements to the tax system; more are envisaged. High rates of taxation, and complexity, encourage participation in the informal sector of the economy. But the lower the rates of tax collection, and the narrower the tax base, the higher the tax rates need to be to maintain government revenues. Streamlining and simplifying the income tax system and lowering tax rates will reduce distortions and will help discourage participation in the informal sector, generating additional revenues in the process.

There is scope, and pressing need, for reform on the expenditure side, too. In spite of earlier pension reforms, the pension deficit widened from 2.5 per cent of GNP in 2000 to 3.5 per cent in 2004; on current trends, without further reforms, it could grow to 7 per cent of GNP over the longer term. The overall social security deficit which also includes health expenditures would be more than double the current 4.5 per cent of GNP in the long run. Such rapid growth in these deficits would divert government resources away from infrastructure, education and other areas necessary for growth.

Plans for further social security reform are already in train. Legislation already submitted to parliament should reduce the annual pension deficit by nearly 1 per cent of GNP over a ten-year period and bring the deficit to below 1 per cent of GNP over the longer term. This will be a major step.

But beyond these key areas, there remains a full agenda of expenditure reform. And privatization of government assets will also contribute to an improvement in the functioning both of the economy as a whole, through its effects on private sector competition, and because it will reduce the burden on the state sector. Competition based on a level playing field for all economic actors – domestic and foreign – is essential for growth.

Finally, a couple of comments on reforms aimed at creating a more hospitable business climate. The 2003 Foreign Direct Investment Law helped level the playing field for foreign and domestic investors. The government has now embarked on reforms aimed at cutting red tape; improving the functioning and predictability of the judicial system; and bringing business standards generally more into line with those of the EU. A more flexible labor market is also badly needed. Labor market rigidities and high minimum wages act as a disincentive to hire new staff. They encourage participation in the informal sector, with consequences for tax revenues and for export growth since informal enterprises cannot export. And labor market inflexibility explains at least some of the current stickiness of the unemployment rate.

The costs of complying with statutory employment legislation remain high and on measures such as the difficulty of hiring workers, and the rigidity of working hours, Turkey currently scores poorly in international comparisons. Liberalizing labor market regulation would greatly improve the business climate and increase employment.

Significant enhancements in Turkish wage and price flexibility will facilitate more rapid and sustained growth; they will help raise real incomes; and they will help reduce poverty. These are objectives that are desirable in themselves. They will also help Turkey converge more closely with the EU and other industrial countries, and so promote the objective of Turkish membership of the European Union. But that is an added bonus – not the main reason for pursuing labor market or any other economic reforms.

Conclusion

Let me conclude. The turnaround in Turkey's economic performance has been remarkable. There is every reason to expect further rapid growth, sustainable over a long period. That will raise real incomes, deliver rising living standards and further reduce poverty: objectives we all endorse. But this can only happen if the economy's growth potential is raised by pursuing further structural reforms.

Timing is crucial. Economic upturns provide the best backdrop for any reform programs. The benefits flow more rapidly, and the costs of adjustment are lower than they would otherwise be. This is a strong argument for continuing now, while the global outlook remains favorable, and while the reform momentum can be maintained.

The payoff from reforms has already been substantial. As reforms continue, the payoff will increase – economic reforms have a cumulatively beneficial impact, the one increasing the returns on all the others. Now is the right moment to press ahead, to extend the scope of the reforms: while the world economy is growing at a healthy pace and when there is the opportunity to ensure that growth can be sustained over a prolonged period. This will help Turkey converge with the European Union. More importantly, it will benefit all of Turkey's citizens.

Thank you.

2. Fiscal policies and sustainability of public finances in the European Union

Jürgen von Hagen

2.1 INTRODUCTION

Membership in the European Union (EU) has important consequences for the conduct of fiscal policies. While fiscal policy remains a national competence, the EU puts various constraints on the fiscal policies of its member states both at the micro and at the macro level. In this chapter, we focus on macro fiscal policies.[1] Constraints on macro fiscal policies arise from two goals of the EU: the wish to coordinate the policies of the member states and the need to maintain sustainable public finances. Formally, these two goals are reflected in two different policy frameworks at the EU level. Coordination works primarily through the Broad Economic Policy Guidelines (BEPG) and several coordination procedures. Sustainability is the focus of the Excessive Deficit Procedure (EDP) and the Stability and Growth Pact (SGP).

The Treaty on European Union (TEU) establishes 'sound public finances' as one of the guiding principles of economic policy in the EU (Art. 4(3)) and that the member states regard their economic policies as a matter of common concern and coordinate them through the ECOFIN Council and on the basis of the BEPG (Art. 99). In this context, the term 'economic policies' is commonly understood to include government tax and expenditure policies. According to Art. 103 of TEU, the Community, its institutions and the individual member states are protected against becoming responsible for financial liabilities of other member states against their will.

EU Procedures with relevance for the conduct and coordination of fiscal policy are the Mutual Surveillance Procedure (Article 99), the Excessive Deficit Procedure (EDP, Art. 104) and the Stability and Growth Pact (SGP, Council Regulations 1466/97, 1476/97, Council Resolution 97/C236/01-02). The EDP sets up a detailed process of monitoring the public finances of the member states with a view to ensuring that they remain sustainable.

It includes the mandate (Article 3 of the Protocol) that the member states of the European Economic and Monetary Union (EMU) should implement appropriate institutions at the national level that enable them to fulfil their obligation for maintaining sustainable finances. The practical meaning of this obligation, however, remains vague.

There is an important distinction between policy coordination and the requirement to maintain sustainable public finances. Coordination seeks to improve upon the results of independent, national fiscal policies. The EU and its core common goods, the Single Market and the EMU can function well without – though perhaps not as well as with – coordination. In contrast, as explained below, sustainability is a necessary condition for EMU to function properly. This distinction explains why the commitment to policy coordination is politically but not legally binding (DG ECFIN, 2002). There are no formal penalties for governments failing to adhere to coordination. In contrast, maintaining sustainability is a legally binding commitment; countries participating in EMU can be penalized if they fail to maintain sustainable public finances.

The TEU also declares a 'sustainable balance of payments' as a goal of economic policy in the EU, committing the member states to avoiding fiscal policies that could lead to balance of payments crises. Should a member state find itself in a currency or balance of payments crisis, nevertheless, the TEU (Art. 199) calls upon the European Commission to investigate the situation and make appropriate recommendations. The article has in view, in particular, the possibility that unilateral actions to counteract such crises could undermine the functioning of the integrated EU markets. If necessary, the European Council can, upon a recommendation from the commission, grant financial assistance to the member state concerned.

This chapter explains the fiscal policy implications of EU membership in more detail and reviews the EU's experience with its fiscal framework. Section 2.2 deals with policy coordination. Section 2.3 discusses the sustainability of public finances. Section 2.4 develops some policy conclusions.

2.2 ECONOMIC POLICY COORDINATION IN THE EU

According to the TEU (Art. 99), member states coordinate their economic policies at the EU level within the Council of Ministers with the participation of all 15 member states and the presence of the European Commission and of the European Central Bank where deemed necessary. The Council of Economics and Finance Ministers (ECOFIN) is the relevant one for the discussion and decisions about government deficits, spending and taxation, while the Employment/Social Affairs Council deals with employment and social policies. The European Commission and the Economic and Financial Committee serve as the secretariats to the Council. In the coordination procedures established by the TEU, the Council adopts policy guidelines and recommendations by majority voting on a proposal from the Commission, thereby following the conclusions of the European Council – the heads of state or government of the member states and the highest level of coordination. Although the title of ECOFIN suggests otherwise, it is noteworthy that the members of this body are far from being a homogeneous group, as the functional and the political role of finance ministers varies considerably across EU member states. The degree to which individual members can enter credible commitments for the macroeconomic policies of their countries is, therefore, variable, too.

The 1997 European Council in Luxembourg agreed to the establishment of the Euro Group, now known as the Euro-12 Group, of the finance ministers of the EMU member states, in recognition of the specific coordination requirements among participants of the euro area. Since the Euro Group has no legislative responsibility, its role is to assess the economic situation and to discuss the major policy issues for the euro area. It is chaired by a minister of a participating EMU member state, including in periods when the EU presidency is held by a non-EMU member. This subgroup of ECOFIN meets in connection with ECOFIN meetings.

The European Commission is present both at Council and Euro-12 Group meetings. The Commission has the right to set the policy agenda for Council meetings and to provide analysis for multilateral surveillance. The Economic and Financial Committee (EFC) has advisory and preparatory functions for the Council meetings. It consists of representatives of national administrations and national central banks, as well as two representatives of the European Commission and the European Central Bank (ECB). While the European Commission and the EFC cover macroeconomic and financial issues, the Economic Policy Committee, which consists of officials from economics ministries, is primarily concerned with structural policies.[2]

According to insider views, the European Council and the Council can hardly be regarded as effective institutions for cooperative decision-making. Padoa Schioppa (1999) argues that the Council is too large a forum to develop concrete policy actions or policy rules. Furthermore, the Council involves too many participants and catches too much media attention to provide an environment for confidential discussions and deliberations.[3] The more informal Euro-12 Group allows a more concentrated debate, since national delegations are restricted to two persons. However, its role is limited since decisions can be taken only at the Council level. Jacquet and

Pisani-Ferry (2000) argue that the Euro-12 Group has played a useful role in developing the quality of economic policy debates among its members, but that the role of this group is largely exhausted with this function.

Table 2.1 presents an overview of the processes of policy coordination in the context of EMU. They include the Broad Economic Policy Guidelines, the process of multilateral surveillance, the Excessive Deficit Procedure and the Stability and Growth Pact, the Luxembourg, the Cologne, and the Cardiff processes.

The Broad Economic Policy Guidelines (BEPGs) consolidate these processes and aim at exploiting the synergies between them. BEPGs also form the reference for the multilateral surveillance procedure, under which the consistency of national economic policies with the BEPGs and the functioning of EMU in general are monitored. The multilateral surveillance procedure includes the possibility of making confidential or public assessments of the policies of individual member states and giving confidential or public recommendations to their governments. The European Council decides by unanimity vote on the BEPG upon proposals by the European Commission and recommendations by ECOFIN.

The European Employment Pact introduced an institutionalized macroeconomic dialogue known as the Cologne Process. This informal dialogue facilitates an open exchange of views among the ECB, a representative of a non-euro area central bank, ECOFIN, the Labour and Social Affairs Councils, the Commission and the social partners at twice-yearly meetings. ECOFIN is represented by the 'troika' of the past, current and subsequent presidencies. The social partners are represented by their respective organizations at the European level. The Cologne Process aims at improving the interaction between wage developments and monetary, budgetary and fiscal policies in order to achieve stronger growth and higher employment while maintaining price stability. The forum is unlikely to play a major role, because the EU federations of trade unions and employers' unions do not have the authority to represent a common view of the respective partners in all the different member countries and, therefore, cannot assure the enforcement of any agreements on guidelines for wage policies at the national level. This, in turn, is due to the institutional heterogeneity of social partner organizations in the member countries (see OECD, 1996).[4]

The Luxembourg Process was launched at the end of 1997 and reinforced by the inclusion of the Employment chapter (Title VIII) in the Amsterdam Treaty. The latter recognizes that member states retain the principal responsibility for employment policies. Nevertheless, Art. 125 calls for the development of a coordinated employment strategy by the member states and the Community and Art. 126 calls upon the member states to contribute to the objectives of this strategy through their employment policies, to regard

Table 2.1 The annual EU procedures and actors involved

Procedures	Form of Coordination and Instruments	Actors	Tasks
Broad Economic Policy Guidelines (Art 99 TEU)	Core of economic policy coordination within the EU defining common objectives. Annual guidelines and recommendations to member states.	Council (EU11 Group) European Commission Member states	The BEPGs defines the economic policy orientations for the EU in accordance with Art 2. The BEPG integrate the different processes mentioned below.
Multilateral surveillance (Art 99 (3) TEU)	Monitoring process. Peer review.	Council European Commission Member states	The process monitors and assesses the economic developments and policies in member states as well as in the Community as a whole. It forms the basis for Community compliance procedure (Art 99 (4)).
Excessive Deficit Procedure (EDP) (Art 104) Stability and Growth Pact (SGP) Regulation 1467/97	Common rules and objectives, Budgetary Surveillance, Pecuniary sanctions. MS submit annually stability or convergence programmes.	European Council European Parliament National governments (finance ministries) European Commission	The EDP and SGP represent an obligation on member states to achieve medium-term budgetary positions close to balance or in surplus.
Luxembourg Process (Art 128 TEU)	Open coordination (guidelines and recommendations to member states). Peer review. Benchmarking, best practices pecuniary incentives (ESF)for MS to provide high quality information. MS submit annually National Action Plans	European Council European Commission National governments (labour and finance ministries)	The Luxembourg Process coordinates the European Employment Strategy. The purpose is to improve the effectiveness of national employment and labour market policies by better focusing on respective problem groups, improving the set of instruments and establishing a continuous evaluation process.

Table 2.1 (continued)

Procedures	Form of Coordination and Instruments	Actors	Tasks
Cologne Process ECOFIN 1999	Informal macroeconomic dialogue at Community level Informal exchange of view,two meetings per year	ECB (+ representative of non EMU CB) European Commission Troika of current, subsequent and preceding presidency of ECOFIN and Labour/Social ministers Social Partners	The Cologne Process aims at improving the interaction between wage developments and monetary, budgetary and fiscal policy at the EU level. The Process was installed to complete the Cardiff and Luxembourg process.
Cardiff Process ECOFIN 1998	Monitoring process within the Single Market: • Identification of good practice • Peer review.	European Commission Economic Policy Committee National governments (economic and finance ministries)	The Cardiff Process is a multilateral review of economic reforms in product, capital and labour markets. The purpose is to improve the market efficiency of member states' economies so as to enhance the favourable environment for growth, high employment and social cohesion.

Source: Von Hagen and Mundschenk (2002).

promoting employment as a matter of common concern, and to coordinate their actions in this regard.

The Luxembourg Process aims at building a coherent approach to structural labour market problems in EU countries. The purpose is to improve the effectiveness of national employment and labour market policies by better focusing on problem groups, by improving the set of instruments and by establishing a continuous evaluation process. The TEU sets up a framework for an annual multilateral surveillance procedure similar to the multilateral surveillance procedure of Art. 99 and in some aspects goes even further than that by giving the Council the opportunity of adopting incentive measures. Specifically, the disbursement of monies from the European Social Fund has been made conditional on the member states' compliance with the Luxembourg Process.

The core of the Luxembourg Process is a shared preference for active labour market policies over both passive policies (that is unemployment insurance and related programmes) and their improvements and the OECD's push for more labour market flexibility.[5] The process consists of monitoring employment policies and their improvements in the member states and the formulation of Council recommendations to individual member states. Even a short glance reveals a lack of substantial foundation of its main elements. Its fundamental weaknesses probably reflect the simple fact that there is no truly 'European' employment problem. A review of the individual labour market performances shows that some countries have achieved full employment, while others have not. Among the latter, some countries have predominantly regional unemployment problems (Italy and Germany), while others have problems with specific social groups, which may be age-related (youth unemployment in France) or skill-related (for example, in the UK). Blanchard and Wolfers (2000) show that the diversity of unemployment performance across EU countries can largely be explained by differences in labour market structures and macro economic shocks experienced in the 1980s and 1990s.

The Cardiff Process monitors the structural reforms and innovations of member states in product, capital and labour markets. The mandate for strengthened structural reforms was given at the European Council in June 1998. It resulted in 15 national reports of reforms concerning the functioning of product, labour and capital markets and a separate report from the Commission. The Lisbon Council reduced the number of reports. In this process the Economic Policy Committee plays a leading role as it conducts a multilateral surveillance (Synthesis Report). Instruments used are peer pressure and an extensive reporting, monitoring and evaluation system. In accordance with the Lisbon Strategy, more emphasis has been put on the identification of best practices.

In sum, economic policy coordination in the EU is a complex network of procedures lacking operational transparency and effectiveness in many respects. The multiplicity of processes reflects the multiplicity of responsibilities at different negotiation levels. From the economic point of view, the distinction of different aspects through the processes is far from being clear-cut. Furthermore, the organization of policy coordination into different processes promotes a compartmentalized approach to policy-making in different areas, which inhibits the recognition and consideration of trade-offs between different policy goals in many areas (von Hagen and Mundschenk, 2002). While effective policy coordination requires the possibility of committing the participants to some joint programme of action or common policies, the current set-up for cooperative policies in the EMU relies essentially on peer pressure and persuasion. This is a direct result of the fact that the EMU member states were unwilling to give up further sovereignty over their economic policies or the result of a lack of consensus.

2.3 SUSTAINABILITY OF PUBLIC FINANCES

In terms of technical economic analysis, sustainability relates to the government's 'intertemporal budget constraint', the requirement that, in the long run, the discounted sum of a government's expected expenditures cannot exceed the discounted sum of its expected revenues. Public finances are sustainable if the government's current and expected future revenues and expenditures meet this requirement (for example, Chalk and Hemming, 2000). Obviously, sustainability does not rule out even prolonged periods of large government deficits, as long as these are compensated by future surpluses. Since the intertemporal budget constraint extends over a very long time horizon and governments can easily promise lower spending or higher revenues in the future, it is obvious that sustainability does not have strong implications for current fiscal policies.[6]

The intertemporal budget constraint establishes an important link between monetary and fiscal policy, which makes sustainability of public finances important for the proper functioning of a monetary union aiming at price stability. This link can be stated in two ways. Traditional analysis sees seigniorage as part of a government's expected revenues. Given an expected stream of expenditures in the future and given an expected stream of tax revenues, seigniorage has to make up for any shortfall of the latter over the former.[7] If closing the gap requires printing more money, inflation will be the consequence. In EMU, the issue is somewhat more complicated, because the governments of the individual member states have given up the right to print money. Seigniorage will be paid to them in the form of central bank profits, but, since the central banks are politically independent and, by virtue of the TEU (Art. 104 and Art. 21.1 of the ECB Statutes), cannot directly monetize public sector deficits, seigniorage should be exogenous to government policies. That is, given an expected stream of expenditures and an exogenous flow of seigniorage, the governments must adjust taxes to assure that the intertemporal budget constraint holds. Otherwise, they would be forced at some point to default on their debts. A fiscal crisis would arise, but it does not create inflation in the monetary union, unless the central bank bails out the troubled government.[8] The critical question here is whether or not the ECB's institutional independence and its determination to safeguard price stability are sufficiently strong for it to withstand any political pressures to provide a bailout.

Alternatively, one may regard the intertemporal budget constraint as a macroeconomic equilibrium condition, which is the essence of the fiscal theory of the price level (Leeper, 1991). Suppose that, initially, the intertemporal budget constraint holds, and let expected tax revenues fall, everything else unchanged. The decline in their tax liabilities will cause households to feel richer than before and raise aggregate demand. Unless the government adjusts its policies, the price level must rise to reduce the real value of households' nominal assets and restore equilibrium. Following this line of reasoning, fiscal deficits can create inflation even if the central bank does not buy additional government debt.

Both views of the issue lead to the conclusion that the EMU needs some rules preventing the national governments from running up excessive levels of debt that would, in the long run, threaten the common good of the monetary union, that is, price stability. This basic insight has left its mark in all documents and decisions leading up to the creation of EMU and is the basic rationale behind the EDP and the SGP. Obviously, the Union's concern for sustainability of public finances in countries not participating in EMU is much weaker. Therefore, member states with derogation from EMU cannot be formally punished for non-compliance with the procedures designed to assure sustainability. However, since participation in EMU is considered the normal case in the EU, even member states with such derogation are subject to the unconditional obligation of maintaining sustainable public finances, and compliance with the relevant procedures is an important part of qualifying for the adoption of the euro.

The difficulty with this basic conclusion is in the question of how to translate it into a framework that guides and constrains the governments' fiscal policies effectively. In a world with perfect information and no transaction costs, one could adopt a policy rule stating in detail what governments should do under what circumstances to meet the intertemporal budget constraint. In reality, the world is too complex and uncertain to do that. A simple fiscal rule limiting annual government deficits or debts is of little use under such circumstances, because it would constrain the governments' fiscal policies either too much or too little in the short run. Either way, it would lack credibility. In the first case, because it may force sovereign governments under some circumstances to adopt policies that are unreasonable or even damaging for their own countries; in the second case, because it would not bind government actions sufficiently in the short run.

Furthermore, simple rules are not adequate in the EU context of supranationality, because a rule must treat all member states equally, even if they are unequal. Consider the following example. The annual budget deficit ratio, d, is linked to the ratio of public debt to GDP, b, through the following relationship: $d=[(1+g)(1+\pi)-1]b$, where g is the real trend growth rate and π the long-run average rate of inflation. In view of this relationship, a rule for the annual budget deficit ratio must be based on an assumption about the long-run real growth rate and the long-run rate of inflation, π, if it is to stabilize the debt ratio, b. Given the ECB's desired rate of inflation in the euro area of 2 per cent annually, the allowable deficit ratio is $d=(1+g)(1+0.02)*b$. With $b=0.6$, the allowable ratio is 4.9 per cent for a country like Finland, growing at 6 per cent on average, but only 1.8 per cent for a country such as Germany, whose trend growth rate is about 1 per cent.

Finally, the distinction between sustainable public finances and optimal public finances is again important. Optimal public finances are the solution to an optimization problem, which consists of a set of policy goals, political preferences regarding policy outcomes, resource constraints, and (assumptions about) the laws describing the functioning of the economy. Designing optimal policies is, therefore, by nature a political task. Sustainability is just one of the resource constraints that must be fulfilled in this task, that is, all optimal policies are sustainable, but not all sustainable policies are optimal. In view of this distinction, a careful balance must be sought between constraining long-term fiscal trends to maintain sustainability and making room for optimal policies. The more a framework meant to achieve sustainability constrains short-term fiscal policies, the more likely it is to get in the way of optimal policy choices. Too much emphasis on the short run, therefore, has the result of politicizing the framework for sustainability to an unnecessary extent. The failure to find a better balance between short-term and long-term exigencies for fiscal policy was critical in the recent demise of the SGP.[9]

2.3.1 The Excessive Deficit Procedure and the Stability and Growth Pact

The EDP is the cornerstone of the fiscal framework of EMU. It combines the unconditional obligation on the part of the member states to avoid 'excessive deficits' with a procedure providing a regular assessment of fiscal policies in EMU and, if necessary, penalties for profligate behaviour (Article 104 TEU). The TEU charges the European Commission with the task of monitoring budgetary developments and the stock of public sector debt of the member states, checking in particular their compliance with two reference values for the ratio of the deficit to GDP and the ratio of public debt to GDP. The two reference values are set at 3 and 60 per cent, respectively (Protocol on the EDP). If a member state does not comply with these reference values, and unless the deficit and the debt are approaching their reference values in a satisfactory way, or the excess of the deficit over the limit is exceptional and temporary, the Commission writes a report to the European Council, taking into account whether the deficit exceeds public investment spending and 'all other relevant factors, including the medium-term economic and budgetary position' (Art. 104(3)) of the country concerned.[10] If the Commission considers that an excessive deficit exists, it makes a recommendation to the European Council, which votes on it by qualified majority after taking into account any observations the country concerned may make and the opinion of the Economic and Financial Committee (EFC), which advises the Council in these matters (Art. 114). The decision whether or not an excessive deficit indeed exists is made by ECOFIN.

If ECOFIN decides that an excessive deficit prevails, it makes confidential recommendations to the country concerned on how to correct the situation within a given period of time. If the country does not take appropriate action and does not respond to ECOFIN's recommendations in a satisfactory way, ECOFIN may make its views and recommendations public, ask the government concerned to take specific corrective actions, and, ultimately, impose a financial penalty on the country. In that case, the country would first be required to make a non-interest bearing deposit with the Community. If the excessive deficit still persists, this deposit would be turned into a fine paid to the Community.[11] The Council can abrogate its decisions under the EDP upon a recommendation from the Commission. All Council decisions in this context are made by qualified majority; once a country has been found to have an excessive deficit, its votes are not counted in these decisions.

In the context of the EDP, the numerical criteria for deficits and debts thus serve as triggers for an assessment prepared by the European Commission and made by the European Council. They do not themselves define what an excessive deficit is, nor does breaching them imply any sanctions per se. Since they merely serve as triggers for a more precise assessment of the situation, there is no need to make them responsive to economic circumstances, for example, by redefining them to exclude interest spending or cyclical effects on spending and revenues. These and other circumstances can be accounted for in the Commission's analysis, EFC's opinion and the Council's judgement. In view of the need to balance long-term objectives with short-run constraints on actual policy, such a trigger role is appropriate for the numerical criteria.

An important feature of the EDP is that the governance of the procedure is shared between the European Commission and ECOFIN. The Commission initiates the process, delivers the analytical input to the assessment, and makes proposals and recommendations to ECOFIN. ECOFIN acts as the ultimate judge of fiscal performance. Since ECOFIN is composed of the national finance ministers, all of whom are susceptible to running excessive deficits, this structure has been interpreted as making a group of 'sinners' judge the performance of fellow 'sinners'. Judging the performance of other governments, ECOFIN members have good reasons to be lenient and avoid actions that could be politically costly for fellow members, anticipating that they might be in a similar position in the future. This makes serious judgement and the application of sanctions by ECOFIN unlikely. As a result, the EDP lacks credibility.

In view of this, public fears arose in Germany in the mid-1990s, that the EDP might not suffice to discipline fiscal policies in EMU. Theo Waigel, then Germany's finance minister, responded to these fears by proposing a 'Stability Pact' for EMU, which was later adopted as the 'Stability and Growth Pact' (SGP) by the European Council.[12] The SGP modifies the EDP in several ways. First, it sets up an early warning system strengthening the surveillance of the public finances of the member states. Under the SGP, EMU member states submit annual Stability Programmes to the European Commission and ECOFIN explaining their intended fiscal policies and, in particular, what they plan to do to keep the budget close to the new and stricter medium-term objective of 'close to balance or in surplus'. Implementation of these programmes is subject to ECOFIN's scrutiny. Based on information and assessments by the Commission and the EFC, ECOFIN can issue early warnings to countries that risk significant deviations from the fiscal targets set out in their Stability Programmes. The goal of the Stability Programmes is to achieve and maintain budgetary positions of close to balance or in surplus.

Second, the SGP clarifies the EDP by giving more specific content to the notions of exceptional and temporary breaches of the 3 per cent limit and by defining the rules for financial penalties, and it speeds up the process by setting specific deadlines for the individual steps. Third, the SGP gives political guidance to the parties involved in the EDP, calling them to implement the rules of the EDP effectively and in a timely manner. It commits the Commission in particular to using its right of initiative under the EDP 'in a manner that facilitates the strict, timely and effective functioning of the SGP'.

The rules of the SGP were further developed in a set of ECOFIN decisions regarding the format and content of the Stability Programmes.[13] In October 1998, ECOFIN endorsed a Monetary Committee (the precursor of the Monetary and Financial Committee) opinion, the 'code of conduct' specifying criteria to be observed in the assessment of a country's medium-term budgetary position and data standards and requirements for the programmes. In October 1999, ECOFIN recommended stricter compliance with and timelier updating of the programmes. In July 2001, ECOFIN endorsed an appended code of conduct refining the format and the use of data in the Stability Programmes, including the use of a common set of assumptions about economic developments outside the EMU. The Commission (2000) has produced a detailed framework of interpretation of divergences from the targets set in the Stability Programmes.

Compared to the original EDP, the main impact of the SGP has been to reduce the Commission's role and to raise the importance of ECOFIN judgements and decisions, thus shifting the balance of power from the institutional guardian of the TEU to the representatives of the member states. This could only reduce the credibility of the fiscal framework further. As a result, European public opinion and financial markets have taken the numerical deficit criteria more seriously in recent years than the formal rules and sensible economic reasoning would warrant, anticipating that ECOFIN will tend to avoid serious judgement and the application of penalties. Thus, the SGP has reduced the weight of sound economic judgement and created a perception that the process was more rigid than it really is.

In early 2002, a few months before the national elections in Germany, the Commission noted that the country had missed its Stability Programme targets by a significant margin and was approaching a deficit of 3 per cent of GDP. The Commission proposed to issue an early warning. To avoid that, the German government struck a deal in ECOFIN by which Germany promised to balance the budget by 2004 in return for not receiving an early warning. After its re-election in September, the government revealed that Germany was going to exceed the 3 per cent deficit ratio by a large margin in 2002 and 2003. In January 2003, ECOFIN decided that Germany had an excessive deficit. But, already in May 2003, the Commission found that the German government had made sufficient efforts to reach budget balance and that there was no need to consider fines. It turned out later that Germany did not bring its deficit below 3 per cent of GDP in 2003, nor did it do so in 2004 or 2005. 'Effort', in the Commission's view amounted to mere declarations of intent rather than real policy adjustments – a mistake that is in line with the TEU but a fallacy in real life.

Also in the spring of 2002, the newly appointed French government announced its intention to postpone balancing the budget until 2007, three years later than its commitments from the previous Stability Programme. France had a deficit ratio in excess of 3 per cent in 2002; yet the French finance minister did not respond to the Commission's request for an adjustment programme. In the summer of 2002, the Italian government also stated that it intended to postpone the budget balance required under the SGP. ECOFIN issued an early warning to the French government in

January 2003, and declared that France had an excessive deficit in June 2003. In June and July 2004, ECOFIN declared that the Netherlands and Greece had excessive deficits. In July 2004, ECOFIN also found that several of the new member states which had entered the EU in May of that year had excessive deficits, that is, the Czech Republic, Cyprus, Hungary, Malta, Poland and the Slovak Republic.

Meanwhile, the governments of Germany, France and other countries had started pushing for a reform of the SGP, allegedly asking for more 'flexibility'.[14] Specifically, Germany wanted to have its large net contribution to the EU budget and the alleged fiscal costs of German unification recognized as excuses for running large deficits. In December 2004, ECOFIN decided to suspend the ongoing procedures under the EDP until after a reform of the SGP. The European Council adopted such a reform in March 2005. Its main points are the following:

(1) The medium-term objective for national budgetary positions to be 'close to balance or in surplus' can now be differentiated according to national circumstances, allowing room for more budgetary manoeuvre, taking into account the need for public investment, and taking into account the fiscal consequences of structural reforms.
(2) A clarification of the term 'exceptional and temporary' excess of the deficit over the reference value of 3 per cent of GDP, considering 'as exceptional an excess over the reference value which results from a negative growth rate or from the accumulated loss of output during a protracted period of very low growth relative to potential growth' (European Council, 2005, p. 33).
(3) A clarification of the term 'all other relevant factors' in the assessment of a country's deficit, taking into account the fiscal consequences of structural reforms and 'financial contributions to fostering international solidarity and to achieving European policy goals, notably the unification of Europe' (p. 34).

The latter would allow Germany to use German unification as a convenient excuse for its lack of fiscal discipline. Notice the prominence of the terms 'structural reforms' and 'potential output growth', which are widely open to interpretation and concern matters for which the Commission has no competence. In view of the huge uncertainty of any estimates of the fiscal consequences of structural reforms[15] and potential output growth, national governments will be able to specify whatever they wish as excuses for large deficits.

Clearly, the request for more flexibility in the EDP and the SGP was odd, because the procedures contained a lot of room for judgement from the beginning and the numerical criteria were never meant to be binding thresholds. While many economists participating in the public debate affirmed the need to take into account cyclical conditions, public investment and the quality of economic policies, they seemed to overlook the simple fact that judgements of this kind were already possible under the existing rules.[16] Thus, the real issue between the national governments and the Commission was the governance of the procedures, that is, who has the right to exert judgement when a country's fiscal policy is being assessed. The political outcome confirms that this view is correct. In principle, specifying the nature of possible excuses for large deficits restricts the scope of economic judgement that can be brought into the procedure and, therefore, is a loss of flexibility, not an increase. But the real purpose of the reform was to further curtail the Commission's influence in the process, and this has been achieved. With ECOFIN now dominating the assessment of sustainability, the procedure has further damaged the credibility of the framework.

2.3.2 Patterns of Fiscal Adjustment

In 1992, the EU's average debt ratio was almost 60 per cent of GDP – hence the 60 per cent limit foreseen in the Maastricht Treaty.[17] It climbed to almost 75 per cent in 1997, the base year for the May 1998 decision on which countries could enter EMU. Since 1997, the average debt ratio has fallen to 63 per cent. In contrast to what EU officials and politicians like to tout, the data do not show that the Maastricht process for fiscal consolidation was successful.

Several qualifications apply. First, the increase in the average debt ratio was driven mainly by debt expansions in five states: Germany (from 44 per cent to 61 per cent), France (from 40 per cent to 56 per cent), Spain (from 48 per cent to 70 per cent), Italy (from 109 per cent to 124 per cent) and the UK (from 42 per cent to 55 per cent). While Belgium and Luxembourg almost stabilized their debt ratios, the Netherlands and Ireland enjoyed falling debt ratios during this period. The debt ratios of the other states were stabilized or fell after 1992.[18] Do the EDP and SGP work more effectively in small EMU states than in the large ones? To answer this question, Table 2.2 reports the changes in the debt to GDP ratios for large states (with GDP in 1997 of at least 7 per cent of EU GDP), Germany, Spain, France, Italy and the UK; intermediate states (with GDP between 2 and 7 per cent), Belgium, the Netherlands, Austria and Sweden; and small states (with GDP of less than 2 per cent of EU GDP), Denmark, Greece, Ireland, Luxembourg, Portugal and Finland. The combined GDP of the large states is 80 per cent of EU GDP, that of the intermediate states 13 per cent, and

Table 2.2 Government debt since 1992

Period	Change in debt ratio (per cent)			
	All EU states	Large states	Intermediate states	Small states
1992–1997	15.8	18.8	4.1	3.3
1998–2003	−4.7	−4.9	−10.5	−7.1

Source: European Economy Statistical Appendix Spring 2002, Fall 2003.

the small states have a combined GDP of 7.7 per cent of EU GDP. The table shows that, between 1992 and 1997, the average debt ratio of the small states increased by just 3.3 per cent, much less than that of the large states, where it rose by almost 19 per cent. Between 1998 and 2003, the small states achieved an average reduction in their debt ratios of 7 per cent, more than the 4.9 per cent of the large states. Intermediate states reduced their debt ratios on average by 10.5 per cent.

This suggests that the fiscal framework is indeed more effective in the small than in the large states, which implies that it is most effective where it matters the least, since a fiscal crisis in a small EMU member state would hardly threaten the stability of the common currency. In contrast, a fiscal crisis in a large state might do that, and there the fiscal rules seem much less effective.

The second qualification is that the observation of fiscal consolidations in some EU states during the 1990s cannot simply be attributed to the Maastricht Process. Since most European countries had had sizeable fiscal expansions during the 1970s and 1980s, a period of consolidation could be expected in the 1990s anyhow. A study of European fiscal policy in the 1990s (Hughes-Hallett et al., 2001) considers this argument in detail. It shows that most the observed consolidations in the 1990s could well be expected just by extrapolating patterns of fiscal behaviour of EU states in the 1970s and 1980s. The evidence of a 'Maastricht effect' speeding up or enforcing consolidations is weak at best.

2.3.3 Discretionary Fiscal Policy since the Start of EMU

Fiscal outcomes such as deficit ratios are determined both by fiscal policy and endogenous economic developments. As noted by Blöndal (2003, p. 8), annual economic growth rates are the most important determinants of fiscal performance in the short run. It is, therefore, necessary to separate the effects of policy from the effects of economic growth to see how much of the observed developments can be attributed to government policy as opposed to windfall gains and losses from strong economic growth and recessions. In this section, we use the growth-accounting approach proposed in Hughes-Hallett et al. (2001) for that purpose. Separating the effects of growth and policy requires some assumption about the economic growth to changes in this ratio. To do this, we start from the observed primary surplus ratio, s, for a given year:

$$s_t = \frac{R_t - G_t}{Y_t} = (r_t - g_t), \tag{2.1}$$

where R denotes government revenues, G non-interest government spending, Y GDP, and $r = R/Y$, and $g = G/Y$. The annual change in this ratio is:

$$\Delta s_t = \frac{\Delta R_t - \Delta G_t}{Y_{t-1}} - \frac{\Delta Y_t}{Y_{t-1}}(r_t - g_t). \tag{2.2}$$

We define a 'neutral' fiscal policy as one which keeps the average tax rate and the volume of government spending unchanged over the previous year, that is, $r_t = r_{t-1}$ and $\Delta G_t = 0$. With this definition, the contribution of economic growth to the change in the surplus ratio is:

$$\Delta s_t^g = \left(\frac{\Delta Y_t}{Y_{t-1}}\right) g_t. \tag{2.3}$$

Using this definition, we obtain the policy-induced change in the surplus ratio or the fiscal impulse as:

$$\Delta s_t^P = \Delta s_t - \Delta s_t^g. \tag{2.4}$$

This definition attributes any change in the average tax rate and all changes in government spending to fiscal policy.[19] We use this part as an indicator of discretionary fiscal policy, since it measures the active contribution of any policy actions to observed changes in the deficit ratio. Note that a positive value indicates a discretionary fiscal contraction, while a negative value indicates a discretionary fiscal expansion.

Table 2.3 reports the averages of the fiscal impulses for the EU countries. The table shows that the average fiscal impulse in 1999–2003 was more expansionary than the 1992–2003 average in all EU countries except Austria and Portugal. Thus, fiscal policy became more expansionary in all EU countries except Austria and Portugal after the start of EMU in 1999. The changes are significant in eight EU countries, that is, Belgium,

Table 2.3 *Fiscal impulses in the EU*

Country	Average 1992–2003	Average 1999–2003	*p*-value
Belgium	−0.67	−1.10	0.05
Denmark	−1.22	−1.28	0.17
Germany	−0.62	−0.98	0.08
Greece	−0.89	−2.28	0.00
Spain	−0.75	−0.81	0.41
France	−1.05	−1.48	0.10
Irish Republic	−2.70	−3.17	0.20
Italy	−0.38	−1.01	0.08
Luxembourg	−2.00	−2.44	0.05
Netherlands	−1.34	−1.58	0.58
Austria	−0.98	−0.77	0.45
Portugal	−0.92	−0.71	0.36
Finland	−1.03	−1.54	0.19
Sweden	−1.39	−2.58	0.07
United Kingdom	−1.18	−2.04	0.06

Note: *p*-value is the corresponding one-sided test for the mean of 1992–98 being larger than the mean of 1999–2003.

Source: Own calculations.

Germany, Greece, France, Italy, Luxembourg, Sweden and the UK. Note that this group includes all large countries except Spain. This is significant, as the threat of not making it into EMU due to lax fiscal policies was no longer hanging over the European countries once EMU had started. Elsewhere, we have dubbed this observation 'consolidation fatigue' (von Hagen and Harden, 1994). EU governments used the first chance for relaxing fiscal policy.

To gain some further insights into the conduct of fiscal policy in the EU, von Hagen (2005) estimates a panel regression using the pooled fiscal impulses of all member states except Luxembourg, for which we do not have the fiscal data for all years of the 1980s. The model uses past fiscal impulses, real GDP growth, and the ratio of public debt to GDP as control variables. The results indicate, first, a positive reaction of the fiscal impulse to a past increase in the debt ratio both in the 1980s and the 1990s. This can be regarded as a necessary condition for fiscal sustainability, as the debt ratio would be unbounded without such a reaction. The result also confirms the finding in Hughes-Hallett et al. (2002) that the likelihood of fiscal consolidations in EU and OECD member states during the period from 1960 to 1999 rises when the debt ratio increases. This reaction is the same in the 1980s and the 1990s.

Second, the average fiscal impulse is significantly more expansionary after 1999. This confirms the hypothesis of consolidation fatigue. The fiscal rules may have had some effect in the desired direction between 1991 and 1998, when the penalty for exceeding the deficit limits was large.

Third, the more expansionary fiscal impulses after 1999 occur predominantly in election years. This indicates that governments in the EU use fiscal expansions systematically to enhance their chances of re-election. This result is consistent with similar findings in Buti and van den Noord (2004). It suggests that the fiscal framework of EMU does not keep governments from creating political budget cycles.

2.3.4 Patterns of Fiscal Adjustment

At the European Council in Lisbon in 2000, the EU called upon its members to improve the 'quality' of public finances. Without defining precisely what the 'quality' of public finances means, the Council recognized that the structure of public spending and taxation has important consequences for economic growth and decided that the EU member states should aim at a more growth-friendly structure of public finances. Endogenous growth theory broadly suggests that a shift from taxing factor incomes to taxing consumption and a shift from public consumption and transfer spending to public investment has positive growth effects (Aghion and Howitt, 1998). Empirical results in this area are mixed, but they suggest that fiscal policies do have effects on growth.[20]

Subsequently, we characterize the fiscal policies of EMU member states to assess the strength of this conjecture. We do this with a series of cross-section regressions focusing on the period since 1997. While the cross-sections have obvious data limitations, the following bits of evidence add up to a picture that underscores the importance of the structure of fiscal adjustments and taxes and spending more generally.[21] We start by noting that the fiscal rules of the EDP and SGP focus on a reference value for public debt relative to GDP. There are two ways to reduce this ratio, slowing down the growth of nominal debt or speeding up the growth of GDP. Since inflation is no longer under the control of domestic monetary policy, the latter is equivalent to speeding up real GDP growth. The first question we look at considers the choice of the EMU government between these two options.

Let $d = B/Y$ be the ratio of public debt, B, to GDP, Y. The relative contributions of growth in public debt and growth in real GDP to the change in this ratio in country i can be written as:

$$C_i = 100\left(\frac{1+b_i}{1+g_i} - 1\right), \tag{2.5}$$

where b is the growth rate of nominal debt and g is the growth rate of real GDP. If $C_i > 0$, the growth of public debt contributed more to the change in the debt ratio than the growth of real GDP, otherwise, real GDP growth dominated.

Figure 2.1 shows a plot of C_i against the real growth rates of the EU countries for two time periods, 1992–97 and 1997–2003. Positive values on the x-axis indicate that the change in the debt ratio during the period considered was due to growth rates of public debt in excess of the growth rate of real GDP. This was true in almost all EU countries in the first period. In contrast, public debt grew less than real GDP in all countries since 1997. Significantly, Figure 2.1 also shows a strong correlation between the average real GDP growth rate over the post-1997 period and the relative contribution of GDP growth to the change in the debt ratio. Such a relationship did not exist in the first half of the 1990s.

Figure 2.2 gives a plot of the relative contributions of debt and real GDP growth against the change in the debt ratio during the periods under consideration. In the earlier period, when debt ratios increase, this was due to debt growing much faster than real GDP. In the later years, however, the pattern is reversed. Countries that achieved a large decline in the debt ratio are countries that achieved high real GDP growth rates relative to the growth rate of debt over this period. Countries that achieved little real growth relative to debt growth also did not manage to reduce their debt ratios significantly. Figure 2.2 thus suggests that a successful strategy to reduce the debt ratio is one that focuses on growing out of the debt burden rather than one that focuses on slowing down the growth rate of debt while neglecting economic growth. Taking figures 2.1 and 2.2 together, a clear message emerges. Without reviving economic growth, a significant reduction in the debt burden is unlikely. Taking the two periods together, another message is that rising debt burdens come from a lack of control over public sector debt. But to reduce an excessive debt burden, controlling debt is only a necessary condition. This suggests that the fiscal framework of EMU is ill conceived. The focus on deficit and debt ratios alone would be justified if EMU had started in a period in which public debt burdens could be regarded as compatible with long-run equilibrium. Given that a reduction in the debt burden is necessary, particularly in the large countries, the policy framework pays too little attention to the role of economic growth in achieving sustainable public finances.

Next, we turn to public sector revenues and spending. In Figure 2.3, we look at the structure of public sector revenues and growth. We call the sum

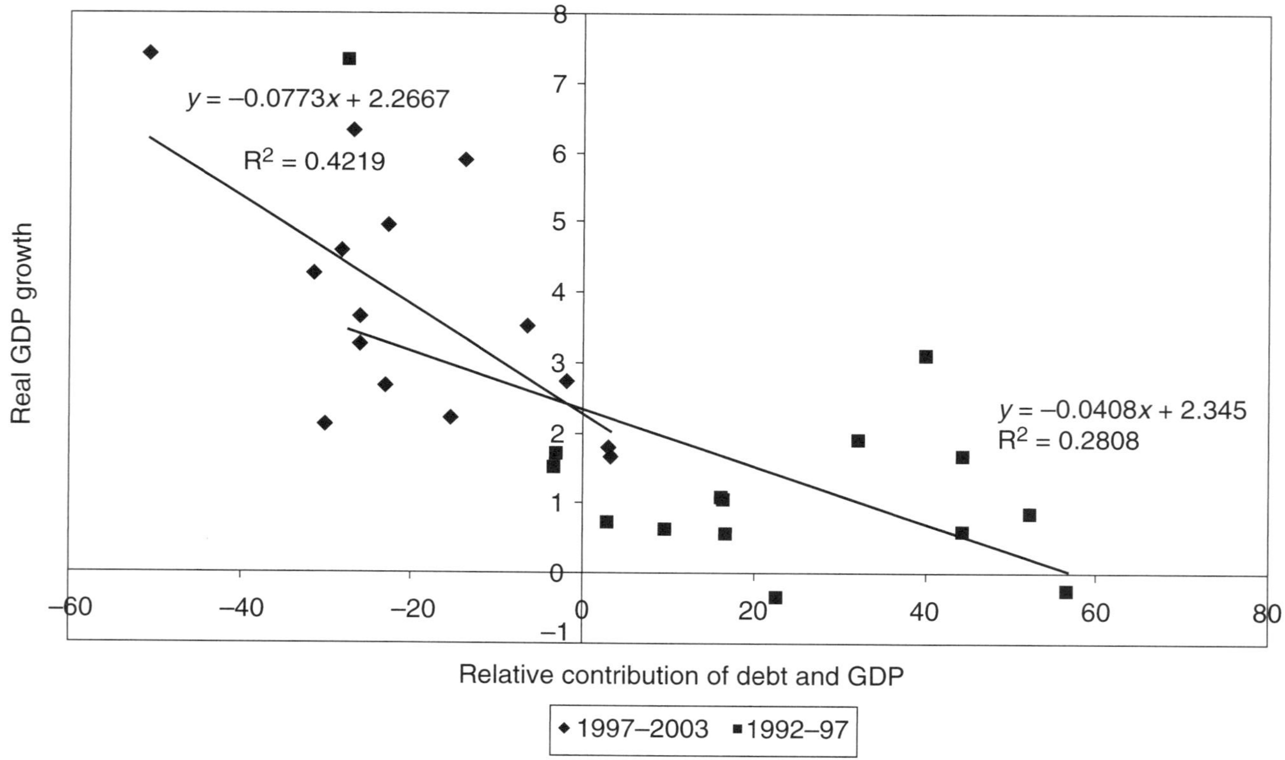

Figure 2.1 Fiscal adjustment

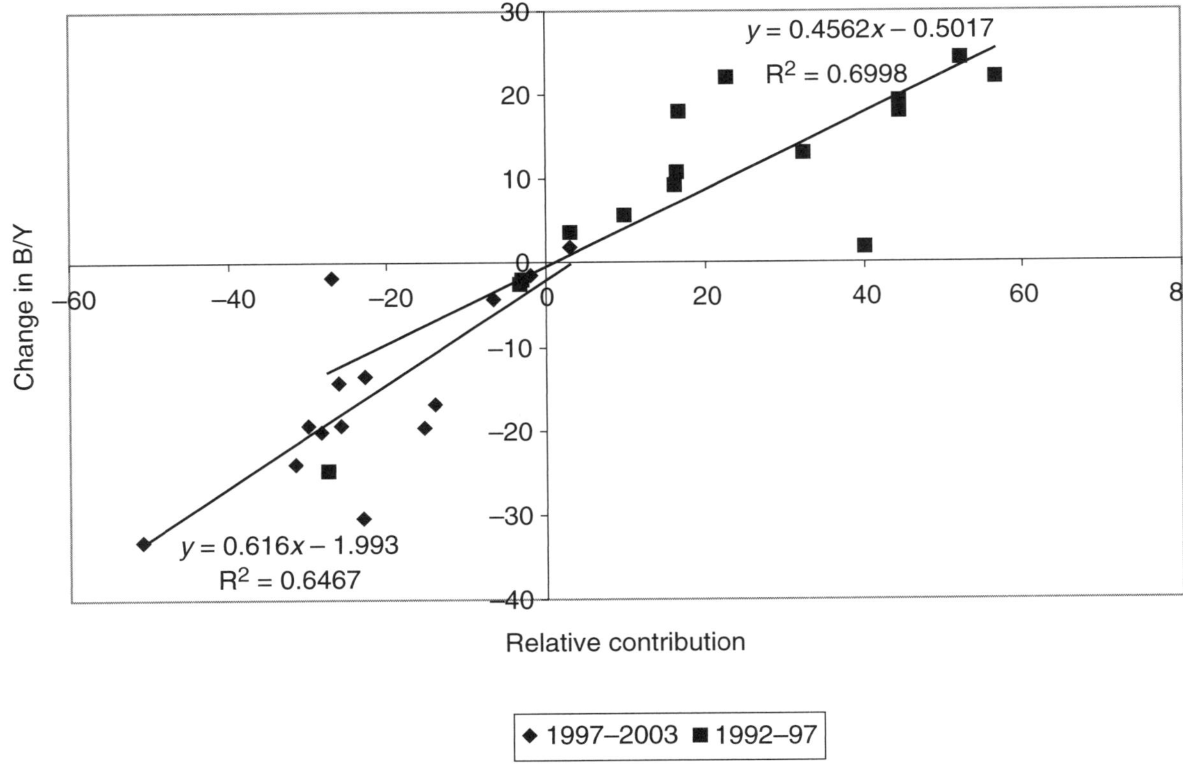

Figure 2.2 *Change in debt ratio*

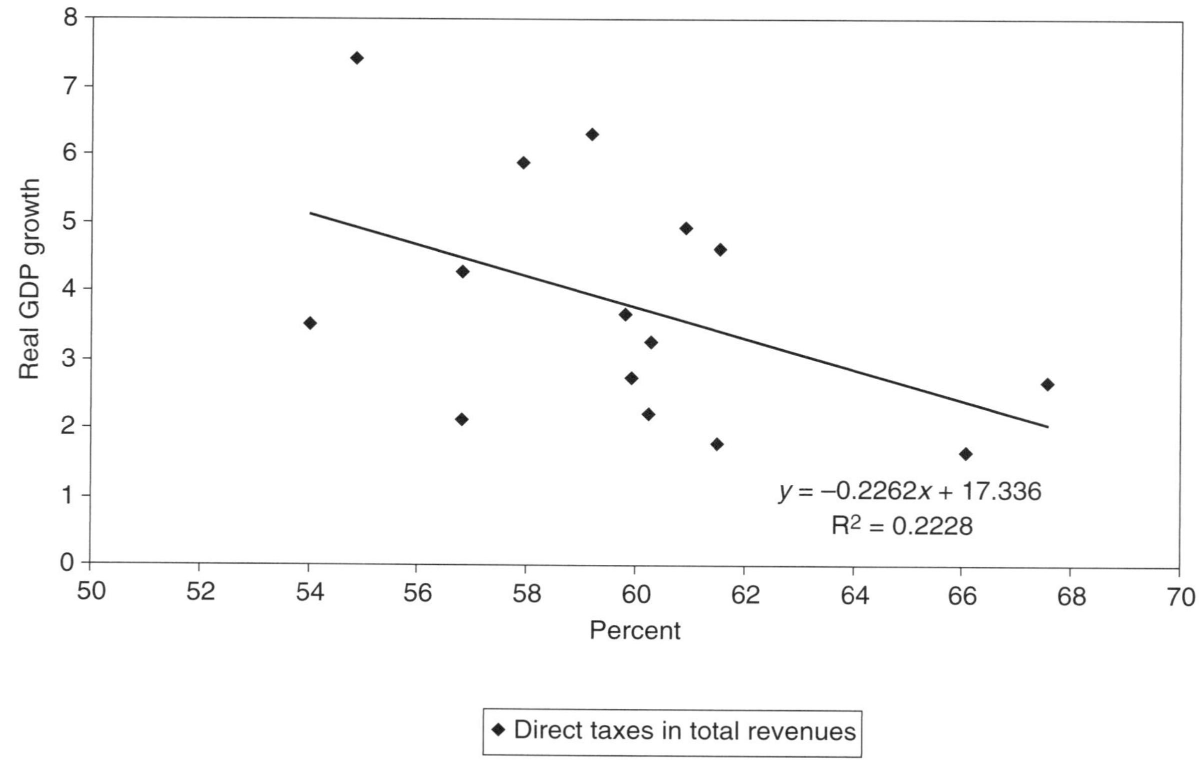

Figure 2.3 *Revenues and growth*

of taxes on income and wealth and social security contributions 'direct' taxes. Figure 2.3 shows a negative association between the share of direct taxes in total government revenues and real GDP growth over the period 1997–2003. Countries relying heavily on direct taxes as a source of income had weaker growth than countries relying more strongly on indirect taxation. In Figure 2.4, we look at the share of public investment and social transfers in total expenditures. The figure shows that countries with higher shares of public investment experienced higher growth rates, while countries with higher shares of social transfers in total spending suffered from weak growth.

Finally, in Figure 2.5, we look at the correlation between fiscal consolidation and real GDP growth. We do this by plotting the growth rate of public debt together with the growth rate of real GDP for the two time periods, 1992–97 and 1997–2003. Figure 2.5 and the two regressions indicate that there is no significant correlation between these two. High growth rates of public debt in the early period apparently did nothing to stimulate economic growth, and lower growth rates in the latter period did not reduce growth. Nor does the figure give much credence to the concept of 'non-Keynesian' effects of fiscal consolidations, that is, the notion that a reduction in public debt would have positive growth effects by stimulating private investment and consumption (Giavazzi and Pagano, 1990). Such effects would lead us to expect higher growth rates for those countries where public debt actually shrank in the period under consideration.

Obviously, the present bivariate framework is not sufficient to achieve a strong conclusion on this matter. Nevertheless, it is in line with the results from a larger econometric model presented in Hughes-Hallett et al. (2001), which does not indicate 'non-Keynesian' effects of the fiscal consolidations in Europe in the past decade. In passing, we note that our evidence here points to a methodological problem of earlier studies of such effects. Specifically, most studies identify fiscal consolidations as periods of significant reductions in public debt or deficit ratios, and 'non-Keynesian' effects as episodes where consolidations go along with vigorous economic growth. The European experience suggests that such episodes may have more to do with policies that succeeded in stimulating growth by restructuring public spending and taxation and reducing tax burdens than with a reduction in public debt or deficits.

2.4 CONCLUSIONS

EU membership has important implications for fiscal policy at the national level. These implications result from the participation in policy coordination and the obligation to maintain sustainable public finances.

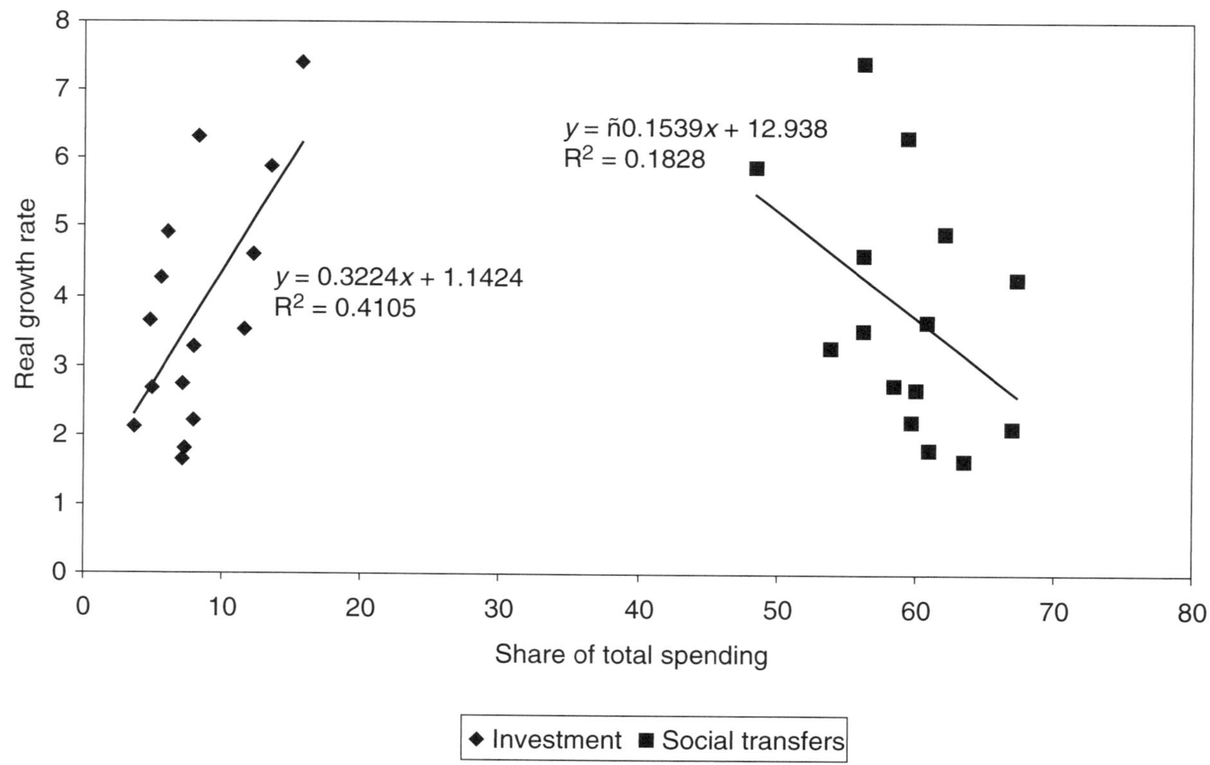

Figure 2.4 *Spending structure (%)*

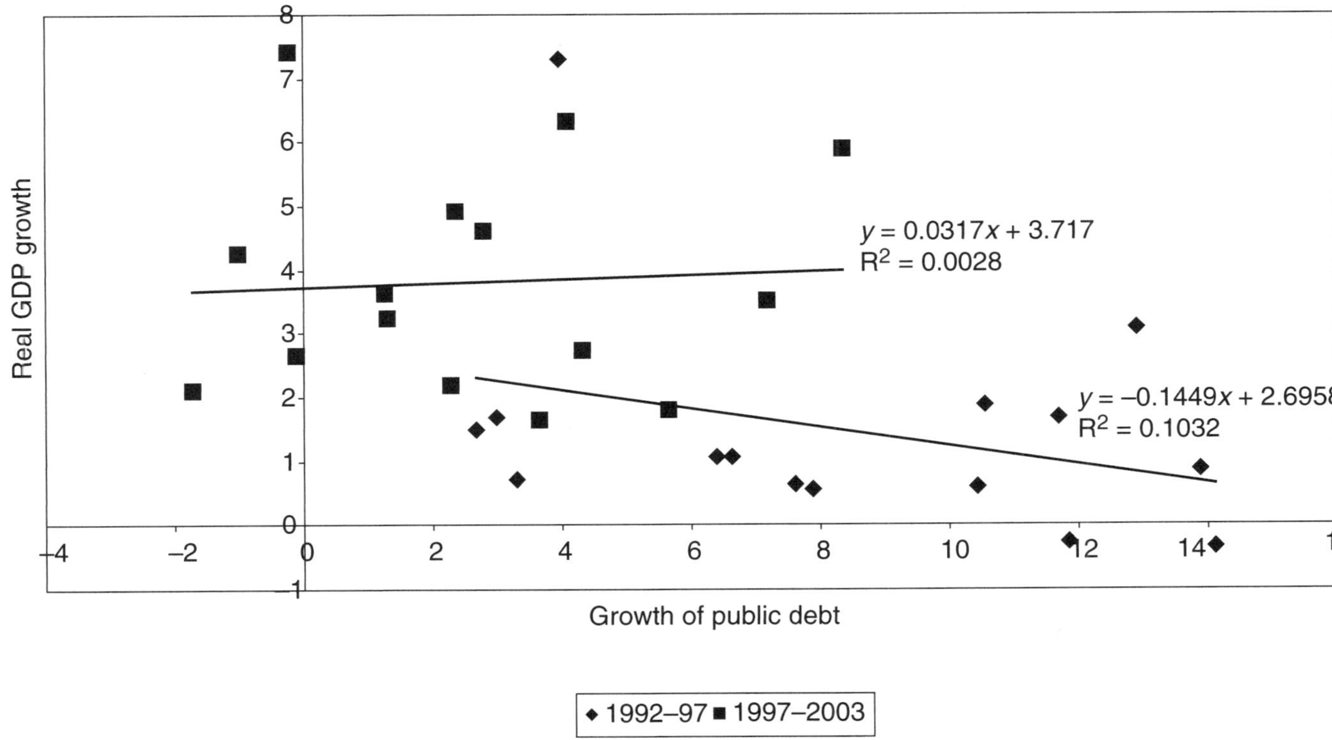

Figure 2.5 Fiscal adjustment and growth

Policy coordination is centred on the Broad Economic Guidelines, which include targets for the quality and the conduct of fiscal policy. As we have shown, the EU has created various networks and processes of coordination. The overarching paradigm of these processes is the method of 'open coordination', which limits coordination to the exchange of views, declarations of intent and efforts to exert peer pressure. In the end, however, policy coordination is not binding and has not resulted in much common action. The main reason for this lack of effectiveness is probably simply the absence of truly 'European' policy problems in many areas, and the unwillingness of the national governments to delegate more competences to the EU level. Nevertheless, participation in the various policy processes is a requirement of EU membership. This creates the need to prepare appropriate reporting tools and frameworks and to abide by the procedural calendars. In contrast, the obligation to maintain sustainable public finances is a binding one in the EU, and the processes for enforcing it are, in principle at least, much stronger.

Nevertheless, the institutional framework of the Excessive Deficit Procedure and the Stability and Growth Pact seem to have done little to discipline fiscal policies especially in the large member states. Based on this judgement, the recent demise of the Stability Pact will not have important consequences. In a union of sovereign member states, common agreements can only be effective if they are supported by the larger economies. This was obviously not the case with regard to the fiscal framework of the EU in the last decade. The implications for a country striving for membership are fairly clear. First, there are technical requirements to be met. Accession countries must create the reporting tools and frameworks foreseen by the Excessive Deficit Procedure and the Stability and Growth Pact. Second, the Copenhagen Criteria for EU membership, laid down at the June 1993 EU Summit, call for 'the existence of a functioning market economy' and the 'ability to take on the obligations of membership, including adherence to the aims of political, economic, and monetary union' (for example European Commission, 2003). A review of the accession reports shows that the Commission regards macroeconomic stability as an important element of the assessment of these criteria. To achieve entry to the EU, fiscal performance must be disciplined enough to keep deficits and debt levels reasonably low.

Third, the numerical criteria of the Excessive Deficit Procedure and the Stability and Growth Pact must be observed to obtain membership in the monetary union, which almost certainly will come later than entry to the EU. After that, experience suggests that sustainability effectively becomes a much less binding obligation, because the governance of the procedures meant to enforce sustainability has been captured by the national governments who are unwilling to penalize one of their own for lack of discipline. Finally, sufficient economic growth is the most important condition for securing and maintaining sustainability of public finances. The experience so far suggests that fiscal policy can contribute to that by reducing the tax burden on labour and capital and the share of transfers in total spending. So far, the EU has not been able to commit its larger members to such policies.

NOTES

1. Fiscal policy constraints at the micro level arise both from the common external trade policy and the Single Market policy of the EU and regard taxation, border tariffs, the regulation of financial markets, and the conduct of public enterprises. See the TEU for details.
2. Under to the Lisbon Strategy, structural policies should gain more prominence on the policy agenda.
3. Italianer (1999) states that because of the abundance of accompanying officials the focus of attention has shifted towards the twice-yearly informal meetings of ministers of finance and central bank governors which often managed to give decisive political impulses to the EMU process.
4. Wyplosz (1999) argues that further centralization at EU level is also hindered by the diverging labour costs throughout Europe where in Germany labour costs are five times larger than in Portugal.
5. The Luxembourg Process and the OECD Job Strategy recommend both that incentives to work are increased within tax and social benefits schemes, and recognize the increasing relevance of 'flexibility' or 'adaptability' for labour market performance. In particular, both recommend that regulatory and administrative burdens be decreased for new business start-ups, and emphasize the job-creation potential of the service sector. The Luxembourg guidelines, however, do not emphasize market flexibility to the same extent as the OECD Jobs Strategy. Unlike the OECD Jobs Strategy, the Luxembourg guidelines do not advocate reforms of employment protection legislation, and do not emphasize the role of wage flexibility and wage dispersion in job creation.
6. To distinguish sustainability from solvency, the former is sometimes defined as the requirement that the intertemporal budget constraint holds with unchanged fiscal policies. See for example Croce and Juan-Ramon (2003) or Perotti et al. (1998) who use an operational definition of sustainability as the absence of a need for large policy adjustments. While assessments of sustainability are conventionally based on expectations for revenues and expenditures, Barnhill and Kopits (2003) suggest a method of evaluating sustainability in the presence of uncertainty.
7. For example, Sargent and Wallace (1981).
8. Note that, while the ECB cannot legally bail out a government in fiscal difficulties by buying its debt directly, it can still do so indirectly, if it wants to. A bail-out could be ex post, with the central bank buying up large amounts of government debt in the market, or ex ante, with the central bank holding down interest rates to reduce the government's interest payments.
9. For a more detailed analysis see below and Fatas et al. (2003). There is also a possibility, however, that constraints on short-term policies aiming at sustainability, such as numerical deficit rules, improve the performance of short-term fiscal policies (for example Beetsma and Debrun (2004; 2005). These authors consider scenarios where unconstrained short-term policies are optimal from the point of view of the government in power, but not from the point of view of the representative citizen, for example, because of distortions arising from the political system. However, arguments of this kind ignore the fact that there are better ways of correcting the underlying distortion.

10. According to Art. 104(3) the Commission may also prepare a report if a member state complies with the criteria but the Commission sees the risk of an excessive deficit nevertheless.
11. Note that neither the deposit nor its conversion into a fine affect the budget of the country in question, as both are financial transactions.
12. For an account of the genesis of the SGP, see Stark (2001).
13. See European Commission (2002a, p. 23).
14. See Fatas et al. (2003) for a review of the reform debate and proposals.
15. See Beetsma and Debrun (2004) and IMF (2004) for a discussion.
16. For example, the European Commission (2002b) and Buti et al. (2003) propose focusing on structural balances rather than the actual deficit, a suggestion that was already incorporated in the 2001 Code of Conduct. Giavazzi and Blanchard (2002) call for a 'golden rule' excluding investment spending from the budget, which the EDP rules hint at. Coeuré and Pisani-Ferry (2005) recommend that the emphasis should be shifted to the debt ratio.
17. The 3 per cent deficit limit under the EDP derives from the 60 per cent debt limit assuming an average nominal GDP growth rate of 5 per cent in all EMU member states.
18. Austria's and Finland's debt ratios increased after 1992, but these countries were not bound by the EDP at the time.
19. Alternatively, one might use the OECD's cyclically adjusted budget balances. These estimates, however, are based on past data and policies. If the introduction of fiscal rules induced changes in the co-movements of cyclical output and budget balances, they could be quite misleading. Buti and van den Noord (2003, 2004) use a similar approach and come to similar conclusions regarding fiscal policy in the early years of EMU.
20. See for example Kneller (2000), Fölster and Henrekson (1999), Tanzi and Zee (1997).
21. To facilitate reading the following figures, note that an R-square of 0.20 in the following regressions corresponds to the 10 per cent critical value, and an R-square of 0.26 to the 5 per cent critical value of the F-distribution of a test for statistical significance.

REFERENCES

Aghion, P. and P. Howitt (1998), *Endogenous Growth Theory*, Cambridge, MA: MIT Press.

Asdrubali, P., B. Sorensen and O. Yosha (1996), 'Channels of interstate risk sharing: United States 1963–1990', *Quarterly Journal of Economics*, **111**, 1081–110.

Athanasoulis, S. and E. van Wincorp (1998), 'Risksharing within the United States: what have financial markets and fiscal federalism accomplished?', Research Paper 9808, Federal Reserve Bank of New York.

Atkeson, A. and T. Bayoumi (1993), 'Do private capital markets insure regional risk? Evidence for the US and Europe', *Open Economies Review*, **4**, 303–24.

Balassone, F., D. Franco and S. Zotteri (2002), 'Fiscal rules for sub-national governments: what lessons for EMU countries', Rome: mimeo, Banca d'Italia Research Department.

Barnhill, T.M. and G. Kopits (2003), 'Assessing sustainability under uncertainty', IMF Working Paper 03/79, Washington, DC.

Beetsma, R. and X. Debrun (2004), 'Reconciling stability and growth: smart pacts and structural reforms', IMF Staff Papers 51, 431–56.

Beetsma, R. and X. Debrun (2005), 'Implementing the stability and growth pact: enforcement and procedural flexibility', CEPR Discussion Paper 5005, London: CEPR.

Blanchard, O. and F. Gïavazzi (2002), 'Reforms that can be done: improving the

SGP through a proper accounting of public investment', mimeo, Department of Economics, Massachusetts Institute of Technology, MA.

Blanchard, O. and J. Wolfers (2000), 'The role of shocks and institutions in the rise of European unemployment: the aggregate evidence', *The Economic Journal*, **110**(462), C1–C33.

Blöndal, J. (2003), 'Budget reform in OECD member countries: common trends', *OECD Journal of Budgeting*, **2**(4), 7–25.

Buti, M. and P. van den Noord (2003), 'Discretionary fiscal policy and elections: the experience of the early years of EMU', OECD Economics Department Working Paper 351, Paris: OECD.

Buti, M. and P. van den Noord (2004), 'Fiscal policy in EMU: rules, discretion and political incentives', Economic Papers 206, Brussels: European Commission.

Calmfors, L. (2001), 'Unemployment, labour market reform and monetary union', *Journal of Labor Economics*, **19**(2), 265–89.

Chalk, N. and R. Hemming (2000), 'Assessing fiscal sustainability in theory and practice', IMF Working Paper 00/81, Washington, DC.

Coeure, B. and J. Pisani-Ferry (2005), 'Fiscal policy in EMU: towards a sustainability and growth pact?', *Oxford Bulletin of Economic Policy*, **21**(4), 598–617.

Croce, E. and V. Hugo Juan-Ramon (2003), 'Assessing fiscal sustainability: a cross-country comparison', IMF Working Paper 03/145, Washington, DC.

DG ECFIN (Directorate General for Economic and Financial Affairs, European Commission) (2002), 'Coordination of economic policies in the EU: a presentation of the key features of the main procedures', Euro Papers 45, Brussels: European Commission.

ECOFIN (2002) (European Council), 2407th Council Meeting (ECOFIN), 6108/02 Presse 28, mimeo, Brussels.

European Commission (1977a), 'Report of the study group on the role of public finance in European integration' (McDougall Report), vol. I, Studies: Economic and Financial Series A13, Brussels.

European Commission (1977b), 'Report of the study group on the role of public finance in European integration' (McDougall Report),vol. II, Studies: Economic and Financial Series B13, Brussels.

European Commission (2000), 'Public finances in EMU 2000', Brussels.

European Commission (2002a), 'Coordination of economic policies in the EU: a presentation of the key features of the main procedures', Euro Paper 45, DG ECFIN.

European Commission (2002b), 'Strengthening the co-ordination of budgetary policies, communication from the commission to the Council and the European Parliament', ECFIN/581/02-EN rev3, Brussels, November 21.

European Commission (2003), 'Strategy paper and report'.

European Council (2005), 'European Council Brussels 22 and 23 March 2005 Presidency Conclusions', Doc. # 7619/05 Brussels 23 March 2005, www.eu2005.lu/en/actualites/conseil/2005/03/23conseileuropen/ceconcl.pdf

Fatas, A., A. Hughes-Hallett, R. Strauch and J. von Hagen (2003), Stability and Growth in Europe – Towards a Better Pact, London: CEPR.

Fölster, S. and M. Heniekson (1999), 'Growth and the public sector: a critique of the critics', *European Journal of Political Economy*, **15**, 337–58.

Giavazzi, F. and M. Pagano (1990), 'Can severe fiscal contractions be expansionary? Tales of two small European countries', in O. Blanchard and S. Fischer (eds), *NBER Macroeconomics Annual*, Cambridge, MA: MIT Press.

Gordo, L. and P. Hernandez de Cos (2000), 'The financing arrangements for the regional (autonomous) governments for the period 1997–2001', Working Paper 3, Bank of Spain, Madrid.
Hughes-Hallett, A., R. Strauch and J. von Hagen (2001), 'Budgetary consolidation in EMU', Economic Policy Paper, 148, European Commission, Brussels.
Hughes-Hallett, A., R. Strauch and J. von Hagen (2002), 'Budgetary consolidations in Europe', *Journal of the Japanese and International Economics*, **16**, 512–35.
Hüttner, B. (1999), 'Österreichischer Stabilitätspakt, Maastricht Defizit und Länderhaushalte', Das öffentliche Haushaltswesen in Österreich, **40**(1–3), 93–105.
International Monetary Fund (2004), World Economic Outlook 2004, Washington, DC: IMF.
Italianer, A. (1999), 'The euro and internal economic policy coordination', *Empirica*, **26**, 201–16.
Jacquet, P. and J. Pisani-Ferry (2000), 'La coordination des politiques economiques dans la zone euro: bilan et propositions', in Conseil d'Analyse economique, *Questions Européennes*, La documentation française, Paris.
Kneller, R. (2000), 'The implications of the Comprehensive Spending Review for the long-run growth rate: a view from the literature', *National Institute Economic Review*, **171**, January, 94–105.
Kneller, R., M.F. Bleaney and N. Gemmel (1999), 'fiscal policy and growth: evidence from OECD countries', *Journal of Public Economics*, **74**, 171–90.
Leeper, E. M. (1991), 'Equilibria under active and passive monetary and fiscal policies', *Journal of Monetary Economics*, **27**(1), 129–47.
Mundschenk, S. and J. von Hagen (2002), 'The political economy of policy coordination in Europe', *Swedish Review of Economic Policy*, **8**, 11–41.
OECD (1996), *OECD Employment Outlook*, Paris: OECD.
Padoa Schioppa, T. (1999), 'Europe's new economic policy constitution', in D. Currie, A. Donnelly, H. Flassbeck, B. Hall, J. Lemierre, T. Padoa-Schioppa and N. Wicks (eds), *Will EMU Lead to a European Economic Government?*, London: Centre for European Reform.
Perotti, R., J. von Hagen and R. Strauch (1998), *Sustainability of Public Finances*, London: CEPR.
Pisani-Ferry, J. (2001), 'The EMU's economic policy principles: words and facts', paper prepared for the DG ECFIN Workshop on the Functioning of EMU: Challenges of the Early Years, Brussels, 21–22 March.
Pisani-Ferry, J. and J. von Hagen (2002), 'Why the EU is not like economists want it to be?', mimeo, ZEI University of Bonn.
Prodi, R. (2002), 'A stronger, better stability and growth pact', speech manuscript, European Parliament, Strasbourg, 21 October.
Sargent, T. and N. Wallace (1981), 'Some unpleasant monetarist arithmetic', *Federal Reserve Bank of Minneapolis Quarterly Review*, **5**(3), 1–18.
Stark, J. (2001), 'Genesis of a pact', in A. Brunila, M. Buti and D. Franco (eds), *The Stability and Growth Pact*, Basingstoke: Palgrave.
Tanzi, V. and H. Zee (1997), 'Fiscal policy and long-run growth', IMF Staff Papers **44**, 179–209.
Von Hagen, J. (1999), 'Co-ordination of economic policies and employment', in A. Lamfalussy, L.D. Bernard and A. Cabral (eds), *The Euro-Zone: A New Economic Entity?*, Brussels: Bruylant.
Von Hagen, J. (2000), 'Fiscal policy and intranational risk sharing', in G.D. Hess and

E. van Wincoop (eds), *Intranational Macroeconomics*, Cambridge: Cambridge University Press.

Von Hagen, J. (2005), 'Fiscal rules in the EU and Japan', mimeo, ZEI University of Bonn.

Von Hagen, J. and I.J. Harden (1994), 'National budget processes and fiscal performance', *European Economy Reports and Studies*, **3**, 311–418.

Von Hagen, J. and S. Mundschenk (2002), 'The functioning of policy coordination in EMU', in A. Sapir and M. Buti (eds), *EMU and Economic Policy in Europe: The Challenge of the Early Years*, Cheltenham, UK and Northampton, MA, USA: Edward Elgar.

Wyplosz, C. (1999), 'Towards a more perfect EMU', CEPR Discussion Paper 2252, London: CEPR.

COMMENTS

Taner M. Yiğit

In analysing the sustainability of EU fiscal policies, the author does a very good job in balancing the EU political structure and its economic consequences. In his study on the EU-15, he initially focuses on the structure of fiscal policy coordination mechanisms in the EU to find that the monitoring of fiscal prudence became much politicized, and that the larger countries with more political power tend to be less disciplined in their fiscal policies. He later conducts empirical tests, showing that (i) the likelihood of consolidation increases with debt ratio, that is, countries with larger initial debt burdens are more disciplined in their fiscal policies; (ii) the countries joining the EMU fall into a consolidation fatigue, noticeably relaxing their fiscal policies; and finally (iii) using growth accounting one can calculate the fiscal impulses that are independent of growth in the EU-15, illustrating that large fiscal impulses occur in election years.

Following his diagnostic analysis, he continues with several recommendations toward both the improvement and better evaluation of fiscal performance in the European Union. The first of these is the possibility of conflicts between the long and short-run targets, necessitating that the members should reconsider the balance between optimal and sustainable policies and not just concentrate on yearly debt or deficit ratios. Secondly, the author notes that rather than simply looking at the ratios, policymakers should dissect them into their components, namely growth and debt (or deficit) to separate out growth-promoting policies from political impulses. Finally, he emphasizes that monetary and fiscal policies should be better coordinated since the ECB is central and independent while fiscal policies are decentralized and national. In fact, he suggests that the EU should even consider aggregation in the evaluation of fiscal performance and planning (as in its monetary policies) for a healthier long-run growth in the EU region.

It is difficult to disagree with many of the facts stated above. Therefore, in the discussion below, I choose to extend and complement the author's analysis by examining the ten new members of the EU and finish with some comments on the implications of the findings for the Turkish economy. After having gone through a costly transition period (except Cyprus and Malta) in the early 1990s the ten new member countries transformed their economies, in return experiencing higher growth and much lower inflation rates, eventually starting accession talks with the EU in 2000. With EU convergence in many areas, they ended their accession talks in 2002 with the consensus that they were ready for membership in 2004. When it comes to their fiscal prudence, however, the picture is completely different, more in line (maybe worse) with the findings of the analysis above.

Examining the deficit and debt to GDP ratios in figures 2C.1a and 2C.1b, we do not see a bright fiscal outlook. Despite the mixed signals we get from the deficit to GDP ratio and the debt to GDP ratios (almost all below the 60 per cent threshold), we witness increases in the debt ratios of almost all countries, especially after the beginning of the accession talks. We also note that some of the countries starting below the 60 per cent threshold go over it by 2004 while only Hungary displays the opposite trend. Inspecting Table 2C.1 on debt and deficit averages and the results from a separate study by Kočenda et al. (2005), we notice an increase in the debt ratios after the accession talks for almost all countries. In the deficit section, we also cannot help but observe the similarity with the EU-15 in the violation of the 3 per cent deficit rule by the larger countries (the Czech Republic, Hungary, and Poland).

We next run regressions similar to those of the author to measure the contribution of debt growth in the ten new member countries to their overall debt to GDP ratios. The outcome of these estimations (illustrated in figures 2C.2a and 2C.2b) shows a strong correlation between output

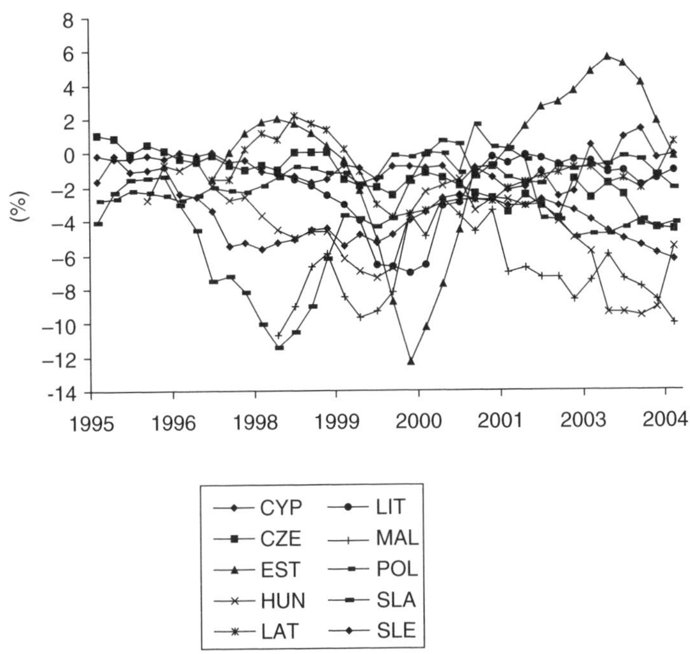

Figure 2C.1a *Deficit to GDP ratio in ten new members of the EU*

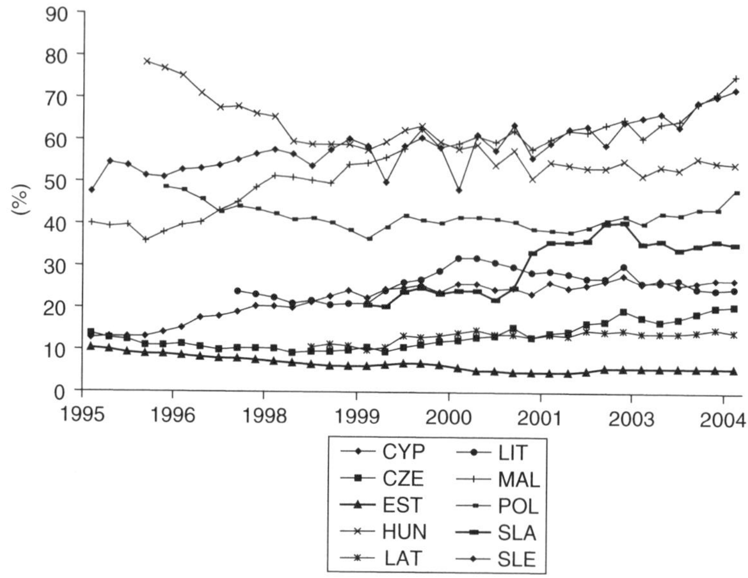

Figure 2C.1b *Debt to GDP ratio in ten new members of the EU*

Table 2C.1 *Deficit and debt ratios before and after the beginning of accession talks with the EU*

	Average deficit/GDP		Average debt/GDP	
	1997–2001	2001–04	1997–2001	2001–04
Cyp	−4.28	−3.93	60.58	66.35
Cze	−3.83	−7.55	14.78	27.48
Est	−0.68	1.10	6.10	5.30
Hun	−5.85	−5.65	60.68	56.25
Lat	−2.90	−2.20	12.73	15.30
Lit	−3.10	−1.95	20.03	23.10
Mal	−8.90	−7.08	57.43	63.15
Pol	−2.33	−3.25	40.00	39.98
Sla	−7.23	−6.90	37.73	46.18
Sle	−2.43	−2.35	24.83	27.13

growth and debt ratio coupled with a higher debt growth than output growth before 2000. These results could be observed by the high R^2 and all the points in Figure 2C.2a lying in the positive quadrant. After the beginning of the accession talks (Figure 2C.2b), the relation is still strong and in

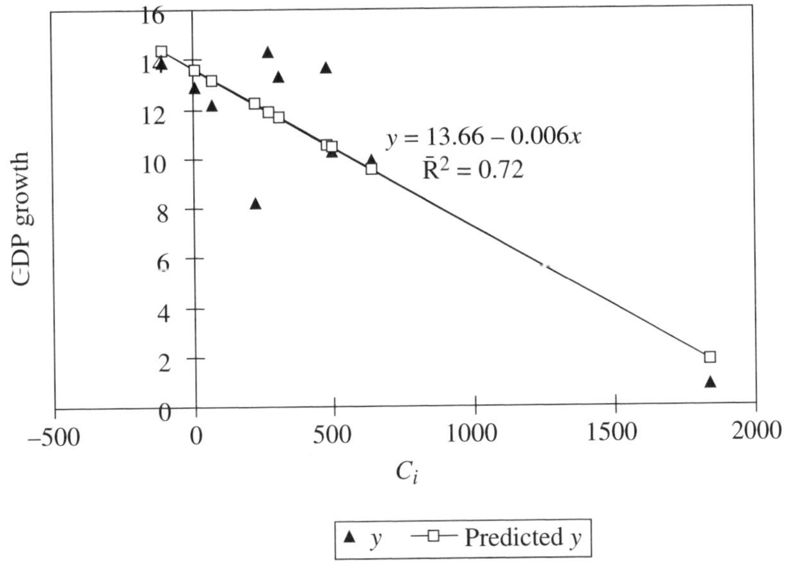

Figure 2C.2a C_i *versus output growth, 1997–2001*

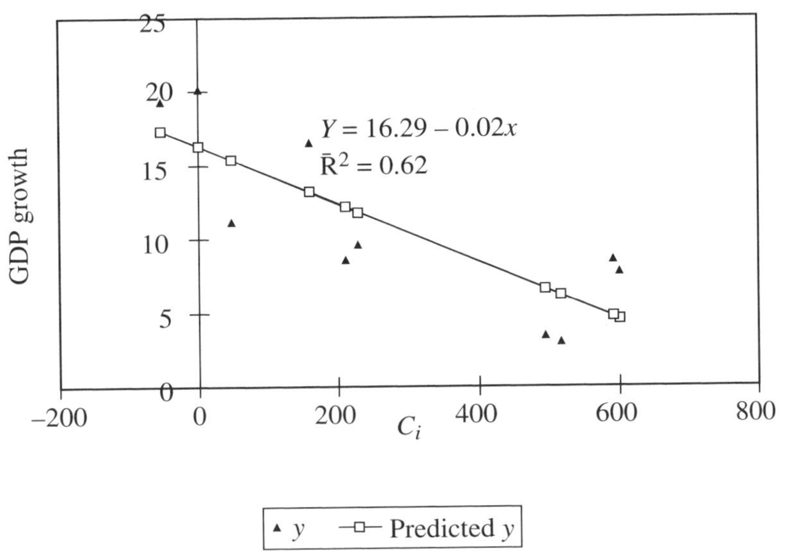

Figure 2C.2b C_i *versus output growth, 2001–04*

the positive quadrant, unlike the trend in EU-15 towards higher GDP growth rate than debt growth after the switch to the EMU. The contribution of debt growth to debt to GDP ratio (C_i) even increases for half of the ten countries. Apparently, these five new members of the EU, while turning their attention to convergence with the EU in many other economic criteria, have overlooked the need for fiscal discipline.

Summarizing our findings in this discussion and Kočenda et al. (2005), we find evidence for (i) the likelihood of consolidation increasing with debt ratio, in other words, countries with a large debt burden following a fiscal discipline while the ones with initial low debt burden behave in the opposite fashion, (ii) consolidation fatigue after the beginning of accession talks, (iii) debt growing faster than output, (iv) no correlation between GDP and debt growth rates in either period, implying that the increase in the ratios were mainly due to fiscal impulses, and finally (v) Baltic countries and Slovakia proceeding more seriously with public reforms than countries such as the Czech Republic where progress is slower.

As a further extension to the study above, one can draw lessons for new candidates, for instance Turkey needs to adhere strictly to the IMF stability programme dictating the 6.5 per cent primary surplus. While this discipline should be sustained even after the end of the programme in 2008, policymakers should also promote growth-enhancing policies to further help the improvement in the debt to GDP ratio of the country. The continuation of the present strong growth performance along with sustainable fiscal policies would provide easier access for Turkey into the EU with fewer burdens for the EU economic region.

Reference

Kočenda, E., A.M. Kutan and T.M. Yiğit (2005), 'Pilgrims to the Eurozone: how far, how fast?', Bilkent University Discussion Paper 05/01.

3. Fiscal policy challenges, sustainability of public finances and EU accession: the case of Turkey

Graham C. Scott*

3.1 INTRODUCTION

This chapter examines the implications of EU succession for the fiscal policies and public finances of Turkey. I begin by summarizing recent fiscal and economic events leading into and emerging from fiscal and financial crisis and the causes of what occurred. The chapter reviews the record of attempts to reform fiscal institutions over the past decade and suggests what shaped the agenda and explains the slow progress until the aftermath of the crisis. Turkey's very ambitious and well-designed reforms of fiscal institutions, which are now under way, are described, together with some thoughts on the risks and challenges of implementation. EU accession is then discussed within this context and some final remarks summarize the key messages.

Turkey's rapid descent into economic and fiscal crisis and its remarkably successful response to it are well documented and I need only summarize the key features of these events to set the stage for my reflections on these events and to inform readers who are not familiar with recent developments in Turkey's government finances.

The Organization for Economic Co-operation and Development (OECD, 2004) report captures the situation succinctly in its executive summary, which also provides a concise précis of this chapter.

> Turkey is at a crossroads. After hitting the most severe crisis in its recent history in 2000–2001, the economy bounced back and is now among the fastest growing economies in the OECD. A new institutional framework for monetary and fiscal policies etc opened a window of opportunity to escape from the three traps of low confidence, weak governance and high informality which underpinned the boom and bust cycle of the past and to embark durably on a higher growth path. Success will depend on fully implementing and completing the new policy framework.

My personal perspective on these issues comes partly from my experiences in New Zealand as the head of its finance ministry at a time when the country experienced a fiscal crisis, which it steadfastly resolved over a period of ten years. My perspective also comes from twelve years working on fiscal policy and public sector management reform in some forty countries at various stages of development. From this work I have learned that what is taught in macroeconomic textbooks about fiscal policy is the tip of an iceberg, made up of the complex fabric of micro policies and the institutions that implement them. To understand fiscal outcomes you need to have a deep and practical understanding of the policies and institutions that created them. There are no shortcuts.

3.2 BACKGROUND SITUATION AND PERSPECTIVES ON TURKISH FISCAL POLICY

Turkey experienced the most severe economic crisis in its recent history in 2000–01 followed by a remarkable recovery. Gross Domestic Product (GDP) dropped 7.5 per cent in 2001 but recovered to grow by 8 per cent and 6 per cent in the following two years. The recovery has been based on productivity growth and strong consumption, investment and export demand. This has been underpinned by the institutional reform of the Central Bank that, from my perspective, is particularly interesting as it is very similar in concept to the reform of the Central Bank in New Zealand in the 1980s and has produced even more dramatic declines in inflation. The inflation rate dropped from 69 per cent in 2001 to 18 per cent in 2003 and 9 per cent in 2004.[1] Further declines to single figures have followed for the first time in 30 years. Fiscal policy has also involved a remarkable turnaround based on an agreement between the International Monetary Fund (IMF) and the government targeted on primary surpluses of 6.5 per cent of Gross National Product (GNP). There has been progress with eliminating off-budget funds and quasi-fiscal activities are more restricted. But it is essential in thinking about future fiscal strategy to understand what drove the fiscal crisis that occurred and what has brought about its relief.

A feature of this story has been the developments in relation to the public debt. The paper by Caroline Van Rijckeghem (2004) analyses the story in fine detail and its key conclusions are important for this chapter so I will touch on them quickly. Appendix 3.1 summarizes briefly some of the key statistics and analysis behind these conclusions.

Following Van Rijckeghem, the pattern shows reasonably clearly what the weaknesses in the fiscal position can be attributed to:

(1) Large risk premia in interest rates caused by a lack of credibility in economic policy and, in particular, inadequate financial sector policies (duty losses are a particular example of this);
(2) State Economic Enterprise (SEE) policies;
(3) Social Security policies;
(4) Contingent liabilities in infrastructure developments; and to a lesser extent, primary deficits.

Given the turnaround in fiscal policy and monetary policy, the important issues to reflect upon are the extent to which these measures have put the fiscal problems of Turkey behind it by addressing, in a fundamental way, the underlying causes of the problem. Or is there reason for concern that these problems have not been dealt with robustly and more is needed? Looking further ahead is there reason to think that even if what has been done does address the causes of past problems, there are new issues in fiscal strategy and the reform of fiscal institutions that should be addressed with greater vigour?

3.3 THE CHALLENGES AHEAD FOR A SOUND SUSTAINABLE FISCAL FRAMEWORK

The recovery from financial crisis points to vital lessons about how to stay away from crises of a similar nature in the future. There is also the imperative to address serious and long-standing weaknesses in fiscal institutions that were there before the crisis and endured through previous financial disturbances in the 1990s. The government is pressing ahead with an impressive range of initiatives with the intention of sustaining the fiscal improvements, as can be seen for example in the Pre-accession Economic Programme (PEP). But the historical record suggests caution in assuming that critical initiatives to reform fiscal institutions will be achieved as planned.

Moving from Quantitative to Qualitative Fiscal Adjustment

In fact it is fair to say that the long-running debate and agenda on reform of fiscal institutions and public administration has had a life of its own, which is only loosely related to the periodic financial disturbances. While the weakness in the structures of fiscal policy such as SEE performance, contingent liabilities, duty losses, and so on, obviously contributed greatly to the crisis, there is far more at stake in fiscal reform than addressing those particular issues.

Also it would be a mistake to be too confident that measures that have enabled a primary surplus to be achieved in the aftermath of a crisis and within the confines of an IMF programme can be sustained in the longer term. Even if they could, there will be difficult trade-offs to face between top-down measures to set ceilings on spending categories and impose tight central discipline on the one hand while on the other achieving the other goals of good fiscal policy, which are to improve allocative and productive efficiency. Modern performance-enhancing public management is about balancing management freedom and accountability for results. This is rarely consistent for long with the imposition of stern central disciplines and detailed control from the centre over finance and human resource management. By the same token, fiscal control at the macroeconomic level is only consistent with devolution, decentralization and management freedom if there are in place advanced systems, processes and institutions to ensure that these freedoms are exercised responsibly, within budget, efficiently and accountably and driven to strive for ever improving standards of service.

Turkey's fiscal and public management institutions have been inadequate in terms of the three dimensions of fiscal performance, that is, macro-fiscal control, effective prioritization of scarce resources and performance improvement in the delivery of services by the state. Balancing these three goals is a challenge anywhere and so a vital question for the authorities in Turkey is how to sustain macroeconomic stability while scoring well on the other two goals. This goes to the heart of the issues of the sustainability of the restored fiscal situation. If stability has been bought at the expense of resource allocation and the quality of services, then the political mandate for the means by which stability was attained will wane, as it appears to have done in the past.

Sustainable sound fiscal policy for the future will involve years of determined progress on a daunting range of issues concerning policy frameworks, resource allocation, effective and efficient service delivery and accountability. Fiscal strategies will have to be cast in a medium-term framework, aligned with national and local development strategies and social needs and with the priorities and politics that are embedded in the political system. Simply put, there needs to be a shift from the quantity of fiscal adjustment to the quality of fiscal adjustment through the creation of policies and institutions that meet these challenges. This is not easy to achieve anywhere and will be a challenge in Turkey. The existing system, as I noted in my work on the Public Expenditure and Institutional Review (PEIR, 2001), was too tight in respect of the central government activities funded by the budget and too loose elsewhere.

Support for this institutional perspective comes from OECD (2004) which characterizes the future policy requirements as addressing three 'traps', firstly in confidence in political and macroeconomic stability, secondly in governance in the sense of the quality of public institutions and public services, and thirdly in informality, which is undermining legitimate business activities and eroding the tax base.

Turkey's own plans and its recent accomplishments all have elements of reform of fiscal institutions. However, to avoid mistaking intentions, plans and even laws for accomplishments in terms of the outcomes of improved fiscal institutions, it is worth rehearsing the legacy of diagnostics as to why Turkey found itself in crisis and then looking more closely at the accomplishments and plans.

The Legacy of Weak Fiscal Institutions

There have been numerous diagnoses of Turkish fiscal institutions in the last five years or so, both by the Turkish Government and other authoritative Turkish sources and also in partnership with international organizations.

In the context of the eighth five-year development plan the special ad hoc Committee on Restructuring of Management of Public Finance and Financial Transparency made a short statement of the problems in the fiscal system. As it saw them, the principle of unity and generality in budgeting had been lost, budgets were inflexible, and the efficiency of the provision of services had been undermined by the budgeting process and the complex and lengthy fund allocation and expenditure processes. The focus was very short term. The World Bank's Public Financial Management Project and certain aspects of the 2000–02 Stability Programme were designed to attend to these shortcomings, but there was a lack of follow-through due in part to what was translated into the English draft as 'chauvinism' within public agencies and their departments.

The committee went on to make a full set of recommendations that, if implemented, would bring Turkey up to the best international standards of fiscal management. Anne Krueger, First Deputy Managing Director, IMF, remarked in a statement after the IMF Board approval of $1 billion stand-by credit to Turkey: 'To be sustainable, the achievement of the overall budget targets will need to be underpinned by decisive reforms in public employment and budget mechanisms.'

The PEIR, which was done in partnership between the Turkish authorities and the World Bank in 2000–01, describes the problems in the fiscal system in the following terms:

(1) Resource flows and resource management processes are highly fragmented;

(2) Fiscal discipline is undermined by non-transparent quasi-fiscal policies and accumulation of fiscal risks which have been exacerbated by poor financial sector governance;
(3) There is little strategic policy or plan guidance to resource allocation; ad hoc processes dominate; and
(4) Antiquated, compliance-oriented budget regulations inhibit operational efficiency and also fail to provide effective financial control.

The PEIR pointed to major weaknesses in procurement, problems in completion of infrastructure projects and in allocating funds to high pay-off areas of public expenditures for example public health programmes.

In a significant speech to a conference of ministers, officials and academics, Ferhat Emil (2000), a senior Treasury official, said of the system:

> It is a fact that Turkish Budgeting System and Expenditures management, at this juncture where we are about to enter the second year of a stability program covering a three-year period, needs to be transformed now in a more substantial way from one that is oriented to handling daily problems into a structure that is geared to solving medium-term problems. Otherwise, the Turkish Budgeting System stands at a point where it is about to lose its function as the instrument of fiscal policy and resource allocation.

He spoke also on that occasion of the problems of circumvention of the budget system due to its rigidities and the need for more flexibility and concern for performance.

Researchers at the Turkish Economic and Social Studies Foundation (TESEV) analysed Turkish fiscal institutions in depth in numerous articles and in a book of conference proceedings published in 2000 (Atiyas and Sayın, 2000) that summarized a lot of expert opinion at that time. This book contains an article by Atiyas and Sayın on good practice benchmarks for fiscal transparency and also an article by Dedeoğlu, Emil and Erden which provides a long list of budget provisions that reduce fiscal transparency and fiscal discipline. These include supplementary appropriations, transfers between appropriations and issuance of non-cash debt. This book also contains an article by Hürcan, Kızıltaş and Yılmaz applying the Transparency Code of the IMF to Turkey to arrive at a poor score of 50–60 out of 100.

Moving from Treasury to TESEV, Emil has written a short but definitive critique of the fiscal machinery and how the measures that have been taken address these (Emil, 2004). His critique of the expenditure system is briefly that:

(1) Aggregate fiscal management is weakened by the inability of the budget to encompass and report on quasi-fiscal activities or 'hidden deficits', which he estimates were 10–12 per cent of GNP;

(2) Neither the five-year development plans nor discretionary policies generally are linked to the budget, which is short term and lacks credibility with the agencies;
(3) Excessive controls over budget implementation do not however prevent waste and inefficiency;
(4) Fiscal transparency is undermined by a lack of common accounting standards; and
(5) A significant part of the government finance is not subject to audit examination, despite the existence of the Court of Accounts and other multiple control and inspection bodies.

Why had this transparently unsatisfactory situation been allowed to develop and why was it so resistant to urgently needed reform? Some discussion of this is important for thinking about the conditions for maintaining momentum for improvement in the future from the initiatives taken since these commentators made their remarks.

At a conference in December 2001,[2] the then Minister of Finance Sümer Oral said that the problems could have been avoided if the authorities had reacted earlier. He said reform was difficult because of resistance from various groups. Why was there such resistance to changes that were so widely recognized as being overdue?

My answer to this question is that a long period of political instability had resulted in a very weak capacity at the top of the government to make strategic decisions and act in the wider collective public interest. At the political level, these problems were compounded by the divisions among the parties to the coalition governments. Over time, governments resorted to increasingly non-transparent public financial management in support of ad hoc decision-making. This undermined effective fiscal management and allowed the accumulation of large expenditure deficits, debt and fiscal risks. Poor governance of the finances also added to the implicit and explicit liabilities of the government.

The problems of leadership were exacerbated by the problems in the key institutions of government. At the level of the senior executive levels of the key central agencies, there were deep divisions and rivalries accentuated by the central agencies (the Ministry of Finance, Treasury and State Planning Organization) falling under different parties in the coalition government.

Multiple agencies with unclear mandates acted in non-cooperative ways to block progress or seek to achieve gains at the expense of others. For example, there are multiple audit institutions, none of whom perform an effective audit function, which still leaves significant parts of government without audit or oversight. Reforms to clarify the relationships between the audit agencies and to ensure that there was a recognized supreme audit authority were blocked.

At the same conference in 2001, a large group of senior officials in a workshop[3] agreed, with only a few exceptions, that the problems highlighted in the PEIR were real and that there needed to be action on three levels to implement a solution:

(1) High-level political agenda-setting and mandating of working groups;
(2) Developing legislation to underpin and consolidate the framework of a new system of public expenditure management; and
(3) Organizing the central ministries to work with line ministries, autonomous agencies and client groups to develop and implement solutions by working together.

So we can ask whether the changes that have been made and are now under way are meeting these requirements and what the longer-term plans are to raise the quality of fiscal adjustment?

Accomplishments and Plans for the Future

Following the crisis the reform agenda includes very significant institutional reforms as well as policy adjustments. It is backed by the National Convergence Programme to the EU *acquis communautaire* and the IMF stand-by arrangements and underpinned by the Government Action Plan. The creation of the independent central bank, which is to target the rate of inflation, is central to macroeconomic stabilization. This is producing even more astonishing results in terms of inflation than the precedent from New Zealand which pioneered this approach in the late 1980s.

Fiscal policy is driven by the agreement with the IMF to target a primary surplus of 6.5 per cent of GNP. There is a strong institutional element in the reform as most off-budget activities have been phased out and quasi-fiscal arrangements are much harder to implement. Build–Operate–Transfer (BOT) arrangements for infrastructure have been stopped to avoid the creation of new contingent liabilities.

The agenda for change in the fiscal system to bring the public expenditure laws and systems up to international standards, is well under way, as spelt out by the Ad Hoc Committee on Restructuring of Management of Public Finance and Financial Transparency, as part of the work for the 8th Development Plan. Two new laws have been adopted to strengthen the budget and control systems. The Public Finance and Debt Management Law effective from January 2003 sets borrowing limits for central government and principles for effective debt and risk management. It addresses the problem of contingent liabilities and places restrictions on local government borrowings under Treasury guarantees. It also sets rules for accounting for debt and for recording and budgeting for certain fiscal risks.

The Public Financial Management and Control Law, which was passed in 2003 and became effective in 2006, is constructed as a very advanced model of modern public finance by international standards and addresses the weakness of the present system. Its purposes are simply:

> to regulate the structure and functioning of the public financial management, the preparation and implementation of the public budgets, the accounting and reporting of all financial transactions, and financial control in line with the politics and objectives covered in the development plans and programs, in order to ensure the effective, economic and efficient collection and utilization of public resources as well as accountability and fiscal transparency.

Article 5 of the law contains 'fundamental principles' which address most or all of the basic purposes of a high-performing system of public finance and management. It re-establishes the unitary nature of the budget as covering all aspects of the public finances and establishes clear objectives in terms of transparency, accountability, strategic planning and performance-based budgeting. Looked at broadly, it is an impressive law and tackles, head-on, the widely accepted diagnosis of the serious problems in the existing system. Ultimately, however, its benefits will depend on the details of the law and the processes and practices it engenders.

It brings local authorities and social security institutions under the coverage of the budget. There are sanctions for exceeding appropriation limits. It enhances the strategic dimension of fiscal policy as it requires the government to declare a medium-term fiscal framework with provisions for a multi-year budgeting framework. It provides for expenditure ceilings at the start of the budget process which should promote better prioritization.

Article 9, which mandates strategic planning and performance-based budgeting, is internationally innovative but whether this is successful will depend on the details of the controls that are mandated elsewhere in the law. As I have already emphasized, getting the balance between freedom for and central control over managers is the central challenge for any country pushing for a performance driven management system. Emil (2004) expresses concern in this regard that ex ante financial controls are made more complex by the law.

The law provides for accrual accounting to be adopted, although it leaves the budget on a cash basis. While this is a sensible compromise for the time being for administrative services, it will be important to get international accounting standards throughout the reporting of all activities where cash accounting is seriously misleading in reporting on the performance of an organization.

An important step forward is the new mandate to the Court of Accounts to do performance auditing, although this will raise major issues in building capability.

Risks and Challenges

Getting these laws drafted and passed in the parliament must have been a daunting task and it has been done with effectiveness and coherence. But passing laws of this kind is always easy compared with implementing them, which is only beginning in many aspects. What is the evidence today that implementation will succeed, keeping in mind the requirements for successful change that were thought to be necessary by the workshop of senior officials in 2001 and quoted above?

It is clear that there has been a sea change in willingness to finally tackle long-standing, widely accepted, well-researched and serious weaknesses in fiscal policy and fiscal institutions. There has been a breakthrough, which is somewhat surprising to me given the sense of seeming despair I sensed amongst many senior officials when I was last in Turkey in 2001.

This is encouraging, but it is important to remember that there have been bursts of reform before; for example, in tidying up SEEs and other matters. But the piecemeal approach in the past did not add up to a movement for continuing improvement in fiscal policy which kept Turkey from descending into crisis once more. What is there this time that provides comfort that the reform movement is well grounded and will have the determination to keep going for the ten years or so that it will take to build the fiscal institutions, capability and culture right across the public sector at all levels of government?

Change management of this kind requires clear goals, extraordinary persistence over time, strong leadership, public commitment and willingness to make some sacrifices. It also requires cooperation across the bureaucracy and willingness to dampen down old rivalries, and politicians who will conduct their contests for power in ways that do not sacrifice the wider national interest in effective fiscal policy to narrow sectoral interests.

Turkey has at the same time addressed long-standing issues about its highly centralized public administration system in which the central government has dominated the local governments. The ambitious decentralization to local government that is under way transfers major spending powers to provincial administrations and municipalities. While the aims of this are to improve the quality and responsiveness of services and enhance autonomy, there have to be worries over whether this will lead to a loss of fiscal control at the local level just at the time it is being regained at the centre. As the OECD report (OECD, 2004, p. 14) notes:

> It is therefore of crucial importance to fully apply the new fiscal and debt management framework to sub-central entities in order to limit their overall borrowing and prevent off-budget and quasi fiscal spending.

I strongly endorse this as the experiences of other countries in devolution show how difficult it can be to get a coherent and politically workable decentralization starting from a highly centralized system. Thailand and Vietnam are two countries grappling with similar issues and, in doing so, facing a lot of problems in practical and political terms.

Further, as is emphasized in the OECD report (2004, p. 61), there must be concern over the fact that there will be strong pressures for additional spending in social security, health, education, infrastructure in less developed regions, the wages bill for public sector employees and other areas of spending. Expenditures, excluding debt service, rose 8 per cent from 1995 to 2003 mainly due to protection of the income levels of various groups (ibid.). It is a concern that even the prospective fiscal relief from reduced debt will not provide the headroom to meet these demands. As the OECD (ibid.) puts it starkly:

> Turkey's tax revenues and primary expenditures as a percentage of GDP because of the heavy source cost of public debt, was one of the highest in the OECD. In contrast, neither GDP per capita not the quality of public services and institutions had converged toward OECD levels.

So there must be a risk to the refreshing fiscal reform movement that is now under way that it might falter as others have before it and for similar reasons. Additionally there must also be a risk that new pressures, new spending on social services, higher public sector wages, and decentralization will seriously stress the political system as it tries to restore the government balance sheet to good health and restrain expenditure demands at a time of rising expectations. There must also be risks that the upgrade in public sector capability and performance that is a necessary condition for the goals of the legislation to be met, will outstretch the capacity and willingness of government organizations to change. A final risk comes from the large informal sector, which is limiting the government's ability to collect tax revenue. This touches on the large and important issue surrounding governance and transparency beyond the area of fiscal policy. This is beyond the scope of this chapter although it is an essential contextual influence on whether the fiscal reforms can be achieved.

3.4 THE EU INFLUENCE ON FUTURE FISCAL POLICY

Prospective accession to the EU will increasingly raise issues that intrude on the development of Turkey's fiscal policies and institutions, but how, when and to what effect? What should Turkey do to ensure that these intrusions are beneficial to its future fiscal management and outcomes? It is impossible to know the answers at this point of course, but I will share some preliminary thoughts from an observer who is about as far away from the action as it is possible to be.

At the outset of the process of convergence with EU fiscal policy frameworks, there is no apparent misalignment with Turkey's fiscal reforms, as the reforms to address past crises and institutional weakness are all in the direction of convergence with the EU. The general macroeconomic principles and requirements of the Stability and Growth Pact (SGP) and the procedures under Article 99[4] are all in general accord with what the Turkish Government has decided to do anyway, and are backed by the International Financial Organizations. As the Pre-accession Economic Programme (PEP) says:

> Further improvement of the existing social policies and thereby an increase in the welfare of the society will be possible by achieving a permanent stability in the economy through continued implementation of the current macroeconomic policies. The proposed economic policies in this program aim at attaining a sustainable growth rate performance, lowering the inflation to single digit levels permanently, ensuring convergence of the fiscal deficits and the public debt stock to the GDP ratios towards EU averages, bringing the inter-regional development differences of Turkey to EU levels, and thereby letting the per capita income level of Turkey converge towards the EU averages. These targets, set in the framework of Maastricht and Copenhagen economic criteria, constitute the main perspective in the determination of economic policies during the EU accession period. (Republic of Turkey, 2004)

It is reasonable to expect that this harmony between national goals and EU requirements will continue while the momentum of reform is maintained. However, if momentum is lost, then the EU requirements will become a helpful pressure that is likely to be in Turkey's longer-term interests, but this alignment may not always be the case. Also, while these pressures may be regarded as helpful by economists, they may prove to be very difficult for politicians.

The effects of accession not only on Turkish fiscal policy but also on EU fiscal policy will largely depend on how the Turkish economy adapts to its future membership and therefore cannot be foreseen. I will make only a few general observations about matters that do seem reasonably clear in relation to expenditure and revenue policies and deficits.

Fiscal Discipline through Accession

The *acquis* is based on a common macroeconomic policy framework for all members to facilitate the working of the European Economic and Monetary Union (EMU). This begins loosely but gets progressively more constraining with the adoption of the *acquis* after accession and even more so when the euro is introduced.

In the pre-accession phase the emphasis is on the Copenhagen economic criteria. There are no binding constraints imposed by EU legislation on budgetary policy, although there are impacts in the areas of independence of thc ccntral bank and its financing of the public sector and financial institutions in particular. Turkey has already addressed these issues.

With accession, the common policy framework provides strong reinforcement of fiscal discipline. Budgets become subject to the excessive deficit procedure and the non-punitive parts of the SGP. Economic policies become a matter of common concern and hence subject to policy coordination and multilateral surveillance procedures.

After accession Turkey will become subject to the SGP, the core commitment of which is for budgets that are close to balance or in surplus.

> This will allow Member States 'to deal with the normal cyclical fluctuations while keeping the government deficit within the 3 per cent reference value'. The Pact, in other words, aims to prevent the emergence of excessive deficits as defined by Art. 104 while allowing the automatic stabilizers to operate during a recession. It sets the framework for the use of the fiscal policy instrument for all Members States. In addition, it is the fiscal counterpart to the single monetary policy of the euro area and it underpins an adequately co-ordinated policy mix. (EU Commission, 2002)

In order to allow for cycles and instability in the economy, the SGP implies large structural surpluses for the more volatile economies if they are to stay within the 3 per cent ceiling – or a generous definition of the time scale over which compliance is assessed.

A point of some importance to Turkey in the SGP is that the Commission takes account of the relative sizes of the fiscal deficit and investment expenditure, which helps to avoid a problem of fiscal restraint crowding out high return investment expenditures.

The key principle behind the EU accession process as it affects fiscal policy is to elevate it to a more important policy instrument. This reflects the underlying belief that the burden on monetary policy is reduced over time through policy convergence and finally, entry to the EMU and use of the euro. At some future time these pressures will be considerable when Turkey joins the monetary union. However, for the foreseeable future, much stronger external pressures on the government for disciplined fiscal policy will come from the domestic and international financial markets and the IMF. Declines in confidence in capital markets will quickly translate into exchange rate instability and force governments to correct any errors in fiscal policy.

I should make it clear, however, that I do not see this as a reason for early entry into the EMU or use of the euro in order to create stronger pressures for fiscal reform. The risks would be too great. As Calvo and Mishkin (2003, p. 100) conclude in their study of exchange rate regimes in emerging market countries:

> the key to macroeconomic success in emerging market countries is not primarily their choice of exchange rate regime, but rather the health of the countries' fundamental macroeconomic institutions, including the institutions associated with fiscal stability, financial stability and monetary stability. In general, we believe that less attention should be focused on the general question of whether a floating or a fixed exchange rate is preferable and more on these deeper institutional arrangements.

Turkey's new arrangements for monetary and exchange rate policies seem to be serving their purpose quite well and in my view it is appropriate for some of the adjustment pressures to emerge in exchange rate changes for the foreseeable future. These adjustment pressures will be severe in the light of the goal of convergence. GDP per capita in Turkey is 29 per cent of the EU average, its GDP is about 2 per cent of the EU-25 GDP or half that of the ten new member states. Its population is 15.5 per cent of the EU-25. Turkey has large regional disparities with the richest region having GDP per capita of 46 per cent of the EU-25 average, while the poorest regions have about 8 per cent. The potential benefits to Turkey are very large if the adjustment goes well but this will require macroeconomic and financial stability, efficient management of the public finances, investment in human and physical capacity and policies to reduce large regional disparities in line with EU norms. The European Central Bank rather understates this message in saying 'A well-defined institutional framework is important to support the long-run growth of the economy and "high quality" public finances play an important role for its functioning' (Alfonso et al., 2005, p. 31).

The ultimate effect of EU economic arrangements is to place much of the burden of adjustment and stabilization on fiscal policy, leaving the central bank to focus on its primary goals of constraining inflation and the stability of the financial sector. However, this demands that fiscal policy and fiscal institutions are operating to a very high standard of capability and effectiveness. A premature entry into the EMU could put unmanageable strains on fiscal policies and institutions that are not ready to carry those burdens.

Expenditure Policies

EU accession will place many fiscal demands on Turkey to meet mandated standards in many areas. Some commentators note for example the very large costs that meeting EU environmental standards will incur. Turkey's contribution to the EU budget can be estimated under current rules at 1 per cent of Gross National Income (GNI).

EU Subsidies

It is technically possible to make estimates of what Turkey would receive under current EU policies and precedents. By one estimate, under the present EU rules, Turkey would be the largest net beneficiary of agricultural and regional subsidies in an amount equal to 14 per cent of the EU budget (Flam, 2003, p. 37). Such estimates are, however, misleading, as EU policies will continue to change and it is notable that the levels of subsidy agreed to in the negotiations for the last group of accession countries progressively fell below previously established norms. As Turkey has 7 million people employed in agriculture compared with 10.4 million in the EU, the extension of the Common Agricultural Policy (CAP) to Turkey could have enormous fiscal effects post-accession. Structural and cohesion funds to address regional disparities could similarly reach huge sums under existing rules many years in the future. Turkey should not count on receiving vast subsidies from the EU.

Revenue Policies

On the subject of tax revenues, other commentators have noted that Turkey's policies are not much out of alignment with EU principles and directives. There are particular issues to address concerning excise duties and regional and investment tax concessions, some Value Added Tax (VAT) adjustments and the removal of some protectionist tax provisions. The effects of EU accession on Poland's tax system are perhaps a useful precedent for Turkey to study.

Some Observations from Experience of Other EU Accession Countries

The experiences of previous accession countries that have been through the process that Turkey is now entering contain valuable lessons. Among the so-called EU-8,[5] each country's experience is unique and general lessons are not easy to discern. For example with regards to fiscal policy the Baltic countries, especially Estonia, have not found meeting the fiscal requirements of the EU economic framework particularly onerous whereas other countries have. Estonia is a small tight-knit country with high capability in its government and well integrated into Scandinavia.

The precedents of the more advanced of the former Eastern European countries are more relevant to Turkey. In the group of countries made up of Poland, Hungary, the Czech Republic and Slovakia, medium-term fiscal targets as laid out in pre-accession programmes have been missed and deficits have exceeded the limits. This reflects mainly delays in reforming and rationalizing expenditure programmes but also lower revenues associated with cuts in income tax rates. Some of these countries have ambitious targets in their convergence programmes but without clear, detailed plans as to how these will be achieved. The lesson to be taken is that it is dangerous to agree to difficult targets, without first thinking through how they are to be achieved within the promised time frames.

3.5 CONCLUDING REMARKS

My fundamental conclusion is that sustaining the current economic recovery in Turkey requires permanent resolution of the issues that led to the contribution of fiscal policy to the crises that have happened. In particular it requires resolution of weaknesses at the political level in giving strategic direction to the economy and at the senior executive level in providing coordinated fiscal management up to the standard of world best practices that are being initiated. This would be necessary whether Turkey was joining the EU or not, as the challenges associated with EU accession discussed are the same as those relating to transition and globalization.

The Turkish authorities have set themselves an ambitious agenda and the comments of international organizations reinforce just how much has to be done. The OECD (2004) for example reflects the consensus by recommending challenging reductions in grants to local government and increasing powers for local taxation, user charges and private provision of public services on top of the reform of central fiscal institutions.

There are very positive initiatives under way, but the question arises as to whether the momentum can be maintained for as long as it will take to complete the changes.

Under the pressure of the crisis and the IMF, much of the attention was focused on the banking sector. The restructuring and closure of banks and the establishment of a stronger regulatory regime has attracted much of the political focus and occupied the capacity and attention of senior economic managers. But the broader public sector reforms were slow to get under way. There was initially a lack of leadership and a lack of coherence across the range of reforms that required integration. Instead, there were ad hoc ministerial committees supported by equally ad hoc technical committees focused on particular issues. Some of these were responses to conditions on loans from the International Financial Institutions, which added to the fragmentation that threatened public sector and fiscal reform. Recent plans to reform the institutions of public finance have however achieved a notable consistency of architecture and the challenge now is to implement it in the years ahead. But failures in inter-agency teamwork have been a common pattern in the past, which must be resolved for real progress to be made this time.

The problem in Turkey seems to me to originate in the nature of the Turkish political system and the culture of its government institutions. The pattern is one of fragmentation in political parties and factions, rapid turnover of leadership, short-term focus, and attention to specific and special interests at the expense of the interests of the country as a whole. In the institutions of government there is an emphasis on seniority and tradition and a reluctance to take risk and innovate. The government fiscal institutions reflected the fragmentation in the political system and put territorial interests high on their agendas at the expense of coordination. There are poor ethical standards in many areas. These patterns are certainly not unique to Turkey and I have seen them elsewhere in countries in Asia, Latin America and the former Soviet Union.

However, for success in reforming fiscal institutions and policies, there need to be behavioural changes in Turkey, including putting an end to these patterns.

Anand Rajaram who led the World Bank's PEIR work, said in a speech to a conference in Ankara in 2001[6] that the budget is 'common property' and as with all common property, the problem is how to maintain it and keep it in good condition when users have private incentives to exploit it to their own ends and at the expense of the common good.

It follows that democratic countries need an overarching system of constitutional, legal and administrative provisions to ensure that the service of the special interests through the budget does not outweigh the wider interests of the public as a whole. Without such provisions, fiscal policy favours special interests over the wider interests of ordinary people and also favours the interests of today's beneficiaries of public expenditure at the expense of future taxpayers who will bear the interest burden of debt. This happens commonly because hard decisions about priorities are avoided, leading to total expenditure outstripping the revenues available. The budget process lacks the ability to say 'no' or to declare that some things are more important than others. Also without such provisions the government may be delivering benefits to particular groups in the community but through systems of management that generally inhibit the provision of good quality services that are widely available to the general public.

At the same conference in December 2001 the then Minister of Finance commented that the public sector management reforms and fiscal system reforms that were needed would redefine the state itself. Turkey was not ready for this. Perhaps it is now. Turkey is quite capable of designing a long-term public sector reform strategy with appropriate support from its international partners. EU requirements will in the longer term be a powerful force for shaping the change but it is up to Turkey to ensure that its fiscal institutions and public management not only serve its national priorities, interests and culture but that they rise to the best international practices, which are not always European models and standards.

APPENDIX 3.1

The Causes of the Fiscal Crisis

This appendix provides information in support of the statements in this chapter on the causes of the fiscal crisis. It draws on Van Rijckeghem (2004). Further detailed data and analysis of debt can be found in the Public Debt Management Report (Treasury, 2005).

Public sector debt exploded from 29 per cent of GNP in 1990 to 80 per cent in 2002 including a leap of 34 per cent in 2000–01. This growth was not steady but rather moved in a series of large steps corresponding to economic crises in 1991, 1994, 1998 and 2001, the last of which was the most damaging. These crises sent shockwaves through the public finances as state-backed financial institutions crashed. Opening exposures of the public finances to changes in interest rates and exchange rates were brought to charge. Other forms of contingent liabilities emerged from the shadows of non-transparent fiscal reporting. Quasi-fiscal activities such as credit subsidies also came into the fiscal books of the government, as off-budget institutions failed.

The visible part of the fiscal picture, the current flows of revenue and expenditure through the budget, were not the cause of the problem. According to the IMF definition of the primary deficit, it averaged only 0.4 per cent of GDP from 1991–2002. In years when the IMF programmes were in place, there were on average primary surpluses of 2 per cent of GDP. Large primary deficits in the early 1990s were replaced after 1994 by moderate deficits due to progress with some structural reforms which led to improvements in fiscal control in the central government, extra-budgetary funds and SEEs. These more than offset the increases in 'duty losses' from public financial institutions and social security deficits. In 2000 the duty losses were brought under control as the interest rates declined.

Van Rijckeghem (2004) provides a broader definition of the primary deficit of the public sector than the IMF definition, which takes into account one-off items, uncaptured primary expenditures of state banks, the withholding of tax revenues on government bonds and in-kind foreign financing. This produces an estimate of the primary deficit of 2.7 per cent of GNP on average over the period, which would still not be of particular concern and is obviously not an explanation for the rapidly deteriorating fiscal situation.

Within this wider definition of the public sector, the non-financial public sector deficit over the period, according to IMF data, was on average 0.4 per cent. This reflected an average 1.8 per cent primary surplus at the consolidated budget level and primary deficits at other levels of 2.7 per cent.

Despite the primary surpluses, Treasury debt grew rapidly due to on-budget and off-budget transfers, mostly to SEEs and social security. Off-budget transfers were in the form of issuing non-cash debt and taking over guaranteed debt of extra-budgetary funds, SEEs and local authorities. Budgetary transfers to SEEs and social security institutions were on average 2.7 per cent during 1991–2002. Extra-budgetary transfers were over 2 per cent per year on average during 1992–2002. This includes covering foreign exchange losses and losses from open market operations at the central bank. It also includes state bank duty losses.

The government's financial position was very vulnerable to fluctuations in the economy and in financial markets and it was government policies that had created this vulnerability. In 2001 the cost of recapitalizing state banks was 2 per cent of GNP. For the period 1997–2002 on average, recapitalization of banks added 1.2 per cent of GNP in expenditures per year. The currency crises of 2000–01 contributed to these costs by increasing banks' cost of funds, non-performing loans, and losses on open foreign exchange positions. For state banks, the stock of unpaid duty losses was some 12 per cent of GNP at the end of 2001, but the high cost of overnight funding of state banks during, and in the wake of, the February crisis then added 4.4 per cent of GNP.

A further explanation arises from the social security deficits. Primary deficits before transfers of the social security institutions were small in the early 1990s but rose rapidly from the mid-1990s to reach 3.6 per cent of GNP in 1999, with huge trend increases projected in the future. The 1999 social security reform arrested this trend and the social security deficit before budgetary transfers fell to 2.5 per cent and 2.9 per cent respectively in 2000 and 2001. The upturn in 2002, of 4.1 per cent of GNP deficit, due mostly to health expenditures, indicates continuing problems.

SEEs have been a source of budgetary instability and stress due to policies affecting prices and costs, especially wages. The aggregate primary deficit for the SEEs was substantial in the early 1990s, improved thereafter due to some reform and then deteriorated again at the end of the decade reaching 2.7 per cent of GNP in 2000.

Contingent liabilities flowing from government support for infrastructure developments have also been a major threat to fiscal stability. Although the full statistical picture is not clear, World Bank analysis of a set of projects show that existing price guarantees and take-or-pay guarantees could cost $8–10 billion for the period to 2010. While there have been issues around guarantees for local government borrowing, they do not seem to have been a major cause of fiscal deterioration.

Macroeconomic dynamics are the most important part of the explanation for the fiscal problems that have arisen. Real interest payments have been a main driver of the debt build-up. The IMF estimates are that real interest payments were 6.2 per cent of GNP on average over the period. However, according to Van Rijckeghem, SEE and social security losses early in the decade set the stage for the vicious cycle of debt that occurred. The debt would have been roughly stable over the period if it were not for the losses from these sources early in the decade, and even declined were it not for the duty losses, other things being equal. Such vicious cycles have caused many fiscal crises in many countries and can become catastrophic if not arrested before debt servicing ratios become intolerable.

NOTES

* The author wishes to acknowledge help in locating reference materials, discussions and comments from many people and would in particular like to acknowledge assistance from Şerif Sayın, Ferhat Emil, Anand Rajaram, Izak Atiyas, Dana Weist, Graham Ingham, Mark Griffiths, Kasi Mathai, Mark Horton, Erdem Başçı, Sübidey Togan, Hakan Yılmaz, Murat Üçer and Carole Hoult. Responsibility for the contents of this chapter is entirely mine.

1. December to December rate of change of Consumer Price Index.
2. Conference on Public Expenditure Reform for Effective Government (10 December 2001), Ministry of Finance of Turkey and the World Bank, Ankara.
3. Workshop on Managing a Comprehensive PEM Reform to link Policies, Plans & Budgets for Effective Government (December 2001), Hilton Hotel, Ankara.
4. Treaty Establishing the European Community, Part Three, Community Policies, Title VII, Chapter 1 Economic Policy.
5. Czech Republic, Estonia, Hungary, Latvia, Lithuania, Poland, Slovenia and Slovakia.
6. Conference on Public Expenditure Reform for Effective Government (10 December 2001), Ministry of Finance of Turkey and the World Bank, Ankara.

REFERENCES

Alfonso, A., W. Ebert, L. Schuknecht and M. Thone (2005), 'Quality of public finances and growth', European Central Bank, Working Paper Series No 438, February.

Atiyas, I. and Ş. Sayın (eds) (2000), *Transparency in Public Finances*, Turkish Economic and Social Studies Foundation (TESEV).

Calvo, A.G. and S.F. Mishkin (2003), 'The mirage of exchange rate regimes for emerging market countries', *Journal of Economic Perspectives*, **17**(4), 100.

Emil, F. (2000), Presentation to Seminar on Public Expenditure and Institutional Reform, Ankara, 26 October.

Emil, F. (2004), 'Public budget, accountancy and control systems in Turkey', Formez Workshop, Naples, December.

EU Commission Directorate General Economic and Financial Affairs (2002), 'The macroeconomic policy framework for EU membership and euro area participation: the role of budgetary policy', Conference on EU Accession-Developing Fiscal Policy Frameworks for Sustainable Growth, Brussels, 13–14 May.

Flam, H. (2003), 'Turkey and the EU: politics and economics of accession', Institute for International Economic Studies, Seminar Paper 718, February, p. 37.

Gönenç, R., W. Leibfritz and E. Yılmaz (2005), 'Reforming Turkey's public expenditure management', OECD Economics Department, Working Paper No. 418.

OECD (2004), *Economic Survey of Turkey*, October.

Public Expenditure & Institutional Review, PEIR (2001), Government of Turkey and The World Bank.

Republic of Turkey (2004), Pre-accession Economic Programme, Ankara, November.

Treasury (2005), Public Debt Management Report (February), prepared by Turkish Treasury (www.treasury.gov.tr).

Van Rijckeghem, C. (2004), 'Turkish debt 1990–2002: how did we get here?', Sabancı University and TESEV.

COMMENTS

Erdem Başçı

This paper is insightful and very helpful in understanding the fiscal stance in Turkey. It points out the chronic problems of Turkey in fiscal domain really well. However, it does not address the significant improvements in fiscal policy and the structural changes that have taken place in recent years. Therefore, in my comments, I would like to emphasize some of the recent achievements.

My comments are organized as follows: first, I will present the achievements of the current economic programme. Second, I will summarize how we see the future regarding inflation and fiscal indicators. Finally, I will touch upon some of the issues overlooked in Dr Scott's paper.

Macroeconomic problems of Turkey in the past, namely low and volatile growth together with high and volatile inflation, were mainly due to fiscal imbalances. The aim of the current economic programme is to eliminate these imbalances, strengthen the Turkish economy and place it on a sustainable growth path, by means of an ambitious list of key structural reforms in the fiscal area and the banking sector.

Thanks to tight monetary and fiscal policies accompanied by a significant amount of institutional and structural reforms, Turkey has recently achieved a remarkable growth performance. At the same time, inflation came down to single-digit levels after more than thirty years. The gains from the programme are clearly reflected in the high growth rates and low inflation figures. The Turkish economy has been the fastest growing economy among OECD countries during the last three years with an average GNP growth rate of 7.9 per cent. Inflation has dropped significantly from 68.5 per cent in 2001 to a single digit, 9.3 per cent as of the end of 2004. In this context, the Turkish experience is a successful case of credible disinflation with remarkable growth.

Despite many internal and external shocks, in each of the last three years the Central Bank has undershot its inflation targets, which are determined together with the government. Establishing an independent central bank has been one of the key factors in this success. Determination of the inflation target jointly with the government was also helpful. The government has set public wages and salaries in line with the inflation targets. A fundamental parameter for disinflation is the Central Bank's credibility gap, that is, the difference between people's expectations of end of year inflation and the targeted rate. There has been a noticeable narrowing in the Central Bank's credibility gap; it indeed disappeared altogether in 2005. Regarding the future, we feel quite comfortable that we will reach our

8 per cent end-year target for 2005. Our inflation targets are planned as 5 per cent and 4 per cent for 2006 and 2007 respectively, which means inflation will be converging towards rates prevailing in other OECD countries as well as the EU averages.

On the fiscal side, primary surplus is the main fiscal policy target of this programme. This was set as 6.5 per cent of GNP for the last three years. Turkey has produced the highest primary surpluses during this period. In 2002, 2003 and 2004 the realizations were 4.1, 6.3 and 6.9 per cent respectively. Thanks to such high levels of primary surpluses, the public sector borrowing requirement decreased drastically from 12.3 per cent of GNP in 2002 to 3.9 per cent in 2004. Interest payments have also dropped significantly, from 23.3 per cent of GNP in 2001 to 13.2 per cent in 2004. This ratio is projected to fall to 11.7 per cent of GNP in 2005. As a result of the high primary surpluses and the fall in the interest burden as well as the appreciation of the Turkish lira, the share of the public net debt stock in GNP reduced significantly from 90.5 per cent in 2001 to 63.5 per cent in 2004.

Turkey has signed a new stand-by agreement with the IMF in line with the Pre-accession Economic Programme, which was submitted to the EU Commission on December 2004. In both documents, primary surplus is seen as 6.5 per cent of GNP for the 2005–07 period. Consistent with such large primary surpluses, the public sector borrowing requirement is projected to decrease to levels as low as 0.5 per cent of GNP in 2007. Taking account of the performance in the last three years, we attach great importance to achieving this target in the future as well. More importantly, according to these projections, Turkey's budget balance will have already fulfilled the corresponding Maastricht criterion by 2007.

All in all, there have been significant improvements in the fiscal position of Turkey. However, in his chapter, Dr Scott mainly draws attention to institutional factors such as quality of fiscal adjustment and inter-agency teamwork.

Regarding the quality of fiscal adjustment, it is worth emphasizing the recent efforts in this area. Improving transparency and accountability in the management of public expenditures is essential to ensure the effective use of public resources. A key starting point is a comprehensive and transparent budgeting process to make sure resources are not diverted to extra budgetary funds that lack oversight and control. Budget formulation and execution procedures must be strengthened through an effective system of incentives and monitoring of results. To make it all work, a strong system of accountability, on both revenue and expenditure sides, is needed.

In this context, Turkey has taken important steps, primarily in three areas, namely tax reform, public expenditure reform and social security reform. To begin with, the parliament recently approved the new tax administration legislation, according to which the Ministry of Finance is responsible for the determination of tax policy, while the Revenue Administration is to carry out tax administration as a strong and semi-autonomous entity under the Ministry of Finance.

In the area of public expenditure reform, positive developments have taken place as well. First, the Public Financial Management and Control Law has been enacted and will be implemented in 2006. Second, a new Public Procurement Law is in place in order to modernize the Turkish procurement system by making it comply with the standards of the European Union. Third, public sector employment policy is being rationalized by means of a comprehensive review of civil and public service wage and employment structures, and the newly adopted legislation establishing a code of ethical conduct for civil servants. Last, there is ongoing work to rationalize public investments and increase funds available for scientific research.

Apart from the tax and public expenditure reforms, a comprehensive social security reform is also necessary for the sustainability of public finances in Turkey. Within this framework, the draft pension and health reform law proposes a unified pension system and a separate unified health system. Further, parametric changes in the system and establishment of a universal health insurance scheme are also on the agenda.

There are noticeable improvements in the area of inter-agency teamwork as well. I want to give two specific examples. At the end of every year, Turkey prepares the Pre-accession Economic Programme, under the coordination of the State Planning Organization, with contributions from the Treasury, the Central Bank and all related ministries and institutions. This year's document, the programme submitted to the EU Commission on December 2004, is one of the best examples of inter-agency teamwork. The second example is the improvement in the coordination between the Treasury and the Central Bank in monetary and debt management policies.

To conclude, given his international experience and especially his previous work on Turkey, Dr Scott's paper is rather sceptical about the future of the fiscal stance. Central banks are regarded as the most conservative institutions. Yet, given the recent progress, as a central banker I must say that I am *cautiously optimistic* about the future of fiscal policy in Turkey.

4. Monetary policy in the euro area: lessons from five years of the ECB and its the implications for Turkey

Fabio Canova and Carlo Favero*

4.1 INTRODUCTION

The end of 1998 witnessed an experiment of historical importance in monetary policy, an experiment which was challenging, exciting and, at the same time, risky. Launching the European Central Bank (ECB) and establishing it as a credible and respected institution capable of managing the transition from a number of central banks to a European one and of communicating and interacting with the central banks of other major developed countries, introducing a new currency and setting solid foundations for maintaining its international value and harmonizing banking regulations and supervisory activities constituted a complex and ambitious agenda whose implementation required effective measures and ingenious action that had to be dealt with effectively and with ingenuity. The costs of disrupting the monetary and credit markets of such a large group of countries were rightly considered to be huge. Many, both in financial markets and overseas, doubted that accomplishing such a formidable feat was possible. Those who were more optimistic worried about the possibility of successfully achieving the goals within a reasonable time frame. The difficulties encountered in the 1980s and 1990s in managing and maintaining a system of fixed exchange rates, the heterogeneities of member's economies and of policymakers' preferences and the historical differences in laws and regulations were clear stumbling blocks in the minds of academics and market observers, and all contributed to make the starting of ECB operations and the related transformations a one-time extraordinary and, in many ways, unpredictable event.

Yet, six years later, one can only be amazed by the results such a young institution has managed to achieve in such a short amount of time. We had terrorist attacks and sneaky wars; we had oil prices swinging up and down, as they have not done since the beginning of the 1990s; we had a number of food price crises; we had confusions about the effects and complaints about the way the euro changeover took place; we had plenty of bickering among politicians looking to locate their countries strategically in the euro arena. Still, on average, the inflation rate was at its lowest level in decades; financial markets behaved in an orderly manner in responses to shocks which could have had catastrophic consequences, and slowly but surely the ECB is establishing itself as a credible and solid decision-maker. Despite the generally poor state of the European economy and the weak growth outlook, much of which is related to the structural imbalances of the euro area economies, such as low productivity, low participation rate, ageing populations, language and institutional barriers to labour movements, the ECB has resisted political pressures from national and EU governments to pursue more expansionary policies and to relax the strict corset imposed by the price stability goal. The short-term (and short-minded) gains and popular approval that came with it were rightly weighted against the much more problematic long-term costs arising from the more inefficient unemployment and inflation trade-off which would have been established as a consequence of such actions. Available publications, speeches by board members and the president of the ECB have repeatedly tried to explain to the public and the markets what the targets of monetary policy are, what strategies and operational frameworks shape policy decisions, what monetary policy can and cannot do so as to enhance the transparency of the policy process. The understanding that expectations formation is crucial to enhancing or disrupting the transmission of monetary policy decisions and that the best outcome that monetary policy actions can achieve is anchoring inflation expectations is present in the major public statements of ECB officials.

Clearly, we should be grateful that potentially disruptive shocks pass over our heads with very little effect on our everyday life, bank accounts and welfare. Nevertheless we, as probably other commentators, feel that some of these achievements may have been obtained despite what the ECB has done and that there is ample room for improvement in strategy, in communication and also, probably, in the decision-making process. We also believe that the experience of other central banks has taught us important lessons and that these experiences can be used as benchmarks to compare words, actions and outcomes in the euro area. Finally, the recent expansion and the predicted further enlargement to the east of the EU poses important questions and challenges to those who run monetary policy which, although surely present in the mind of ECB officials, are not entirely spelled out in the official publications.

Given this background, this chapter addresses three interrelated issues. First, we discuss what modern theory tells us about the monetary policy strategy that should be adopted by central banks and contrast it with the one employed by the ECB. In the process we review accomplishments (and failures) of monetary policy in the euro area over the last five years and suggest some changes which, in our opinion, would help to reduce the tensions created by the low correlation between words and actions, streamline the understanding that markets have of the policy process and, as a consequence, improve its transparency, and more clearly anchor expectation formation. We also briefly touch on the issue of the euro changeover and discuss the nature of the gap between actual and perceived inflation. Second, we examine the transmission of monetary policy decisions in the euro area and in a few potential new member countries and third, we try to infer on the basis of this analysis the effects which are likely to occur when Turkey joins the EU and then the euro club. Much of the analysis here uses the experience of past newcomers to provide a scenario of the probable gains and warns against having too high expectations regarding the economic improvements that membership of the EU/euro will produce.

The chapter is organized as follows. Section 4.2 describes the monetary policy strategy favoured by academic economists, confronts it with that of the ECB and of other central bankers and makes some suggestions for improving the coherence between words and actions and the framework for policy formation. Section 4.3 focuses on the transmission of monetary policy shocks in the euro area and in some Central European countries. Section 4.4 describes the likely effects of joining the EU and then the euro will have on the Turkish economy. Section 4.5 concludes.

4.2 MONETARY POLICY: THEORY AND PRACTICE

Since the beginning of the 1990s, there has been a revolution in the way central banks see their mandate and communicate with the markets and the public. Previously, central banks were secretive institutions, which spent little time clarifying their objectives and their strategies, and often surprised or confused market participants with their setting of policy instruments. A secretive approach was preferred, in part, because it was thought to provide a good shield against political oversight, an important precondition to achieve central bank independence (see for example Mishkin, 2004). In the last 15 years, central banks have dealt with political pressures in a completely different manner. Almost all policymakers, both in the industrialized and the developing world, now recognize that transparency and improved communication with the public are key ingredients in running a successful monetary policy, both in the sense of allowing markets smoothly to predict and to adjust to policy changes and of effectively anchoring inflation expectations. To gain public support and to build confidence, central banks have now engaged in a capillary information process, and to acquire credibility they have improved both the accountability and the transparency of the policy decision process. As a consequence, a plethora of speeches, documents and publications describing the goals and the targets of monetary policy, highlighting what monetary policy can and cannot do, and in general, the philosophy and the strategy behind policy decisions are now available on the official websites of many central banks.

For academic economists, a good monetary policy is easy to design and the basic ingredients which make policy successful easy to characterize. What turns out to be complicated is how to make the general principles contained in such a prescription operational. As Svensson (2004) puts it:

> The principles for good monetary policy are simple: perform *flexible inflation targeting* . . . The practice of constructing (inflation) forecasts and of deciding the appropriate instrument rate is quite complicated . . . and requires collecting and processing of vast amounts of data, thorough analysis, and skilful combination of judgment and model results.

Various central banks have taken this recipe seriously and altered policies to adhere as close as possible to this simple and general principle. Strangely enough, the Fed, the ECB and the Bank of Japan – the central banks of the three major economies of the world – have not followed this lead and have instead continued to be quite opaque in characterizing their policy strategies and/or in explaining their decision-making process, even though in public appearances some officials (see for example Poole, 1999 and 2001) also appear to favour the principles underlying an inflation targeting strategy.

Why is flexible inflation targeting the favourite choice of academics? Because such a policy directly affects inflation expectation – the key mechanism for transmitting monetary policy decisions – and does this in a transparent and straightforward way. Policy actions, in fact, produce changes to the economy primarily through expectations formed, first, in the financial markets and, later, in the household and firm sectors. Central banks set a target rate for their instruments but it is expectations about the level of that target in the future which determine interest rates all along the yield curve. In particular, expectations about how the central bank responds to likely scenarios in the future determines the expected inflation rate. Assuming that the objectives of the central bank are sound, the success of monetary policy critically depends on market expectations and market confidence. When expectations are accurate and confidence high, markets understand what a central bank does and have no incentive to deviate from the set path of inflation. When expectations turn out to be wrong and/or confidence low, private agents may try to gain from strategically influencing the expected inflation rate with the setting of their choice variables.

What makes flexible inflation targeting appealing relative to other strategies? First, flexible inflation targeting requires the publication of forecasts of inflation and of all the variables needed to produce inflation forecasts, for example output and/or unemployment. Publications of these numbers increases central banks' accountability; gives them the right incentive to generate good forecasts, and as a by-product, enhances credibility if the forecast record is consistently on target over time. Second, given that monetary policy affects the economy with delays which are random in time and magnitude, flexible inflation targeting focuses policy actions on the medium run and therefore reduces the importance of day to day responses to inflation variations. Third, since monetary policy works through the expectations of future instrument settings, rather than via the current choice of the instrument rate, and since expectations of the future level of inflation and output matter for current pricing and production decisions, flexible inflation targeting helps in the management of expectations. Hence, publications of inflation forecasts, increased transparency and improved public understanding of the policy decision process could all help to increase monetary policy effectiveness.

The existence of an operational medium-term objective is important in anchoring both inflation expectations and the level of nominal variables. Its absence in the 1970s and 1980s was one of the reasons why markets paid so much attention to short-run policy actions and seemingly routine speeches by policymakers. In comparison, in the 1950s and 1960s central bank actions received less attention because the long-term policy objective was defined by gold standard arrangements. Hence, the public's estimate of the long-term inflation rate was not much affected by speeches or short-term policy actions even though, in retrospect, agents should have paid more attention than they did to central bank choices, since they produced an environment which was inconsistent with the survival of the gold standard.

Why is inflation targeting difficult to implement? A central bank that follows such a strategy needs to assess the future path of inflation and of other macroeconomic forces and the future path of the instrument rate. Furthermore, it needs to communicate to the markets how it will adjust the instrument rate in response to unexpected events or economic developments that make the future path of inflation deviate from the target. The first of these activities requires considerable staff work and the development of models which are able to predict future (rather than tracking past) tendencies in the economy. A variety of models are needed for the task because models are simplified and stylized constructions, hardly capable of capturing the detailed interrelationships present in the real world.

Furthermore, considerable ingenuity is needed to judge the outcome of forecasting exercises, for example, when deciding if an inflation path is unlikely or very likely or when predicting policy decisions and how long it will take for them to take effect. Finally, a clear description of the steps to be taken once permanent deviations from the target occur, needs to be made. Clearly all of these activities are subject to errors: it does not take a magician to recognize that the future is largely unforecastable, that information about economic indicators is lumpy and frequently revised, that human judgement, even a prudent one, is bound to make mistakes, and that models are just that, mathematical constructions, often unable to adjust automatically if the structure of the economy changes. For this reason central bank communication is critical in conveying not only the goals of monetary policy and the strategy to achieve them but also the difficulties involved in the decision-making process. We are convinced that markets already have a deep understanding of how monetary policy works and of the difficulties existing in formulating policy in face of uncertainty. Often, when new information accrues, central banks and the markets are in close agreement about the action required to keep the economy on a steady course. Nevertheless, the better markets understand how and why a central bank reaches its decisions, the better they will be able to respond to new information and the closer their reactions will be to that of the central bank. When this occurs a smoother and more efficient transmission of policy changes to the economy's product, labour and capital markets will take place. Transparency in a general sense simply means providing the fullest explanation possible of policy actions and the considerations underlying them, in as timely manner as possible.

It is important to stress that the actual value for the inflation target is not nearly as important as is the decision to choose a target and to create a benchmark for making policy transparent and accountable. Furthermore, while setting an inflation target helps to run monetary policy smoothly, it is by no means a necessary precondition for achieving a low and steady inflation rate. For example, in the USA no inflation target has ever been announced. Yet, the path of US inflation in the last 15 years does not significantly deviate from that experienced by the best inflation targeters.

4.2.1 The Monetary Policy Strategy of the ECB

The original monetary policy strategy of the ECB, announced by the Governing Council in October 1998, included three defining features: a strict focus on price stability, meaning that other objectives, such as output or employment stability, were given little or no consideration; a target range for inflation (below 2 per cent), which was tougher than the one adopted by inflation targetting central banks such as the Bank of England; and a 'two pillar' framework for the conduct of monetary policy, which assigned a prominent role to monetary aggregates (first pillar), imposed the announcement of a quantitative reference value for M3 growth, and clustered into the second pillar a wide range of economic and financial indicators providing a broad outlook for price stability.

All three defining features of such a strategy have been criticized. For example, Begg et al. (2002) found the strict focus on price stability an unnecessary straitjacket in light of the development following the events of 2001 and the threat of deflation that loomed as a consequence, while Gali et al. (2004) consider a serious strategic mistake, even from an ex ante point of view, the tough anti-inflationary stance adopted by the Governing Council. Finally, a list of articles too long to be referenced here criticized the two pillar strategy, using terms ranging from controversial to patently wrong and ill-conceived. In particular, what attracted the attention of commentators was the artificial separation of information into two pillars, the emphasis on monetary aggregates, and the reliance on a quantitative reference value for M3 growth which, even with various definitional adjustments, has been repeatedly surpassed in many months since the ECB started its operations.

In a key press release issued in May 2003 and in the Monthly Bulletin of June 2003, the ECB announced that it had evaluated the soundness of its monetary policy strategy in light of the economic outcomes obtained in the first three and half years of operations. Such an evaluation led to a series of clarifications, qualifications and changes which could alter the way Governing Council decisions will be taken in the future. The reaction to this update in the strategy has been mixed. Several observers have noted the extraordinary continuity between the new guidelines and those of 1998 and regard the changes as little more than cosmetic, especially in relationship to the current situation in the euro area, characterized by meagre output and employment prospects, the dissolution of the Growth and Stability Pact and an inflation rate, which although relatively low, has often and persistently exceeded the upper bound set by policy in the months preceding June 2003. Furthermore, its persistent nature indicated that the return to the selected range was not expected to occur very soon. Others have underlined that the updated strategy is simply an attempt to convince the public that everything is under control and that there is nothing to worry about (see Gali et al., 2004). Finally, more benign observers noted that the new strategy takes a step in the right direction of making the rhetoric square better with the facts, but considered the step an insufficient one.

There are three cornerstones to the new strategy. First, the issue of price stability is refocused into the medium term, the risks of deflation explicitly examined and the presence of inflation differentials in the euro area given consideration. Second, the target range for inflation is qualified as being 'below but close to 2 per cent'. Third, the labels and the importance of the two pillars are reshuffled while the control of monetary/credit aggregates has acquired the role of an 'escape clause' to prevent discretionary traps and self-fulfilling expectations and to guarantee a more robust approach to inflation stabilization.

How is one to interpret these alterations? Figure 4.1 plots the record of HICP (harmonized index of consumer prices) inflation in the euro area since 1999. Clearly, relative to the goal (below 2 per cent inflation), the outcome is nothing to cheer about. Narrowing the focus to persistent and sizeable deviations from the target only, a similar conclusion needs to be drawn: the ECB failed to meet its objectives. Given this observation, the new focus on medium-term dynamics and the qualification 'close to' could then be interpreted in at least four different ways. It could be an attempt to make objectives and statements more consistent with the outcomes; it could be a tacit recognition that the ECB, as a new central bank, does not have yet the ability fully to control inflation and definitively not in the short run; it could also be an indirect way of allowing revisions of the target rate of inflation in the near future (the 2 per cent threshold should not be considered an upper bound but the mid-range of the target inflation rate) and for justifying persistent deviations from the target; or it could simply be a cover up for expansionary policies designed to limit the risks of deflation and the coexistence within the euro area of regions facing deflationary and inflationary pressures. Lacking more information on the exact motivations of the ECB, it is hard to take a stand on which interpretation is most likely to be true. In our opinion, all arguments have some validity and could explain the readjustment in the rhetoric of ECB statements. In practice, the explicit explanation of the medium-term focus and the qualification of 'below but close to 2 per cent' may make very little change in the way the policy discussion proceeds and the Governing Council takes decisions.

The negative assessment contained in Figure 4.1 must however be put in a historical perspective. Over the last five years the rate of inflation has been remarkably stable and low when compared to the previous 30 years. Failure to meet the (overly optimistic) objectives should therefore not detract from the fact that inflation fears were almost absent from public perceptions (except for the euro changeover period, see later on); that in many countries unions agreed to nominal wage increases for medium-term contracts roughly in line with the target level inflation; and that a stable environment was largely maintained. In other words, differences between the target and the actual rate of inflation did not trigger important nominal wage adjustments nor did they produce large welfare costs. Perhaps this is not surprising. The Bundesbank also repeatedly failed to meet its objectives, in both the 1980s

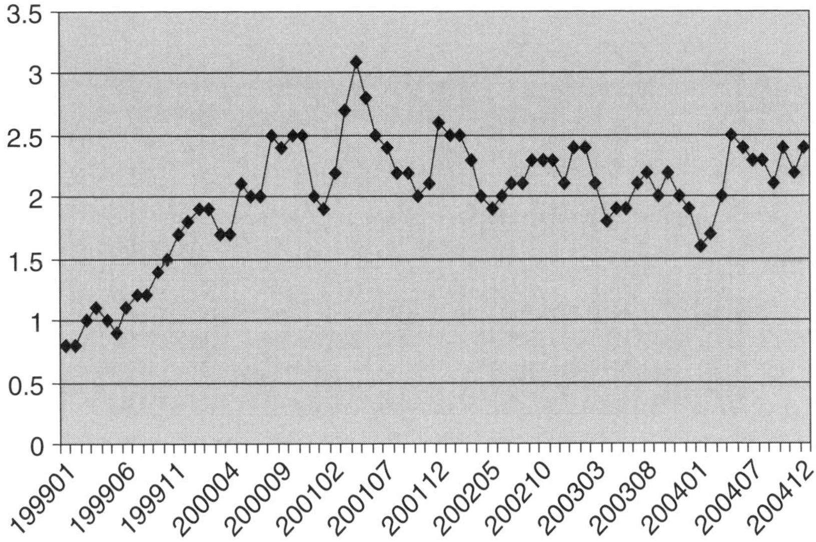

Figure 4.1 HICP inflation (%)

and the 1990s. Yet, German inflation was always under control, even when it was drifting away in other countries, and there were never any doubts about the credibility of the Bundesbank as a tough inflation fighter (see Siklos and Bohl, 2003). Hence, despite its inability to meet its goals and the communication problems noted below, the ECB has been, overall, successful in keeping the actual rate of inflation close to the target rate.

4.2.2 Inflation Expectations

One of the most remarkable achievements of the first five years of the ECB has been the ability to control inflation expectations. Given past experiences this is no small feat and the ECB has often stressed in public statements that, despite the difficult environment, there were hardly any indications in the last five years that inflationary expectations were getting out of control. Gali et al. (2004) are less enthusiastic about the outcome and indicate that, over the last couple of years, inflation expectations are slowly but surely creeping up. While this could be due to the qualifications contained in the strategy revision of 2003, in particular regarding the target rate of inflation and the relative importance of unexpected inflation and deflation episodes, it could also indicate that the public are not so upbeat about the current state of inflation and that the ECB could lose control of inflation expectations in the years to come.

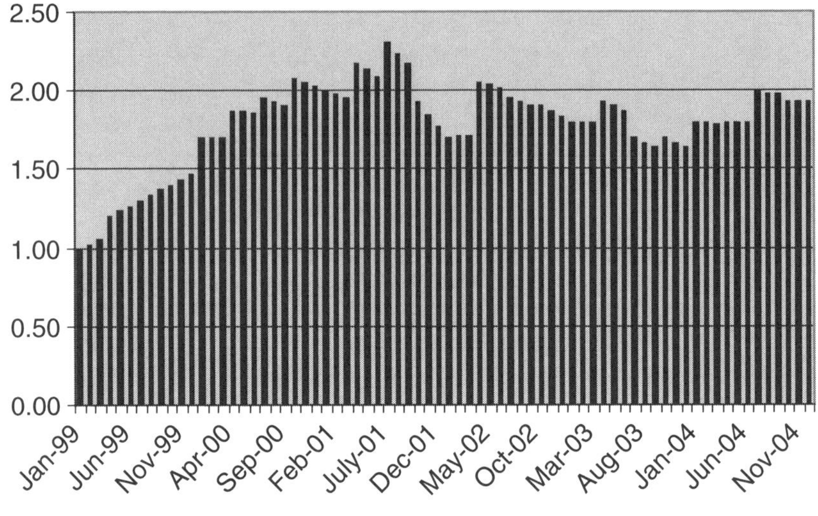

Figure 4.2 *Inflation expectations (%)*

Figure 4.2 presents evidence supporting both claims: it reports the weighted average of inflation expectations constructed by *The Economist's* poll of forecasters. *The Economist* asks forecasters every month to give an opinion of where the inflation rate will be at the end of the year. Since there are typically two observations for each forecasting horizon and since the information available at the beginning of the year is less precise than the information at the end, we weight the information appropriately. Clearly, inflation expectations by professional forecasters have been below 2 per cent for almost the entire period from January 1999 to November 2004. Therefore, the ECB is right to rejoice about this achievement. However, as Gali et al. (2004) have pointed out, inflation expectations in the last two years are somewhat higher than previously.

While suggestive, poll data is subject to a large amount of measurement error. In particular, there is a tendency to report numbers which are close to the mean outcome to avoid being singled out as inaccurate when the actual outcome deviates from the expectation, and this is true even when deviations are not systematic. A better way to check inflation expectations is to look directly at the term structure of interest rates and extract the information which is contained in the actual financial market data.

Fluctuations in yield to maturity of long-term bonds can be very useful in measuring expectations on long-term inflation by market participants. However, measuring expected inflation from yield to maturity on long-term bonds requires the solution of a signal extraction problem. In fact, nominal

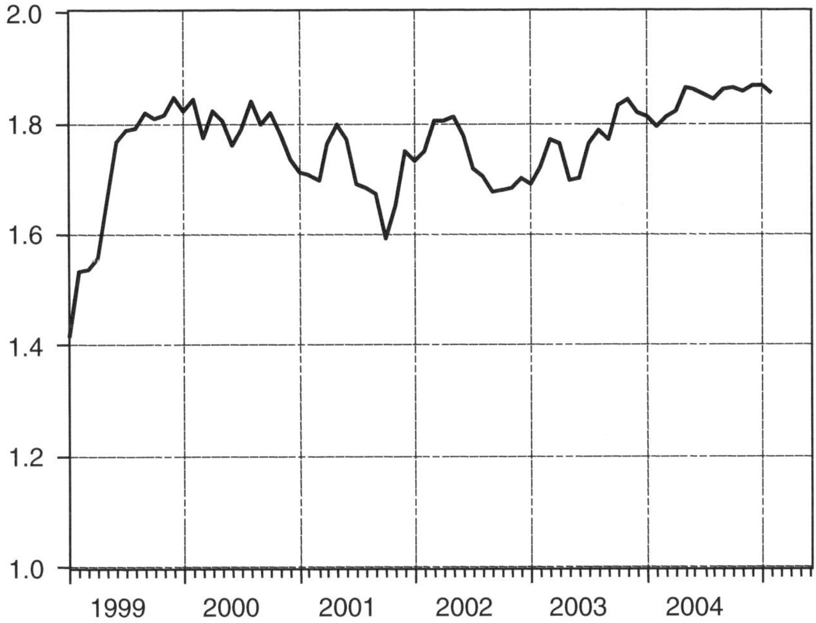

Figure 4.3 Break-even inflation from 10-year French OAT (%)

yields to maturity on long-term bonds reflect both real long-term interest rates and inflation expectations, two variables that are not observable. To solve the signal extraction problem and understand what financial markets tell us about inflation expectations we take two different approaches. First, we examine the break-even inflation implied by index-linked French obligations assimilables du Trésor (OATs) 10-year bonds. The difference between the yield to maturity of a nominal French Bond and an index-linked bond with the same characteristics is a direct measure of expected inflation over the residual life of the two bonds. The break-even inflation implied by ten-year bonds index OAT (OAT – I FRANCE 1998 3 per cent 25/07/09 INDXLK) and nominal 10-year French OAT(OAT FRANCE 1998 5.25 per cent 25/04/08) is reported in Figure 4.3.

The trend of the series confirms Gali et al.'s (2004) observation on the tendency of inflation expectations over the last two years, and the pattern of Figure 4.3 replicates quite closely the one present in Figure 4.2 since 2001. Break-even inflation, however, is not a perfect measure of expected inflation as the characteristics of the two bonds used to compute this quantity are never the same. To complement this measure, we therefore examined the pattern of long-term expected inflation implicit in yield to maturity of

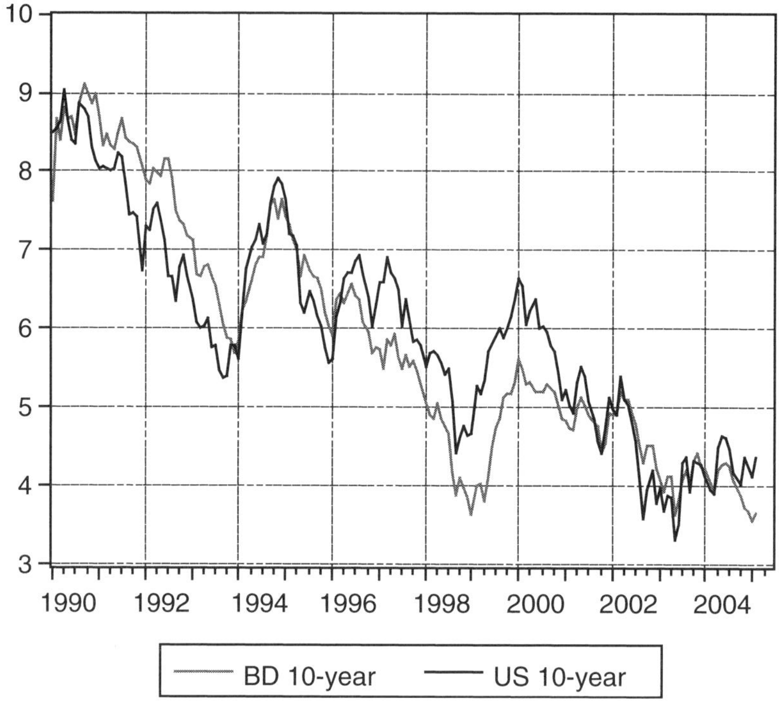

Figure 4.4 Ten-year US and German bonds (%)

long-term bonds in Germany and the USA at the 10-year maturity. As Figure 4.4 clearly shows, there has been a clear tendency in US and German bonds to move together from 1990 onwards.

Favero and Tristani (2005) consider several explanations for the high and stable contemporaneous correlation between US and German long-term interest rates. First, the expectations model suggests that the level of the term structure depends on the average of all future monetary policy rates. Therefore, a high correlation of long-term rates is compatible with any contemporaneous correlations of policy rates, provided that the correlation between the average of future expected policy rates is high. Second, if term premia are important and if there is a world factor in the 'appetite for risk', then it is possible that long-term rates are more strongly correlated across countries because they are heavily affected by risk premia. Third, if the Fed is the dominant monetary policy authority, the monetary policy of the Fed is responsible for the common pattern in long-term interest rates across the ocean. Given that Favero and Tristani (2005) conclude that the strong co-movements between US and German long-term rates is primarily due to

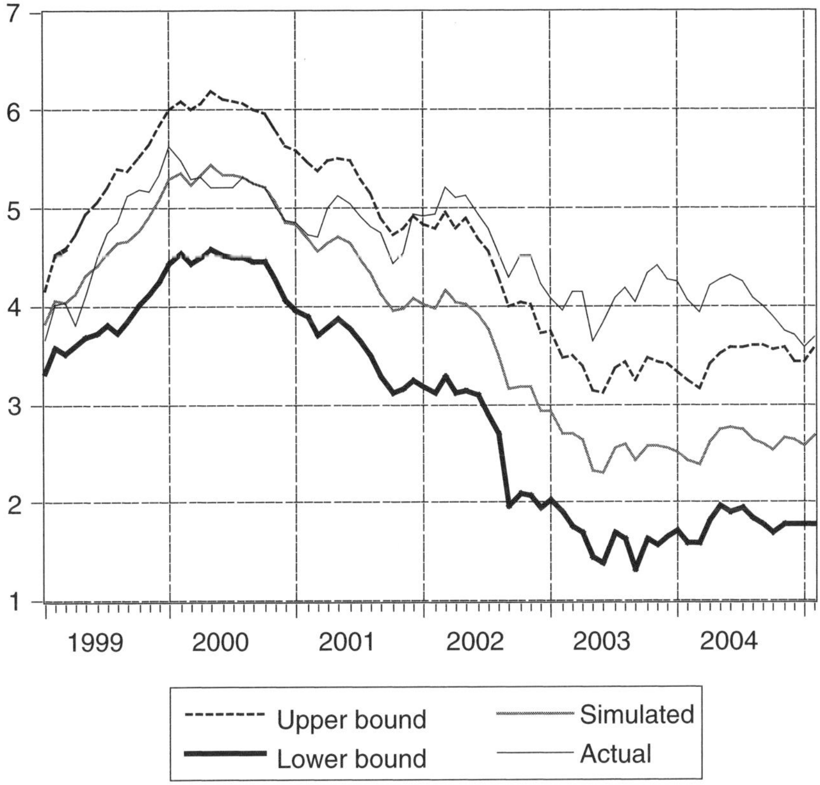

Figure 4.5 Actual and simulated German 10-year rates

the common path of expected monetary policy (mostly driven by common fluctuations in the US and German inflation and output gap), it is interesting to assess the performance in simulation over the sample when the ECB has been operational of a model where the relation between US and German long-term rates is estimated over the sample where the Bundesbank was operational. We have estimated from 1990:1 to 1998:12 an ECM relationship between US and German long-term rates and then stochastically simulated the model from 1999:1 onwards using the actual path of US long-term rates in the simulation. The results of our exercise are reported in Figure 4.5: we plot the actual German 10-year rates along with the simulated ones and their associated 95 per cent confidence interval.

Figure 4.5 is consistent with the idea that inflation expectations have been increasing slightly in the last few years. In fact, simulated long-term interest rates are very close to actual ones over the first two years of ECB existence but tend to drift upwards, getting closer first and eventually slightly outside of the upper bound of the confidence interval, over the last few years.

In summary, the ECB appears to have managed to anchor inflation expectations, probably more because of the good faith that the markets and the public had in the institution than because of the consistency between deeds and the inflation record produced over its first five years of life. Refocusing the strategy and qualifying the targets can therefore have beneficial effects. In particular, much clearer statements, explicitly stating what the medium-run is, which policies should be used in case persistent deviations from the target emerge and what the target (and its range) is, would probably make monetary policy actions more transparent and predictable.

4.2.3 Communication

There appears to be a substantial difference in the tone and the content of speeches and statements posted at the ECB site and those found at, for example, regional Fed sites or in other smaller but more receptive central banks, such as the Riksbank or the Federal Reserve Bank of New Zealand. ECB statements and speeches are often opaque; the rationale given for policy choices is at times contorted and its theoretical justification somewhat weak; explanations given for certain strategic decisions are improbable and, at times, more obvious reasons are given no consideration. Those of the others are crisper, the message is clearer, to a point that a first year undergraduate student in economics would be able to correctly understand their meaning, and transparency is maximized (compare for example Trichet speech (27 November 2003), Poole speech (30 November 2001) and Sherwin speech (1 July 1999)).

Perhaps, this is not surprising. Since the euro area is a new entity, the transmission of policy shocks to the region is still somewhat uncertain, the consequences of ECB choices are not yet fully understood and, in general, learning is still under way. Opaqueness may therefore reflect difficulties in the learning process. However, letting the public know that there are considerable uncertainties in the current decision-making process and that the ECB and market participants are trying to reach mutual understanding as to how their decisions interact, is preferable to presenting a smoky and somewhat confusing viewpoint. It should also be clear that the publication of information which is hard to understand or irrelevant and the repetition of concepts which sound foreign to the public will not make communication easier or more fruitful. In this respect, one cannot overlook the fact that high-ranking officials in a number of central banks around the world were in academia before they took policy jobs while, currently, this is hardly the case at the ECB. Not only is an academic background important in keeping in touch with new developments and the refinement of old theories, it is also important because academic discipline forces officials to strip issues down to their basic components, leaving aside peripheral arguments. This process is the same whether communicating to the markets, whether explaining a concept in a classroom or arguing a viewpoint in a professional conference. As Poole (2001) puts it, 'the easiest way to be sure you understand an issue is to explain it to the others, in a class, a journal article, a lecture, or in meeting minutes. Transparency is a great spur to developing coherent views, and surely is beneficial to policymakers to be coherent in their own thinking.' Communication and transparency will surely improve in the future as the details of the euro area economy become better known. Better communication and transparency may ameliorate the effectiveness of policy, enhance accountability and reduce informational noise in the markets. Recognizing the limits to policymaking, given the available information, is an honest way to achieve this goal.

There are indications that financial markets did not initially have a good understanding of the ECB strategy and of the reasons behind some policy actions (see Sims and Wessel, 2000 or Issing, 2001). The situation does not seem to have improved in later years: for example the survey reported in De Haan et al. (2004) indicates that professional economists did not rank the ECB as a highly transparent central bank. But, apart from surveys, what does the available empirical evidence tell us about the communication (and the implied credibility) of the ECB? A recent article by Jansen and De Haan (2004) addresses exactly this issue by examining to what extent statements of various European central bankers have been different or contradictory and how ECB communication has improved over time. They found that there is considerable noise in public statements and several sources of noise are highlighted. First, national central bank presidents have made at least as many statements as members of the ECB Executive Board and there is no evidence that this trend has been reversed over the years. When information emanates from different sources it may generate confusing messages and make the public think that there are different and separate decision-making units. Second, statements on interest rates, inflation and output growth have been contradictory. While confusion on the stance of interest rates has diminished over time and statements have become more correlated, disagreements about the current and prospective levels of inflation and growth have increased over the years. Third, different groups of central banks have followed different communication strategies around ECB Governing Council meetings. In particular, while the ECB Executive Board has observed radio silence, national central bank officials tended to communicate more (rather than less) before these meetings. Interestingly, some of these features appear to have been engendered by Bundesbank officials. In fact, Siklos and Bohl (2003) found that the Bundesbank has suffered similar problems in communicating with the public over the years.

Wilhelmsen and Zaghini (2005) address the related issue of monetary policy predictability in the euro area in comparison to 13 other countries with different monetary policy strategies and regimes. Their result is interesting but somewhat mixed: the volatility of one-month interest rates on the days of the policy change is larger in the euro area than in inflation targeting countries, such as Sweden, Australia or the UK. On the other hand, there is little difference in the predictability of interest rate movements in the USA, the euro area and Switzerland and in inflation targeters. Furthermore, in both sets of countries, policy changes are quickly incorporated in the term structure of interest rates.

4.2.4 Pillars

The other major adjustment in the ECB monetary policy strategy was the requalification of the two-pillar strategy. The first pillar, now termed economic analysis, is used to identify short to medium-term risks to price stability; the second, now termed monetary analysis, is used to assess the medium/long-term trends of inflation and to cross-check the results obtained from the economic analysis.

Several observations about the reshuffling of the labels and the reweighting of the two pillars can be made. First, it appears that the role of monetary factors has been rightly de-emphasized, that the reference value for M3 growth (at 4.5 per cent) is no longer an alternative policy target – probably because the target was consistently and consecutively exceeded over the first four years of operations (see Figure 4.6) – and that the control of monetary aggregates now involves monitoring a large range of monetary and credit statistics, not simply the growth rate of M3.

Second, it appears that policymakers believe that when analysing price developments, it is important to have an explicit time series perspective, separating high frequency movements from more persistent trends. They also appear to believe that factors driving short-term, high frequency movements are distinct from those driving long-term fluctuations. Third, implicit in the formulation of the new policy framework is the idea that monetary factors predict, in an unconditional sense, inflation dynamics in the medium/long-run better than any other variable. Finally, cross-checking the information coming from economic and monetary analyses, appears to be important in the eyes of ECB officials to ascertain the soundness of the course of policy. In particular, it is thought to avoid problems connected with myopic overactivism (see Issing, 2001) – if inflation is not

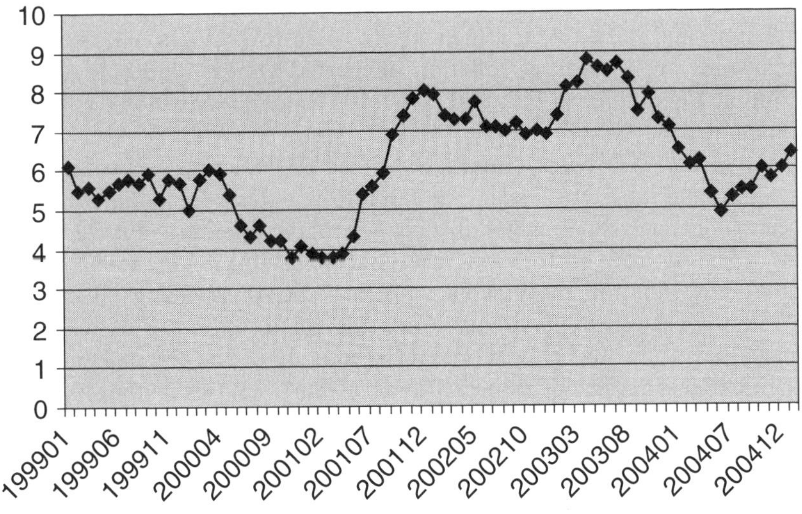

Figure 4.6 *M3 growth*

a unit root process, inflationary/deflationary pressures will eventually subside with no need for any policy intervention – to eliminate instabilities associated with multiple equilibria produced by standard Taylor rules (see for example Christiano and Rostagno, 2001) and to allow a more robust inflation stabilization approach. To people like ourselves, who earn part of our living analysing the relationship between prices, money and real activity, the general principles which constitute the foundations of such an approach appear not only to be based on an old fashion idea of the macroeconomic interdependencies, questioned or discredited in many academic papers, but also to contrast with the empirical evidence available in the euro area.

Macroeconomic time series typically display high frequency, random movements and more persistent, longer term fluctuations. One characteristic of inflation, noted in many academic chapter (see for example Roberts, 1997), and now also well understood in policy circles, is its tenacious and persistent nature, at least since the 1970s. The recent ECB conference on inflation persistence in the euro area, held in Frankfurt in December 2004 indicates that such a concern is also present in the agenda of some ECB policymakers. Persistence means that periods of relatively high inflation tend to be followed by further periods of relatively high inflation and that the duration of the fluctuations on either side of the target tends to be relatively long. It is important to stress that this was not necessarily the case in the nineteenth century and in the early twentieth century prior to the

Second World War. Price deflation occurred almost as often as price inflation, and inflation movements were mean-reverting in nature, that is, high and low periods of inflation alternated almost randomly (see for example Friedman and Schwartz, 1960, 1963 and more recently Cooley and Ohanian, 1991).

While the ECB has systematically failed to state precisely what short, medium and long-term mean, one can think of short fluctuations as those occurring and dissipating within a year or so; medium-term fluctuations as those lasting from 18 to 60 months, and long-term fluctuations as those producing inflation movements with periodicity exceeding 60 months. While the cut-off points are arbitrary and the division can be refined to make the arguments below more precise, it is should be obvious that there is little that economic or monetary analysis can do to predict the amplitude and the nature of short-term movements of inflation except, perhaps, through ex post introspection. The indicators monitored in the economic analysis (GDP and its components, fiscal policy, labour market conditions, balance sheet positions and so on) are not typically available on a very short-run basis and when they are, they are subject to substantial amount measurement or revision error. Moreover, the relationship between monetary and credit aggregates and short-term inflation movements is recognized to be tenuous and, in general, unreliable for predicting inflation fluctuations. Hence, short-term inflation fluctuations are broadly unpredictable, and only detailed micro information (for example the impact of weather on non-processed food production or the pass-through of oil price increases to gas pumps) could help us to improve our understanding and our forecasts of the dynamics of short-term price changes.

The rest of this subsection provides evidence on four related and, in our opinion, important issues: (i) there is little information in the inflation data which would help us to pin down and predict fluctuations which last longer than 60 months, even taking into account the artificial data set constructed by ECB staff to examine the dynamics of the pre-1999 European economy; (ii) given the persistence of the inflation process, it is impossible to further distinguish fluctuations with periodicity ranging from 18 to 60 months – these are persistent, medium-term fluctuations – and even if this distinction was possible it would not help to understand the nature of inflation dynamics; (iii) as a consequence of (ii); shocks which are temporary in nature may take a long time to dissipate; (iv) monetary aggregates have little predictive power for medium-term inflation fluctuations whenever past inflation is used in prediction, both in the euro area as a whole and in the major member countries. On the contrary, an index constructed using information coming from a variety of disaggregated international data helps to track and forecast movements in euro area inflation reasonably well since 1990.

Table 4.1 Dynamics of HICP inflation (year to year rate)

	1970–2004	1990–2004	1999–2004
Volatility	0.38	0.26	0.11
Faction of variance due to medium cycles	0.90	0.82	0.77
Persistence	0.76	0.50	−0.25

Table 4.1 presents statistics summarizing the dynamics of headline (HICP) inflation for the euro area. It reports, first, a measure of volatility of the series; second, the fraction of the variance of inflation due to medium-term fluctuations; and third, a measure of persistence for the samples 1970–2004, 1990–2004 and 1999–2004. The share of the inflation variance due to medium-term frequencies is obtained by extracting the relevant information from the spectrum of the series with a band pass filter, while a measure of persistence is obtained by summing up the estimated AR coefficients of the inflation process. The spectrum is a useful device for our purposes since it allows us to split inflation movements into orthogonal short, medium and long-term fluctuations, much in the same fashion as a prism allows us to divide a light beam into its constituent components – from the infrared (low frequency) to the ultraviolet (high frequency) waves.

Four features of Table 4.1 are worth commenting upon. First, the bulk of the inflation fluctuation in the euro area are of medium-term nature – both high and low frequency variations are minor. Second, the volatility of inflation at all frequencies is smaller in the second and third samples. This conforms to the idea that inflation has become less volatile over the last 15 years, thanks, in part, to the larger credibility that central banks of member countries have acquired since the early 1990s. Third, the overall bulk of the fluctuations since 1999 is also of a medium-term nature. Fourth, there is also a decline in the estimated inflation persistence in the latter two samples, consistent for example with the analyses of Cogley and Sargent (2005), Canova and Gambetti (2004) for the USA and Benati (2002) for the UK. Nevertheless, while the estimated persistence for the 1999–2004 sample is significantly different from the estimated persistence obtained in the other samples, standard tests fail to detect any statistical difference in the persistence measures in the first two sub-samples. In sum, Table 4.1 overwhelmingly indicates that inflation in the euro area is a persistent process and that the majority of the fluctuations are of a medium-term nature.

Is it possible to decompose medium-term fluctuations further, say, into short–medium (18–36 months) or medium–long (36–60)? It turns out that such a division is artificial for two reasons. First, the magnitude of the fluctuations is roughly the same over two frequency ranges. Second, a shock that significantly moves inflation for at least 18 months will also move inflation for more than 36 months. We show this in two ways. First, by displaying the cumulative multiplier of a shock to the univariate process for inflation computed by summing up responses from 18 to 36 months and from 36 to 60 months. Second, by showing that persistent output gap shocks – such as those experienced in the euro area over the last three years – produce significant inflation dynamics over both frequency ranges. To demonstrate this point, Figure 4.7 presents the response of inflation to a typical output gap shock. It is clear that inflation is persistently displaced from its long-run path, and that output gap disturbances can induce longer inflation fluctuations than those the first pillar of the new ECB strategy is supposed to capture – a typical shock is not completely dissipated even after 10 years. Figure 4.7 also shows how the data give very little support to the notion that, in the medium-run, monetary variations are tightly

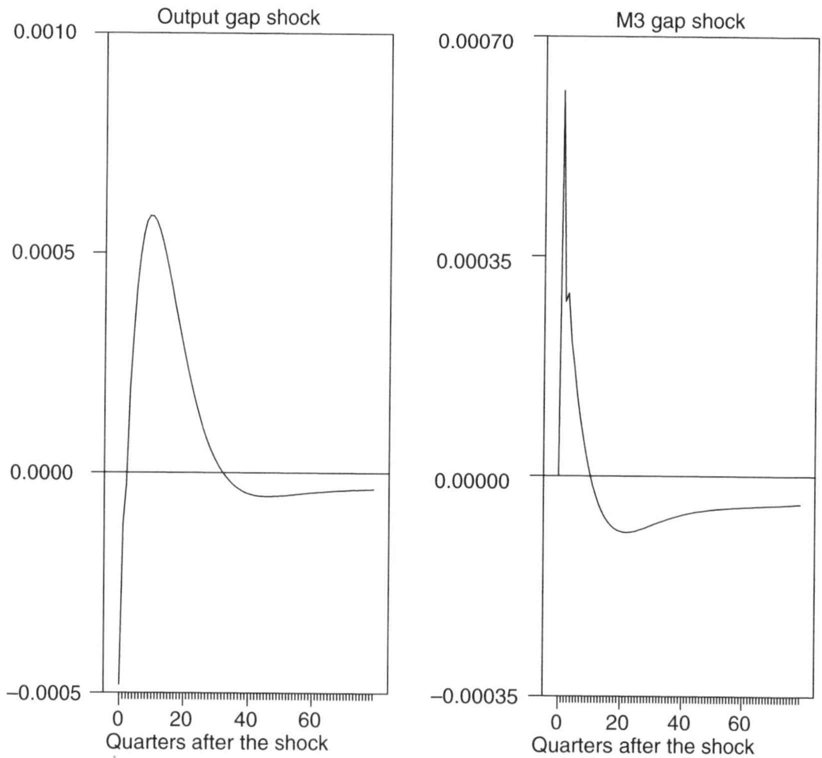

Figure 4.7 Inflation responses

linked to inflation developments. In fact, unexpected increases of M3 growth from target produce inflation dynamics which are smaller in size and shorter lived than those produced by output gap disturbances and that are roughly insignificant after about two and half years. To put this another way, over the medium term, the percentage of inflation variance explained by output gap shocks (25 per cent) is larger than the one explained by M3 gap shocks (only 11 per cent). It is important to stress that this result is independent of the sample. For example, had we excluded the last five years from our analysis, a period where M3 growth was persistently above its target, probably because of negative return obtained on many financial assets, the same outcome would have been obtained.

While suggestive of the lack of a tight link between medium-term movements of inflation and money growth, this evidence may be still regarded as inconclusive by staunch monetarist believers. Further evidence on this issue is obtained by analysing the predictive power of various forecasting models for inflation. Canova (2002) examined this issue in detail for the G-7 countries. Two of his results are particularly important here. First, a simple univariate AR model is as good as a model which, in addition to past inflation, uses M3 growth rates to forecast inflation at one or two year horizons for Germany, Italy and France in the five years leading to the creation of the ECB. Second, a model which uses an index combining the information contained in a number of lagged G-7 variables, not only outperforms a model which uses M3 growth but also substantially reduces the mean square forecast error of a simple univariate AR model. Taken, together, these results suggest that there is information in the cross-section of the G-7 countries which is helpful in predicting domestic inflation in the medium run and that M3 growth, while useful for in-sample fit, has no use in out-of-sample prediction exercises.

Since the index model available in-house at the ECB has been shown to have a consistently good forecasting record over the 1990s (see Canova and Ciccarelli, 2003) and has also been demonstrated to be superior to a number of alternative benchmarks over the first five years of the euro (see Anzuini et al., 2005) it is somewhat surprising that its informational content is systematically neglected in the policymaking process and that, in general, international information is ignored in predicting medium-term trends of inflation. Since inflation is not only a persistent process, but also highly correlated across countries, information concerning the state of inflation from other areas of the world not only helps more accurately to predict domestic medium-term trends, but also provides a more coherent explanation for its causes, both of which make policy decisions, in general, easier.

All of this should be obvious to a keen observer. Globalization means also that shocks which had an important national component in the past

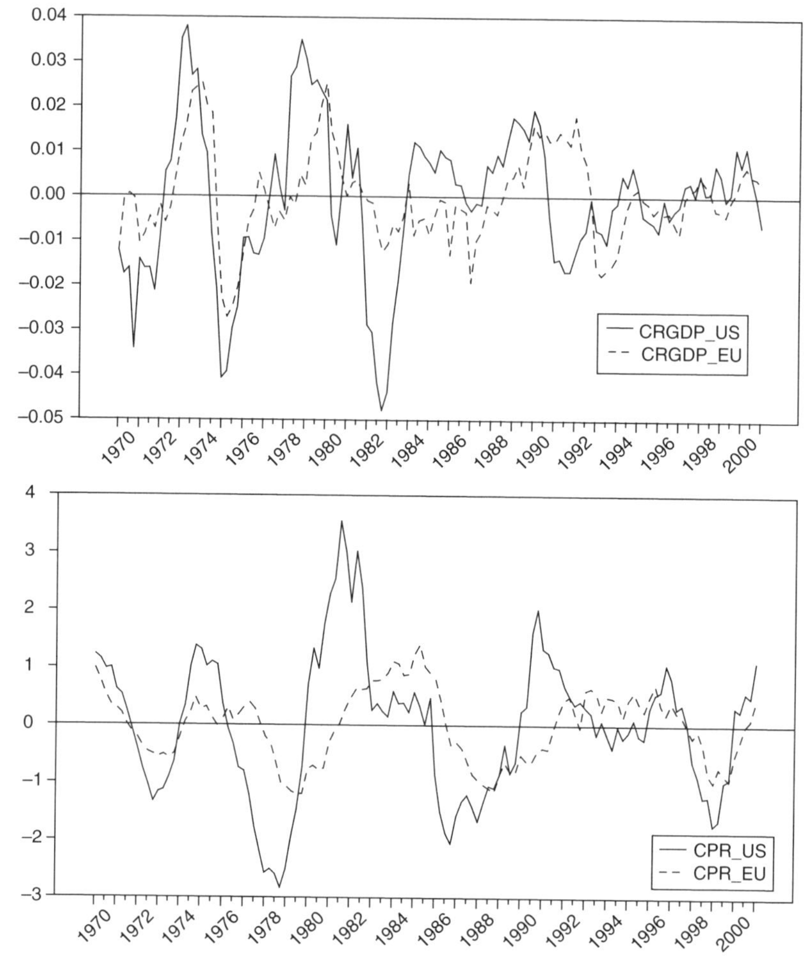

Figure 4.8 Cyclical component of output and inflation in the USA and the euro area

are now swamped by movements which are common in nature. Figure 4.8 reports the dynamics of cyclical output and inflation in the euro area and the USA from 1970 to 2000. It is easy to see that the ups and downs of inflation and output in the USA are followed by ups and downs in inflation and output in the euro area, with about 4–5 months delay. Given this evidence, one is left wondering why monetary aggregates and not international variables have such prominence in the ECB strategy. Monetary aggregates do not seem to be the major source of inflation fluctuations in the medium run, nor do they help to forecast medium-term trends of inflation once obvious information is used. Clearly, this does not mean that monetary (and credit aggregates) should be set aside either in the analysis or the decision-making process. But, in our opinion, even the reduced emphasis that the revised ECB strategy puts on them is unwarranted: monetary and credit aggregates should not be strategically singled out from all other information and given predominance in the policy discussion.

In conclusion, the artificial split of inflation fluctuations into those explainable with economic analysis and those interpretable with monetary analysis, the lack of appreciation of the tight links between short-run shocks and medium-term movements in inflation and the failure to entertain a global perspective in evaluating medium-term trends of inflation could have been sufficient to seriously endanger the price stability goal. Despite this, inflation has been around the 2 per cent level for the last five years and inflation expectations have been anchored. Perhaps, the markets and the public learned to discount 'incredible' statements of ECB officials and, more pragmatically, looked at facts when deciding a course of action to take.

4.2.5 Where Do We Leave Output Concerns?

Central bankers, whether they are inflation targeters or not, are extremely reluctant to discuss concerns about output fluctuations (see for example Mishkin, 2004). There are many important reasons which may explain this reluctance. First, announcing that a central bank has two objectives (price stability and elimination of the output gap) may confuse market participants and make it more likely that the public sees the elimination of short-run output fluctuations as the mission of a central bank. It is well known that such a perception may lead to expectation traps: prices and wages could rise because the public knows that the monetary authority is likely to accommodate these increases by pursuing expansionary policies which prevent the output gap from enlarging. Discussing monetary policy objectives in terms of output fluctuations may therefore lead to a loss of inflation-fighting credibility which may worsen the actual inflation-output trade-off. The experience of the 1970s is still very vivid in the mind of macroeconomists and the risks now are probably as large as they were back then. Second, the announcement that a central bank also has output objectives can lead short-sighted politicians, such as those running many euro area countries, to exacerbate time consistency problems. In particular, they can pressure central banks to pursue overexpansionary policies in order to yield short-term gains by exploiting the unemployment and inflation trade-off. Third, in announcing that output fluctuations are important it is necessary to take a stand on what potential output is now and how large it will be in the future and to operationally measure deviations from it. Both academic economists and central bankers know how difficult it is to quantify potential output using real time data and the distortions that can be created with imperfect information (see for example Orphanides, 2001). Furthermore, statistical output gap measures do not necessarily have a close relationship with relevant theoretical ones. For example, a New Keynesian Phillips curve requires marginal costs to be operational and the output gap enters the specification only after additional assumptions on the nature of the production function are made. Finally, announcing a second objective requires specifying how inflation and output concerns are weighted in the decision-making process and what is the loss function used by policymakers, which creates a number of practical complications for the decision-making process. For example, it is necessary to state clearly what is the relative importance of the two objectives, and how and in what situations committee members may decide to change the weights and design ways for extracting information from committee members who are not used to thinking in these terms.

Despite the rhetoric and the theoretical reasons for shying away from output gap concerns, central bankers' actions show that output fluctuations are very much in their minds. As shown in Begg et al. (2002), a rule where the short-term nominal interest rate responds only to the output gap fits the time path of interest rates in the 1999–2002 period reasonably well, both in the USA and in the euro area. Furthermore, it appears to be superior to other rules which also make short-term interest rates respond to inflation or expected inflation. Extending their exercise up to the end of 2004 changes very little in their conclusions.

From an academic point of view there is nothing wrong with such a reduced form rule and, in fact, it is consistent with the prescriptions of many models currently used by economists. However, an interest rate rule of this type underlines once again that the ECB (and the Fed for that matter) lacks transparency and this adds to the already mentioned communication problems, at least to the extent that the words do not match the deeds; and may lead to a medium-term erosion of confidence in other elements of central bank transparency that are beneficial for the economy. The term 'inflation nutters' minted by Mervyn King a few years ago is very much present in the mind of market participants and such a perception may lead to a renewal of discussion of the support for central bank policies and independence.

One simple way to communicate to the public that output fluctuations are important without reducing the emphasis on the medium-term inflation objective is to state, as suggested for example by Mishkin (2004), that large shocks may move the actual inflation rate far away from the target, in which case sticking to the inflation objective may cause unacceptably high output losses. Such shocks do occur in the real world and a policy that recognizes their presence helps markets to behave in an orderly fashion, makes it clear when and how medium-run objectives can be temporarily set aside and, at the same time, sets up ways to gradually return to the inflation objective. Clauses of this type are present for example in inflation targeting regime countries such as the UK. Furthermore, Brazil successfully implemented a policy of this type when a major exchange rate shock hit the local economy (see Fraga et al., 2003).

Luckily, and despite the events of the last few years, the euro area economy has been shielded from those large shocks which would have required a temporary suspension of the inflation objective. Nevertheless, one must be aware that, for example, the events of September 2001 have dramatically increased the volatility and persistently worsened the perceptions of agents about the future prospects of the world economy. Chronic problems such as the ageing population, low productivity and low participation rates also combine to create an environment where output may remain permanently below its potential. Stressing that these are important concerns in the euro area, that they have to be addressed if the output–inflation trade-off has to be permanently improved, and underlining the fact that the ECB can do nothing to solve these problems other than exert pressure on national and EU governments, could be an important way to demonstrate that the ECB is not an 'inflation nutter' and create the consensus needed to implement those changes which may improve efficiency. Similarly, the presence of overexpansionary fiscal policies in many member countries and the increased heterogeneity that can be expected when EU newcomers adopt the euro pose serious threats to the price stability objective and open up the possibility that persistent and undesirable inflation differentials will result in the euro area. Warnings of this nature, describing the mechanics which transform overexpansionary fiscal policy in an overexpansionary output process and the way in which these pressures represent a threat to medium-run price stability can kill two birds with one stone: they may help to establish the link between output gap and inflation process and to indicate who has responsibility for keeping interest rates up, despite the fact that the strong euro decreases both the share of imported inflation and the importance of oil price swings.

4.2.6 The Euro Changeover

The introduction of euro banknotes and coins (the cash changeover), which occurred during the early months of 2002, was followed by a number of complaints from consumer associations in euro area countries. These concerns have ranged from losses due to increases in transaction costs to the alleged inflationary effects produced by the change in the unit of account. Goodhart and Pappa (2003) tried to measure the size of transaction costs using supermarket prices and waiting time at cashier lines in the months surrounding the change. They found that there was a temporary increase in transaction time with a sunk cost roughly equal to yearly opportunity costs incurred by consumers in withdrawing cash from banks.

On the second issue, several observers have reported that consumers' 'perceived inflation' (based on qualitative judgements) was systematically larger than actual inflation and in countries such as Italy, Germany, Greece, Spain and the Netherlands there are numerous reports about the price increases brought about by the changeover. In Germany the euro has became known as the 'Teuro' – teuer means expensive! In Italy, such a phenomenon was more marked than in other countries. The Italian media and consumers' associations frequently reported extraordinary price increases. Among them, those recorded by restaurants gave rise to heated controversies. According to a survey conducted in an Italian region, one-third of citizens blamed restaurants for excessive increases, a percentage second only to the share of respondents who blamed food prices. Gaiotti and Lippi (2005) examine the veracity of these arguments by looking at a panel of restaurants' price-setting behaviour in the year of the changeover and in the neighbouring ones. Their empirical micro-based analysis shows that a sizeable average price increase took place in 2002 (about 9 per cent). This increase however was slightly smaller than that recorded in the previous year (about 10 per cent). Furthermore, it appears that these increases were related to rising demand and costs. While the authors suggest caution in attributing the inflationary effect exclusively to the introduction of the euro banknotes, we find the evidence in striking contrast to the hypothesis that the euro changeover led to a doubling of prices by Italian restaurants. This widespread perception might be ascribed to the substantial price increase which took place in this sector but over a longer period. In fact, between 1998 and 2003 the average price of a meal rose by 40 per cent; in the 10 per cent of restaurants recording the largest increases the increase is 75 per cent. Nevertheless, it is true that the changeover has moved public attention away from inflation rates to the general price level, prompting the attribution of the whole increase to the introduction of the euro.

Interestingly, the data are consistent with both the 'menu cost' and the 'market power' hypotheses. In fact, the evidence shows that much of the aggregate price increases during the changeover were due to a greater number of prices being revised, rather than to individual price increases. Also, market structure affected price dynamics after the changeover. In 2002 and 2003 the increases were largely due to price jumps in the countryside and in the provinces, two locations traditionally characterized by a smaller degree of competitiveness.

What lessons can one learn from this experience, in particular, for countries which are planning to adopt the euro? First, the change of unit of account will induce substantial time costs. Second, it may lead to a faster convergence of regional price levels than experienced in the past. Third, price increases are going to be more marked in rural areas and therefore more likely to be perceived by the consumers who are used to much more sluggish price changes. All in all, appropriate diffusion of information and capillary education in non-urban areas are crucial to preventing the emergence of a dangerous gap between perceived inflation and actual inflation such as has induced considerable discontent with the euro in the past few years.

4.2.7 A Tentative Conclusion

What conclusions can one draw from the evidence we have presented? It appears to us that the ECB has largely done its job. Over the last five years inflation has been low, expectations have been kept under control and markets have behaved smoothly in response to unexpected and possibly disruptive disturbances. The ECB, however, deserves a much lower score as far as communication is concerned. In particular, the two-pillar strategy employed to achieve a low inflation outcome turns out to be 'incredible'; output concerns are present but never spelled out in a way that makes explicit not only their importance but also their connection with excessive fiscal policy and price stability; and markets do not seem to have a clear understanding of how the policy process works nor seem to be very sure of how policy will change when it is expected to change. So far, opacity and poor communication have not threatened the price stability goal. But they might in the near future unless decisive steps are taken.

4.3 THE TRANSMISSION OF POLICY IMPULSES

4.3.1 The Euro Area

Considerable evidence exists on the transmission of monetary policy shocks in the euro area (see for example Angeloni et al., 2003; Peersman, 2004). While results somewhat depend on the study, the sample, the country and the exact methodology employed to identify disturbances to the policy rule, it is generally agreed that a shock which unexpectedly increases interest rates makes output and inflation decline, even though the magnitude and the timing of the decline are pretty much uncertain. This uncertainty is due to many factors: the magnitude of the policy impulse, the sensitivity of credit and/or investment aggregates to interest rate changes, the expectations of the public and, as a consequence, the reaction of the yield curve. Since most of the evidence for the euro area as a whole is based on synthetic data reconstructed for the pre-ECB regime, we provide some evidence concerning the effects of policy shocks on industrial output growth, inflation and the dollar-euro rate using monthly data for the period 1999:1–2005:1. Clearly, since the sample is short, estimates are likely to be noisy. Furthermore, the sample we analyse is somewhat special, very rich with other unexpected events, and therefore may not truly represent the 'normal' features of the transmission of monetary policy shocks. Nevertheless, our exercise may give us some indications of whether important changes have taken place after the establishment of the ECB.

Figure 4.9 plots the responses of the three variables to a 25 basis points unexpected increase in short-term interest rates where the unexpected increase in the short-term rate is identified via a liquidity effect (an interest rate increase must decrease narrow monetary aggregates like M1). A few important features of the figure are worth discussion. First, an increase in the short-term interest rate appreciates the euro and makes industrial production growth decline, while inflation first declines and then increases. This pattern which, to a large extent, reproduces the dynamics present in the pre-ECB era is fairly standard: higher domestic short-term interest rates attract foreign investors seeking higher return opportunities and, at the same time, cool down domestic economic activity. Second, the effect on industrial production growth is of an order of magnitude larger than the one on inflation. This pattern is less standard but easily interpretable. Typically, the output effects of monetary disturbances are small. However, output data are not available at the monthly frequency and industrial production is only a small percentage of output in the euro area (roughly 20 per cent). Therefore, while the effect on industrial output is large, the effects on the service and the agricultural sectors are probably small, making the total output response considerably smaller. Notice also that once the monthly effect is cumulated at the quarterly frequency the total response is likely to be negligible.

Third, the largest industrial output growth and exchange rate responses are instantaneous while the largest inflation response is typically observed after about six months. While the location of the maximum response is not pinned down with clockmaker's precision, it seems that in the last five years, monetary policy disturbances were transmitted to the euro area economy much more quickly than in the past. While many explanations could be found for this change, a quicker transmission is consistent with the idea that the public understands central bank actions better than in the past. Fourth, the effects of a monetary policy disturbance dissipate relatively

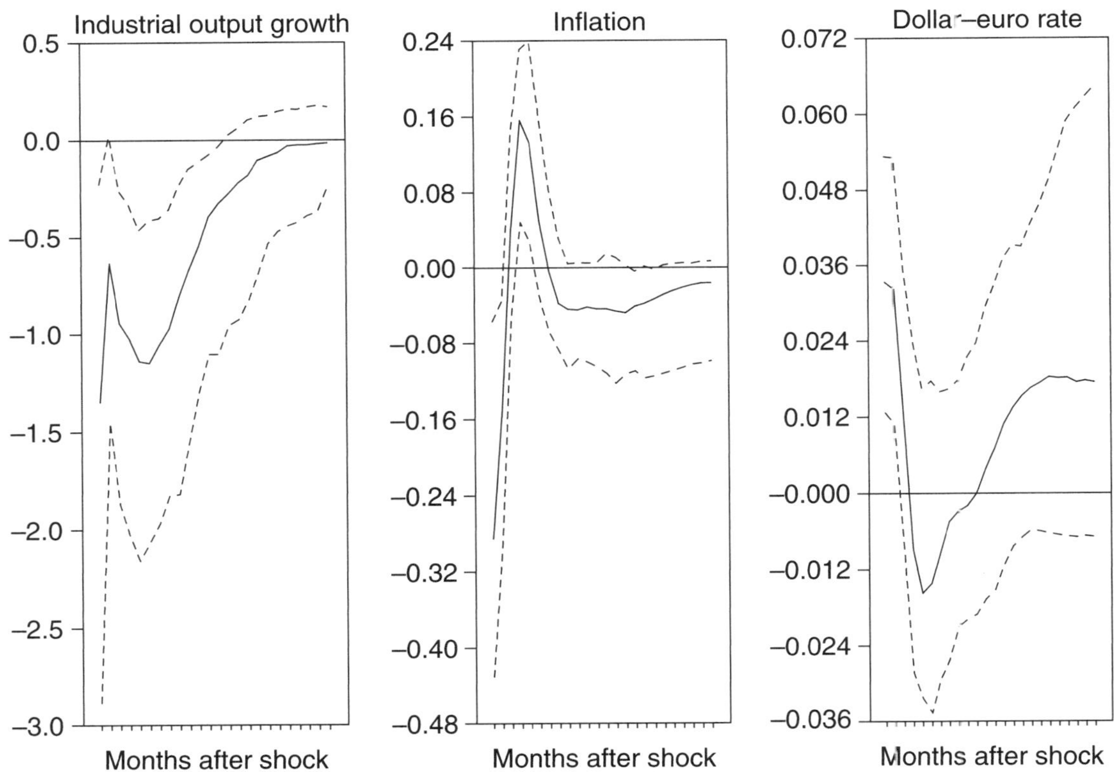

Figure 4.9 *Responses to an interest rate shock, 1999–2001*

quickly and after about 9–12 months the responses of all three variables are insignificantly different from zero.

To sum up, it looks as if monetary policy is a powerful lever for industrial output growth in the short run while the effects on inflation are more sluggish – and this is very much consistent with the evidence presented in the previous section. We think this is good news. Monetary policy has the ability to alter the short-run path of output growth and inflation if it wishes to do so and can do it relatively quickly. However, unexpected changes in short-term interest rates are unlikely to have any medium-term effect on industrial output growth, inflation or, for that matter, the dollar-euro exchange rate. Surprising market participants cannot be the medicine to remedy structural imbalances or to ease frictions. Unsurprisingly, market participants quickly learn about the possibility of being surprised.

4.3.2 The New EU Members

There is a growing body of literature showing how monetary policy shocks are transmitted within the ten new members of the EU and some effort has been made in comparing differences in the responses of these countries with those of the existing euro area (see for example Ganev et al., 2002; Suppel, 2003; Anzuini and Levy, 2004; Jarocinski, 2004). The main conclusion of all these studies is that, despite important differences in the structure of the economies, the transmission of policy shocks in the old and the new members of the EU is similar. That is to say, contractionary domestic monetary policy shocks reduce output growth and inflation and, although with some heterogeneities, tend to appreciate the local currency. While the qualitative pattern is similar, the quantitative effects in the old and the new members of the EU are different. In particular, interest rate responses tend to be more persistent in the new EU countries and price responses stronger in the medium term but less persistent. All in all, monetary policy appears to have stronger but more delayed price effects in these countries.

Many reasons may account for the differences. For example, since these countries are more open than the euro area, the exchange rate channel becomes stronger. Moreover, the fact that these countries are less financially integrated, that they have somewhat inefficient financial markets and that they have large amounts of trade credit may make them more responsive to monetary policy. Is this good or bad news for the possible adoption of the euro by these countries? In our opinion, it dramatically depends on the reasons that make transmission different. If the heterogeneities between old and new members are the results of structural differences, premature adoption of the euro may force adjustments to shocks to take place in relative prices. If these adjust slowly, damage can be done. On the other hand, if the heterogeneities in transmission are due to lack of central bank credibility, the adoption of the euro could make the transmission of policy shocks quicker and the output costs smaller. In our opinion, central banks in the new EU countries are quickly gaining reputation and credibility. In addition, the fact that many of them follow inflation targeting strategies makes us conjecture that it is probably the first reason, the presence of important structural differences, which is at the heart of the problem.

There is much less evidence in the literature on the effects of shocks originating in the euro area for new EU members and on the relative size of domestic versus external shocks (one exception is Benczur et al., 2004). Both questions are important. It is often claimed that small open economies are subject to a considerable amount of external (and uncontrollable) shocks. If fluctuations in the periphery of the EU are largely attributable to shocks originating in the euro area there is scope for coordination activities between policymakers, both to avoid unnecessary shocks and to respond jointly to unforeseen circumstances. Clearly, having dominant external shocks is insufficient to justify common policies, the extra condition being that these shocks should have similar effects on the variables of the two areas. Observing different effects, however, it is not necessarily a drawback for integration as it may indicate the presence of a self-correcting mechanism across regions. Interestingly, Benczur et al. (2004) report that while some of the domestic fluctuations in the new EU members are due to external shocks, the vast majority of the fluctuations come from domestically induced disturbances. In other words, while one should worry about shocks generated in the euro area, there is still ample room to put the house in order before considering the consequences of intensifying external links and eliminating the equilibrating effects of exchange rate movements.

Given that external shocks are less important than domestic ones, what is the channel through which euro area shocks are transmitted to the local economies? Consider a contractionary monetary policy shock in the euro area. Since, as we have seen, such a shock has a temporary but sizeable effect on industrial output, it is conceivable that the demand for goods by euro area firms will decline. If there are large trade links between the euro area and the new EU member countries, the demand for locally produced goods will also decline and this will have depressing real effects. The magnitude and the importance of this channel obviously depends on the degree of interdependencies and integration between the two areas. Note that the opposite can also occur as a beggar-thy-neighbour policy may reduce output growth in neighbouring countries (see for example Mackowiak, 2005).

The previous section has also shown that the euro typically appreciates when the ECB increases interest rates, as financial capital flows to take advantage of higher returns. However, depressed local demand conditions may also induce industrial capital to move away from the area, and this is especially true when there are complementaries in production. Therefore a 'capital' channel may act exactly in the opposite direction to the trade channel, reinforcing the beggar-thy-neighbour effect, making the final outcome on the new EU countries uncertain. Also in this case, the level of financial integration and the degree of international capital mobility determines the magnitude and the persistence of this effect. Separating the two channels is difficult (see Canova, 2005), but such an exercise may provide useful information to policymakers in order to design the proper reaction to disturbances.

Which channel dominates in the actual data? Do we see industrial output in new EU countries contracting or increasing in response to contractionary monetary policy shocks? Do we see inflation responses which positively or negatively correlate with inflation responses in the euro area? Given the short sample and the fact that only quarterly data for new EU countries is available, the analysis is very tentative and subject to both large measurement errors and small sample biases. In Figure 4.10, we report the responses of industrial output growth, inflation and nominal exchange rate in Poland, the Czech Republic and Hungary when a contractionary monetary policy shock hits the euro area. While there are important similarities with the responses of Figure 4.9, differences are also noticeable. For example, in response to tighter monetary policy in the euro area, industrial output growth declines in Hungary and Poland but increases in the Czech Republic. That is to say, for the latter country the capital/beggar-thy-neighbour channel seems to be stronger. Inflation is typically temporarily reduced in all three countries, but the effect becomes positive and significantly so after about two quarters. This is similar to what occurs in the euro area. Furthermore, in the Czech Republic and Hungary, the currency temporarily appreciates and then strongly depreciates so that the observed inflation response could be the result of increased import costs. In Poland the picture is more complicated: in fact, the nominal exchange rate first depreciates as economic activity contracts and then appreciates after about a year, therefore making the interpretation of inflation responses difficult.

In sum, and tentatively speaking, it appears that both channels of transmission are present and that their importance depends on a number of factors. Of the three countries, the Czech Republic appears to be the most integrated with the euro area economy and the one that seems to benefit most when contractionary policy shocks hit the euro area economy. Interestingly, inflation responses in all three countries mimic those in the euro area,

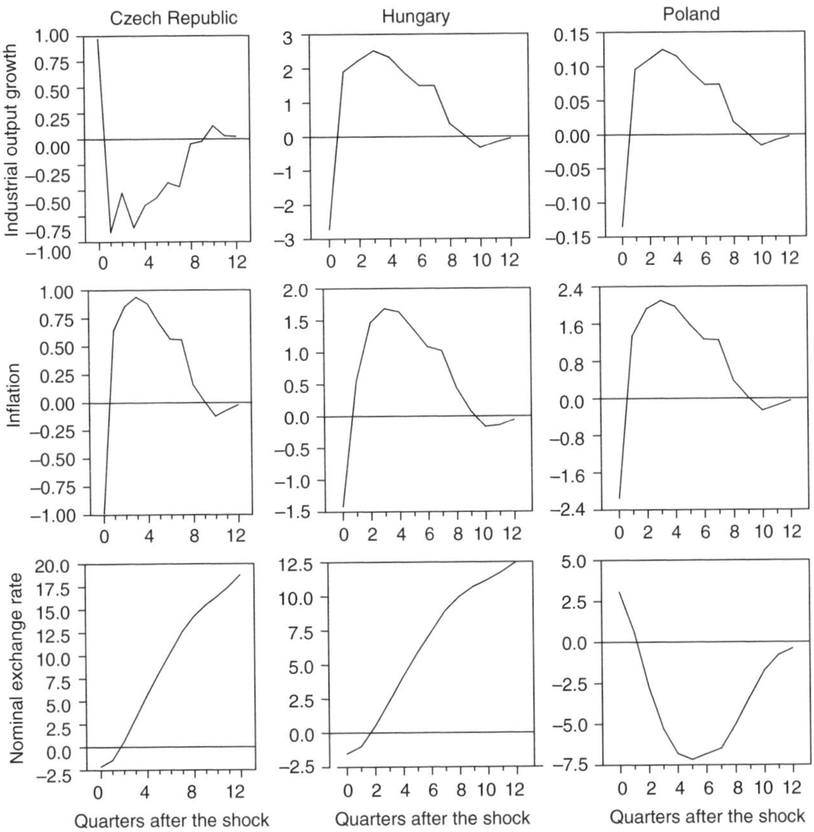

Figure 4.10 Responses to euro area monetary policy shocks

suggesting that, perhaps, some implicit coordination between central banks is already taking place. The heterogeneities present in the transmission of euro area monetary policy shocks to these three countries will probably be magnified if the sample is extended to consider other new EU members.

These heterogeneities, if confirmed, should be carefully analysed when the decision to adopt the euro is considered. Rushing into a single currency may be dangerous: without the exchange rate channel to resolve imbalances, larger heterogeneities in the responses to monetary policy may magnify the pattern of real and inflationary differentials already present in euro regions, therefore making monetary policy more difficult and less effective. From the information presented in Figure 4.10, one can predict that shutting down the exchange rate channel may turn out to be less of a problem for the Czech Republic and Hungary. However, there is considerable uncertainty regarding the consequences of such a choice. Therefore, gains from a less volatile environment must be weighted against the costs of having one less channel to absorb domestic and international shocks.

4.4 IMPLICATIONS FOR TURKEY

4.4.1 Joining the EU

Among the prospective newcomers to the EU and the euro, Turkey is the largest and the most densely populated. What are the likely consequences of joining the EU club? Would joining the EU foster a process of income convergence between Turkey and Europe? Would the adoption of the euro cause major changes in the way euro area shocks in general, and monetary policy shocks in particular, are transmitted to the Turkish economy? Most of these questions cannot have a direct answer since they involve a change of regime which is unprecedented in the history of Turkey. However, the now relatively long list of countries acceding to the EU and having comparable stages of development to Turkey has taught us important lessons which, to a large extent, are also applicable to Turkey.

A few years before accession took place, Canova and Boldrin (2002) examined in detail the economic prospects of the Central European countries (CECs) and compared their economic conditions to those of Greece, Spain and Portugal when they joined the EU. Unsurprisingly, they found striking similarities between the two experiences. In fact, although the political and historical circumstances of accession were different, macroeconomic conditions in the CEC resembled those of the earlier joiners in terms of cultural characteristics, political past, structural and socioeconomic features, GDP per capita and labour productivity relative to the EU average, share of employment in agriculture and openness of the economy (the latter measured by exports plus imports over GDP). Table 4.2 reproduces some of their data: for Central European countries, 2000 is used as a benchmark, for Spain and Portugal we average conditions existing in 1985 and 1986, while for Greece we average the conditions existing in 1980 and 1981. It is clear that in terms of backwardness (the share of employment in agriculture), relative income per capita and labour productivity (Spain is the exception here) the two experiences are very similar. One important difference is that the CECs were much more open than Spain, Portugal and Greece were 20 years ago, but this could be the result of a general trend toward stronger interdependencies between advanced and less advanced economies. In fact, not only trade interdependencies were stronger, but also capital flows were considerably larger than those of the

Table 4.2 Indices of similarity

	Openness	Employment in agriculture	Relative GDP per capita	Relative labour productivity
Spain 1985–86	0.29	0.15	0.62	0.95
Portugal 1985–86	0.56	0.22	0.49	0.44
Greece 1980–81	0.42	NA	0.55	0.52
Czech 2000	1.44	0.05	0.59	0.47
Estonia 2000	0.87	0.07	0.41	0.34
Hungary 2000	1.23	0.07	0.53	0.47
Latvia 2000	1.02	0.14	0.30	0.30
Lithuania 2000	1.06	0.19	0.30	0.26
Poland 2000	0.63	0.25	0.41	0.34
Slovak 2000	1.60	0.08	0.49	0.47
Slovenia 2000	1.20	0.10	0.73	0.50
Turkey 2003	0.60	0.35	0.14	0.25

three early newcomers. Perhaps more importantly for our purposes, between 40 and 70 per cent of the trade of the CECs in 2000 took place with EU countries and about 70 per cent of foreign direct investments came from the EU (Germany, in particular). One more feature emphasizes the similarities between pre-accession Central European countries and Spain and Portugal in the early–mid-1980s: labour market dynamics. In fact, the rapid expulsion of workers from agriculture and from traditional industrial sectors, an equally fast increase in unemployment and reduction in the labour force participation rates, and the creation of a substantial and a long-lasting stock of long-term unemployed – at around 40–50 per cent of total unemployment – are significant features of both transition processes.

Given these observations, Canova and Boldrin (2002) estimated that the costs and the gains that the CECs would enjoy joining on the EU would probably be comparable to those experienced by the previous three newcomers, a prediction which is so far confirmed by the available data. In particular, their economic and econometric analysis predicted that most of the convergence gains would take place in the years leading to accession and after that the old and the new EU members would experience a roughly similar growth path. That is to say, inequalities between the core and the periphery of the EU existing at the time of accession are unlikely be eliminated and instead should be expected to persist for a least a few decades.

Why is it a good idea to compare the Central European countries with Mediterranean ones and not with Ireland, which was equally backward when it joined the EU in 1976 and experienced extraordinary growth in the late 1990s? There are several reasons why this comparison is inappropriate. The most important one is that Irish growth did not occur in a vacuum. If the CECs were willing to adopt the policies that Ireland implemented in the last decade of the twentieth century, including aggressive labour market reforms, productivity incentives, tax reductions, financial market deepening, and new legislation to eliminate local market inefficiencies, a much rosier picture would probably result. Accession, however, does not necessarily come together with good national policies. Since history and social norms matter, Canova and Boldrin (2002) conjectured that sweeping changes in labour, financial and capital markets were unlikely to occur and, as far as we can tell, have so far not occurred.

Where does Turkey stand relative to previous EU newcomers? Table 4.2 suggests that the numbers for Turkey in 2003 are comparable to those of the Mediterranean countries in the mid-1980s. A few differences however are worth stressing. Turkey is relatively more open than earlier Mediterranean EU joiners; as open as Poland was in 2000 but, in general, less open then the average CEC. Moreover, more than 50 per cent of the trade in goods and services is already with EU countries. Therefore, while one should expect this share to increase as membership is granted, its currently high level suggests that gains from improved trade interdependencies are probably not going to be very large. Second, the share of the population employed in agriculture is still large compared to the CECs, and is approximately the same as in Romania and Bulgaria, two other countries knocking at the doors of the EU for membership. This indicates that the job-shedding process in traditional sectors, typical of economies in transition, has yet to take place in Turkey, even though the economy is relatively open to trade in goods and services. Hence membership of the EU may bring substantial transitional labour costs which, from an ex ante point of view, are better incurred before joining the club than afterwards (for this issue compare the experiences of East Germany and the most dynamic CEC). Third, income per capita is low relative to the European average despite the fact that the contribution of the service sector to GNP is roughly as large as in the EU. Therefore, while the adjustments, improvements and elimination of inefficiencies which need to take place for membership to be granted will probably spur a fast process of convergence, the mere size of the differences in income per capita makes even the 50 per cent of EU average threshold an ambitious goal for the years to come. Hence, considerable income transfers will have to take place from the core of the EU to Turkey to avoid large cross-regional inequalities. Finally, labour productivity is low relative to the EU average and, once again, comparable to the figures for Bulgaria and Romania. Given that foreign direct investment comprises a risible fraction of GDP (less than 1 per cent in 2002, 2003 and 2004), one would expect them to soar as membership is granted but to make little difference in terms of labour productivity growth in the next few years.

There is a sense in which some of the aggregate numbers presented in Table 4.2 are a bit misleading. In fact, as has happened in the majority of previous EU accession countries, cities quickly converge to the EU city average while the countryside and rural provinces lag behind both the local cities and the EU non-city average. Furthermore, as recent estimates put the size of the underground economy at about 40 per cent of GNP, income per capita is likely to be larger than official figures report.

All in all, past experience and current economic conditions suggest that placing too high growth expectations on Turkey joining the EU would be misplaced. Membership will help to reduce income inequalities, but it will not necessarily foster the process of economic convergence. Regional transfers which will take place under the structural and cohesion policies have not become growth engines in Greece, Spain and Portugal; they are unlikely to do so in the CECs and there is no reason to expect the situation to miraculously change for Turkey. To be clear: they will have a positive impact on local income, but they are unlikely to change the long-run growth rate of the beneficiary regions. One way of making structural and cohesion funds more effective in generating real convergence is to condition their reception on the implementation of the structural reforms mentioned below. The availability of such funds could in fact significantly decrease the transitional costs of structural reforms and may represent a unique opportunity for the EU actively to foster projects with the highest rate of social return. As far as we know, such conditionality is absent and is not planned to be instituted in the future.

In general, to achieve long-run growth at rates higher than the average EU level, an appropriate mix of EU and national policies is needed. This includes fostering trade integration with the EU and setting up the environment for international capital flows, restructuring public spending and containing public debt, creating supply side incentives by proper reforms of fiscal and social insurance policies, setting a competitive level of labour income taxation and, last but not least, establishing free movement of capital and labour. Based on historical experience, two types of policies appear to be particularly relevant. First, public programmes for long-term income support, corporate subsidies and other forms of income transfer have negative effects on economic growth. Second, labour and capital mobility are good for growth and economic convergence. The adoption or continuation of various transfer and/or regulation policies aimed at eliminating labour migration, in particular, is misplaced and damaging. Fear of migrations has been magnified by skilful EU politicians: migrations in past enlargements have been small. There is no reason to expect this to be large were Turkey to join the EU.

4.4.2 Transmission of Euro Area Shocks to Turkey

A significant literature examines the transmission of monetary policy shocks within Turkey, and in many papers the analysis is conducted with modern applied macroeconomic tools (see, to cite only a few, Gündüz, 2000; Berument, 2001; Şahinbeyoğlu, 2001). Interestingly, the outcome of these exercises appears to agree with the general conclusions we have reached for both euro area countries and CEC. For example Berument (2001), who uses the spread between the interbank rate and the depreciation of the local currency as a robust indicator of monetary policy over the last 15 years, found that positive innovations in this variable lead to a fall in prices and output and to an appreciation of the local currency. Furthermore, he finds that while the fall in output is temporary, prices and nominal exchange rate effects appear to be permanent. On the other hand, Şahinbeyoğlu (2001), simulating a small open economy model calibrated to match the high inflation experience of Turkey, finds that in response to a policy contraction, output falls while the inflation rate and the nominal exchange rate first fall and then increase. Relatively speaking, the effects appear to be larger in magnitude and more persistent than those observed in the euro area and also larger than those experienced in the CECs. The broad similarity of the qualitative pattern of transmission could be due to the fact that Turkish financial markets are relatively free of regulation. Therefore, since market forces are allowed to operate roughly in the same way in Turkey and the EU, the transmission of policy shocks is similar to the one observed in the most advanced countries of the world. Clearly, magnitude difference can be related to the historical experience of Turkey, which over the last 25 years witnessed repeated bursts of hyperinflation, capital flight and political instability. All of these features make the exchange rate channel stronger than in other countries and this may lead to stronger reactions of prices and foreign exchange rates to monetary policy disturbances.

There is very little evidence, however, on how euro area monetary policy shocks are transmitted to Turkey. Knowing the features of transmission and the channels through which it occurs is crucial in predicting how trade integration and, later, the adoption of the euro will affect the Turkish economy. For example, if trade matters most, the transmission of euro area shocks will probably change as membership is granted but we should not expect significant changes when the euro is adopted. Once again the analysis is tentative since the sample is short, the Turkish economy has experienced huge local shocks over the last five years and it is slowly

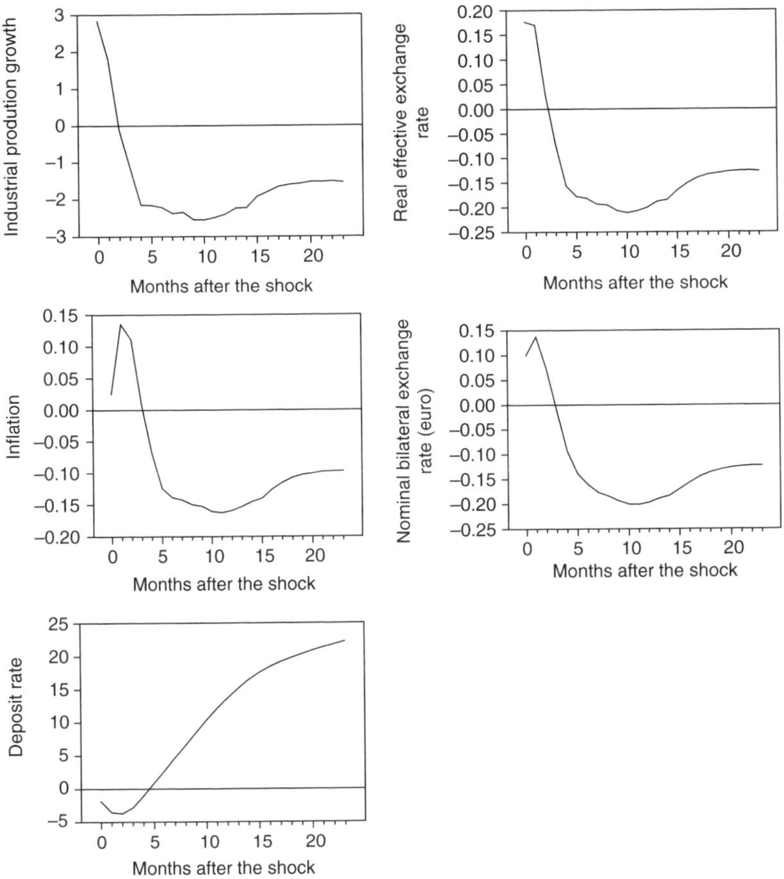

Figure 4.11 *Responses of Turkish variables to a monetary policy shock in the euro area, 1999–2005*

converging to inflation rates which are more moderate than those experienced in the 1980s and 1990s.

Figure 4.11, which reports the responses of industrial production growth, the inflation rate, the deposit rate, the real effective exchange rate and the nominal bilateral exchange rate with the euro for the sample 1999–2005 indicates that tightening the stance of monetary policy in the euro area produces adjustments in the Turkish economy which are of considerable size and have significant persistence. Interestingly, a temporarily higher interest rate in the euro area is accompanied by a decline in Turkish interest rates and this tends to boost industrial output growth and inflation and depreciate the local currency. This initial effect is reversed in three or four months after which production growth and inflation fall, interest rates increase and both the real effective and the nominal exchange rates appreciate. While the domestic pattern of responses is internally consistent, the initial negative effect on deposit rates is more puzzling and requires, at a minimum, further careful investigation.

One possible reason for the perverse response of the deposit rate is that a contractionary monetary policy shock in the euro area may turn out to represent a terms of trade shock for Turkey. In fact, as Hakan Berument (2001) has pointed out the majority of Turkish exports is denominated in euros while the largest portion of imports is denominated in dollars. Therefore, euro appreciation following the ECB contractionary policy shock represents a positive wealth effect for Turkey, which may produce a switch between saving and consumption and therefore decrease interest rates and boost domestic demand and inflation. Note that while such a terms of trade effect dominates in the very short run, the standard response of interest rates, inflation and real activity shows up three or four months after the shocks.

In summary, contractionary policy shocks in the euro area are accompanied by responses in interest rates, inflation and the nominal exchange rate which are somewhat different and more persistent than the ones observed in the new EU countries. If these patterns are confirmed in future studies, it would appear that transferring monetary policy decisions to the ECB could destabilize the Turkish economy. On the other hand, in the unlikely case that Turkey would adopt the euro soon, the task of the ECB would become considerably more complicated as regional differences in response to monetary shocks would be greatly magnified. Finally, it appears that both the trade and the financial channels matter for transmitting euro area shocks to Turkey. Therefore, the trade integration expected from EU membership and the deeper financial and monetary links that will come with a single currency may alter both the intensity and the shape of responses presented in Figure 4.11.

4.5 CONCLUSIONS

This chapter has two parts. First, we reviewed the monetary policy strategy currently favoured by academics and contrasted it with the one employed by the ECB. In the process we highlighted the accomplishments and failures of monetary policy in the euro area over the last five years and suggested changes that could streamline the understanding that markets have of the policy process and, as a consequence, improve its transparency and more clearly anchor expectation formation. We showed that the good inflation outcome experienced over the last five years was obtained despite some flaws in the ECB strategy and policies. We have conjectured that market participants discounted the noisy signals present in the public statements of the newly established institution and looked more pragmatically at actions and outcomes. This initial honeymoon effect, which rightly took into account the difficulties and the starting costs faced by a new institution, could turn sour if a more coherent and transparent approach to policymaking is not taken. We showed that if the goal of policy is the control of the medium-term dynamics of inflation, the ECB is neglecting important information which could sharpen the prediction and control of the medium-term inflation dynamics; we argued that the separation between monetary and economic analysis is artificial and that the focus on monetary aggregates as predictors of medium-term inflation trends is misplaced. To the extent that improved inflation forecasts are made and the public understands the uncertain environment in which they are produced, better communication can be obtained, credibility will be fostered and a much more appealing monetary policy strategy will emerge. We also argue that hiding output concerns is not only potentially misleading but also makes it is very difficult to rationalize certain decisions taken in the last five years, albeit only in terms of inflation concerns.

The second part of the chapter examines the transmission of monetary policy shocks in the euro area to the new EU countries and tries to offer some indications of whether and how Turkey will benefit from joining the EU and later adopting the euro. Our analysis reaches a few important conclusions. First, there are substantial similarities in the qualitative features of the response of industrial output growth, inflation and the nominal exchange rate to contractionary domestic monetary policy shocks. However, together with qualitative similarities, magnitude differences should also be emphasized. These differences are easily rationalized once we consider the relative size of the countries, the relative magnitude of the exchange rate channel and the relative credibility of domestic central banks. Second, monetary policy shocks generated in the euro area tend to have asymmetric effects on industrial output in the EU newcomers, while they tend to produce similar effects on inflation and the nominal exchange rate of these countries. Hence the real side of the euro area economy is still substantially different from those of the EU newcomers. We already know from the experience of Germany since unification that monetary integration (coordination) without a preliminary process of convergence of the real economies may create imbalances which are difficult to resolve once the exchange rate is fixed to unity since regional relative prices tend to be sticky. Fostering real convergence between the current and future periphery of the EU should be a major goal of all countries which plan to adopt the euro.

Once real convergence has been obtained, releasing the conduct of monetary policy to the ECB would probably make little difference, as far as transmission of policy shocks are concerned. Third, the real side of the Turkish economy today looks very much as the real side of earlier Mediterranean joiners of the EU. Therefore, while some form of real convergence will surely take place in the period leading to accession, income inequalities and structural heterogeneities are likely to persist for quite some time after membership is granted. While reforms needed to join the EU will probably be beneficial for growth and convergence, one should not expect too much from EU structural and cohesion funds. Such funds have reduced income inequalities between rich and poor regions and in that sense they have played an important cohesive role. However, they have not typically led to higher growth in the funded regions nor have they changed the underlying structural characteristics of poor regions. Therefore, structural changes must take place in Turkey before the admission process is started. The costs of undertaking structural changes are non-negligible but, if properly handled, will turn out to be temporary. The costs of delaying the transformations and waiting for the safety net of EU funds are large and long lasting. Fourth, the transmission of monetary policy shocks in the euro area constitutes a powerful lever on the Turkish economy but, at least for the short sample we have available, they produce somewhat perverse effects. Hence, it is probably premature to think of releasing the control of monetary policy to the ECB.

To conclude, the biggest challenge we see for countries wishing to adopt the euro in the medium term is to make the real side of their economies more dynamic and to find ways to foster growth paths leading to significant real convergence in the years to come. As long as monetary policy keeps its focus on maintaining a relatively stable inflation environment and growth reforms take place, the preconditions for joining the EU and adopting the euro could be met within a reasonable time span.

NOTE

* We thank J. von Hagen and H. Berument for insightful comments, A. Notarpietro for help in collecting and organizing the data and N. Scalzo for the editiorial assistance.

REFERENCES

Angeloni, I., A. Kashap, B. Mojon and D. Terlizzese (2003), *Monetary Policy Transmission in the Euro Area*, Cambridge: Cambridge University Press.

Anzuini, A. and A. Levy (2004), 'Financial structure and the transmission of monetary policy shocks: preliminary evidence from the Czech Republic, Hungary and Poland', manuscript, Bank of Italy.

Anzuini, A., M. Caivano, A. Lamorgese, C. Miani and F. Venditti (2005), 'A panel BVAR model for the euro economy and Italy', manuscript, Bank of Italy.

Benati, L. (2002), 'Evolving post WW II UK economic performance', working paper, Bank of England.

Benczur, P., M. Koren and A. Raftai (2004), 'The transmission of Eurozone shocks to CEECs', manuscript, Central European University.

Begg, D., F. Canova, A. Fatas and D. Lane (2002), 'Monitoring ECB 4', CEPR.

Berument, H. (2001), 'Measuring monetary policy for a small open economy: Turkey', working paper, Bilkent University.

Canova, F. (2002), 'G-7 inflation forecast', ECB working paper 151.

Canova, F. (2005), 'The transmission of US shocks to Latin America', *Journal of Applied Econometrics*, **20**, 229–51.

Canova, F. and M. Boldrin (2002), 'Regional policies and EU enlargement', in L. Pizzauti and B. Funck (eds), *The EU Enlargement to the East*, Washington, DC: World Bank.

Canova, F. and M. Ciccarelli (2003), 'Panel VAR: specification, estimation, testing and leading indicators', CEPR working paper, 3963.

Canova, F. and L. Gambetti (2004), 'Structural changes in the US economy: bad lack or bad policy?', http://www.igier.uni-bocconi.it/~canova.

Christiano, L. and M. Rostagno (2001), 'Monetary growth monitoring and the Taylor rule', manuscript, Northwestern University.

Cogley, T. and T. Sargent (2005), 'Drifts and volatilities: monetary policies and outcomes in the post WW II US', *Review of Economic Dynamics*, **8** (2), April, 262–302.

Cooley, T. and L. Ohanian (1991), 'The cyclical behaviour of prices', *Journal of Monetary Economics*, **28**, 25–60.

De Haan, J., S. Ejiffinger and S. Waller (2004), *The ECB: Communication, Transparency and Credibility*, Cambridge, MA: MIT Press.

Favero, C.A. and O. Tristani (2005), 'Understanding fluctuations in the US and German term structure of interest rates', mimeo, available at www.igier.unibocconi.it/favero.

Fraga, A., I. Goldfajn and A. Minella (2003), 'Inflation targeting in emerging market economies', in M. Gertler and K. Rogoff (eds), *NBER Macroeconomics Annual*, Harvard: The MIT Press.

Friedman, M. and A. Schwartz (1960), *Monetary History of US*, Princeton, NJ: Princeton University Press.

Friedman, M. and A. Schwartz (1963), *Monetary History of UK*, Princeton, NJ: Princeton University Press.

Gaiotti, E. and F. Lippi (2005), 'Pricing behavior and the introduction of the euro: evidence from a panel of restaurants in Italy', *Giornale degli Economisti ed Annali di Economia*, **63**, 491–526.

Gali, J., S. Gerlach, J. Rotemberg, H. Uhlig and M. Woodford (2004), Monitoring ECB 5, CEPR.

Ganev, G., K. Molnar, K. Rybinki and P. Wozniak (2002), 'Transmission mechanism of monetary policy in Central and Eastern Europe', CASE report 52, Center for Social and Economic Research, available at www.case.com.pl.

Goodhart, C. and P. Pappa (2003), 'The transition from national currencies to the euro', *Economic Letters*, forthcoming.

Gündüz, L. (2000), 'Monetary transmission and the bank lending channel', working paper, Beykent University.
Issing, O. (2001), 'The euro area and the single monetary policy', working paper 44, Oesterreichische Nationalbank.
Jansen, D.-J. and J. De Haan (2004), 'Look who's talking: ECB communication during the first years of EMU', manuscript, De Nederlandsche Bank.
Jarocinski, M. (2004), 'Responses to monetary policy shocks in Eastern and Western Europe: a comparison', Universitat Pompeu Fabra (UPF) manuscript.
Mackowiak, B. (2005), 'What does the bank of Japan do to east Asia?', manuscript, Humboldt University.
Mishkin, F. (2004), 'Can central bank transparency go too far?', NBER working paper 10829.
Orphanides, A. (2001), 'Monetary policy rules, macroeconomic stability, and inflation: a view from the trenches', Boards of Governors of the Federal Reserve System Discussion Paper 62.
Peersman, G. (2004), 'The transmission of monetary policy in the euro area. Are the effects different across countries?', *Oxford Bulletin of Economics and Statistics*, **66**, 285–308.
Poole, W. (1999), 'Communicating the stance of monetary policy', speech, http://stlouisfed.ord/news/speeches.
Poole, W. (2001), 'Central bank transparency: why and how', speech, http://stlouisfed.ord/news/speeches.
Roberts, J. (1997), 'Is inflation sticky?', *Journal of Monetary Economics*, **39**, 173–96.
Şahinbeyoğlu, G. (2001), 'Monetary transmission mechanism: a view from a high inflation environment', Central Bank of Turkey working paper 2001/1.
Sherwin, M. (1999), 'Inflation targeting: 10 years on', speech, http://www.rbnz.govt.nz/speeches.
Siklos, P.L. and M.T. Bohl (2003), 'Do words speak louder than actions?', working paper on the conduct of monetary policy at the Bundesbank.
Sims, G. and D. Wessel (2000), 'The ECB can't master communication', *Wall Street Journal*, April 27.
Suppel, R. (2003), 'Comparing the economic dynamics in EU and CEE accession countries', ECB working paper 267.
Svensson, L. (2004), 'Challenges for monetary policy', http://www.princeton.edu/~svensson.
Trichet, J.C. (2003), 'The ECB's monetary policy strategy after the evaluation and clarification of May 2003', http://www.ecb.int/press/key/date/2003.
Wilhelmsen, B. and A. Zaghini (2005), 'Monetary policy predictability in the euro area: an international Comparison', manuscript, Bank of Italy.

COMMENTS

Hakan Berument

I read the chapter, and enjoyed it very much as it was a great learning experience for me. This chapter looks at the effects of the monetary policy setting in the euro area and how this affects Turkey. The chapter has three parts. The first part suggests the optimum monetary policy strategy setting that the central banks should adopt and compares this with European Central Bank practices. The second part examines the transmission mechanism of monetary policy in the euro area to the new member countries. The third part discusses the influence of European Central Bank practices on Turkey. Since the conference is on the possible effect of the EU membership of Turkey on economic outcomes, my comments will focus on the third part.

The authors present Turkey's membership as a threat to price stability due to the different inflation dynamics of each country and heterogeneities in the transmission. It is true that various shocks (including money supply and supply side shocks) affect economic performances differently across countries. For example, increased input prices may benefit some countries and hurt others. Even if the input price increase (say oil) accelerates inflation for all the countries in the euro area, this increase may be more immediate and shorter in duration in some countries but more persistent elsewhere. Here, I would like to elaborate on the issue of tight monetary policy in the euro area. Due to the depth of financial markets, lower price indexation or flexibility in labour markets, new member countries in general, and Turkey in particular, will have relatively shorter periods for output to adjust to a tight monetary policy. Their membership will benefit old members in deceasing their adjustment period, but this increases the adjustment periods of the new members. However, if the majority of shocks come from the domestic economy (for example, Benczur et al., 2004), then there is a possibility of a decrease in domestic volatility due to the stability provided by being a member of the EU and this may bring about a net benefit even if the volatility due to external shocks increases. Therefore, at least on the issue of heteroskedasticity of adjustments, I believe a win/win situation exists for old and new members.[1] However, this does not mean that income differentials will disappear due to internal/external shocks over time. Heteroskedasticity of the adjustment is a problem, there will be cost for new members due to external shocks, but the old members will benefit.

The authors also argue that tight monetary policy affects economic performance in the euro area and Turkey differently. This is clearly a problem because this will increase the volatility of the macroeconomic variables and destabilize the system. Here rather than analyse why this destabilizing effect is present, we will offer just one possible explanation. This is by no means the only possible explanation because further study of destabilizing effects is needed. Even though Turkey would like to be a member of the EU, she has not integrated herself with the EU completely. Her trade composition has an asymmetry in terms of the denomination of the currencies used for international trade. Even if the majority of exports are realized in euros, the majority of imports are realized in US dollars. Therefore, following an increase in euro-dollar parity (when the US dollar value of the euro increases), Turkey will benefit as if there is an improvement in the terms of trade. This will increase the trade balance (Berument and Dinçer, 2005), appreciate the local currency, enhance growth and decrease inflation (Berument and Yücel, 2005; Berument and Paşaoğullari, 2003). If the tight monetary policy appreciates the euro against the US dollar under asymmetric trade denomination, this will increase output and decrease inflation in Turkey.

Figure 4C.1 shows the impulse response functions of the real exchange rate, inflation and output when a one standard deviation shock is given to euro–US dollar parity (see Berument and Yücel, 2005 for the details of the specification and further elaboration of the issue). The figure clearly shows that an increase in parity appreciates the local currency, decreases inflation and enhances growth.

Moreover, as the authors recognize, Turkish economic performance might not be co-moving with the euro area economic performance. Table 4C.1 reports the cross-correlations of Turkish industrial production with that of other sets of countries (see Berument et al., 2005 for the details). Table 4C.1 suggests that Turkish industrial production moves countercyclically to euro area industrial production for the full sample that is considered (note that the sample size for each country is reported in Table 4C.1). However, in order to account for domestic shocks, we perform the analysis for the period that excludes the financial crises in April 1994 and November 2000. Table 4C.2 repeats the analysis for a smaller sample. The basic conclusion that we gather by comparing Table 4C.2 to Table 4C.1 changes all cross-correlation. This may suggest that as the Turkish economy integrates with the euro area, the Turkish economy will move more procyclically with the EU since the likelihood of the occurrence of domestic shocks will decrease. This will further decrease the volatility of the Turkish economy and enhance the growth potential of the euro land economies.

The authors also argue that membership in the EU will not bring much benefit to Turkish labour productivity: 'One would expect them to soar as membership is granted but to make little difference in terms of labour

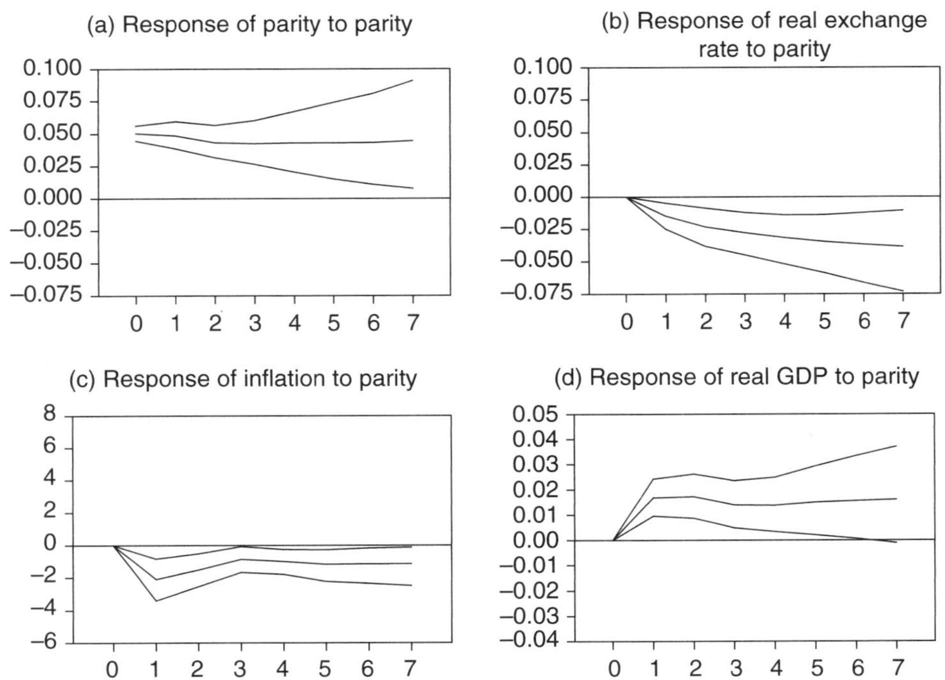

Note: The central line in each panel presents the impulse response function. The surrounding lines are the 68% error bands obtained from the Bayesian procedure, based on Sims and Zha (1999).

Figure 4C.1 Impulse response functions

Table 4C.1 *Cross-correlations with industrial production of Turkey and other countries*

Country/region	Period	St. Dv.	−12	−11	−10	−9	−8	−7	−6	−5	−4
(United States)	01/85–02/03	6.8	**−27**	−24	−20	−16	−13	−9	−5	−1	5
(Japan)	01/85–02/03	6.8	6	7	8	8	8	9	10	11	13
Belgium	01/85–12/02	6.8	12	8	11	7	6	5	4	2	4
(Ind. countries)	01/85–02/03	6.8	−10	−9	−9	−7	−6	−5	−4	−2	1
Portugal	01/85–06/02	6.9	−8	−9	−9	−4	−1	2	5	9	15
(Norway)	01/85–02/03	6.8	6	7	4	6	6	5	7	11	10
Slovakia	01/92–10/02	8.8	30	26	23	22	22	20	17	14	10
Finland	01/85–02/03	6.8	−32	**−32**	−32	−30	−29	−26	−23	−21	−17
Greece	01/85–04/02	6.9	−7	−8	−6	−8	−8	−2	−5	0	0
The Netherlands	01/85–02/03	6.8	5	**10**	7	5	3	3	4	4	3
Italy	01/85–04/02	6.8	9	9	6	7	6	6	6	4	2
Spain	01/85–12/02	6.8	4	4	0	2	3	1	2	−1	−2
Czech republic	01/92–02/03	8.3	**45**	43	39	32	26	19	13	9	5
Austria	01/85–02/03	6.8	−9	−6	−11	−12	−11	−13	−12	−13	−14
France	01/85–01/03	6.8	0	−2	−4	−5	−7	−9	−11	−12	−11
(Canada)	01/85–01/03	6.8	**−32**	−31	−30	−31	−30	−28	−25	−23	−19
Luxembourg	01/85–04/02	6.8	−18	−16	−14	−17	−16	−22	−26	−25	**−28**
United Kingdom	01/85–01/03	6.8	−21	−22	**−24**	−23	−23	−22	−22	−21	−20
Germany	01/85–12/02	6.8	−3	−6	−8	−8	−10	−11	−11	**−13**	−10
Sweden	01/85–06/02	6.9	**−19**	−17	−18	−16	−15	−13	−14	−14	−15
Hungary	01/85–12/02	6.8	**−25**	−24	−23	−22	−21	−21	−20	−20	−18
Denmark	01/85–12/02	6.8	2	−1	−7	−9	−13	−17	−16	−19	−20
Ireland	01/85–01/03	6.8	−5	−9	−13	−18	−23	−28	−32	**−34**	−34
Slovenia	12/91–02/03	8.6	−8	−10	−15	−20	−24	−28	−28	−28	−28
Euro zone	01/98–01/03	12.8	−23	−26	−29	−32	−35	−36	−37	−37	−37

Notes:
Standard deviations are calculated as $(1/\sqrt{n})$.
Maximum values (in absolute value) for each row are highlighted as bold and underlined.
The names of the current EU member states are written in bold; those of the new member states and the benchmark countries are written in italics and in parentheses, respectively.

Source: Berument et al. (2005).

productivity growth in the next few years.' I do not agree with the authors. Membership will come with the adjustment of existing institutions and the creation of new ones. These institutions will be likely to affect the workings of the existing markets. Turkey has low labour productivity in informal sectors but high productivity in formal sectors (see, McKinsey and Company, 2003). With the structural adjustments, the role of the formal sector will increase and this will further enhance labour productivity. Thus, within the context that we discussed, I believe that Turkish membership will benefit both the existing members of the EU and Turkey.

−3	−2	−1	0	1	2	3	4	5	6	7	8	9	10	11	12
11	15	19	23	25	25	24	24	23	23	24	25	25	25	25	25
15	15	16	**18**	16	15	11	9	5	2	−2	−4	−6	−7	−7	−7
8	5	**12**	12	6	5	−3	−2	−2	−5	−6	−6	−9	−11	−5	−11
4	6	8	**11**	11	11	9	8	5	4	3	3	2	3	3	3
16	14	12	11	12	15	18	19	19	16	18	22	**22**	19	15	13
8	10	9	8	3	−1	−7	**−14**	−13	−7	−1	−4	−5	−2	−8	−3
7	4	3	−1	−2	−4	−3	−1	−3	−5	−9	−14	−21	−27	−32	**−40**
−14	−9	−4	−2	−3	−5	−7	−8	−7	−6	−3	−2	0	1	2	1
−2	−5	−5	−3	−1	0	−5	0	0	0	0	1	−1	−10	−11	**−19**
2	−2	−4	−4	0	0	−1	−3	−4	1	2	4	0	−2	−5	−6
1	0	−3	−5	−3	−5	−4	−5	−13	−11	−14	−15	**−17**	−14	−13	−13
−3	−5	−5	−5	−7	−8	−6	−9	−9	**−9**	−7	−5	−1	1	3	6
1	−2	−6	−6	−8	−8	−9	−10	−10	−11	−11	−11	−12	−15	−17	−19
−10	−10	−9	−8	−9	−13	−13	−17	−21	−25	**−29**	−29	−26	−22	−17	−10
−10	−10	−8	−9	−8	−8	−6	−4	−1	1	3	6	8	10	**13**	12
−17	−15	−12	−9	−6	−6	−6	−6	−6	−5	−5	−3	0	2	6	9
−23	−22	−16	−9	−4	−1	0	1	−2	3	6	9	13	10	12	12
−21	−18	−15	−11	−5	−4	−2	2	4	7	10	12	12	12	12	9
−12	−9	−11	−12	−11	−10	−9	−8	−8	−5	−3	−1	−1	0	−2	−3
−14	−14	−16	−12	−11	−11	−12	−15	−17	−17	−18	−18	−15	−15	−14	−10
−17	−19	−18	−17	−15	−14	−13	−12	−11	−10	−8	−5	−5	−7	−8	−9
−18	−22	−24	−24	−24	**−26**	−25	−25	−25	−24	−24	−21	−17	−14	−13	−12
−32	−30	−28	−25	−24	−22	−20	−19	−21	−23	−24	−24	−22	−20	−19	−20
−28	−28	−28	−29	−30	**−31**	−29	−28	−26	−24	−24	−21	−19	−16	−13	−10
−36	−39	−42	**−43**	−41	−39	−36	−34	−33	−33	−33	−34	−37	−38	−39	−35

One small note to be added is that the inflation target for the euro is too low. European enlargement requires various structural adjustments, which are likely to create supply-side disturbances. Having too low an inflation target does not allow for easy relative price adjustment for a better allocation of resources and this may create output losses. This is parallel to the authors' statement that 'the 2 per cent threshold should not be considered an upper bound but the mid-range of the target inflation rate'.

Note

1. Berument et al. (2005) argue that controlling domestic shocks will alter the inference gathered from the correlation between domestic and foreign countries on output for Turkey. Therefore, one may claim that domestic shocks represent an important determinant of output volatility in Turkey. Decreasing the volatility stemming from the domestic shocks will help Turkey synchronize its business cycles with those of the European Union.

Table 4C.2 Cross-correlations with industrial production of Turkey and other countries (excluding Turkish crises)

Country/region	Period	St. Dv.*	−12	−11	−10	−9	−8	−7	−6	−5	−4
(United States)	06/94–10/00	11.3	−2	3	7	12	16	21	26	31	36
(Ind. countries)	06/94–10/00	11.3	−8	−3	0	3	5	7	9	12	16
Belgium	06/94–10/00	11.3	7	11	13	8	16	14	13	21	17
The Netherlands	06/94–10/00	11.3	4	7	9	4	6	7	8	8	13
(Japan)	06/94–10/00	11.3	13	16	18	20	19	18	18	18	19
Luxembourg	06/94–10/00	11.3	−10	−11	−5	−4	4	4	4	11	8
(Norway)	06/94–10/00	11.3	5	5	8	9	10	11	10	12	12
France	06/94–10/00	11.3	−26	−22	−21	−18	−13	−10	−6	−3	−2
Germany	06/94–10/00	11.3	−21	−18	−16	−12	−10	−9	−5	−2	2
Spain	06/94–10/00	11.3	−26	−24	−22	−18	−11	−7	−3	−1	1
Euro zone	01/98–10/00	17.2	34	37	35	35	34	32	31	35	34
Slovakia	06/94–10/00	11.3	−2	−3	−4	−3	1	4	4	5	5
Greece	06/94–10/00	11.3	−11	−14	−14	**−17**	−14	−10	−5	0	0
Hungary	06/94–10/00	11.3	**−33**	−29	−27	−26	−22	−20	−17	−13	−11
Finland	06/94–10/00	11.3	**−32**	−32	−29	−27	−24	−22	−18	−14	−12
Portugal	06/94–10/00	11.3	−1	−2	0	5	4	2	3	2	3
Austria	06/94–10/00	11.3	−20	−17	−18	−19	−17	−15	−14	−12	−12
Sweden	06/94–10/00	11.3	−24	−22	−21	−19	−20	−19	−18	−17	−12
Denmark	06/94–10/00	11.3	−16	−13	−12	−11	−11	−16	−16	−10	−11
(Canada)	06/94–10/00	11.3	**−30**	−29	−27	−25	−22	−20	−19	−18	−18
Italy	06/94–10/00	11.3	−27	−25	−26	−26	−22	−20	−18	−13	−12
Czech Republic	06/94–10/00	11.3	−8	−8	−8	−11	−12	−13	−16	−16	−16
United Kingdom	06/94–10/00	11.3	−28	−27	−27	−29	−29	−30	−30	−28	−25
Slovenia	06/94–10/00	11.3	**−34**	−33	−32	−32	−30	−28	−27	−28	−29
Ireland	06/94–10/00	11.3	−20	−24	−28	−32	−37	−41	−44	−45	−45

Notes:
Standard deviations are calculated as $(1/\sqrt{n})$.
Maximum values (in absolute value) for each row are highlighted with bold and underlined.
The names of the current EU member states are written in bold; those of the new member states and the benchmark countries are written in italics and in parentheses, respectively.

Source: Berument et al. (2005).

References

Benczur, P., M. Koren and A. Raftai (2004), 'The transmission of Eurozone shocks to CEECs', manuscript, Central European University.

Berument, H. and N. Dinçer (2005), 'Denomination composition of trade and trade balance: evidence from Turkey', *Applied Economics*, **37**, 1177–91.

Berument, H. and M. Paşaoğullar (2003), 'Effects of the real exchange rate on output and inflation: evidence from Turkey', *Developing Economies*, **41** (4), 401–35.

Berument, H., Z. Kılınç and E. Yücel (2005), 'Business cycles in Turkey and European Union countries: a perspective to membership', *Sosyo Ekonomi*, **1** (1), 11–26.

−3	−2	−1	0	1	2	3	4	5	6	7	8	9	10	11	12
40	45	50	53	52	50	49	46	46	45	48	51	53	56	57	**58**
18	21	23	**23**	17	12	7	2	−1	−3	−2	−1	0	4	7	11
23	22	22	21	21	2	4	3	−5	−4	−16	−14	−14	−11	−16	−9
13	14	**19**	17	12	6	−1	0	6	−4	−3	−5	−9	−7	−11	−13
18	19	18	17	9	4	−3	−8	−14	−16	−19	−23	**−25**	−23	−21	−19
14	13	16	16	17	17	**20**	19	10	18	19	19	15	15	15	14
10	8	8	10	15	7	−7	−14	−17	−16	−19	−22	−29	−31	**−33**	−32
2	4	8	9	6	8	9	12	12	15	20	24	26	30	30	**35**
5	8	9	9	8	4	2	0	2	5	12	12	15	18	19	**23**
4	6	7	6	3	3	5	3	2	3	9	17	21	24	27	**35**
32	22	13	3	−9	−18	−28	−38	−49	−56	−61	−61	**−65**	−60	−57	−49
5	4	4	3	1	−3	−5	−9	−17	−23	−26	−31	−38	−45	−52	**−55**
3	6	2	1	1	1	0	4	1	4	0	4	3	−2	−11	−14
−9	−6	−3	1	1	−2	−1	1	−1	0	0	3	7	13	16	22
−9	−6	−4	0	−2	−3	−4	−3	2	5	7	12	15	21	24	26
4	1	0	0	0	**5**	−2	−2	−3	−2	−3	−2	−3	2	−1	0
−8	−7	−5	−4	−9	−12	−14	−18	−21	−27	**−34**	−25	−19	−14	−8	−2
−10	−11	−11	−9	−15	−19	−28	−29	−32	**−33**	−33	−31	−27	−22	−12	−10
−9	−8	−7	−10	−12	−12	−12	−17	−23	**−25**	−23	−21	−17	−11	−10	−7
−18	−17	−16	−14	−14	−15	−15	−16	−16	−14	−10	−3	4	11	17	24
−14	−14	−12	−15	−19	−20	−18	−21	−28	−32	−29	−31	−34	−34	−31	**−35**
−16	−15	−15	−15	−15	−19	−20	−21	−27	−32	−35	−38	−41	−44	−48	**−49**
−24	−23	−23	−23	−26	−30	**−31**	−27	−25	−21	−15	−12	−9	−3	2	6
−30	−30	−30	−32	−31	−30	−27	−26	−26	−26	−27	−25	−21	−15	−13	−10
−45	**−46**	−45	−45	−45	−45	−44	−43	−43	−43	−43	−42	−41	−39	−38	−39

Berument, H. and E.M. Yücel (2005), 'Effects of USD-euro parity on economic performance for a small open economy under unbalanced trade denomination: evidence from Turkey', *Applied Economics*, forthcoming.

McKinsey and Company (2003), 'Turkey: realization of productivity and growth (in Turkish)' (Türkiye: verimlilik ve büyüme atılımının gerçekleştirilmesi), working paper.

Sims, C.A. and T. Zha (1999), 'Error bands for impulse responses', *Econometrica*, **67** (5), 1113–56.

5. Monetary policy challenges for Turkey in the European Union accession process

Fatih Özatay*

5.1 INTRODUCTION

After being officially recognized as a candidate state at the Helsinki European Council, the Turkish government announced its own National Programme for the adoption of the *acquis communautaire* on 19 March 2001. A turning point towards full membership came on 17 December 2004, when a date for starting the membership negotiations was given to Turkey.

According to the Treaty Establishing the European Community, the economic and monetary integration process consists of three phases. The first phase covers the period of candidacy for the European Union (EU). In this phase, the candidate countries choose their own monetary policy and exchange rate policy. However, they have to make necessary changes in their legislation to ensure central bank independence. The second is the accession phase and starts with EU membership. This phase consists of two stages: the period before joining the Exchange Rate Mechanism of the European Monetary System (ERM II) and the ERM II period. ERM II membership can take place any time after EU accession. It is an exchange rate arrangement with fixed but adjustable central parities and a fluctuation band of ± 15 per cent. The minimum period of ERM II membership is two years prior to the convergence assessment. In the final phase, member countries are expected to join the European Monetary Union (EMU) and adopt the euro.[1]

In this chapter, the EU accession process is analysed from the perspective of monetary policy. Problems that can be faced by the monetary authorities after becoming a member (the second and third phases) are not discussed. Since May 2001 Turkey has been implementing an ambitious stabilization and structural change programme to address the accumulated problems of more than three decades of imprudent policies and the eventual 2000–01 crisis. Because of this, the accession process cannot be analysed in isolation from the process of the 'normalization' of the Turkish economy.

In the aftermath of the 2000–01 crisis the banking sector was in turbulence and required immediate action. The rescue operation increased the public debt to gross domestic product (GDP) ratio sharply to almost 100 per cent. In mid-May 2001, just three months after the February crisis, Turkey started to implement a new programme. Monetary authorities found themselves conducting monetary policy under fiscal dominance.[2] Since then, fiscal dominance has put severe constraints on the implementation of monetary policy. With the determined implementation of the programme the fiscal dominance has begun to lose its power. However, it is an open question whether the fiscal dominance period has come to an end or is even close to the end.

While sound macroeconomic policies and structural reforms, such as those Turkey has been implementing since May 2001, are necessary for improving economic fundamentals and creating a positive trend in macroeconomic variables, a considerable amount of time is needed to reduce the vulnerability of an economy that has accumulated problems to changes in international and domestic risk factors over the years. This points to the fact that challenges to monetary policy over the medium term will not only arise from the EU accession process, but that fiscal dominance and the transition period to monetary dominance will also create problems.

This chapter aims to analyse how monetary policy authorities can address such problems arising from two different sources. In order to achieve this aim, the importance of fiscal dominance for the conduct of monetary policy should be analysed. This is the subject matter of the Section 5.2. The problems that may arise in the normalization period and the EU accession process and possible answers to them are discussed in the Section 5.3. The current structure of the balance sheet of the Central Bank of Turkey (CBT) is a clear reflection of the macro economic imbalances of the past. This structure is briefly analysed in the same section and some future policy implications are underlined. This section also briefly compares the CBT law with that of the European Central Bank (ECB) and identifies the necessary amendments to the former. The final section concludes the paper.

5.2 FISCAL DOMINANCE AND MONETARY POLICY: MAY 2001–04

In highly indebted economies in which the real rate of return on government securities is in excess of the economy's growth rate, and in the absence of a significant tightening of fiscal policy, that is, under fiscal dominance, either monetary policy sooner or later has to be accommodative or default is inescapable. This well-known fact severely limits the conduct of an active monetary policy. This section first presents a model of debt repudiation to show the importance of default risk as the main driving force of the economy under the fiscal dominance regime. The model points out the crucial role played by fiscal discipline and market expectations in the continuation of sound policies for attaining a good equilibrium (low default probability, low real interest rates and low debt burden). Second, this section gives brief information regarding post-crisis economic policies and outcomes in Turkey. The outcome of the programme has been impressive. However, there have been occasional deviations from this main trend throughout the post-crisis period. The positive main trend and deviations from this trend are documented and their reasons are discussed in the light of the model. Thirdly, challenges to monetary policy are analysed.

5.2.1 The Model

We consider a two-period Barro and Gordon (1983) model with two types of agents: the government and the private sector composed of many atomistic agents. The government can borrow in the first period with a (gross) interest factor R. There is no borrowing in the second period as it is the 'end of the world'. The government collects taxes (x) to pay its liabilities in the second period:

$$x = (1 - \theta)Rb + u, \tag{5.1}$$

where θ ($0 \leq \theta \leq 1$) is the proportion of total debt (Rb) that is going to be repudiated by the government and u is a shock. It is assumed as in Obstfeld (1996) that it is uniformly distributed on the interval $[-\lambda, \lambda]$. A negative political development is represented by a positive value of u and it either necessitates a rise in x or θ. Note that, for expositional simplicity, the exogenous value of government non-interest expenditures is assumed to be zero.

The private sector is risk-neutral and does not observe political shocks at the time of purchasing government bonds (b). It simply decides what the probability of debt repudiation is in the second period, and requires an interest factor accordingly:

$$R = \frac{R^*}{1 - \theta^e}. \tag{5.2}$$

In this equation, R^* is the risk-free interest factor and θ^e is the expected proportion of total bonds that is going to be repudiated by the government ($0 \leq \theta^e \leq 1$).

Taking θ^e as given, the government chooses an optimal level for θ by minimizing a loss function subject to its budget constraint given by Equation (5.1). The loss function is quadratic and has two items. The first cost is incurred due to taxation as, for example, in Calvo (1988), Missale and Blanchard (1994), and Sachs et al. (1996). The second cost arises due to repudiation. Calvo (1988) states that this can be considered as transaction costs (as legal fees and so on) associated with debt repudiation. There is no incentive for inflation for the government in our model. This may arise, for example, due to inflation-indexed debt. This assumption simplifies the model and makes it analytically more tractable. This fact is known by the private sector and expected inflation is zero. The loss function is as follows:

$$l = \frac{1}{2}\alpha x^2 + \frac{1}{2}(\beta\theta Rb)^2, \tag{5.3}$$

where α is the relative importance given to taxation by the government and β stands for the cost per unit of repudiated debt ($0 \leq \beta < 1$).

Using equations (5.1) and (5.2) in (5.3), the minimization problem of the policymaker acting at his/her discretion reduces to setting θ optimally by minimizing the following loss function, taking θ^e as given:

$$l = \frac{1}{2}\alpha\left[\frac{R^*b(1-\theta)}{(1-\theta^e)} + u\right]^2 + \frac{1}{2}\left[\beta\frac{R^*b\theta}{(1-\theta^e)}\right]^2. \tag{5.4}$$

The solution to this problem gives:

$$\theta = \frac{\alpha}{(\alpha + \beta^2)}\left[1 + \frac{(1-\theta^e)}{R^*b}u\right]. \tag{5.5}$$

If the government fully honours its obligations, then $\theta = 0$. Using this in Equation (5.4), the loss that the government incurs is found to be:

$$l^h = \frac{1}{2}\alpha\left(\frac{R^*b}{1-\theta^e} + u\right)^2. \tag{5.6}$$

The government loses credibility through not honouring its debt and this represents a cost for the government, as in Sachs et al. (1996).[3] Denoting this loss by c ($c>0$) and substituting (5.5) in (5.4) for θ, the loss incurred under repudiation is given as:

$$l^r = \frac{1}{2}\frac{\alpha\beta^2}{(\alpha+\beta^2)}\left(\frac{R^*b}{1-\theta^e}+u\right)^2 + c. \quad (5.7)$$

The condition for repudiation is given by:

$$l^r < l^h. \quad (5.8)$$

Note that this condition always holds when $c=0$. That is, if there were no costs stemming from credibility losses due to repudiation, then the government would always repudiate its debt. Plugging l^h from Equation (5.6) and l^r from Equation (5.7) into (5.8) gives the critical value of shock u^* such that $u>u^*$ triggers a repudiation.

$$u^* = \frac{\sqrt{2c(\alpha+\beta^2)}}{\alpha} - \frac{R^*b}{1-\theta^e}. \quad (5.9)$$

Note that as the level of the inherited debt stock or expected repudiation increases, the critical level of shock that triggers repudiation decreases, which obviously increases the probability of repudiation.

The analysis up to now assumes the public's expectations as given. However, private sector agents are rational and aware of the government's optimization problem. They have all the information, except that they do not observe political shocks at the time of purchasing bonds. They rationally form their expectations for θ as:

$$\theta^e = E(\theta) = Pr(u<u^*)E(\theta|u<u^*) + Pr(u \geq u^*)E(\theta|u \geq u^*), \quad (5.10)$$

where E is the expectation operator and $Pr(.)$ is the probability of the event (.). Using Equation (5.5) for θ, taking into consideration the fact that if $u<u^*$ then $\theta=0$, and remembering that u is uniformly distributed at the interval $[-\lambda, \lambda]$, Equation (5.10) further gives:

$$\theta^e = \frac{2R^*b\alpha(\lambda-u^*) + \alpha(\lambda^2-u^{*2})}{4\lambda R^*b(\alpha+\beta^2) + \alpha(\lambda^2-u^{*2})}. \quad (5.11)$$

The important thing to note from equations (5.9) and (5.11) is that $(du^*/d\theta^e)<0$. That is, the expectations are self-fulfilling. On the one hand, as the private sector expects the government to increase the portion of debt that it is going to repudiate in the second period, the maximum level of shock necessary to trigger repudiation decreases. On the other hand, as this critical level of shock decreases, θ^e increases. And, note from Equation (5.2) that, as θ^e increases, the private sector demands a higher interest rate to purchase government securities.

Now, we have two unknowns (θ^e, u^*) and two equations (equations (5.9) and (5.11)) to solve them. Defining $m = \sqrt{2c(\alpha + \beta^2)}$ and substituting (5.11) for θ^e in (5.9), a quadratic equation is obtained for u^*, which yields two values for u^*:

$$u^*_{1,2} = \frac{1}{\alpha}[-\lambda(\alpha + 2\beta^2) + m \pm \sqrt{4\lambda(\alpha + \beta^2)(\lambda\beta^2 - \alpha R^* b) + m^2}]. \qquad (5.12)$$

Substituting these values for u^* in Equation (5.11) corresponding values for θ^e can be obtained. Using Equation (5.2), this will further give two values for R. In Table 5.1, the results of a simulation analysis that is performed to obtain these values for different values of credibility cost (c) are provided. Values of the credibility cost, minimum level of shock that is necessary to trigger repudiation (u^*), upper limit of this shock (λ), and real debt stock (b) can all be thought of as percentages of GDP. The following parameter values are chosen: $\lambda = 0.5$, $b = 0.1$, $R^* = 1.03$, $\beta = 0.2$ and $c \in [0.03, 0.06]$. The value of the real debt stock may seem low at first glance. Note, however, that we consider the average annual debt burden of the government in the period analysed rather than its total commitments, which makes this specific value

Table 5.1 Multiple equilibria and credibility cost of repudiation[a]

	Credibility cost of repudiation (c)			
	0.03	0.04	0.05	0.06
Minimum level of shock that is necessary to trigger repudiation (u^*_1)	0.026	0.191	0.322	0.436
Expected repudiation ratio (θ^e_1)	0.729	0.630	0.490	0.254
Minimum level of shock that is necessary to trigger repudiation (u^*_2)	−0.414	−0.453	−0.474	−0.487
Expected repudiation ratio (θ^e_2)	0.874	0.888	0.897	0.903

Notes:
a. Credibility cost (c), level of shock (u^*), upper limit of shock (λ), and real debt stock (b) can all be thought of as percentages of GDP.
Parameter values chosen are as follows: Repudiation costs except credibility costs as a percentage of total amount of debt repudiated: $\beta = 0.2$; Relative importance attached to taxation in the loss function: $\alpha = 0.4$; Risk free real interest rate factor: $R^* = 1.03$; $\lambda = 0.5$; $b = 0.1$.

a realistic one. Given that the magnitude of the immediate cost of the 2001 crisis to the government was an amount comprising 30 per cent of GDP and that this cost increased in the subsequent months, and further that in the post-crisis period any shock that forced the government to halt the implementation of the International Monetary Fund (IMF) supported programme would have been a similar burden on the budget, the upper limit of political shock (λ) is taken as 50 per cent of GDP. We assume that the government cares more about repudiation than about taxes ($\alpha = 0.4$). For these reasonable parameter values, this model yields multiple equilibria. For example, with $c = 0.05$, the minimum level of shock to trigger debt repudiation is 32.2 per cent of the GDP, and the corresponding expected debt repudiation ratio is 0.49. However, despite no change in the fundamentals, a sudden change in market sentiment lowers this minimum level of shock sharply and increases the debt repudiation ratio to 0.90.

These results are similar to the results obtained from second-generation crises models in the sense that they give rise to multiple equilibria. However, our results are obtained from a model that focuses mainly on the financing alternatives of the inherited debt stock for the government and analyses the impact of expectations of debt repudiation on interest rates. In this sense, it deviates from this literature. Our model is an extension of Calvo (1988) by introducing uncertainty, but the methodology used is different and more akin to Obstfeld (1996).

5.2.2 Policy Framework of the Post-crisis Period and the Outcome: May 2001–04

The model presented in the preceding section shows the importance of fiscal discipline and market expectations in the continuation of sound policies for attaining a good equilibrium. Note that the effect of fiscal discipline on market expectations can be analysed in two alternative ways in the model presented. First, fiscal discipline means a lower level of inherited debt stock at the beginning of the second period; hence a higher threshold value for u^* (the critical level of shock above which debt repudiation is realized) and lower values for expected debt repudiation ratio and real interest rate. Alternatively, for the second period, one can introduce real government expenditures on the right-hand side of Equation (5.1). An increase in government expenditures (fiscal laxity) then reduces the threshold level of u^*.

Policy framework of the post-crisis period

Throughout the post-crisis period in Turkey, the primary budget surplus to Gross National Product (GNP) ratio targets were rather ambitious. Despite a temporary deviation due to political chaos in the second half of 2002, the realizations were almost in line with the targets: 5.5 per cent in 2001, 4.1 per cent in 2002, 6.3 per cent in 2003 and 6.5 per cent in 2004 versus a 6.5 per cent target. Simultaneously, the public sector reduced its deficit from 21.1 per cent of the GDP in 2001 to 7 per cent in 2004. Additionally, the risk exposure of public debt stock has decreased through a successful debt management policy: the share of foreign exchange denominated (or indexed) debt in the total public debt has also been reduced considerably. Similarly, the floating rate part of domestic debt stock has shrunk significantly.

There has been substantial progress in structural reforms. Just after the crisis the CBT gained instrument independence. State banks were restructured; the number of branches and employees were reduced sharply. Problematic banks were removed from the system. The regulatory and supervisory framework was reinforced. The capital adequacy ratios of banks were increased. Vulnerability to various mismatches was minimized. Blanket guarantees were eliminated. A new comprehensive law on credit institutions in line with EU standards was passed. The public sector has also been undergoing a reform process. Redundant positions (more than 10 per cent of total state economic enterprises' employment) were eliminated. A hiring limit was implemented. The agricultural support system was redesigned. Independent regulatory and supervisory agencies were formed. Steps were taken to enhance transparency, budget discipline and accountability in the public sector. Various laws were enacted to improve the investment environment.

At the beginning of 2002, the CBT announced that it was going to implement implicit inflation targeting, which is still the current monetary policy framework. The core of formal inflation targeting is included in this framework. That is, first, given that the main aim of the CBT is to achieve price stability, short-term interest rates (the main policy tool of the CBT) have been changed based purely on the inflation outlook. Second, whenever a decision was taken on interest rates, the rationale behind that decision was explained to the public in press releases. However, up to the beginning of 2005, some elements of formal inflation targeting were missing: for example, the public did not know the meeting dates of the monetary policy committee.

One of the most important elements of the programme that was implemented after the crisis is the floating exchange rate system. The exchange rate policy of the CBT was made more transparent at the beginning of 2002. In the meantime, the main principle has been that market conditions would determine exchange rates. That is, the CBT stressed that it would not interfere with the level or trend of the exchange rate. It also announced that it could intervene in case of excess volatility. Based on the main principle, however, the CBT has also pledged to limit the incidence of such intervention. In addition, at the beginning of 2002, the CBT explicitly instructed the markets that, first, on condition of strict implementation of the programme and in the absence of large external shocks, the dollarization process would lose its importance, eventually leading to a reverse dollarization process, and second, favourable balance of payments conditions (a rise in capital inflows) would probably arise. Third, although the exchange rate regime was floating, the level of foreign exchange reserves was important for three main reasons: Turkey had debt repayments forthcoming to the IMF; international investors gave a special emphasize to the level of reserves; the CBT wanted to clear its balance sheet of some types of foreign exchange liabilities, such as deposits of workers abroad. Fourth, given the importance of the level of reserves (in this case, regardless of the exchange rate system), provided that at least one of the conditions stated in the first two items materialized, it was going to build up reserves through rule-based, transparent, and pre-announced purchase auctions.

The outcome

At the end of 2001, the programme started to show its strength; inflation expectations have followed a downward trend, the inflation rate has almost continuously declined and the public debt to GDP ratio has been significantly reduced. The Turkish economy first started to recover and then to grow, despite extremely tight fiscal policy. There is no doubt that this phenomenon is not unique to Turkey; it was observed in some other countries in the 1980s, leading to the development of so-called 'expansionary fiscal contractions' in economic literature.[4] The main negative developments were the deterioration of the current account deficit and the high unemployment rate (Table 5.2).

Through foreign exchange purchase auctions, the CBT purchased $0.8 billion in 2002, $5.7 billion in 2003 and $4.1 billion in 2004. Since at least one of the conditions stated in the first two items above were absent, the CBT did not open purchase auctions in nine months in 2002, six months in 2003 and seven months in 2004.[5]

However, one should also note that there were temporary deviations from the main trend. As discussed above, the main reason is that despite sound policies and reforms, economies that have inherited a host of problems due to imprudent policies in the past need a considerable period of time to overcome these problems. During this period, such economies remain vulnerable to shifts in market sentiment due to changes in international and domestic risk factors. Any development that increases concerns about the viability of fiscal discipline has the potential to move the economy into a bad equilibrium. For instance, negative domestic political

Table 5.2 Selected macroeconomic indicators: March 2001–March 2005 (%)

	Growth rate[a]	Expected inflation[b]	Consumer inflation[a]	Interest rate[c]	Public debt stock/GDP	Current account deficit/GDP	Budget deficit/GDP	Unemployment rate
2001.03	−1.0	n.a.	37.5	193.7	72.1	4.2	7.0	8.5
2001.06	−9.8	n.a.	56.1	88.4	98.2	1.9	9.2	6.7
2001.09	−7.5	64.8	61.8	87.6	105.1	0.1	13.4	7.8
2001.12	−10.3	69.8	68.5	74.1	99.7	−2.4	16.0	10.4
2002.03	2.3	43.6	65.1	68.4	91.1	−2.2	20.3	11.5
2002.06	8.9	35.2	42.6	72.2	95.0	−0.7	17.3	9.3
2002.09	8.0	34.3	37.0	62.2	92.2	−0.1	13.9	9.6
2002.12	11.7	31.0	29.7	49.8	87.4	0.8	14.1	11.0
2003.03	8.1	27.3	29.4	59.9	87.6	2.1	12.6	12.3
2003.06	3.9	25.4	29.8	46.0	81.7	2.9	14.4	10.0
2003.09	5.5	20.5	23.0	32.2	76.3	2.5	12.8	9.4
2003.12	6.1	19.1	18.4	27.9	78.6	3.3	11.1	10.3
2004.03	11.8	11.8	11.8	24.4	76.8	3.9	9.7	12.4
2004.06	14.4	11.5	8.9	27.5	78.2	4.4	7.6	9.3
2004.09	5.3	10.5	9.0	25.4	77.1	4.9	7.6	9.5
2004.12	6.3	10.0	9.3	23.1	73.5	5.2	7.0	10.0
2005.03	4.8	7.6	8.7	17.0	72.9	5.3	5.9	11.7

Notes:
a. Percentage change with respect to the same period of the previous year.
b. Expectations Survey of the Central Bank, expected year-end consumer price inflation.
c. Average compounded interest rate realized in Treasury auctions, weighted by net sales.

Sources: Central Bank of Turkey, State Institute of Statistics, State Planning Organization.

news releases, sovereign rate cuts, bad news from the IMF or an upward cycle in interest rates in the developed world could trigger such concerns. However, one should note that as time passes such vulnerability decreases.

Evidently, Turkey was not immune to this condition. Even a brief glance at the evolution of secondary market interest rates, the exchange rate, and eurobond spreads would reveal this fact (figures 5.1a, 5.1b, 5.1c). Regarding the interest rate and spread, while the main trend is downwards, there were sharp increases in both of the variables from time to time. A similar phenomenon applies to the exchange rate. Emir et al. (2005) analysed the relative importance of the effects of macroeconomic news (surprises in fundamentals), US interest rates and domestic political, EU and IMF-related news releases on secondary market interest rates in the period May 2001–December 2002 using daily data. They have shown that

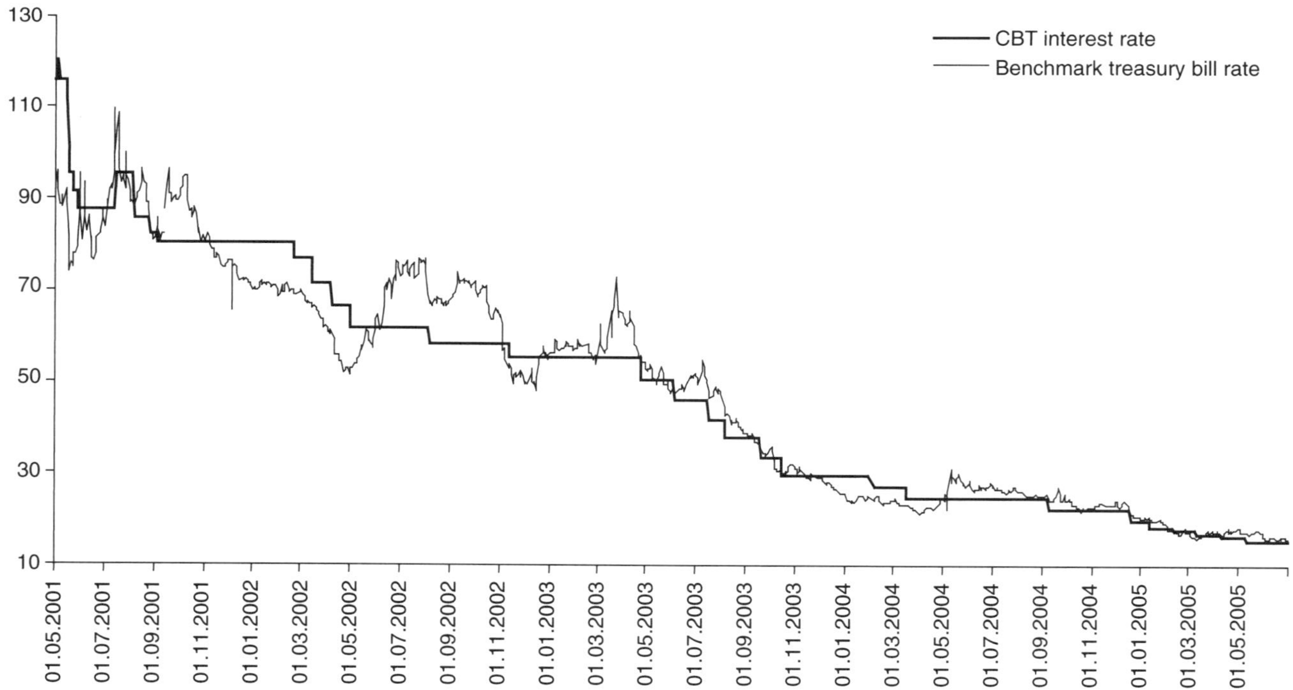

Figure 5.1a *Evolution of interest rates, 1 May 2001–30 June 2005 (%)*

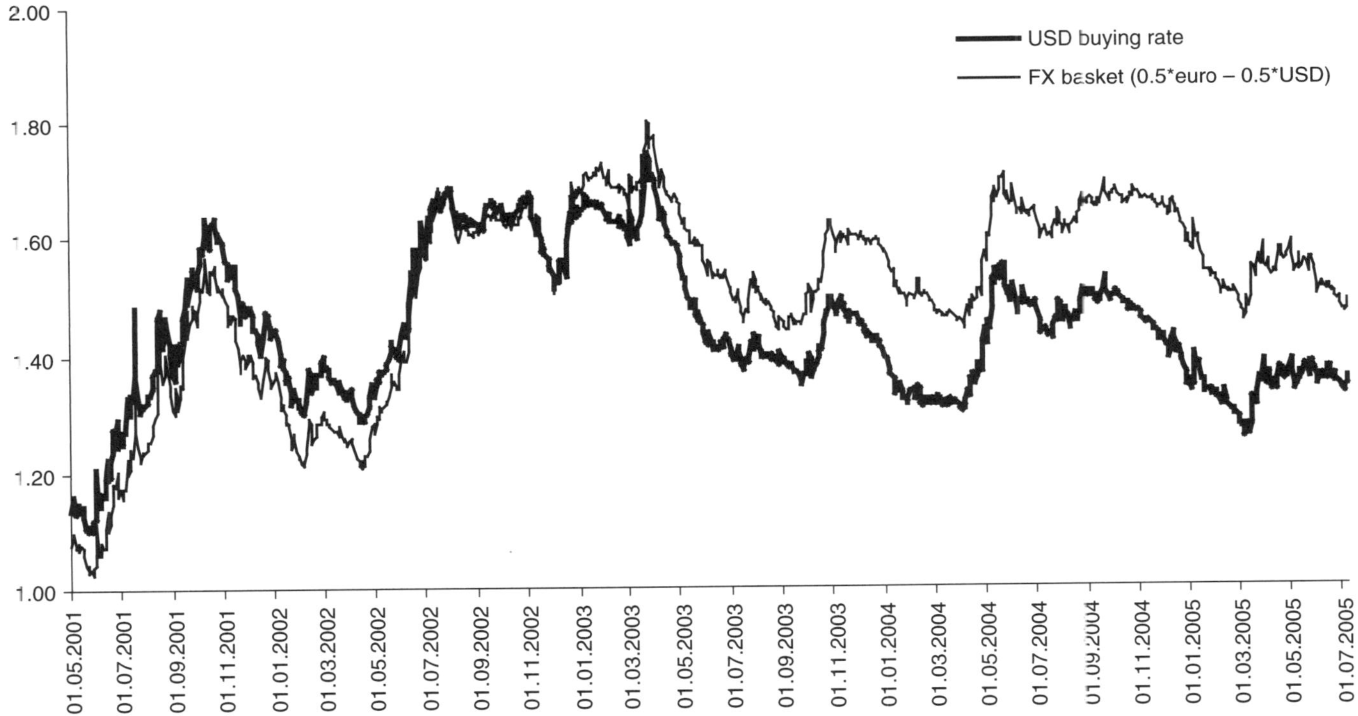

Figure 5.1b *Evolution of exchange rates, 1 May 2001–8 July 2005 (million TL per foreign currency)*

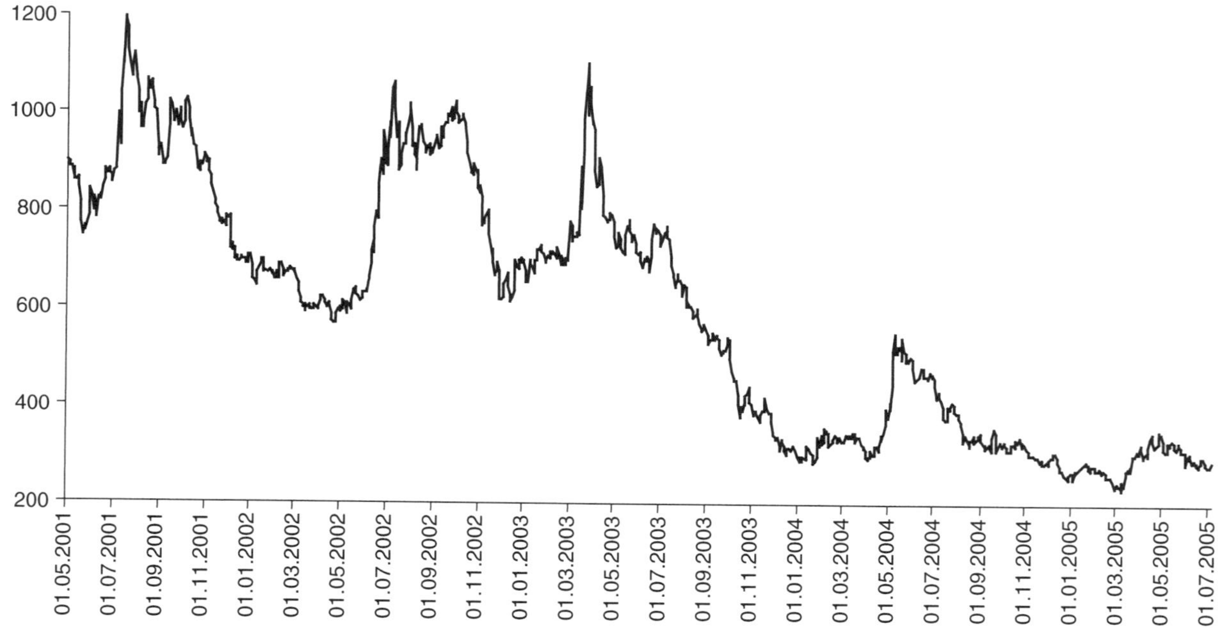

Note: Throughout this paper EMBI refers to the Turkish component of EMBI +. It is an index number calculated by JP Morgan and is generally used as a measure of markets' assessment of the probability that Turkey night default on its debt obligations. EMBI spread in the difference between the yield on a dollars-denominated bond issued by Turkey and a corresponding one issued by the US Treasury.

Figure 5.1c *Eurobond spread, 1 May 2001–7 July 2005 (EMBI-Turkey)*

macroeconomic fundamentals (credit ratings and central bank overnight changes) were among the determinants in changing interest rates. However, both positive and negative political news (not all kinds of news, but news related to fulfilling conditions of the IMF programme), adverse EU related news, and IMF announcements also had very significant influence on these rates. Note that this finding is in line with our interpretation of the developments in the post-crisis period.

5.2.3 Challenges to Monetary Policy under Fiscal Dominance: 2001–04

Eurobond spreads, domestic interest rates and exchange rate fluctuations

The striking point in figures 5.1a–c is the positive and close relationship between the daily evolution of Eurobond spreads, the exchange rate (value of Turkish Lira (TL) against an equal weighted basket of euro and dollar), and the secondary market Treasury bill rate during the May 2001–December 2004 period. More formally, Table 5.3 presents the contemporaneous correlation coefficients between these variables for different periods. The correlation coefficients are positive and very high, with the exception of 2 January–31 December 2004. A positive correlation between the rate of change of the exchange rate and interest rate is something that the portfolio model would not predict.

Blanchard (2005) presents a formal model to explain this phenomenon, which is apparently at odds with the portfolio model. The positive association between the exchange rate and the interest rate arises from the default risk. A rise in the interest rate due to an increase in the default risk triggers capital outflows and causes the domestic currency to depreciate (capital outflow occurs). On the other hand, in Blanchard's model, a rise in the interest rate without any accompanying change in the default risk (for example due to a rise in riskless rate that does not change the risk appetite of foreign investors and debt service of the country) would cause appreciation (due to a rise in capital inflows) as the portfolio model predicts. Blanchard (2005, p. 76) using Brazilian data concludes that:

> When fiscal fundamentals are wrong – i.e. when debt is high, when a high proportion of debt is denominated in foreign currency, when the risk aversion of investors is high – an increase in the interest rate is more likely to lead to a depreciation than to appreciation. And fiscal conditions were indeed probably wrong, in this specific sense, in Brazil in 2002.

Favero and Giavazzi (2005, p. 85–6) note that:

> All financial variables in Brazil fluctuate in parallel with the EMBI spread, most notably the exchange rate. The channel through which fluctuations in the EMBI

Table 5.3 Contemporaneous correlation coefficients between Eurobond spreads, the exchange rate and the Treasury bill rate

	Treasury bill rate	Eurobond spread	Exchange rate
1 May 2001–31 December 2004			
Treasury bill rate	1.00	0.86	0.85
Eurobond spread	0.86	1.00	0.63
Exchange rate	0.85	0.63	1.00
2 January 2002–31 December 2004			
Treasury bill rate	1.00	0.73	0.83
Eurobond spread	0.73	1.00	0.46
Exchange rate	0.83	0.46	1.00
2 January 2003–31 December 2004			
Treasury bill rate	1.00	0.68	0.93
Eurobond spread	0.68	1.00	0.62
Exchange rate	0.93	0.62	1.00
2 January 2004–31 December 2004			
Treasury bill rate	1.00	−0.30	0.52
Eurobond spread	−0.30	1.00	0.29
Exchange rate	0.52	0.29	1.00
1 April 2004–30 June 2004			
Treasury bill rate	1.00	0.93	0.89
Eurobond spread	0.93	1.00	0.92
Exchange rate	0.89	0.92	1.00

> spread are transmitted to the exchange rate are capital flows: an increase in the country risk premium leads to a sudden stop of capital flows and to a (real) depreciation which is needed to generate the trade surplus required to offset the decrease in net capital inflows. In turn, fluctuations in the exchange rate induce corresponding fluctuations in the public debt to GDP . . . Domestic interest rates at all maturities are also affected by fluctuations in the EMBI spread. In the case of the policy rate, the Selic, the mechanism works via the exchange rate: exchange rate fluctuations move inflation expectations, and the central bank, as we shall document in this paper, looks at inflation expectations when deciding on the level of the Selic . . . Domestic interest rates at longer maturities are affected by the EMBI spread in two ways: indirectly, through the Selic . . . and directly because long term interest rates reflect term premia which are affected by default risk even at relatively short maturities.

These observations relating to Turkey and Brazil both have important repercussions on the conduct of monetary policy. However, before turning to this issue, the impact of exchange rate fluctuations on inflation in Turkey should be discussed. Kara et al. (2005) analysed the impact of exchange rates on domestic prices in Turkey. Some of their findings can be summarized as follows. First, they show that the pass-through of exchange rates to domestic prices has declined in the post-2001 period in comparison with earlier episodes. Second, despite the reduction in the pass-through, they found that the impact of the exchange rate on inflation, especially in traded goods, is still notable. Third, switching to the floating exchange rate regime and implementing an ambitious disinflation policy have contributed to the reduction in the pass-through. Fourth, the pass-through is stronger in periods of positive output gap than the periods of negative output gap. Moreover, the pass-through, on average, is higher during periods of depreciation.

Repercussions on the conduct of monetary policy

An inflation targeting central bank should respond to an increase in the probability of an upsurge in future inflation by raising its policy rate. Now, suppose that in a highly indebted economy, the pass-through effect is significant. In this economy, negative political developments which increase concerns about debt sustainability would not only increase interest rates, but also weaken the domestic currency. The reasoning behind this is similar to what is discussed above. On the one hand, an increase in the probability of debt repudiation would cause new subscribers to ask for higher rates to compensate for an increase in default risk, while on the other hand, demand for foreign currency denominated assets would increase; hence the weakening of the domestic currency would occur. Consequently, a central bank that raises its policy rate in response to a potential rise in inflation due to weakening of the currency faces two related problems. First, a rise in its overnight rate could signal to the markets that 'things are not going in the right direction', which could obviously increase the perceived default risk and hence, the real interest rate and exchange rate. Second, both indirectly with the first effect and directly by raising the cost of borrowing, such a response in policy would increase the debt burden of the Treasury and jeopardize debt sustainability. The domestic currency would depreciate in these circumstances, which is inflationary given our significant pass-through assumption. This means the plan to increase the short-term interest rate to cope with inflationary pressures would backfire.

A counter-argument would be that a central bank which does its job by raising interest rates will be credible and such a credible policy decision will more than offset the negative effects on inflation stated above. Analysing which argument is correct is not an issue that this chapter addresses. However, the probability of the backfiring of raising interest rates in such circumstances is not something that can be disregarded immediately. Given this probability, the effectiveness of inflation targeting in such economies is asymmetric: cutting policy rates does not pose such problems (provided that such a cut is warranted by the inflation outlook), whereas raising them does. The model presented in Blanchard (2005) shows in what conditions and in what ways inflation targeting can have adverse effects. Blanchard (2005) further argues that Brazil found itself in such a situation in 2002 and 2003. Studying the recent experience of Brazil, Favero and Giavazzi (2005) show how the effectiveness of monetary policy depended on the fiscal policy regime in the same period. Aktaş et al. (2005) derived a 'model-based' default risk series for Turkey during the 1999–2003 period by introducing an unobserved components model with time varying parameters. They found that the arguments of Blanchard (2005) and Favero and Giavazzi (2005) are also valid for Turkey.

In the post-crisis period, the CBT raised its overnight rate just once – in July 2001 – and the reactions of the markets were adverse. The interest rates in all maturities moved upwards and the TL depreciated. With a jump in debt to GDP ratio after the 2001 crisis, the CBT has taken the influence of the fiscal policy regime into consideration and attached a special importance to it. In its various press releases, the CBT explicitly stated the multiple equilibria phenomenon and the importance of fiscal discipline to reduce real interest rates, to help in the fight against inflation and to reach higher growth rates. For example, the following paragraphs are taken from the press release of 2 January 2002:

> In designing monetary policy and exchange rate policy for the period ahead, it is assumed that (i) a fiscal discipline based on a high primary surplus will be attained; (ii) long-term commitments regarding fiscal discipline and public sector restructuring will be tackled . . . (iv) economic reforms boosting the economic fundamentals and prospects of the Turkish economy will persist . . .
>
> However, the experience in 2001 has demonstrated once again that correcting economic fundamentals does not always guarantee success. In the period between the February 2001 crisis and August of the same year, and for a month following the attacks on September 11, interest rates remained high and the Turkish Lira continued to depreciate despite improvements in economic fundamentals. Thus, concerns were raised about Turkey's ability to roll over domestic debts. As a result, the interest rate went up further due to increased risk premium, and the exchange rate was in an upward trend. These dynamics have further increased the concerns about the sustainability of domestic debts. In other words, a self-fulfilling process, feeding on itself, was observed.
>
> . . . restoring economic fundamentals alone does not suffice for reaching the targets. Therefore, we announced on 17 August 2001 that similar economic fundamentals might generate very different results. This stems from the expectations of economic agents. With similar economic fundamentals, optimistic

expectations will direct the economy towards a lower interest rate and exchange rate equilibrium, while pessimistic expectations will do the opposite. In technical terms, there can be more than one equilibrium to be attained at any time in an economy.

. . . the prospects of achieving fiscal discipline in 2002, the persistence in structural reforms and the impending supplemental reserve facility from the IMF have changed economic expectations into a positive mode. As a result of the change in expectations, interest rates declined substantially and the bubble in the exchange rate exploded, as we have already drawn attention to in our earlier press releases.

. . . In 2002, we will begin by monetary targeting and at the same time implement a monetary policy focused on the 'future inflation' . . . In other words, this is an 'implicit inflation targeting' . . . We will openly initiate the inflation targeting regime whenever the necessary conditions emerge. We had to postpone the introduction of inflation targeting due to concerns about the sustainability of domestic debt. Deepening concerns did not allow the short-term interest rates to be used against inflation. As stated above, recent positive developments have shelved discussions on the sustainability of domestic debt. With the realization of the economic environment envisaged for 2001, there will be no place for such discussions in 2002. Therefore, the continuation of an uninterrupted reform process in 2002 and the realization of primary surplus will remove one of the obstacles in the way of inflation targeting.

5.3 THE EU ACCESSION AND THE CHALLENGES TO MONETARY POLICY DURING THE TRANSITION AND THE MONETARY DOMINANCE PERIODS

According to the Treaty on the EU the economic and monetary integration process consists of three phases. The first phase covers the period of candidacy for the EU. The second is the accession phase and starts with EU membership. In the final phase, member countries are expected to join the EMU and adopt the euro. In the first phase, candidate countries choose their own monetary policy and exchange rate policy. However, they have to make necessary changes in their central bank laws. In this section, first, challenges to monetary end exchange rate policy in the first phase are discussed. Then, the necessary amendments to the CBT Law are analysed.

5.3.1 Farewell to Fiscal Dominance?

While the debt to GDP ratio has declined sharply in the last three years, it is still high. The question now arises whether or not fiscal dominance still continues in Turkey? Giving a proper answer to this question is highly important from the perspective of monetary policy. The discussion above implies that the impact of tightening monetary policy in a monetary dominance economy may be significantly different to that in a fiscally dominance economy.

In the last couple of years the Turkish economy has faced a number of important external shocks. The first one was the Iraq war, during which real interest rates jumped and the real value of the TL dropped significantly. The second one followed the announcements of the US Federal Reserve Bank (FED) and the subsequent interpretations of a possible aggressive tightening during the first half of 2004. The terrorist bombing attacks in Istanbul reinforced the negative impact of FED announcements. Despite these shocks, the main macroeconomic indicators stayed on the right track. This points to the increased resilience of the Turkish economy.

The results of Aktaş et al. (2005) shed some light on this issue. They show that default risk reached a peak during the third quarter of 2001, when the debt to GDP ratio attained its maximum level. The first half of 2002 witnessed a significant improvement, whereas it once again picked up slightly from the beginning of 2003. They used data up to the end of 2003. The important points to note are that, first, their findings are in line with our 'main positive trend with temporary deviations from the trend' argument and second, these results show also that the Turkish economy is moving towards a monetary dominance period.

The Eurobond spreads could be used as a proxy for the importance of the fiscal dominance. For new members of the EU, Eurobond spreads have generally hovered around 50 basis points throughout 2004. The lowest level of Turkish Eurobond spreads was attained in February 2005 with 280 basis points. At the time of writing (March–April 2005), the spread was 350 basis points. To put it another way, the default risk level is much lower compared to the recent past, but the absolute value of the spread is still sizeable (Figure 5.1c).

Further contradictory examples can be provided. However, the important point to note is that the Turkish economy is in a transition period and day by day is getting closer to a 'normal economy' (monetary dominance stage). The continuation of fiscal discipline and the restructuring of the institutional set-up play a vital role in maintaining this normalization process.

5.3.2 The New Three-Year Programme, the EU Accession and Risks

The discussion above implies that, in the short run, the main driving force of economic prospects will be the new programme for the period 2005–07, which is supported by a stand-by agreement with the IMF. Fiscal and monetary discipline is again at the core of the programme; consequently as of 2006, the CBT started the implementation of formal inflation targeting. The primary budget surplus to GNP ratio will be kept at 6.5 per cent for the extent of the new programme. There will be three important structural reforms: social security reform (second phase), tax reform and financial services reform and the related laws have been submitted to parliament. The second anchor will be the EU accession process. While the role of the EU accession is going to be more visible in the medium to long term, it will nevertheless reinforce the positive impact of the new programme.

Based on these two anchors, it is natural to expect a positive (main) trend in macroeconomic variables. The three key reforms will help to remove structural barriers to achieving lower real interest rates, by deepening the financial sector and increasing the quality of fiscal discipline. The downward trend in real rates will be strengthened by macroeconomic discipline. Hence, further reductions in the debt to GNP ratio, real interest rates and inflation are going to be observed. As discussed above, this environment will again be conducive to economic growth.

More formally, consumer inflation targets are 8, 5 and 4 per cent respectively for 2005, 2006 and 2007. The ratio of public sector net debt (according to the IMF definition) to GNP is projected to decline to 61 per cent at the end of 2007 from a level of 70 per cent at end-2004. The new programme assumes that growth will be led by increased investment and exports and moderated to around 5 per cent. This should lower the current account deficit to around 4.3 per cent of GNP in 2005 and subsequently lower figures for the remainder of the programme.

Some risks also exist, primarily the potential destabilizing effect of the deterioration in the current account deficit in 2004. However, this potential risk is not very high due to several reasons. First, an important factor behind this deterioration was the very high growth in 2004 (9.9 per cent) and a slowdown was projected for 2005. Second, various one-off tax incentive policies led to a jump in demand for automotive sector products. This factor, by increasing both passenger car imports and intermediate goods imports for the manufacture of domestic automotive products, was responsible for a significant part of the widening in the current account deficit. Such incentives have been eliminated from the tax system. Third, there is no longer a currency mismatch in the banking sector.

Another source of risk is the EU accession process. While, as mentioned above, this process is shown to be one of the two powerful anchors for the Turkish economy, stressful periods can occasionally arise during the process, due to domestic discussions regarding meeting various necessary criteria and/or debates on Turkish membership in member countries.

During these periods, negative developments especially in exchange rates, interest rates and expectations could occur.

5.3.3 The First Challenge to Monetary Policy: Raising its Policy Rate

In July 2004 – more than three years after the start of the programme, when the debt to GDP ratio was much lower, the inflation rate was down by 60 percentage points and at a single digit level and inflation expectations were in line with the end year target – in its quarterly monetary policy report, the CBT emphasized the positive inflationary outlook, but added that should the outlook change it would not hesitate to increase the overnight rates. The reaction of the markets was adverse: the secondary market interest rate increased and the TL depreciated.

This points to the difficulties that the monetary authorities are going to face in the transition to monetary dominance period. There is no doubt that the necessary condition to overcome this problem is the continuation of implementing sound macroeconomic policies. However, given recent experience, another condition should be met: convincing economic agents that the Turkish economy is close to a monetary dominance period. This necessitates a good communication policy.

In January 2005, the CBT announced that formal inflation targeting would start in January 2006. Moreover, it named 2005 as a transition period and announced a plan to increase the transparency of its implicit inflation targeting framework. This shows that, based on positive developments in macroeconomic indicators and the declaration that the (ambitious) fiscal discipline is going to continue in the new programme period, the CBT judges that the economy is close to a monetary dominance regime.

While the importance of fiscal dominance will decrease the closer the economy is to the monetary dominance period, monetary authorities will nonetheless have to address significant problems arising, paradoxically, from the implementation of sound policies towards macroeconomic stability, structural change and EU accession. This is the challenge to monetary policy stemming from a possible reversal in dollarization and a surge in capital flows. These issues are analysed below.

5.3.4 A Pleasant Problem: Reverse Dollarization

The Turkish economy is a highly 'dollarized' economy. Reinhart et al. (2003) define a composite index to measure the degree of dollarization in a country. This index is the normalized sum of bank deposits in foreign currency as a share of broad money, total external debt as a share of the GNP, and domestic government debt denominated or linked to a foreign currency as a share of total domestic government debt. Using this measure, they classify 90 developing countries into four degrees of dollarization using data in 1996–2001: very high, high, moderate and low. Turkey is in the high dollarization group. In addition, they determine the variety of dollarization prevalent in each country at any point in time on the basis of two separate criteria: the degree of domestic dollarization (measured by the first and third item of their composite index) and the amount of foreign borrowing by the private sector. They define four varieties. Countries where at least 10 per cent of broad money or of domestic public debt is denominated in a foreign currency and where the stock of private non-guaranteed external debt is more than 10 per cent of the total debt are defined as Type I economies. Turkey is a Type I economy.

Figures 5.2a, b and c show the evolution of the three elements of composite index for Turkey which is calculated as in Reinhart et al. (2003). Bank deposits in foreign currency as a share of broad money are shown in Figure 5.2a, based on monthly data from June 1996–June 2005. Figure 5.2b shows the evolution of total external debt as a share in GNP (quarterly data). Figure 5.2c is for domestic government debt denominated in or linked to a foreign currency as a share of total government debt (monthly data). The evolution of the indicators of domestic dollarization (figures 5.2a and c) followed a declining trend after the end of 2001. However, this trend was not without interruptions and there were occasional reversals. Further, the current values of both of the ratios are high.

Starting from the one-digit levels of the 1960s, the inflation rate followed an upward trend in the second half of the 1970s and reached 107 per cent in 1980. With the stabilization and structural adjustment programme of 1980 it fell to 25 per cent in 1982, but after that it once again picked up and hovered around 80 per cent in the second half of the 1990s. In 1984, partly as an element of the financial liberalization process and partly due to high inflation levels, the Turkish government gave residents the right to hold foreign currency deposits in the banks. In 1989, the capital account was liberalized. The high inflation period and the underlying imprudent policies on the one hand, and legal developments on the other, accelerated the dollarization process in the 1980s and 1990s. Given that the disinflation process has been continuing for more than three years, the inflation rate is at one-digit levels, and the implementation of prudent policies and structural reforms are going to continue in the new three-year programme, the question that arises is whether a reversal in the dollarization process is likely to start.

Reinhart et al. (2003) shed some light on this issue. They examined the evidence on successful de-dollarization. At first glance their results are not particularly encouraging for the de-dollarization prospects for Turkey. The

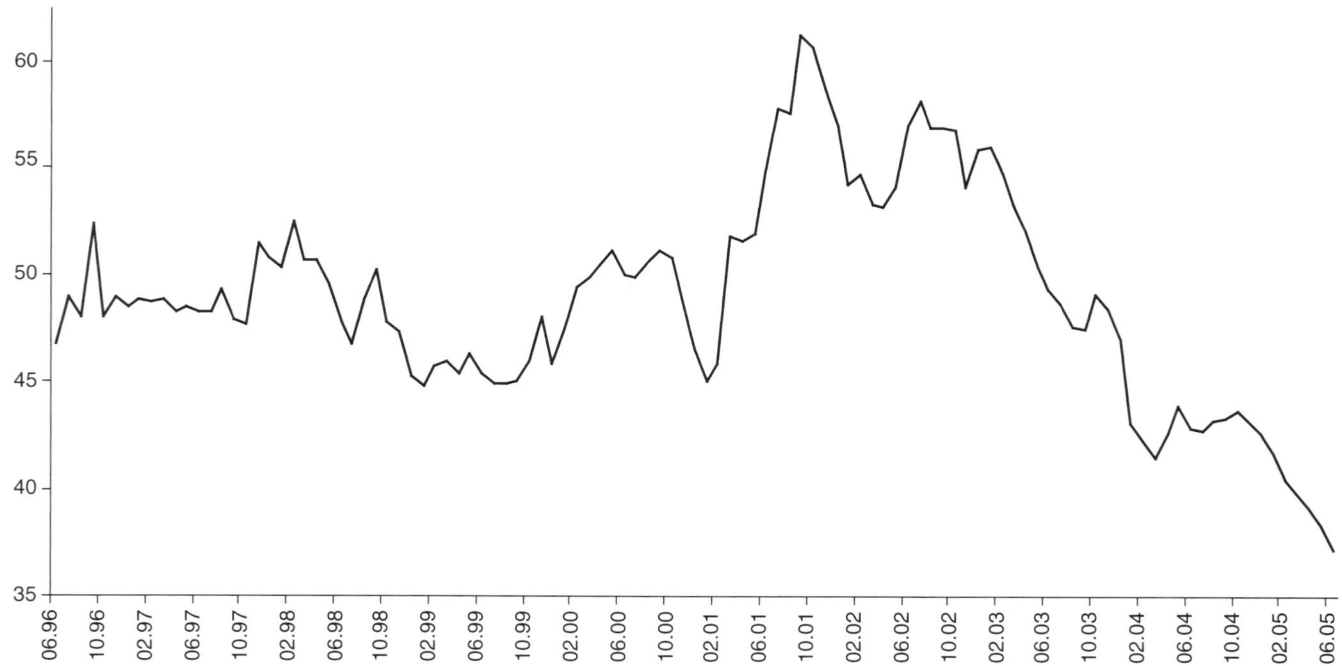

Note: Broad money = M2 + foreign currency deposits.

Figure 5.2a Bank deposits in foreign currency as a share of broad money, June 1996–June 2005 (%)

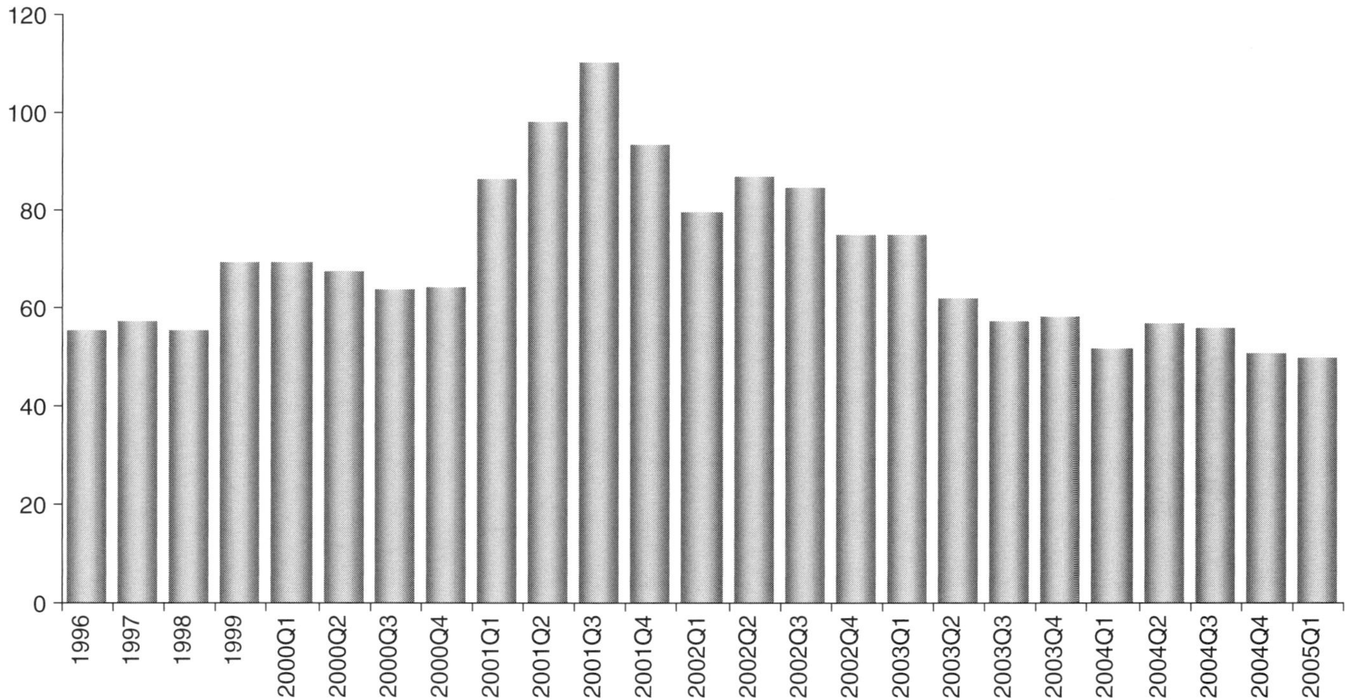

Figure 5.2b *Total external debt/GNP, 1996–2005Q1 (%)*

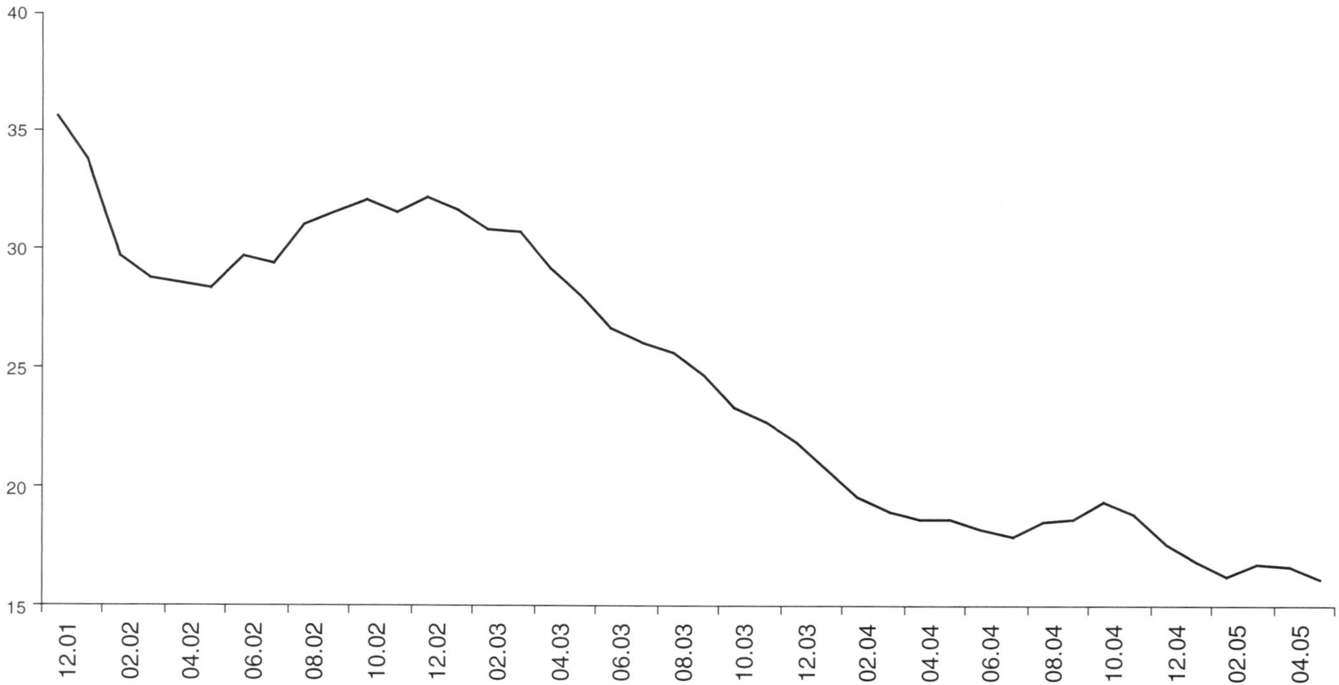

Figure 5.2c *Foreign currency denominated and linked domestic public debt as a share of total domestic public debt, December 2001–May 2005 (%)*

experience of the 85 countries in their sample shows that reducing inflation is generally not sufficient to undo domestic dollarization for at least five-year-plus horizons. One of the reasons they put forward is that 'a country with a poor inflationary history will need to maintain inflation at low levels for a long period before it can significantly reduce the probability of another inflation bout' (Reinhart et al., 2003, p. 31). They conclude that:

> Israel and Poland appear as the only two cases on record of large and lasting reversals of deposit dollarization that had minimal side effects on financial intermediation and/or capital flight. In both cases the de-dollarization started almost at the same time as the authorities embarked on a (eventually successful) disinflation program centred around a strong exchange rate anchor, and the domestic financial system offered assets with alternative forms of indexation (Israel) or very high real interest rates (Poland). (p. 48)

Will Turkey be the third country to achieve this? Three points suggest an affirmative answer to this question. First, Turkey has been implementing an ambitious macroeconomic stability and structural reform process for almost four years and a similar programme is going to be implemented for another three years. Second, the EU accession process (provided that Turkey remains on the right track) is a powerful anchor to curb expectations for destabilizing policies. Hence, the new programme and the accession process have the potential to significantly reduce the probability of another inflation bout, the main block, according to Reinhart et al. (2003), to starting a de-dollarization process. Third, economic agents have increasingly held more TL-denominated financial assets in their portfolios since 2002, albeit with temporary deviations from this main trend (Figure 5.2.a).

A reverse dollarization process means a decrease in foreign exchange demand and an increase in foreign exchange supply, which will certainly put appreciation pressure on the domestic currency. This will be a problem, but admittedly after more than three decades of high inflation and a depreciation-depreciation cycle, which ended in the last quarter of 2001, it will be a pleasant one: hence the title of the subsection – 'pleasant problem'.

5.3.5 Surge in Capital Inflows

Table 5.4 shows foreign direct investment (FDI) inflows to Central and Eastern European (CEE) countries during the 1999–2004 period. The striking fact is that FDI inflows to Turkey have been at a very low level both in absolute terms and compared to new members of the EU and candidate countries. Doubtlessly, the main underlying reason is the macroeconomic disorder of more than three decades preceding May 2001. The improvement of macroeconomic fundamentals since then and the EU accession process

Table 5.4 Capital inflows to some of the CEE countries, 1999–2004 (% of GNP)

	1999	2000	2001	2002	2003	2004
Czech Republic						
Current account balance	−2.5	−4.9	−5.4	−5.6	−6.3	−5.2
Net errors and omissions	0.1	−0.5	0.8	0.2	0.6	−0.6
Total financing requirement	−2.4	−5.4	−4.6	−5.4	−5.6	−5.8
Total inflows	2.4	5.4	4.6	5.4	5.6	5.8
FDI (net)	10.6	8.9	9.0	11.2	2.1	3.7
Portfolio (net)	−2.4	−3.2	1.4	−2.1	−1.2	2.2
Credits and others	−3.0	1.2	−2.9	5.3	5.3	0.2
Reserve assets	−2.8	−1.5	−2.9	−9.0	−0.5	−0.2
Hungary						
Current account balance	−7.9	−8.6	−6.2	−7.3	−9.0	−8.9
Net errors and omissions	−0.8	−0.3	0.1	0.3	0.4	0.0
Total financing requirement	−8.7	−9.0	−6.1	−7.0	−8.6	−8.9
Total inflows	8.7	9.0	6.1	7.0	8.6	8.9
FDI (net)	6.4	4.7	6.9	4.2	0.8	3.7
Portfolio (net)	4.0	−0.8	2.9	2.4	3.5	7.5
Credits and others	3.1	7.4	−3.8	−2.4	4.7	−0.3
Reserve assets	−4.9	−2.3	0.2	2.8	−0.4	−2.0
Poland						
Current account balance	−7.7	−6.0	−2.9	−2.6	−2.2	−1.6
Net errors and omissions	1.3	0.2	0.9	−0.8	1.1	1.3
Total financing requirement	−6.4	−5.8	−2.0	−3.4	−1.1	−0.3
Total inflows	6.4	5.8	2.0	3.4	1.1	0.3
FDI (net)	4.5	5.6	3.1	2.0	1.9	2.4
Portfolio (net)	0.4	2.2	0.4	0.5	0.8	4.4
Credits and others	1.6	−1.6	−1.8	1.2	−1.0	−6.1
Reserve assets	−0.1	−0.4	0.2	−0.3	−0.6	−0.3
Slovak Republic						
Current account balance	−5.7	−3.4	−8.4	−8.1	−0.9	−3.5
Net errors and omissions	−0.1	0.2	0.5	1.2	0.1	0.4
Total financing requirement	−5.7	−3.2	−7.8	−6.8	−0.8	−3.1
Total inflows	5.7	3.2	7.8	6.8	0.8	3.1
FDI (net)	3.6	10.0	7.4	16.9	1.6	3.1
Portfolio (net)	3.2	4.1	−1.2	2.3	−1.7	2.0
Credits and others	2.8	−6.4	2.3	2.8	5.5	2.1
Reserve assets	−3.8	−4.5	−0.7	−15.2	−4.6	−4.1
Romania						
Current account balance	−3.6	−3.7	−5.5	−3.3	−5.8	n.a.

Table 5.4 (continued)

	1999	2000	2001	2002	2003	2004
Net errors and omissions	2.2	0.3	1.8	−1.9	−0.5	n.a.
Total financing requirement	−1.4	−3.3	−3.7	−5.2	−6.3	n.a.
Total inflows	1.4	3.3	3.7	5.2	6.3	n.a.
FDI (net)	2.9	2.8	2.9	2.5	3.2	n.a.
Portfolio (net)	−2.0	0.3	1.4	0.8	1.0	n.a.
Credits and others	1.2	2.7	3.2	5.8	3.9	n.a.
Reserve assets	−0.7	−2.5	−3.8	−3.9	−1.8	n.a.
Turkey						
Current account balance	−0.7	−4.9	2.3	−0.8	−3.3	−5.1
Net errors and omissions	0.9	−1.4	−1.1	0.1	2.1	0.9
Total financing requirement	0.2	−6.3	1.2	−0.7	−1.2	−4.2
Total inflows	−0.2	6.3	−1.2	0.7	1.2	4.2
FDI (net)	0.1	0.1	1.9	0.5	0.5	0.6
Portfolio (net)	1.9	0.5	−3.1	−0.3	1.1	2.7
Credits and others	0.6	4.2	−8.9	0.5	1.4	2.4
Reserve assets	−2.8	1.5	8.9	0.1	−1.7	−1.4

Sources: IMF; IFS and individual countries' official websites.

provide the potential to change this picture. Of course this will not happen overnight, in a base line scenario it will materialize in the medium run.

The picture is entirely different regarding other types of capital inflows. While such inflows to Turkey and other CEE countries have surged over the past two years, the largest recipient of emerging market flows into the region has been Turkey (38 per cent in 2004). After the positive decision from the EU in mid-December 2004 and the redenomination of the TL (which allowed Euroclear to handle new TL-denominated bonds), multilateral institutions, international banks and export credit agencies have started to issue new TL denominated bonds, a new phenomenon for Turkey, but one which was also observed in new EU member countries during their accession process. The value of such bonds in the first four months of 2005 reached $3.3 billion. Such issues increase demand for longer maturity Turkish Treasury securities and lead to more capital inflows.

As long as the new programme and the EU process remain on track, these observations and the experience of new member states point to the increased probability of a surge in capital inflows to Turkey. In the short term, capital inflows will be more in the form of portfolio and loan flows, which currently are and will continue to be sensitive to changes in the interest rates in the developed world and the risk-appetite of foreign investors. As time passes, the importance of foreign direct investment will increase.

5.3.6 Handling Capital Inflows and a Reversal in Dollarization: The Second Challenge to Monetary Policy

Both a reversal in dollarization and a surge in capital inflows will put appreciation pressure on the new TL. What can the CBT do to overcome this problem? In answering this question, four points should be taken into consideration. First, according to its law, the main objective of the CBT is to achieve price stability. Furthermore, the CBT has been implementing implicit inflation targeting since 2002 and started to conduct formal inflation targeting in January 2006. Second, given the vulnerability of the economy to changes in markets sentiment in the post-crisis period, the floating exchange rate regime became one of the important stabilizing pillars of the programme. The new programme is also based on the floating exchange rate regime. Third, the public sector and the CBT have significant amounts of foreign debt repayments due in the period 2005–07. Fourth, an important part of the reserves of the CBT is actually its liabilities to Turkish workers abroad. Note that since the mid-1970s the CBT has acted like a deposit bank, because since then workers abroad have had the right to hold foreign exchange deposits in Turkey. The interest cost of these deposits is an important cost item for the CBT and the CBT plans to get rid of this facility.[6]

The evolution of the pass-through effect in Turkey is discussed in Section 5.2 above. As stated, while there has been a significant drop in this effect in the post-crisis period, it is still high. An increase in foreign exchange supply due to a surge in capital inflows and possible reverse dollarization will contribute to the ongoing disinflation process by putting appreciation pressure on the new lira. In these circumstances, being an inflation targeting central bank, the CBT will have room for manoeuvre to reduce interest rates. Note that this policy response has been effectively used by the CBT since 2002 and by other countries in the region (namely, the Czech Republic, the Slovak Republic, Hungary and Romania) during the accession process.

A second policy response that can be used jointly with rate cuts is international reserve build-up. Significant amounts of foreign debt repayments of the public sector and the desire of the CBT to get rid of its liabilities to Turkish workers abroad point to the importance of the level of reserves for Turkey regardless of the exchange rate regime. A surge in capital flows and reverse dollarization have the potential to create an opportunity to increase the level of reserves. However, the build-up mechanism should be in line with the implemented exchange rate regime. In fact, as emphasized in Section 5.2, the CBT has followed this strategy for the last three and half years. The main principle has been that the exchange rate is determined by market forces, and the CBT does not have any exchange rate target under the floating exchange rate regime. Therefore, the CBT has purchased foreign exchange through market-friendly auctions: the mechanism through which the CBT purchased foreign exchange and how much it was going to purchase daily were set in advance and announced. Whenever the reverse dollarization process and capital inflows stopped, the CBT also stopped opening purchase auctions. In other words, it has not been aggressive in reserve accumulation.[7]

While this two-pillar strategy seems to be feasible given recent experience, it has a limit. In easing monetary policy, the CBT's capacity for manoeuvre will be determined by other factors behind the disinflation prospects brought by the pass-through effect. First of all, as discussed above, the pass-through effect itself has been losing its importance. Second, an easing cycle can jeopardize the inflation outlook from other channels. Just to give an example, a rapid credit extension can be observed due to this easing. The level of reserves cannot be increased indefinitely. Besides, an optimal level of reserves can be defined and the accumulation process brings the sterilization/un-sterilization dilemma to the forefront. While an un-sterilized accumulation strategy can undermine disinflation prospects, a sterilized strategy has well-known costs[8] attached to it and self-fulfilling potential.

This two-pillar monetary policy strategy can first be reinforced through an appropriate debt management strategy of the Treasury, which could aim to reduce foreign exchange denominated and/or indexed portion of the public debt. Second, reducing the vulnerability of the economy to sudden stops and reversal by reducing currency mismatches in the banking and corporate sector will be a strong policy response. However, these are outside the scope of this chapter and are not further analysed here.

5.3.7 The Need to Change the Structure of the Balance Sheet of the CBT

The balance sheet of the CBT is rather a peculiar central bank balance sheet that reflects the macroeconomic imbalances of the past. The share of foreign currency liabilities of the central bank in its total liabilities was 67 per cent at the end of 2004. In other words, two-thirds of its liabilities were denominated in currencies of which the CBT is not a supplier. To give another example, the currency issued was only 18 per cent of the total liabilities of the CBT in the same period. Another interesting peculiarity, that the CBT has been operating like a commercial bank since the

Table 5.5 Balance sheet structure of the CBT, 1999–2004

	1999	2000	2001	2002	2003	2004
FX[a] liabilities/ Total liabilities (%)	87.8	94.2	83.6	72.3	68.5	66.9
Non-residents' deposits/ Total liabilities (%)	44.7	41.8	25.9	31.1	31.5	33.4
Banks' FX reserves/ Total liabilities (%)	23.1	25.4	17.2	14.5	13.3	17.8
TL liabilities/ Total liabilities (%)	12.2	5.8	16.4	27.7	31.5	33.1
Currency issued/ Total liabilities (%)	18.4	22.3	8.8	10.3	14.0	18.0
OMO[b]/Total liabilities (%)	−18.5	−30.9	2.1	12.9	10.8	4.9
Memo items (million YTL)						
Net domestic assets	−938	2485	20475	7520	7819	9094
Net foreign assets	4818	3303	−12672	2907	7048	12042
Base Money (NDA + NFA)	3879	5788	7803	10427	14867	21136

Notes:
a. FX denotes foreign currency.
b. OMO denotes net open market operations.

mid-1970s, was touched on above. The share of foreign exchange deposits of workers abroad in the total balance sheet was 33 per cent at the end of 2004 (Table 5.5).

Another challenge for the monetary authorities is, therefore, to change this awkward balance sheet structure. Based on a smooth EU accession process and implementation of the new three-year programme, the CBT aims to clear its balance sheet of deposits of workers abroad in a smooth manner. While this aim has been made public, a detailed plan has not been yet announced. To achieve this aim, the spread between the interest rate that the CBT pays on such deposits and the rates of alternative assets has been considerably reduced in the last three years. However, the spreads are still significant. The CBT will continue to reduce these spreads in a cautious manner. Close coordination with the Treasury can help in this respect. To this end, a team is currently working on whether the Treasury can assume these liabilities by issuing securities. A questionnaire has been applied to the holders of these deposits to gauge their reaction to such a voluntary swap operation. The second important part of total foreign exchange liabilities of the CBT is the required reserves denominated in foreign currency, which are held by commercial banks. The evolution of this portion will be determined by the reverse dollarization process.

5.3.8 Necessary Amendments to the CBT Law

The CBT law was amended on 25 April 2001. Since that date it has had instrument independence according to Article 4: 'The primary objective of the Bank shall be to achieve and maintain price stability. The Bank shall determine at its own discretion the monetary policy that it shall implement and the monetary policy instruments that it is going to use in order to achieve and maintain price stability.' The CBT staff has continuously discussed various issues towards EU accession with the ECB. One of the issues is the statute of the CBT with regard to the requirements of central bank independence. In a highly tentative assessment, several items have been identified as problematic.

The most important of these is the lack of goal independence. Article 4 II b of the CBT law states 'The Bank shall determine the inflation target with the government and shall in compliance with the said target adopt monetary policy. The Bank shall be the ultimate body authorized and responsible to implement monetary policy.' This is criticized for not being compatible with the Treaty. Based on this criticism, the CBT law has to be amended. However, note that instrument independence is in line with central bank independence and, moreover, goal independence has been criticized for being undemocratic.[9]

Article 3 states 'The Bank may, by Board decision, become a member of international finance, economic and professional organizations as a shareholder with the consent of the government.' This has been criticized on the grounds that the right of the government to approve the Bank's participation in international monetary institutions is not compatible with the Treaty and the Statute.

Article 15 (3) states 'The General Assembly shall have the following duties and powers: to release members of the Board and the Auditing Committee.' Given that Article 8 guarantees the Treasury a majority stake in the shares of the CBT, Article 15 is criticized for permitting an external political influence enabling pressure to be put on members of the Board, which is incompatible with Article 108 of the Treaty.

ECB experts also find articles 19 and 33 to be problematic. According to these articles, the salaries and remuneration of Board members and the salaries and the representation allowances of the Governor and Vice-Governors shall be determined by Council of Ministers. Instead of this, the ECB proposes an amendment to this article with the aim of clarifying that salaries and remunerations are fixed for the term of the office of these members.

An amendment to Article 24 – to ensure that members of the Audit Committee act in an independent manner and within a clearly defined mandate – also seems necessary.

Article 26 states 'The Governor may, in case of his/her dissent from the decisions of the Board, postpone the execution of any decision and may demand that it be reconsidered at the next meeting. In urgent circumstances, the Board shall convene upon the instruction of the Governor and reconsider the issues under dispute. In the event of a disagreement between the Governor and the Board, the Prime Minister shall act as an arbitrator.' This is considered to be incompatible with Article 18 of the Treaty.

Referring to Article 42: 'The Prime Minister may have the operations and accounts of the Bank audited. The Prime Minister may request any information in this regards from the Bank.' This is found to have the potential of undermining the independence of decision-making required by Article 108 of the Treaty.

Another problematic article concerns grounds for the dismissal of governors. Article 28, second paragraph, states 'The Governor may be excused from office through the same procedure applied for his/her appointment, only in cases in which the prohibitions stated in Article 27 are violated and in which there is no longer any responsibility for him/her to perform the duties entrusted by this Law.' This paragraph is found not to be compatible with Article 14.2 of the Statute of the European System of Central Banks (ESCB).

Article 20, first paragraph, states, 'The term of office of Board members shall be three years.' This has been criticized on the grounds that the members of the Board are involved in the performance of ESCB related tasks ('to take decisions concerning monetary policy . . .') and therefore the same minimum rules for the security of tenure of office as are applicable to the governors (five years) have to apply to all members of the Board.

5.4 CONCLUDING REMARKS

Turkey is a candidate country for full membership of the EU. The initial period of the EU accession process – 2005 to 2007 – will witness the implementation of the three-year IMF backed programme. If the programme remains on track, this period will at the same time be the transition period from fiscal dominance of the post-crisis period to monetary dominance.

This chapter has analysed possible challenges that both the EU accession and transition processes pose to the monetary authorities, since one cannot be analysed without the other. The problems that may arise and are well documented in literature for new member countries in the period following membership (the pre-ERM II and ERM II phases and the adoption of the euro) are not discussed.

The first challenge for the monetary policy authorities will arise from the difficulties inherited from the fiscal dominance period. Given that the programme that has been implemented since May 2001 is successful, this problem will lose importance in the initial phase of the EU accession process. The second and, it is argued, the main challenge to monetary policy, will stem from a surge in capital inflows and the reverse dollarization process. A two-pillar monetary policy response is envisaged: a non-aggressive market-friendly reserve accumulation strategy and policy rate cuts provided that the inflation outlook looks promising. The third challenge is the need for a radical change in the balance sheet structure of the CBT, which is a mirror image of past macroeconomic imbalances. Fourth, the CBT law should be amended to comply with the Treaty.

NOTES

* The views expressed in this chapter are those of the author and should not be interpreted as reflecting those of the Central Bank of the Republic of Turkey.

1. For further details see ECB (2003).
2. As pointed out by Sargent and Wallace (1981), when public debt is high and the real rate of return on government securities is in excess of the economy's growth rate, tightening monetary policy by reducing the growth rate of money can result in higher, rather than lower inflation. Under these conditions, a contractionary monetary policy will initially lower seigniorage revenue and require that additional debt be issued; an increase in the deficit and the following rise in the stock of debt will eventually require an increase in seigniorage. This situation has been dubbed as 'fiscal dominance of monetary policy'. In contrast, if the government adjusts the primary deficit to limit debt accumulation, an eventual increase in seigniorage will not materialize; such a regime has been called 'monetary dominant'. Under fiscal dominance, monetary policy has to accommodate any fiscal policy to prevent default, whereas monetary dominance is the opposite. See also, for example, Tanner and Ramos (2002).
3. This is a credibility cost to the government and different from transaction costs associated with debt repudiation that are considered in Equation (5.3).
4. Sustainability of public debt is the key here. The evolution of the debt to GDP ratio is a function of the real growth rate, the real interest rate, and the primary budget surplus to GDP ratio. Leaving monetary policy aside, a government can only control its budget and affect real interest rates through this channel. A tight fiscal policy will increase confidence in debt sustainability and hence curb the default premium, provided that it is held credible by the private sector. While this would reduce real interest rates, there is a high probability that fiscal discipline, on the other hand, would increase consumer and business confidence. In a nutshell, fiscal discipline may be conducive to growth, despite its negative impact on growth through a decline in government demand in such economies. It may more than offset the contractionary effect of a decline in government demand through two main channels: first, through a decline in real interest rates, as discussed above; and second, a reduction in default risk and a consequent increase in consumer confidence in the initial phase and business confidence in the following periods would stimulate private demand. In the initial phase of the post-crisis period the fear of loss of jobs would cease, hence pent-up demand would increase, which would naturally be followed by an overall increase in private consumption and private investment. Another significant point to note is that a stronger financial sector, as a result of structural reforms and a stable currency (especially in highly dollarized economies), would reinforce such offsetting effects.
5. The important point to note is that these auctions, unlike volatility interventions, were not discretionary. They were rule-based and known to the public. Provided that the

aforementioned conditions were satisfied, the CBT announced how much and via which mechanism it was going to buy foreign exchange in these daily auctions at the beginning of each month. Finally, the CBT revised its auction procedure, effective from 22 December 2004. A yearly programme was announced to minimize the distortionary effects of possible changes in daily purchase amounts at the beginning of each month on the operation of the foreign exchange market.

6. This issue is discussed in the following section.
7. The details are provided in Section 5.2.2.
8. Sterilization, especially a prolonged one, can impose heavy financing costs on the monetary authorities. See, for example, Calvo et al. (1993) for the desirability of sterilized intervention.
9. On this issue, see for example Fischer (1994).

REFERENCES

Aktaş, Z., N. Kaya and Ü. Özlale (2005), 'The price puzzle for emerging markets: evidence from the Turkish economy using "model based" risk premium derived from domestic fundamentals', the Research Department Working Paper, CBT, 05/02.

Barro, R.J. and D.B. Gordon (1983), 'A positive theory of monetary policy in a natural rate model', *Journal of Political Economy*, **91**, 589–610.

Blanchard, O. (2005), 'Fiscal dominance and inflation targeting: lessons from Brazil', in G. Giavazzi, I. Goldfajn and S. Herrera (eds), *Inflation Targeting, Debt, and the Brazilian Experience, 1999 to 2003*, Cambridge, MA: MIT Press, pp. 49–80.

Calvo, A.G. (1988), 'Servicing the public debt: the role of expectations', *American Economic Review*, **78**, 647–61.

Calvo, A.G., L. Leiderman and C.M. Reinhart (1993), 'Capital inflows and real exchange rate appreciation in Latin America: the role of external factors', *IMF Staff Papers*, **40**, 108–51.

ECB (2003), 'Policy position of the governing council of the European Central Bank on exchange rate issues relating to the acceding countries', http://www.ecb.int ('Press release' section).

Emir, O.E., F. Özatay and G. Şahinbeyoğlu (2005), 'Effects of interest rates and news on the daily interest rates of a highly indebted emerging country: evidence from Turkey', the Research Department Working Paper, CBT, 05/08, forthcoming in *Applied Economics*.

Favero, C.A. and F. Giavazzi (2005), 'Inflation targeting and debt: lessons from Brazil', in G. Giavazzi, I. Goldfajn and S. Herrera (eds), *Inflation Targeting, Debt, and the Brazilian Experience, 1999 to 2003*, Cambridge, MA: MIT Press, pp. 85–108.

Fischer, S. (1994), 'Modern central banking', in F. Capie, C. Goodhart, S. Fischer and N. Schnadt (eds), *The Future of Central Banking*, Cambridge: Cambridge University Press, pp. 262–308.

Kara, H., H.K. Tuğer, Ü. Özlale, B. Tuğer, D. Yavuz and E.M. Yücel (2005), 'Exchange rate pass-through in Turkey: has it changed and to what extent?', the Research Department Working Paper, CBT, 05/04.

Missale, A. and O.J. Blanchard (1994), 'The debt burden and debt maturity', *American Economic Review*, **84**, 309–19.

Obstfeld, M. (1996), 'Models of currency crises with self-fulfilling features', *European Economic Review*, **40**, 1037–47.

Reinhart, C.M., K.S. Rogoff and M.A. Savastano (2003), 'Addicted to dollars', NBER Working Paper, 10015.
Sachs, J., A. Tornell and A. Velasco (1996), 'The Mexican Peso crisis: sudden death or death foretold?', *Journal of International Economics*, **41**, 265–83.
Sargent, T. and N. Wallace (1981), 'Some unpleasant monetarist arithmetic', *Federal Reserve Bank of Minneapolis Quarterly Review*, **5**, 1–17.
Tanner, E. and A.M. Ramos (2002), 'Fiscal sustainability and monetary versus fiscal dominance: evidence from Brazil, 1991–2000', IMF Working Paper, WP/02/5.

COMMENTS

Ricardo Hausmann

In 'Monetary policy challenges for Turkey in the EU accession process', Fatih Özatay explains Turkey's fight against fiscal dominance and its impressive recovery thanks to its large primary fiscal surplus. The author goes on to explain the implementation of inflation targeting and its effects and challenges, and how to face up to a new period of monetary dominance in the context of large capital inflows and de-dollarization. This is excellent, and a 'must read' for anyone interested in the topic.

The chapter mainly summarizes policies of the post-crisis period, and lays out future challenges facing Turkey during the first phase of the accession to European Union, that is, the candidacy period.

The main emphasis is on fiscal dominance, and a simple model is developed to emphasize the importance of fiscal discipline and market expectations. I will first summarize the chapter and leave the discussion of the model to the end.

The post-crisis policy actions include: large primary surpluses (6.5 per cent of GDP) and the associated decline in public sector deficit (from approximately 15 per cent to 7 per cent); movement away from foreign currency denominated (and indexed) and floating domestic debt stock; Central Bank instrumental independence; significant restructuring of state and problematic private sector banks; and other structural reforms such as the reforms of the agricultural support system. Monetary policy, in the meantime, has been 'implicit inflation targeting', so the goal of the Central Bank of Turkey (CBT) is to achieve price stability. Since the crisis in 2001, the exchange rate regime has been floating, and the CBT intervenes only to prevent excess volatility (almost all of these interventions so far are in the direction of buying). At the same time, the CBT has been accumulating reserves through pre-announced auctions, but not in an aggressive manner.

As a result of these policy actions, the economy has been improving. Inflation (and also inflation expectations) is down to single digit; growth has recovered (9.9 per cent in 2004, but this clearly is above the potential); debt to GDP ratio is declining. However, these general trends have been vulnerable to political news and investor perceptions, as exemplified by a few episodes. The current account deficit is also significantly deteriorating. Despite efforts on the fiscal side, monetary policy post-crisis (2001–04) has suffered from fiscal dominance, so the CBT was not altogether free to raise the interest rates when it saw fit.

There are a couple of concerns regarding monetary policy conduct for the coming couple of years. Turkey has signed a new stand-by agreement with the IMF, which aims to continue the fiscal discipline. By the beginning of 2006, the CBT will implement formal inflation targeting, which requires a very firm control over the short-term interest rates. While the effect of fiscal dominance is expected to decline further, it still imposes challenges to monetary policy, particularly in raising the policy rate. Therefore, the chapter hints that managing expectations via improved communication policies is also very important.

Reverse dollarization and capital inflows (mostly portfolio and loan flows) are expected to put further appreciation pressure on the new lira. The CBT is planning to respond through a combination of interest rate reduction and reserve accumulation.

Finally, during the EU accession process, the CBT needs to improve its balance sheet by reducing foreign currency liabilities, and abandoning its role as a commercial bank in accepting deposits from workers abroad. In addition the CBT Law has to be amended to better align with the European Central Bank.

The transition to the European Union is happening at a time when Turkey is in transition from fiscal dominance to monetary dominance. The model presented in the paper concludes that fiscal discipline and the management of expectations are key to making this transition successfully. While this is definitely true, I would argue that the composition of debt is another key component in the drive to end fiscal dominance.

The Özatay Model

The model presented in the paper is elegant and full of intuition. It has a two-period model where the government borrows in the first period, and pays back in the second period by either taxation (x) or repudiation (θ). The loss function of government is a function of taxes and repudiation (transaction cost of repudiation). The debt is assumed to be indexed so there is no incentive for inflation, and accordingly, inflation expectations are set to zero. Therefore, this model captures only the fiscal policy decision on how to finance debt. Implicitly it assumes no role for monetary policy.

Government minimizes this loss function subject to the budget constraint, which is affected by a shock (u) in the second period. The government observes the shock, but the private agents when they lend to government in the first period do not observe it. They set their expectation regarding the repudiation, and determine the rate of interest accordingly. The higher their repudiation expectations, the higher is the lending rate (R).

Taking these expectations as given, government chooses the percentage of debt to be repudiated optimally. The first order condition to this problem determines a threshold level of shock at which government prefers to repudiate as a function of expected repudiation. If the shock turns out to be lower than this threshold, then the government does not repudiate. Note that in case of repudiation, there is an additional cost of credibility loss (c). On the other hand, private agents are rational, and set their expectations given the probability of the shock exceeding this threshold and the respective expected level of repudiation. An important point here that the higher the repudiation expectations, the lower is the threshold, and so the expectations are self-fulfilling. The model has multiple equilibria. For a given level of credibility cost and other fundamentals, the threshold level for the shock and associated debt repudiation can take two values; the bad equilibrium being the low threshold and high repudiation.

The paper draws two conclusions from this model: first the importance of fiscal discipline, through lower debt accumulation (in the first period), and second the importance of expectation management.

I like the intuition provided by the model and would like to make a simple extension in order to highlight the role of debt denomination in the determinants of the threshold and of the determinants of the multiple equilibria. But first let me stress an important point: the relationship between the size of the debt and fiscal dominance is more subtle than the model suggests.

Debt Ratios and Credit Ratings

The Özatay model implies a fairly straightforward relationship between the size of the debt, the repudiation threshold and credibility. This implies that we should observe a relatively close relationship between debt ratios and perceptions of repudiation risk as captured, for example, in credit ratings. Figure 5C.1 shows the relationship between the net public debt to GDP ratio and foreign currency rating of sovereign debt according to Standard and Poor's on average for the period 1992–99. We choose this period because it precedes the Turkish crisis.

Figure 5C.1 clearly shows a very weak relationship at best. The IMF's most frequent clients – Turkey, Brazil and Argentina – appear with similar debt ratios as AAA-rated countries such as Japan, the United Kingdom, Australia and the United States. It might be argued that the reason for this is that public debt is not really paid out of GDP, but only out of the portion of GDP that the government can tax. Since developed countries have a larger tax base, they can service a larger debt. Therefore, a more adequate numeraire for the debt may be the net debt to tax revenue ratio.

Figure 5C.2 shows the relationship between the credit ratings and this measure. The picture does not change much. There is an enormous gap

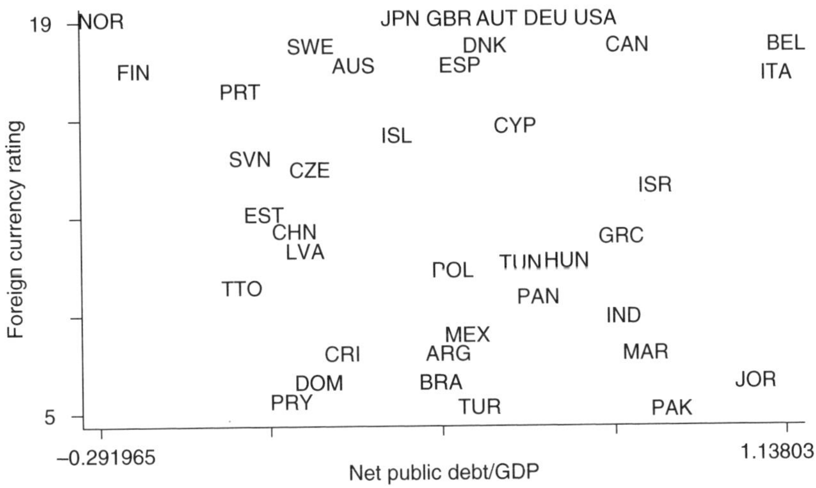

Figure 5C.1 *Foreign currency rating and net public debt to GDP ratio, average 1992–99*

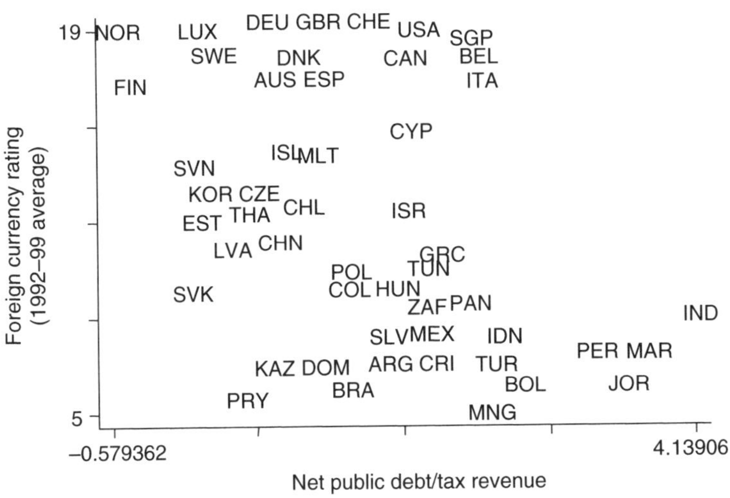

Figure 5C.2 *Net public debt to tax revenue, average 1992–99*

between the ratings of Turkey, Indonesia, Mexico and Argentina on the one hand, and Italy, Belgium Canada and the United States.

So, the question is clear. Why is it that the same debt ratio maps into such different credit ratings? What can countries do – besides lowering their debt ratios – to improve their creditworthiness?

A Simplified Model

To understand the issues involved, let us create the simplest possible model that puts the necessary elements on the table. Let x be the debt to tax revenue ratio of a country.

$$x = \frac{D}{tY}i \tag{5C.1}$$

where D is the stock of debt, Y is output, i is the interest rate on the debt, and t is the tax rate, making x the debt service to tax revenue ratio.

Let us assume a default behaviour similar to the Özatay model: if the variable x exceeds some ceiling $\bar{x}$. If $x > \bar{x}$, then the government is better off defaulting and not paying anything. If $x < \bar{x}$ then debts are serviced in full. Assume investors are risk neutral and hence demand that – in expected terms – they earn the risk-free rate of return ρ. Under these conditions, the contractual interest rate i will have to be high enough to compensate for the states of the world in which the government defaults:

$$i = \frac{\rho}{Pr(x < \bar{x})}. \tag{5C.2}$$

This model can be solved graphically in the space x vs. i (Figure 5C.3). Equation (5C.1) is a ray through the origin with a slope equal to the debt to tax revenue ratio. Equation (5C.2) is a hyperbola that starts at $i = \rho$ and approaches infinity as x approaches $\bar{x}$. We draw three versions of Equation (5C.1) at three different debt to tax revenue ratios. If the ratio is low, the probability of default is essentially null and the interest rate approximates the risk-free rate. If the ratio is very high, there is no combination of x and i that satisfies both equations; the country is bankrupt and has no access to finance. In an intermediate situation, the model exhibits multiple equilibria. The good equilibrium will imply some interest rate spread over the risk-free rate, while the bad equilibrium involves bankruptcy.[1]

Consider now two countries with the same expected debt to tax revenue ratio but where one has a larger variance of x than the other. Figure 5C.4 graphs the difference. It tells us that even though the two countries have the same debt ratio, one country may well have a high credit rating while the other might be bankrupt.

What Would Allow Turkey to Overcome this Fiscal Dominance?

To overcome fiscal dominance, the government must address the level and volatility of x. Looking at this model, one potential method is to lower the

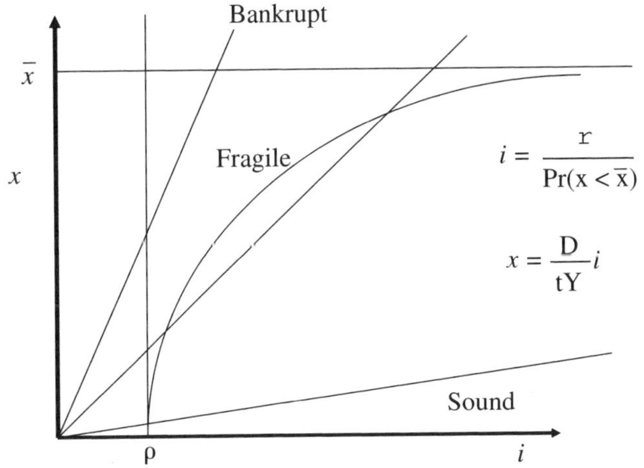

Figure 5C.3 A graphical solution of the model

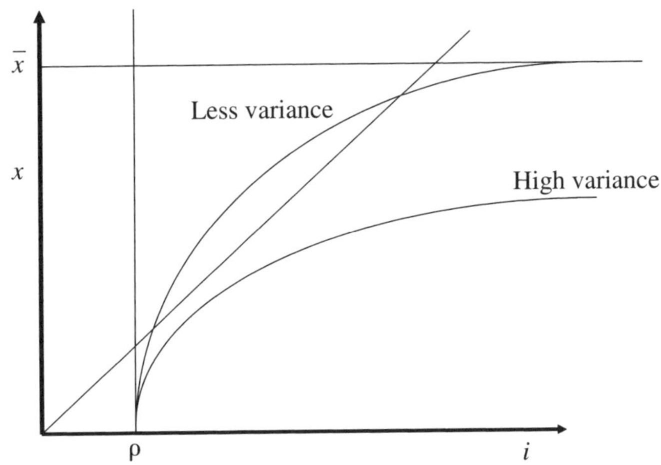

Figure 5C.4 The effect of volatility in the debt to tax revenue ratio

debt to GDP ratio, D/Y. However, the relationship between the debt to GDP ratio and country credit rating is quite weak, suggesting that improving it alone would not help debt sustainability.

Now, what is behind the volatility in x? One possibility is that the denominator, that is, tax revenues, may be volatile. This may happen either because real GDP or the terms of trade may be volatile. However, as I have shown in a previous paper (Hausmann, 2003), this is usually only a fraction of the variance in x. The most important component comes from the volatility in debt service. Consider the composition of debt service and its implications for risk. Debt can be either short-term debt or long-term debt and it can be denominated either in local currency or in foreign currency. If, the debt is long-term fixed-rate and in local currency, the government knows exactly how much it will cost: it knows the stock of inherited debt and the contractual interest rate. If, instead, the debt is short-term, the government knows the stock it inherits, but does not know the interest rate at which it will need to roll over the debt. If the debt is long-term fixed-rate but is in dollars, the government knows how many dollars it will have to pay, but is uncertain about the cost in terms of domestic resources, as it does not know what the real exchange rate will be in the future.

Developed countries have most of their public debt at large maturities and in local currency. By contrast, the debt of many developing countries – Turkey included – is mostly either short-term in local currency, making the variance of x dependent on the variance of the short-term interest rate, or long-term in dollars, making it dependent on the volatility of the real exchange rate.

As Eichengreen et al. (2004) have shown, the collapse in the capacity to pay in most emerging market debt crises comes much more from a drastic weakening in the real exchange rate than from a collapse in GDP. In short, for a country with a public debt composed of short-term local currency instruments and dollar liabilities, the volatility in the debt service to tax revenue ratio is dominated by the volatility of the real exchange rate and of the real interest rate and this dwarfs the volatility of real government revenues. Moreover, the real exchange rate, the real interest and output have the worst possible co variance structure from the point of view of the variance of x. Typically, in bad times, the currency weakens, output is low and real interest rates are high, creating a triple shock to x.

Implications for Turkey

The previous model suggests that improving creditworthiness can be done either by reducing the debt to tax revenue ratio or by lowering the volatility of that ratio. The first strategy requires sustaining a large primary fiscal surplus for a long time. The second strategy requires working on the structure of the debt, extending its duration and denominating it in a unit that better matches the characteristics of the tax revenue flow. Local currency or CPI-indexed obligations are typically better than dollar debt. However, they may also involve a higher interest rate. This creates a trade-off between reducing the expected cost of the debt and reducing its volatility. My impression is that finance ministries and parliaments tend to place too much emphasis on the expected cost and not enough on the volatility aspect. Much more discussion should go into a debt management strategy that optimizes on this margin.

In sum, the chapter by Fatih Özatay presents a great overview of the achievements and challenges facing Turkey and its monetary and fiscal authorities. The chapter includes a very interesting model that highlights the importance of fiscal discipline and credibility. In this note, I have tried to emphasize that beyond the issue of fiscal discipline as reflected in the level of the deficit and the debt, much of the problems of credibility and creditworthiness are associated with the structure of the debt in terms of denomination and duration. Working on this margin may help improve macroeconomic stability in a socially more efficient manner.

Note

1. The first point where the straight line crosses the hyperbola is stable, but the second one is unstable. The economy will either move to the good equilibrium or go bankrupt.

References

Hausmann, R. (2003), 'Good credit ratios, bad credit rating: the role of debt structure', in G. Kopits (ed.), *Rule-based Fiscal Policy in Emerging Markets*, London: Macmillan, pp. 30–52.

Eichengreen, B., R. Hausmann and U. Panizza (2004), 'Currency mismatches, debt intolerance and original sin', NBER Working Paper 10036, to be published in an NBER Conference Book (forthcoming in the *Journal of Economic Development*).

6. Monetary and fiscal policy in Poland during EU accession

Lucjan T. Orlowski*

6.1 INTRODUCTION

The main objective of this chapter is to review the fiscal and monetary policies of Poland for EU accession and to extract their guiding precepts. Only the most essential aspects of fiscal and monetary convergence are examined, with some attention to institutional convergence. An in-depth analysis of institutional convergence falls beyond the boundaries of this study, as its main focus is on the systemic foundations of macroeconomic stabilization policies during the economic transition and in the course of preparations for EU accession. The chapter also examines policy options for the post-accession macroeconomic policy strategy which will focus on preparations for adopting the euro.

This chapter underlines the importance of imposing and preserving fiscal discipline and political stability on the road to Poland's accession to the EU which took place on 1 May 2004, and to the future adoption of the euro. Special attention is drawn to fiscal restructuring and bringing about compliance with the European System of National Accounts. In addition, the implications of the expected net transfers from the EU budget are examined.

The evolution of Poland's monetary policy, which is marked by a passage from a simple policy framework based on a hard peg to a modern, complex regime based on direct inflation targeting (DIT) is examined. With respect to the tasks related to monetary convergence to the euro, the main analytical hypothesis is that the current strict DIT regime is not conducive to adopting the euro. It needs to be more flexible, that is, to incorporate the objective of stabilizing the exchange rate, which, in essence, means the lowering of the exchange rate risk premium. However, it is advised that the central bank's main commitment to the low inflation target is preserved until the very end of the euro convergence.

As this study focuses on the systemic foundations of macroeconomic stabilization policies it does not provide a detailed account of the actual record of real and nominal convergence in Poland. The gradual advancement of

Poland's monetary policy has been so far consistent with the task of laying down solid foundations for a functioning market economy that is capable of withstanding competition within the EU. At the final stage of convergence to the euro, Poland's monetary policy needs to be focused on achieving the convergence benchmarks embodied in the Maastricht criteria. In general terms, this means embracing an appropriate policy framework and a sequence of policy adjustments that will be most conducive to achieving price stability and securing a smooth currency convergence. A proposal for such policy adjustments is outlined in section 6.5 on the sequencing of monetary policy for euro adoption.

The analysis begins with a brief description of the stabilization policies in the early 1990s which established an effective springboard for convergence to the EU/EMU. Next, fiscal policy considerations are discussed, followed by the overview of systemic changes in Poland's monetary policy framework. Subsequently, alternative policy proposals for convergence to the euro are presented. A synthesis of the key policy prescriptions concludes this chapter.

6.2 ADVANCING MACROECONOMIC POLICY: FROM TRANSITION TO EU ENTRY

Policies for the accession of Poland to the EU constitute an extension of stabilization strategies that were enacted at the start of the country's swift transition from central planning to a market economy in the early 1990s. At that time, the initial infusion of economic stability posed a particularly serious challenge to the Polish economy which was plagued by a severe crisis stemming directly from the pitfalls of the communist central planning. Among the most severe rigidities of the previous system were highly regulated prices set at ceilings far below market equilibrium, monopoly structures in the financial and industrial sectors, the execution of the central plan as the main business objective, non-convertible currency, and the arbitrarily-imposed trade ties with the former Soviet bloc (Bruno, 1992).

In order to underpin a decisive departure from the inefficiencies of central planning, the now democratically elected, independent Polish Government instituted a radical programme of reforms in January 1990. The so-called Balcerowicz Plan was aimed at dismantling the most obstructive foundations of the former command economy system (Bruno, 1992; Sachs, 1993). The main precepts of this radical reform programme included far-reaching price liberalization, full currency convertibility on current account, trade liberalization, fiscal consolidation and monetary policy discipline to be achieved through the hard peg of the Polish zloty to the US dollar. As a consequence of massive price liberalization and the incomplete decomposition and privatization of state-owned monopolies, producer and retail prices quickly rose to market equilibrium levels, which spurred a short-lived corrective inflation that on the CPI-basis reached 640 per cent in 1989 and declined below the annual rate of 50 per cent only in 1992.

The early 'shock therapy' programme in Poland was based on the reformers' notion of 'extraordinary politics', that is, that the collapse of the old system created a unique window of opportunity that provided the government with the special mandate to proclaim such reforms. Consequently, strong political will and commitment led to the establishment of the foundations of macroeconomic stability and, later, to the pursuit of macroeconomic reforms for EU accession. Polish society, having vivid memories of the inefficiencies and high social costs of central planning, has strongly endorsed the reform programme and supported the government's commitment to laying down foundations for a functioning market economy capable of withstanding competition within the EU. However, social endorsement has not always been unequivocal as the transition to a deregulated and privatized economy has carried considerable welfare costs, such as the gradual increase in (mostly structural) unemployment that reached a monthly average of 19.8 per cent in the peak year of 2002. (Table 6.1)

The early macroeconomic stabilization policies brought about considerable progress in economic stability in the late 1990s during the more advanced stage of transition and active preparations for the EU accession. This progress is reflected by the set of indicators presented in Table 6.1.

The real economy and financial sector annual data show that Poland's monetary authorities have been able to contain inflation while avoiding economic recession. Yet, in the post-accession period, there is still a need to improve fiscal discipline and enact long-term labour market reforms to ease persistently high unemployment.

As shown in Table 6.1, between 1997–2004 the CPI-based inflation fell from double digits to a low single digit level that in the last three reported years was roughly commensurate with the Maastricht price stability benchmark qualifying for accession to the euro.[1] Yet the ambitious disinflation effort succeeded only by applying very high real interest rates which undoubtedly contributed to a significant slowdown of economic growth in 2001–02. In that period, the inflation adjusted short-term credit refinancing rate was maintained at extremely high levels by the National Bank of Poland (NBP). This rate, which serves as the policy reference rate for NBP, reached its peak of 9 per cent in 2001. Having contained inflation at a sustainable 'safe' level through such highly restrictive monetary policy, the NBP was able to reduce the real short-term interest rate to 2.1 per cent by 2004. Most importantly, high real interest rates helped establish a necessary degree of

Table 6.1 *Selected measures of real and financial stability in Poland, 1997–2004*

	1997	1998	1999	2000	2001	2002	2003	2004
Real GDP growth rate	6.8	4.8	4.1	4.0	1.0	1.4	3.8	5.5
Unemployment rate (ILO def.)	10.9	10.2	13.4	16.4	18.5	19.8	19.2	19.1
CPI-inflation rate	14.9	11.8	7.3	10.1	5.5	1.9	0.8	3.5
PPI-inflation rate	12.5	7.5	5.8	7.9	3.1	0.5	1.6	7.0
Real compensation per employee (whole economy)	21.0	16.0	13.2	11.9	8.0	2.6	4.2	4.8
Labour productivity (% growth)	3.9	2.4	7.0	6.4	1.7	3.7	16.6	6.1
Unit labour cost (% growth)	16.5	13.2	5.8	5.2	11.5	−1.6	−9.7	−2.2
Govt. budget deficit (% GDP)	−4.0	−2.1	−1.4	−0.7	−3.8	−3.6	−3.9	−5.6
Govt. total debt (% GDP)	n.a.	n.a.	40.1	36.8	36.7	41.1	45.4	47.2
Real short-term int. rate (avg. monthly)	8.4	7.7	6.0	7.1	9.0	6.7	4.8	2.1
Bank lending (avg. m. growth rate)	33.8	27.0	26.7	17.6	7.4	4.0	7.1	n.a.
M3 (avg. m. growth rate)	27.9	24.7	20.1	11.9	9.2	−2.0	8.8	9.4
Current account (% GDP)	−3.7	−4.1	−7.6	−6.0	−2.8	−2.6	−2.2	−1.5
PLN-per-EUR (ECU) (avg. monthly rate)	3.54	3.92	4.23	4.01	3.67	3.86	4.40	4.53
Consumer confidence index[a]	103	100	85	80	75	76	77	n.a.
New job offers in '000[b]	916	751	681	606	406	550	730	n.a.

Notes:
a. Ratio of optimistic to pessimistic consumers periodically compiled and reported by *Rzeczpospolita Daily*.
b. Reported by search firms.

Sources: Central Statistical Office, Warsaw; Eurostat; Ministry of Finance, *Macroeconomic Survey* (various issues); *Rzeczpospolita* (various editions).

policy credibility that contributed to declining inflation expectations, which subsequently suppressed wage demands in both the public and the private sector, as reflected by the parallel to inflation decline in real compensation per employee. At the same time, a combination of large direct investments from domestic and foreign sources coupled with a squeeze on wage demands from high unemployment led to the accelerated growth of labour productivity outpacing the growth of labour compensation. As a result, unit labour costs that were still rising during the 1997–2001 period began to recede over the following three years. Along with the monetary easing that has been evident over the recent two-year period, the bank lending and the M3 money aggregate returned to higher growth rates reinvigorating investment and real GDP growth. As a consequence, the declining unit labour costs along with a brisk demand for credit and rising investment have recently contributed to the growth of industrial production and exports. They have also reduced unemployment, albeit at a very slow pace.

As shown in Table 6.1, the macroeconomic stability conditions are strongly correlated with consumer confidence and job market conditions. High unemployment along with a wage squeeze is not conducive to raising consumer confidence and promoting growth in consumption. In fact, the recently renewed economic recovery is mainly driven by the increase in private investment and to some extent by sharply rising exports to the EU. These spending components contribute to a recognizable job creation, as reflected by new job offers, and to a significant improvement in the current account position. Nevertheless, a sustainable economic recovery is likely to depend on higher consumer spending, which is yet to materialize. As a matter of fact, it may take some time for consumer to recover from the recent drop in confidence about future economic conditions. One may hope that the stimulus of the EU accession-related income transfers along with the continuous commitment to a macroeconomic stability that no longer needs to be supported by excessively restrictive policies may ultimately improve this situation.

The disciplined economic policies of the centre-right coalition government pursued prior to 2001 did not help Poland's now-notorious political instability. After losing the 2001 election, the Solidarity government was replaced by a coalition of left-wing parties that was initially less inclined to maintaining fiscal discipline. However, the required commitment to a sound fiscal policy, which is a pillar of the post-EU accession strategy and its focus on convergence to the euro, forced the new socialist government to outline a budget-balancing strategy in its April 2004 Convergence Programme in a way conducive to euro convergence. Nonetheless, unpopular budget cuts cannot immediately improve the confidence of the general public in the economy.

In retrospect, both the pre- and the post-EU accession strategies can be viewed as a logical extension of the macroeconomic policies pursued during the economic transition of the 1990s. The process of navigating the macroeconomic convergence becomes increasingly challenging in Poland due to unfavourable demographic dynamics and the high social costs of disciplined policies.

One may further argue that in order to be successful and sustainable, the convergence strategy in Poland must be highly transparent. Since the

EU/EMU accession entails certain short-run costs, while its benefits are likely to materialize only in the long-run, there is a serious risk that the net social costs will outweigh the benefits in the near future, which may erode public endorsement of the convergence programme. Thus, to sustain social endorsement, the government must fully explain the detailed aspects of the convergence strategies and the expected social costs. Therefore, a high transparency of the convergence programme is a key prerequisite for its overall success.

6.3 FISCAL CONVERGENCE

The main aim of fiscal policy adjustments in Poland in the course of preparations for EU accession included laying the ground for a sustainable fiscal discipline, developing compliance with the European System of National Accounts and reforming the tax system in congruence with Chapter 10 (Taxation) of the EU *acquis communautaire*. Accordingly, Poland had to develop institutional capacity in the area of taxation and in aligning its legislation with that of EU. A number of changes were made in the area of indirect taxation, including VAT and excise duties. In general terms, without resorting to the complexity of the detailed tasks, special attention had to be paid to the scope and definition of VAT rates, particularly the extensive use of zero-rating, as well as to the vast tax exemptions.[2] New taxes were introduced with regard to direct taxation, such as a 20 per cent tax on interest income and a temporary 2 per cent tax on outward capital movements by residents only. Still, on EU entry in May 2004, Poland had to raise VAT and excise taxes on a number of products (including construction materials, tobacco, mineral oils and so on), which induced a short-lived jump in inflation.

As a member of the EU, Poland is obliged to provide the European Commission with a detailed report on fiscal stance, including general government deficit and debt statistics, in accordance with the European System of National Accounts (ESA'95). In preparation for such reports, the Polish Government has redesigned its budgetary process by distinguishing between three basic subsectors of public finance: central government, local government and social security funds. This distinction has proven to be very helpful for enacting appropriate fiscal reforms aimed at decentralizing the budget, streamlining funds to their main intended recipients and broadening the tax base.

Furthermore, in order to develop compliance with the EU budgetary procedures, the Polish Government has enacted a series of legislative documents, including the 'Medium Term Public Finance Strategy' of September 2003, the 'Programme of Consolidation of Public Expenditures' of January 2004 and 'The Convergence Programme' of April 2004. A driving force behind the ongoing fiscal consolidation is the officially declared plan to adopt the euro in the unspecified future. Accordingly, the fiscal authorities are now facing the challenge of maintaining fiscal discipline as stipulated by the EU Stability and Growth Pact (SGP). They are compelled to demonstrate efforts to bring the budget deficit down to 3 per cent in relation to GDP. In fact, the SGP has been used extensively by the authorities as a politically convenient excuse for maintaining fiscal discipline. Aspirations to enter the eurozone provide a compelling justification for the government to reduce budgetary expenditures and, at the same time, to maintain taxes at a level low enough to promote growth and high enough to balance the budget. For instance, in response to the deteriorating budgetary situation, the government adopted an expenditure rule (in 2002) according to which central government spending was limited to an annual rise of 1 per cent above the inflation rate. The need to undergo further fiscal consolidation is quite apparent. As evidenced by the data in Table 6.1, there is a propagation of the general government budget deficit to the degree exceeding the maximum allowed benchmark of 3 per cent of GDP and an increase in public debt getting closer to the maximum of 60 per cent of GDP stipulated by the Maastricht Treaty.

The pronounced acceleration of the general government budget deficit over the past three years poses a serious problem to the implementation of fiscal consolidation. Yet, there are some optimistic developments. The expected increase in economic growth is likely to ease pressure on the deficit and to stabilize the level of indebtedness. Taking into account the faster economic growth that has been recently driven by high investment and exports, the projected decline of the deficit from 4.2 per cent of GDP in 2005 to 1.5 per cent in 2007, as specified in the Polish Government Convergence Programme (Republic of Poland, 2004) appears to be realistic. In order to achieve this ambitious goal, the government needs to reduce expenditures on public administration and on selected social programmes. While it is reasonable to expect reduced costs of debt servicing due to steadily declining interest rates, spending cuts on public administration and social programmes will have to be decisively administered. However, spending cuts on social programmes may pose a major challenge as they are politically unpopular and risky.

Major challenges to a successful implementation of fiscal consolidation can be detected by analysing recent budgetary developments and projections within the three basic subsectors of the budget, as defined by ESA'95 (Table 6.2).

Large central government expenditures that are allocated predominantly to social programmes and public administration constitute the primary

Table 6.2 *General government budget balance and public debt in Poland (ESA'95) (% GDP)*

	2000	2001	2002	2003	*2004*	*2005*	*2006*	*2007*
General government budget balance	−1.8	−3.5	−4.0	−4.1	*−5.7*	*−4.2*	*−3.3*	*−1.5*
Central government	−1.9	−4.2	−4.6	−5.6	*−6.4*	*−5.5*	*−4.8*	*−3.4*
Local government	−0.5	−0.3	−0.3	−0.2	*−0.2*	*−0.4*	*−0.4*	*−0.1*
Social security funds	+0.6	+1.0	+0.9	+1.7	*+0.9*	*+1.8*	*+1.9*	*+2.0*
General government debt	36.6	36.7	41.2	45.3	*49.0*	*51.9*	*52.9*	*52.3*

Note: Ministry of Finance forecasts are indicated in italics.

Source: Republic of Poland, Convergence Programme, Warsaw, April 2004.

area of concern within the consolidated budget. In the 2004 budget, the consolidated expenditures in relation to GDP reached 23.5 per cent for social transfers, 15.1 per cent for public administration, 9 per cent for public consumption and only 2.9 per cent for interest on public debt (Republic of Poland, 2004, p. 26). Since the central government conducts the majority of spending on social programmes and public administration, its deficit level reached 6.4 per cent while the local government deficit was only 0.2 per cent of GDP. Needless to say, the success of fiscal consolidation projected in Table 6.2 will depend on the government's ability and determination to reduce spending in these politically sensitive areas.[3] At the local level, the major accession-related task for governments is to improve their absorptive capacity to dispose the EU transfers related to common agricultural policy (CAP) subsidies as well as structural and cohesion funds.

A serious challenge to fiscal consolidation stems from rising transfers related to the ageing population. The need to foster EU tax coordination and to restructure the public finances in order to prepare for the budgetary consequences of the ageing population was emphasized in the 1999 Commission report on economic and structural reform in the EU (Cardiff II). The gravity of the ageing problem in Poland can be illustrated by the ratio of retired to working age population, which is expected to rise from the recently reported level of 62 per cent in 2002 to the projected 69 per cent in 2010 and 94 per cent in 2050. The large share of retirees, along with the negative growth of the country's total population will impose a serious rigidity on social spending programmes.

Within the next several years, the social security fund is expected to show a rising surplus (Table 6.2). This projected surplus stems from the ongoing contributions to the special 'open retirement funds' by the insured persons, while the first payments from these funds are scheduled to take place only in 2009 (the intended year for adopting the euro!). The changes adopted by the EU Council of Ministers at its March 2005 meeting which now allow for accounting contributions to these funds as budget revenues are of crucial importance for Poland, as their inclusion may help the country meet the Maastricht budget deficit criterion by the time of examination for the euro entry.

In addition to reforming government expenditures, policymakers face the challenge of determining an optimal level and pragmatic rules of taxation. The efforts in this direction pursued by the Polish Government are encouraging. Since 1999, the Ministry of Finance has reduced corporate income taxes from 27 to 19 per cent, closing at the same time many of the existing tax loopholes. It also allowed for accelerated depreciation allowances and established a special fund for restructuring the budgetary obligations of some firms with serious liquidity problems. Personal income taxes have been also significantly reduced. In spite of these reductions in tax rates, tax revenues have been growing steadily. The 2006 Budget Proposal introducing a linear flat tax of 18 per cent (submitted in March 2005 by the Ministry of Finance), if passed by the parliament, should further contribute to higher tax revenues as it will likely translate into accelerated income growth. In addition, tax revenues should also benefit from the existing institutional improvements in tax administration and in the collection system.

It should be further noted that the official programme of fiscal consolidation (Republic of Poland, 2004) will materialize only in the absence of serious threats to financial stability. Among these might be the possibility of a significant depreciation of the Polish zloty (PLN) as well as the danger of renewed inflationary expectations that would have to be restrained by the NBP with higher interest. These would contribute to higher debt service payments. Other dangers include a possible propagation of political risk stemming from the recent corruption scandals involving government officials. In addition, the erosion of public support for the government due to its inability to reduce rampant unemployment may further exacerbate the political risk.

Poland's membership of the EU is likely to improve the state of public finance due to the injection of net transfers from the EU budget. The main components of estimated transfers and contributions to the EU budget are shown in Table 6.3. It should, however, be noted that the presented data are only estimates based on the results of accession negotiations at the December 2002 Copenhagen Summit and do not necessarily reflect actual appropriations and payments which are yet to be disclosed.

Table 6.3 EU appropriations for Poland (EUR million in 1999 prices)

	2004	2005	2006
Total transfers to Poland	**2983**	**5068**	**5498**
Pre-accession assistance	970	823	509
Agriculture (total):	425	1512	1934
1. market measures	135	350	377
2. direct payments	0	557	675
3. development of rural areas	290	605	882
Structural actions (total):	860	1776	2107
1. structural funds	834	1482	1578
2. cohesion funds	26	294	529
Internal policies (total):	285	407	499
1. existing policies	154	266	359
2. institutions building	38	48	46
3. Schengen instrument	93	93	94
Special cash-flow facility	443	550	450
Total contributions by Poland to EU budget	**−1579**	**−2454**	**−2520**
Traditional resources	−123	−213	−214
VAT resource	−194	−304	−310
GNI resource	−1114	−1707	−1752
British rebate	−148	−230	−244
Net appropriations balance	**1404**	**2614**	**2978**

Source: Kawecka-Wyrzykowska (2004).

Among the receipts, structural funds are the largest initial component, followed by CAP subsidies. Structural funds are designated mostly for infrastructural projects thus the data in Table 6.3 reflect mostly granted funds, which may take longer to be actually transferred. The assistance to the agricultural sector is expected to rise in proportion to other receipt items during the years following formal EU entry. CAP payments to Polish farmers will reach respectively 55, 60 and 65 per cent of the level of corresponding subsidies in the incumbent EU member states during the first three years of membership (Kawecka-Wyrzykowska, 2004). This is because full-scale assistance would be extremely expensive for the EU, given the large size of Polands' agricultural employment, which comprised 19.6 per cent of total employment in 2002, while the sector's value added was merely 3.1 per cent of total value added in the economy (European Commission, 2003). Direct payments to farmers are expected to be the fastest growing component among all transfer categories. In contrast, the assistance aimed at strengthening internal policies will rise at a slower rate. These funds are particularly needed in the early stage of membership as they are aimed at strengthening institutions indispensable for the implementation of Community legislation and for reinforcing border controls (the Schengen Instrument). In addition, Poland will receive large direct cash transfers (the Special cash-flow facility) designated to improve absorptive capacity and to cushion the fiscal burden of the initially large contributions to the EU budget.

Poland's contributions to the EU budget will come from three main sources: (1) traditional resources (mainly revenues from import duties and agricultural duties); (2) value added tax (VAT) revenues; and (3) resources based on gross national income (GNI). Along with other EU member states, Poland is also obliged to contribute to the 'British rebate', or special VAT refund scheme granted by the EU to the United Kingdom.

In summary, Poland is expected to be a net recipient of sizeable funds from the EU, estimated at 0.8 per cent of GDP for 2004, gradually increasing to 1.3 per cent for 2005 and 1.4 per cent for 2006.[4] However, the large scale of these net transfers is not automatically guaranteed, as some delays in CAP subsidies due to bureaucratic hurdles have already been reported. In addition, some structural fund appropriations that have already been granted may take some time to materialize.

There is still another important dimension of the necessary fiscal reform, that is, the determination of an appropriate type of fiscal governance. Following a proposal made by Hallerbeg et al. (2004), fiscal policies can be bound by rules, thus following a contract approach, or they can be based on a high degree of finance ministry discretion, consistent with the delegation approach to budgetary decisions. These authors show empirically that, based on the EU experience, coalition governments are more likely to employ the contract approach, while single or majority party governments are likely to delegate the budgetary decision-making power to finance ministers in order to alleviate the coordination problem that is inherent in the fiscal policy process. One may reasonably assume that these findings will also hold for Poland in the near future. Therefore, the design of a fiscal policy framework that is consistent with the delegation approach seems to be a viable option, since a majority party government is likely to prevail in the future, after the recent wave of consolidation of major political parties in Poland.

6.4 MONETARY CONVERGENCE

Concurrently with fiscal reforms, Poland's monetary policy regime had to undergo equally challenging changes during the course of preparations for the EU accession. The general objective of these adjustments was to ensure a sustainable degree of financial stability in the spirit of one of the three Copenhagen EU accession criteria, namely, the task of establishing a well-functioning market economy. In order to generate a stable financial environment, the NBP faced the task of devising a proper monetary policy framework that would, at minimum, effectively contain inflation, mitigate exchange rate risk, and help establish a solid record of policy credibility.

Defining such a policy framework turned out to be an intricate task at the early stage of preparations for the EU accession. The exchange rate anchor had to be given up relatively early, as the combination of currency peg and high, double-digit inflation led to real currency appreciation, which in turn exacerbated Poland's current account deficit and deteriorated the risk structure of capital inflows (the move toward short-term and away from long-term capital inflows). The evolution of the country's exchange rate system is synthesized in Table 6.4.

The hard peg to the US dollar was instrumental in the elimination of the corrective inflation and the diffusion of the monetary overhang in the early 1990s. Once an acceptable degree of financial stability appeared in sight, the monetary authorities enacted a soft peg in the form of the crawling devaluation with a 7 per cent symmetric band around the parity rate on 16 May 1995. A further notable move toward greater flexibility coincided with the official inception of direct inflation targeting in January 1999. DIT is a monetary policy framework that is based on the assumption of long-term price stability as the official policy goal through designation of the official

Table 6.4 Evolution of Poland's exchange rate regime

	Exchange rate regime (Classification)*	Currency basket	Tolerance band
1 Jan. 1990–17 May 1991	hard peg (2)	9500 PLZ/USD	–
17 May 1991–30 Apr. 1993	crawling peg (5)	USD	+/– 1%
1 May 1993–15 May 1995	crawling peg (5)	5-currency basket	+/– 1%
16 May 1995–24 Feb. 1998	crawling band (9)	basket	+/– 7%
25 Feb. 1998–31 Dec. 1998	crawling band (9)	basket	+/– 10%
1 Jan. 1999–11 Apr. 2000	crawling band (9)	EUR 55% USD 45%	+/– 15%
12 Apr. 2000–present	free float (13)	–	–

Note: * The exchange rate classification number is based on the 'fine course' determined by Rogoff et al. (2003, p. 55), and it ranges from the least flexible (no separate legal tender = class 1) to most flexible exchange rate arrangements (free float, class 13; freely falling, class 14, and dual market in which parallel market data is missing, class 15).

Source: Own compilation based on *IMF Annual Report on Exchange Rate Arrangements and Restrictions* (various editions).

target ranges for the inflation rate (Orlowski, 2000). DIT focuses directly on achieving the predetermined inflation target and by this virtue it differs from alternative monetary policy regimes that may aim at lowering inflation in an indirect way, for instance by focusing first on exchange rate stability objective.

With the inception of DIT, the exchange rate band was effectively widened to 15 per cent around the central parity, which in essence denoted abandonment of the exchange rate based monetary regime. Once price stability became the predominant objective of monetary policy, the crawling devaluation mechanism could no longer be maintained since the forced currency weakening promulgated inflation via the active exchange rate channel of policy transmission. In recognition of this threat to price stability, Poland's monetary authorities finally embraced a free float in April 2000.

After abandoning the exchange rate anchor in May 1995, the NBP was prompted to search for alternative regimes that would uphold the necessary policy discipline. As a consequence, it carried out several, rather ineffective policy experiments, beginning with interest rate targeting in 1996. This option proved to be flawed in the presence of sizeable capital inflows which induced large shocks to market interest rates in a continuously vulnerable financial system. For this reason, the NBP moved to monetary base targeting in 1997 and M2 money growth targeting in 1998. These alternatives proved to be ineffective as well, particularly in the presence of some contagion effects from the Asian and Russian financial crises which infused large shocks to money balances. In addition, monetary targeting was not practical in an economy undergoing fast-paced monetization, as reflected by the overall growth of the M2 to GDP ratio from 15 per cent in 1991 to 43 per cent in 2002. As a result, money balances grew at a much faster rate than GDP, contributing to a large instability of income elasticity of money demand, which in turn made monetary targeting entirely implausible (Orlowski, 2004a).

Under such circumstances, inflation targeting appeared to be the only viable option for Poland as it could offer an effective disciplinary anchor for monetary policy which got lost after departing from the currency peg; it could also underpin the authorities' commitment to disinflation (Jonas and Mishkin, 2003; Eichengreen, 2005; Orlowski, 2005a). However, the inception of the DIT framework in January 1999 took place at the earliest possible time or, as argued by Christofferssen and Wescott (1999), even slightly prematurely, since inflation was still running at double-digit levels and a prior record of price stability had not yet been established. In spite of the violation of some prerequisites for the DIT inception specified as essential by Mishkin (2000), the DIT framework was embraced by the NBP as it entailed important benefits, which prevailed over the possible costs of missing overly optimistic inflation targets (Orlowski, 2001b, 2005a). Among the important DIT benefits is the explicit commitment to achieve ambitious and transparent inflation goals. An additional DIT advantage that is particularly pertinent to convergence to a common currency system is its ability to insulate the economy from balance of payments shocks. For this reason, DIT is an attractive policy option for Poland since inflation fluctuations there are predominantly influenced by nominal supply-side shocks, rather than real exchange rate and balance of payments shocks, as is empirically proven by Dibooğlu and Kutan (2005). In hindsight, it is well-established in the literature that inflation targets must be believable in order to be effective; therefore, DIT could be introduced in Poland only when a minimum degree of 'foundational credibility' was in place.

Due to the key strategic objective of reducing inflation from double-digits to a low, sustainable level, a strict variant of DIT (as defined by Svensson, 1999) with year-end, narrowly defined targets appeared to be a viable policy option. As summarized in Table 6.5, the early variant of DIT was based on a strict CPI-inflation target of 6.6–7.8 per cent specified for December 1999. It seemed to be quite ambitious, considering the fact that the average monthly inflation in 1998 was 11.8 per cent (as shown in Table 6.1). The initial actual target realization was far from being satisfactory, as December 1999 inflation was 2 per cent higher than the upper bound of the

Table 6.5 Evolution of direct inflation targeting in Poland

	Type of DIT	Main target(s)	Actual annualized CPI inflation	Corresponding exchange rate regime	Policy transparency	Formal plan for euro adoption
Initial regime Jan. 1999	Strict, single target	CPI inflation: Long-term goal Year-end target 6.6–7.8% Dec.99	Dec. 1999: 9.8%	Crawling devaluation with a wide band	Medium, published inflation reports, no published forecast	n.a.
Current regime (2005)	Strict, single target	CPI inflation trajectory: midpoint 2.5%, +/− 1% tolerance band	Dec. 2004: 4.4%	Pure float	High, published: inflation projection, reports and policy assumptions	Yes, date not specified

Source: Own compilation based on NBP, *Monetary Policy Assumptions* (various issues).

operating target. It should also be noted that a similar mismatch was repeated in the second year of DIT. The target for December 2000 was set at 5.4–6.8 per cent, while actual inflation reached 8.5 per cent. In response to such prolonged target overshooting, the NBP took decisive policy steps to contain inflation to the degree commensurate with its ambitious target. It applied an extremely restrictive course of monetary policy as reflected by the average monthly real short-term (three months T-bill) interest rate, which reached 8.48 per cent during the January 1998–December 1999 period, and an even higher rate of 8.60 per cent between January 2000 and June 2001. As a result, actual inflation at the end of 2001 fell to 3.6 per cent, well below the target of 6–8 per cent, and at the end of 2002 it fell to 1.9 per cent, also considerably below the 4–6 per cent target. In essence, it took approximately two and a half years to bring inflation down to the desired level, or in other words, to align private sector inflation expectations with the central bank forecast. Needless to say, the NBP was successful in establishing a solid ground for policy credibility and price stability, but it did so by applying an extremely restrictive course of monetary policy, which, without doubt, entailed certain welfare costs and contributed to the economic slowdown in 2001–02.

Once a satisfactory degree of financial stability was achieved, the NBP altered the DIT strategy by replacing year-end operating targets with the trend consistent linear inflation trajectory. By doing so, it has improved the transparency and credibility of the DIT regime, in line with the arguments introduced to the literature by King (1996). The trajectory approach is believed to be superior to the year-end target specification for several reasons. The stable linear target allows for expanding the time horizon of low inflation expectations, thus it contributes to lower long-term interest rates and promotes private sector long-term borrowing and investment. Moreover, the linear trajectory is also beneficial for resisting political pressures on the central bank, which is not the case of year-end targets. In principle, the trajectory maintains a steady course that is not subject to negotiations, while year-end targets are annually adjusted, which leaves them exposed to potential pressures.

The current linear inflation trajectory in Poland is formulated in consistency with the precepts of monetary convergence to the euro. The midpoint is set at 2.5 per cent – the rate roughly corresponding with the anticipated Maastricht reference rate. It is surrounded by the symmetric tolerance band of 1 per cent that allows for accommodating possible temporary shocks. In addition, the current DIT policy is highly transparent, as the NBP regularly publishes quarterly and annual inflation reports and discloses its inflation projection to the general public. However, the current strict DIT framework is not fully consistent with the key objectives of monetary convergence to the euro as it focuses exclusively on the inflation target and does not incorporate an exchange rate stability objective. The NBP is continuously committed to the pure float, perhaps due to the technical difficulties in determining a long-run sustainable market equilibrium rate of PLN in EUR terms that could serve as a targeted reference rate.

Modifications of Poland's and other new EU member states' monetary regimes on the final passage towards the euro will have to take into account a number of potential risks (Masson, 1999; Schadler, 2004). Chief among them are risks attributed to asymmetric shocks. In order to mitigate such risks, a clear and transparent monetary policy framework needs to be in place as it will be imperative to explain how disruptions to financial conditions will be dealt with. The effective absorption of exogenous shocks becomes particularly important upon entry to ERM II. Fiscal and monetary policies need to provide capacity to support the limits on exchange rate volatility imposed by this interim mechanism preceding euro adoption. Monetary policy in particular needs to embrace a mechanism of responding to contagion effects of possible future financial crises. For this reason, a continuous commitment to inflation targeting would offer a necessary cushion for absorbing such effects.

It should be noted at this juncture that there is a compelling historical record of Poland's effective responses to international financial crises. Two particular episodes underscore this claim:

(1) the policy of counteracting possible contagion effects of the August/September 1998 Russian financial crisis, and
(2) the strategy of dealing with the May 2004 'accession syndrome'.

The Russian moratorium on repayment of foreign currency debt declared on 29 August 1998 triggered a wave of contagion effects to international financial markets. Poland dealt with the shock relatively well as the government launched the so-called 'de-coupling' from Russia (Orlowski, 2001a). Empirical research on this subject proves that such a strategic approach was indeed successful. There were only mild contagion effects from Russia to Poland (as oppose to the Czech Republic or Hungary) in the aftermath of the crisis (Linne, 1999), particularly with respect to eurobonds (Gelos and Sahay, 2001). This is because the PLN and the Russian ruble displayed a limited co-movement at the time, which was not the case with other Central and East European currencies. In addition, depreciation of PLN in USD terms was considerably milder relative to the fall of other currencies in the region, which might have stemmed from the NBP decision to cut interest rates at that time, while other central banks were forced to raise them in order to prevent capital outflows (Orlowski,

2001a). In an effort to insulate the Polish financial market from Russia's troubles, the NBP, by cutting interest rates, sent a 'signalling effect' to international markets, underpinning the country's systemic resilience to external nominal shocks. In sum, thanks to its strong policy base, Poland weathered relatively well the shocks from the Russian financial crisis (as well as from the 1997–98 Asian crisis) that reverberated across the international financial markets, while many other countries fell victim to recession. Its currency remained strong, capital inflows continued and the banks were not imperilled.

Another noteworthy incidence of asymmetric shocks is related to the May 2004 EU accession. However, that was much easier to deal with than the 1998 disturbance, as Poland's economic policy base and its systemic foundation had become considerably stronger, resulting in the overall nominal shock being milder. The scope of the accession-related real and nominal disturbance is reflected by changes in the selected macroeconomic variables shown in Table 6.6.

Table 6.6 The impact of Poland's EU accession on selected macroeconomic variables

	2003	2004 1st Q	2004 2nd Q
Real GDP[a]	3.8	6.9	6.1
Private consumption[a]	3.1	3.9	3.8
Public consumption[a]	0.4	1.3	2.5
Gross fixed capital formation[a]	−0.9	3.5	3.6
Exports[a]	14.7	16.0	11.3
Imports[a]	9.3	11.3	8.3
Real industrial output[a]	8.6	18.7	16.6
Real labour productivity[a]	11.4	19.6	17.0
Average nominal wage in industry[a]	3.0	6.6	4.8
Unit labour cost of industry (nominal)[a]	−7.5	−10.9	−10.5
Unemployment rate (ILO definition)	19.6	20.7	19.1
HICP inflation	0.7	1.8	3.4
Broad money growth rate (nominal)[a, b]	1.5	5.3	7.1
Net domestic bank credit growth rate (nom.)[a]	5.2	6.2	4.6
PLN per EUR (period average)	4.40	4.78	4.69

Notes:
a. Year-on-year percentage change (period average).
b. Including foreign currency deposits.

Source: Central Statistical Office, Warsaw and Österreichische Nationalbank, *Focus on Transition*, 2/2004.

The real economy effects directly related to the EU accession included the acceleration of real GDP and industrial production in the first quarter of 2004. This phenomenon has been labelled by Polish economic analysts as 'the accession syndrome', which was based on a switch in industrial activity from the second to the first quarter, in anticipation of strong demand following EU entry. Other real effects included a strong increase in investment, a surge in exports of mainly industrial and food products, and a decline in imports. Notably, exports of food products rose significantly, contrary to prior warnings from some politicians and economists about a possible influx of less expensive Western food products following the accession. These fears were entirely unfounded. It should also be noted that in April 2004, on the eve of the accession, exports rose at the annual rate of 41.6 per cent, while imports fell by 58.4 per cent, primarily due to the alignment of tariffs with the common EU rates.

In addition to shocks in the real sphere, EU accession triggered a mild inflation shock, caused mainly by higher VAT rates and excise taxes now aligned with the EU norms. The inflation effect was additionally exacerbated by the decline in domestic supply of certain food products and construction materials which became unexpectedly popular among the buyers in other EU countries.[5] In consequence, HICP inflation rose from the average rate of 0.7 per cent in 2003 to 3.4 per cent in the second half of 2004. Broad money balances showed a proportional increase to inflation.

Without doubt, EU accession augmented economic growth in Poland, primarily through a surge in industrial production, investment and exports. This is a welcome development for monetary authorities because the national income acceleration helps reduce welfare losses stemming from the restrictive DIT policy. As a consequence, the EU accession shocks did not have to be curtailed with active monetary policy responses.

Looking ahead, monetary policy during the final stage preceding euro adoption will have to rely on the continuous commitment to disinflation, but also incorporate the task of lowering the exchange rate risk. Therefore, the strict variant of DIT is no longer a viable policy option during the active preparations for the euro adoption.

6.5 SEQUENCING OF MONETARY POLICY FOR THE EURO ADOPTION

There is a common understanding in the literature that the adoption of the euro means relinquishing monetary autonomy of the candidate countries, but clearly there is no uniform 'one-size-fits-all' policy prescription. The ongoing debate on this subject includes a variety of proposals ranging from calls for a leap to unilateral euroization to a gradual convergence relying on an extended application of flexible DIT. One may however notice that with the passage of time the difference between an early euroization and a gradual policy adjustment becomes increasingly irrelevant. The bottom line is that Poland as well as other new member states will enter the euro system as soon as they complete the fiscal, monetary and institutional convergence prescribed by the Maastricht criteria and go through the two-year minimum quarantine imposed by the ERM II rules.

The proponents of an early adoption of the euro, including Bratkowski and Rostowski (2001), Buiter and Grafe (2002) and Begg et al. (2003) have identified a number of benefits from such a bold move. They include elimination of exchange rate risk, lower transaction costs, a more favourable climate for foreign direct investment and a clear framework for macroeconomic policy discipline. However, a rush to a common currency may also entail large costs, particularly if the institutional convergence is far from complete (Nuti, 2002), making the domestic financial system vulnerable to default risk. In addition, the country entering a common currency automatically relinquishes its monetary autonomy and the option to use exchange rates as a tool for countering nominal (mostly demand-side) shocks. In essence, an early euroization by itself is unlikely to resolve the remaining problems related to the institutional fragility of the real economy and the financial system; neither will it guarantee a necessary fiscal discipline. This is because the institutional deficiencies have much deeper roots than simply the monetary regime, and fiscal problems are a function of more than just the availability of seigniorage revenues (Eichengreen, 2005). For these reasons, the timing of formal euro adoption should matter less than having in place well-coordinated monetary, real and institutional convergence policies. A few more years of monetary independence combined with disciplined fiscal policies may allow enough time for the necessary completion of institutional reforms.

The qualified reservations against a premature euroization along with the Maastricht due process prescribed by the EU authorities have motivated researchers to seek more gradual policy solutions to euro convergence. In general terms, the gradualist proposals are based on various degrees of departure from the current strict DIT regimes. They infuse greater flexibility to various degrees by placing more or less balanced weights on inflation and exchange rate stability targets. It becomes clear that the two extreme solutions, namely a hard peg versus a full flexibility, which have been dismissed in the literature as viable policy options (Fischer, 2001) cannot work for the eurosystem accession programme. This is because the euro convergence necessitates a dual focus on price stability and the exchange rate stability. Thus flexibility becomes pragmatic in order to avoid extreme solutions. A critical task is to cope with the exchange rate risk as well as the interest rate risk, which entails an inflation risk premium when adjusted to real interest rates (Orlowski, 2003; Holtemöller, 2005).

An extreme solution assigning preference to the exchange rate stability is proposed by Bofinger and Wollmershäuser (2001, 2002) who advocate adopting a monetary regime based on flexible exchange rate targeting.[6] In their policy scenario, exchange rate stability becomes the key policy objective, while price stability plays a secondary role, as it is presumed to be derived from less volatile exchange rates. However, their scenario implies a significant regime switch which might prove to be too costly for those new member states that follow DIT policies, including Poland, the Czech Republic and, to a lesser degree, Hungary. This is because the primary commitment to the exchange rate stability objective may entail frequent and costly foreign exchange market interventions, particularly if financial markets continue to be vulnerable to large nominal shocks. In addition, it is highly uncertain whether the monetary regime focusing on exchange rate stability (even in a stricter form than the one allowed by the ERM II) will actually contribute to price stability. This is because the exchange rate channel of monetary policy transmission in the larger NMS such as Poland is rather unstable (Orlowski, 2003).[7] Therefore, a smooth transmission of a more stable exchange rate into low inflation is not automatically guaranteed upon assigning a strong priority to the exchange rate stability.

A more balanced weighting of inflation and exchange rate stability targets is examined by Jonas (2004). His analysis focuses on the 'dual target–one instrument' policy scenario as an extension of the present DIT regimes, which assigns equal importance to the inflation and exchange rate stability targets. A central bank uses interest rates as a single policy instrument to hit these, at times conflicting, targets. Possible conflicts between them may arise in the presence of a simultaneous currency appreciation and high inflation, when both are triggered by large capital inflows. In such a case, a deliberate lowering of the domestic currency value requires an interest rate cut, which in turn may jeopardize realization of the inflation target. Also, higher interest rates aimed at containing inflation are likely to aggravate currency appreciation and promulgate exchange rate volatility. The conflicts between the targets are particularly severe in the presence of the Balassa-Samuelson effect.[8] A number of studies have argued that such an effect is prevalent and contributes to high inflation in transition economies (Buiter and Grafe, 2002; Begg et al., 2003; Mihaljek and Klau, 2004; De Grauwe and Schnabl, 2005). Others, particularly Égert et al. (2003), show that this effect has now evaporated. A compelling empirical study by Blaszkiewicz et al. (2004) shows that the Balassa–Samuelson effect in Poland has been negligible since 1999, while before that it was quite pronounced, contributing between 1.5 and 2 per cent to annual inflation. With the expiration of this effect, the potential conflicts between inflation and exchange rate stability targets have little merit; so do the arguments for an early euroization that are derived on the basis of this effect. The strongest weight on inflation targets is assigned in yet another scenario of gradual policy adjustments proposed by Orlowski (2005b) who introduces the monetary policy framework based on relative inflation forecast targeting (RIFT). This operational framework is a forward-looking extension to the DIT regimes pursued currently by Poland as well as by several other new member states. It constitutes a viable solution for the final passage towards the euro as it is likely to facilitate monetary convergence and ensure a smooth entry to the euro system. Stating briefly, RIFT is based on targeting the differentials between the candidate country and the eurozone inflation forecasts, thus, in essence it is an advanced variant of DIT, which in principle focuses on domestic inflation only. Therefore, RIFT allows for combining a decisive commitment to disinflation with an effective price convergence. In this advanced policy framework the inflation forecast differential becomes the key operating target of monetary policy, while exchange rate stability is treated only as one of the main indicator variables, and not as an auxiliary operating target. RIFT enables policymakers to focus exclusively on price stability as the main objective of monetary convergence. It therefore assigns priority to lowering inflation when a possible conflict between disinflation and exchange rate stability arises.

To underpin a successful monetary convergence to the euro, the proposed RIFT framework assumes a perfect identity between the long-term inflation targets of the candidate country and the eurozone. Therefore, in practical terms, the candidate's inflation based on HICP (harmonized index of consumer prices) can reasonably be expected to converge to less than 2 per cent by the time of the euro adoption. Instrumentalization of RIFT is based on the 'instrument dichotomy', that is, on interest rate adjustments in response to changes in the differential between domestic and eurozone inflation forecasts, while exchange rate stability is secured with foreign exchange market interventions. Thus, in essence, RIFT is an elaborate combination of a forward-looking DIT and a managed float. Shocks to the exchange rate can be curtailed with higher interest rates only if they are destabilizing (elevating the exchange rate risk premium) and potentially threatening to realization of the inflation target.[9]

It seems plausible and necessary to modify the current Polish monetary regime based on strict DIT and the pure float by introducing solutions consistent with the proposed RIFT strategy. The NBP is presently well equipped to consider such regime adjustment as it has developed an advanced inflation forecasting methodology, as well as the ability to apply efficiently indirect instruments of monetary policy implementation. In addition, the RIFT framework is unlikely to interfere with the ramifications of ERM II, since it also incorporates the precept of lowering the exchange rate risk premium. Nevertheless, the operational viability of such a complex monetary policy framework is yet to be tested.

In sum, the current strict DIT in Poland needs to be modified by incorporating the exchange rate stability objective. The same is required of other DIT countries pursuing monetary convergence to the euro (Jonas and Mishkin, 2003; Jonas, 2004; Orlowski, 2005b). Regardless of the selected direction of DIT modification, Poland can and should avail itself of the exchange rate flexibility afforded by ERM II, providing that the 'standard' plus-minus 15 per cent band of currency fluctuations will be upheld, rather than the 'normal' band of 2.25 per cent prescribed originally by ERM I. It is, however, likely that the future band surrounding the official reference rate to the euro will be asymmetric, that is, wider on the appreciation side and much narrower (perhaps only 2.25 per cent) on the depreciation side. Under such circumstances, a tighter than normal stance of monetary policy will be required in order to accommodate the prevalent exchange rate risk premium within the short-term interest rate target. Moreover, frequent interventions will be called for in the presence of even relatively mild shocks to the exchange rate. Due to these constraints, remaining in the ERM II beyond the required two-year minimum period is not advisable.

Reformulation of Poland's monetary policy upon entry to ERM II will take into consideration a proper choice of the PLN per EUR reference rate. This choice is critically important. In principle, the official 'de jure' reference rate should correspond with the 'de facto' rate that is technically perceived as a sustainable long-run equilibrium rate as determined by the financial markets. Mis-specification of the official rate at a level considerably different from the market rate may lead to a number of destabilizing consequences. These can be encapsulated as follows:

(1) A considerably stronger official rate than the market rate may precipitate short-term capital inflows, exacerbating inflation. The unfavourable risk structure of capital inflows may result from expectations of an official devaluation.
(2) A weaker official rate is likely to inflate the domestic value of foreign currency debt and raise the default risk.
(3) Mis-specification of the official rate may effectively narrow the exchange rate tolerance band, as its perceived percentage boundaries

will surround the long-run equilibrium market rate, not the official rate. This scenario will necessitate more frequent, seemingly asymmetric foreign exchange market interventions.

(4) A mis-specified official rate may function as a magnet, pulling the market rate in a wrong, suboptimal direction (Schadler, 2004) that may in turn threaten realization of the inflation target.

(5) In general terms, the greater gap between the official rate and the market equilibrium rate is likely to exacerbate exchange rate risk (volatility) as its choice will appear to be less credible and expectations of rate resetting will arise. This risk will be greater if the official rate is too weak, as the markets are likely to expect either resetting of the official rate or an easing of monetary policy in an effort to adhere to its actual level. The easier policy stance will be suboptimal as it will clearly jeopardize realization of the inflation target.

Considering the serious dangers of the official rate mis-specification, its careful and thorough estimation and determination becomes a critical task. So far, the attempts to determine the long-run equilibrium rate for Poland have produced mixed and rather inconclusive results. Steady-state equilibrium conditions modelled by Golinelli and Rovelli (2005) have arrived at some suggestions. In contrast, Johanssen cointegration tests employed by Orlowski (2004a) have not produced conclusive results due to frequent regime changes, a high exchange rate risk premium and unstable key monetary variables applied in cointegrating equations.

There is a further complexity in the determination of the appropriate reference rate. This stems from the prevalent risk premia that are built into the equilibrium exchange rate (Orlowski, 2004b). Uncertainties about fiscal discipline and political stability may bring down the perceived market rate and demand a much tighter monetary policy stance, that is, higher interest rates encapsulating such exogenous risk premia. Needless to say, the choice of the official rate must take into account the political risk and the fiscal policy outlook. In order to accommodate these risks, the official rate might be set at a slightly higher level than the long-run equilibrium rate perceived by the market.

The process of selecting the appropriate official ERM II reference rate for PLN will require the application of correct procedures and robust formulas. It is imperative not to determine the reference rate too soon (as appears to be the case in Hungary) in order to alleviate the above-listed serious dangers of its mis-specification.

To reiterate, it is advisable for Poland to continue the reliance of its monetary policy on inflation targeting to the very end of the euro convergence process. Yet, DIT needs to become more flexible in order to incorporate the exchange rate stability objective into the framework that will preserve the NBP commitment to price stability. The proposed RIFT framework appears to be viable for accomplishing these tasks.

6.6 A SYNTHESIS: IMPLICATIONS FOR FUTURE EMU ACCESSION

Several important prescriptions for successful EU accession and an effective pursuit of convergence to the euro have emerged from the Polish experience. At the forefront is the ability to maintain fiscal discipline, which is a function of the authorities' resilience to political pressures on government spending. Equally important is the development of a simplified, transparent tax system, ultimately leading to adoption of a flat linear tax set at a low rate that is competitive within the EU.

With respect to adjustments to the monetary regime, the objective of disinflation and price stability plays a critical role for balancing the attainment of long-term economic growth and convergence to the euro. A flexible DIT framework is believed to be conducive to achieving such balance. At the initial stage of convergence to the EU and EMU, a strict DIT supported with high real interest rates was effective for lowering inflation to a manageable, single-digit level. Yet, a strict DIT is not conducive to convergence to the euro, as the task of achieving exchange rate stability, or more precisely, lowering the exchange rate risk will have to be incorporated in the DIT framework.

Following Orlowski (2005b), this study advocates, for the final passage towards the euro, the RIFT framework which prioritizes realignment of the inflation forecast of the candidate and the eurozone and incorporates the exchange rate stability objective (within the ERM II) as the policy indicator variable. Adherence to the relative inflation forecast is achieved primarily by adjusting the differential between domestic and eurozone interest rates, while exchange rate stability is secured with cautiously applied foreign exchange market interventions.

In general terms, a successful completion of the EU/EMU convergence process necessitates enacting policies that would reinforce resilience to various types of financial risk. Among others, disciplined fiscal and monetary policies need to be in place in order to mitigate the exchange rate risk. In the case of Poland, such policies are entirely possible providing that a stable political climate, free of populist claims and pressures, is preserved.

NOTES

* I thank Ali M. Kutan and Jürgen von Hagen for valuable comments and suggestions. I remain, however, solely responsible for the views presented in this chapter and for all possible errors and omissions.

1. The Maastricht inflation convergence requirement calls for a euro-candidate country to achieve sustainable inflation not exceeding 1.5 per cent above the average of the three lowest inflation EU members. The benchmark rate specified in the October 2004 ECB Convergence Report was 3.4 per cent.
2. Specifically, the Ministry of Finance had to introduce equal taxation of goods irrespective of their origin, as well as special VAT schemes concerning travel agents, second-hand goods, investment in gold, and farm products. Special tax provisions had to be granted for intra-Community transactions (European Commission, 2003). During the course of accession negotiations, Poland was granted a number of derogations on VAT adjustments for residential housing, selected goods and periodicals (until the end of 2007), as well as a large number of food products (until the end of April 2008).
3. Yet, the ability to cut spending will pose a major challenge. Following argument by von Hagen et al. (2001), fiscal adjustments are successful if they are based on cuts in transfer payments, rather than on tax increases or cuts in government consumption and investments. Due to unfavourable demographic developments and strong political pressures, there is currently little chance of reducing transfer payments in Poland.
4. Own estimates based on Ministry of Finance data.
5. For instance, in June 2004 domestic prices of beef rose by 13.8 per cent, poultry 13.4 per cent, butter 7 per cent and sugar 48.5 per cent (additionally triggered by hoarding purchases), relative to their level from the year before. Prices of building materials rose 11.4 per cent.
6. A similar recognition of the exchange rate stability target is presented by Natalucci and Ravenna (2003).
7. A more optimistic view is presented by Golinelli and Rovelli (2005) whose empirical tests indicate a seemingly robust channel of monetary policy transmission in the Central European countries, including Poland.
8. The Balassa–Samuelson effect is based on the argument that there is a productivity shock in the tradable goods sector in an open economy, which in turn drives up wages of non-tradables and subsequently contributes to chronic inflation.
9. The debate on designing an optimal monetary policy framework for convergence to the euro focuses mainly on relative importance of low inflation versus exchange rate stability targets. However, equally challenging, yet inadequately addressed, are issues of appropriate choices of policy instruments. The advocated separation of interest rate adjustments in response to the inflation target, and market intervention aimed at stabilizing the exchange rate seems to be in opposition to the calls for integrating both instruments presented by the proponents of using the monetary conditions index (MCI) as an instrument rule. Such a rule is, for instance, endorsed for Turkey by Us (2004). Yet, its implementation might be technically very difficult, if not impossible, at least in the case of Poland. Because the MCI rule-based policy may send conflicting signals about the policy stance, it may inhibit central bank credibility.

REFERENCES

Begg, D., B. Eichengreen, L. Halpern, J. von Hagen and C. Wyplosz (2003), 'Sustainable regimes of capital movements in accession countries', CEPR Policy Paper No. 10.

Blaszkiewicz, M., P. Kowalski, L. Rawdanowicz and P. Woźniak (2004), 'Harrod-Balassa–Samuelson Effect in selected countries of Central and Eastern Europe', Report No. 57, Warszawa: Centrum Analiz Społeczno-Ekonomicznych (CASE).

Bofinger, P. and T. Wollmershäuser (2001), 'Is there a third way to EMU for the EU accession countries?', *Economic Systems*, **25** (3), 253–74.

Bofinger, P. and T. Wollmershäuser (2002), 'Exchange rate policies for the transition to EMU', in Urmas Sepp and Martin Randveer (eds), *Alternative Monetary Regimes in Entry to EMU*, Tallinn, Estonia: Bank of Estonia, pp. 95–132.

Bratkowski, A. and J. Rostowski (2001), 'Unilateral adoption of the euro by EU applicant countries: the macroeconomic aspects', in Lucjan T. Orlowski (ed.), *Transition and Growth in Post-communist Countries: The Ten-year Experience*, Cheltenham, UK and Northampton, MA, USA: Edward Elgar, pp. 125–47.

Bruno, M. (1992), 'Stabilization and reform in Eastern Europe: a preliminary evaluation', IMF Staff Papers, **39** (4), 741–77.

Buiter, W. and C. Grafe (2002), 'Patching up the Pact – some suggestions for enhancing fiscal sustainability and macroeconomic stability in an enlarged European Union', CEPR Discussion Paper No. 3496.

Christofferssen, P.R. and R.S. Wescott (1999), 'Is Poland ready for inflation targeting?', IMF Working Paper No. 99/41, Washington, DC: International Monetary Fund.

De Grauwe, P. and G.G. Schnabl (2005), 'Nominal versus real convergence: EMU entry scenarios for the new member states', *Kyklos*, **68** (4), 537–55.

Dibooğlu, S. and A.M. Kutan (2005), 'Sources of inflation and output movements in Poland and Hungary: policy implications for accession to the economic and monetary union', *Journal of Macroeconomics*, **27** (2), 107–31.

Égert, B., I. Drine, K. Lommatzsch and C. Rault (2003), 'The Balassa–Samuelson effect in Central and Eastern Europe: myth or reality?', *Journal of Comparative Economics*, **31** (3), 552–72.

Eichengreen, B.L. (2005), 'Can emerging markets float? Should they inflation target?', in Rebecca L. Driver, Peter J.N. Sinclair and Christoph Thoenissen (eds), *Exchange Rates, Capital Flows and Policy*, London: Routledge, pp. 10–38.

European Commission (2003), *Comprehensive Monitoring Report on Poland's Preparation for Membership*, Brussels, November 5.

Fischer, S. (2001), 'Exchange rate regimes: is the bipolar view correct?', *Journal of Economic Perspectives*, **15** (2), 3–24.

Gelos, R.G. and R. Sahay (2001), 'Financial market spillovers in transition economies', *Economics of Transition*, **9** (1), 53–86.

Golinelli, R. and R.R. Rovelli (2005), 'Monetary policy transmission, interest rate rules and inflation targeting in three transition countries', *Journal of Banking and Finance*, **29** (1), 183–201.

Hallerberg, M., R. Strauch and J. von Hagen (2004), 'The design of fiscal rules and forms of governments in European Union countries', ECB Working Paper No. 419.

Holtemöller, O. (2005), 'Uncovered interest rate parity and analysis of monetary convergence of potential EMU accession countries', *International Economics and Economic Policy*, **2** (1), 33–63.

Jonas, J. (2004), 'Euro adoption and Maastricht criteria: rules or discretion?', University of Bonn–Centre for European Integration Studies (ZEI): Working Paper B14/2004.

Jonas, J. and F.S. Mishkin (2003), 'Inflation targeting in transition economies: experience and prospects, NBER Working Paper No. 9667.
Kawecka-Wyrzykowska, E. (2004), 'Financial conditions of Poland's accession to the European Union', in Elżbieta Kawecka-Wyrzykowska and E. Synowiec (eds), *Poland in the European Union*, Warsaw: Foreign Trade Research Institute, pp. 13–36.
Kenen, P. and E.E. Meade (2003), 'EU accession and euro: close together or far apart?', Institute for International Economics: International Policy Briefs No. PB03-9.
King, M.A. (1996), 'How should central banks reduce inflation? Conceptual issues', in *New Challenges for Monetary Policy: A Symposium sponsored by the Federal Reserve Bank of Kansas City*, Kansas City, Missouri, pp. 53–92.
Linne, T. (1999), 'Contagion effects of Central and East European currency crises', Halle Institute for Economic Research, Discussion Paper No. 96.
Masson, P.R. (1999), 'Monetary and exchange rate policy of transition economies of Central and Eastern Europe after the launch of EMU', IMF Policy Discussion Paper No. PDP/99/5, Washington, DC: International Monetary Fund.
Mihaljek, D. and M. Klau (2004), 'The Balassa–Samuelson effect in Central Europe: a disaggregated analysis', *Comparative Economic Studies*, **46** (1), 63–94.
Mishkin, F.S. (2000), 'Inflation targeting in emerging-market countries', *American Economic Review: Papers and Proceedings*, **90** (2), 105–9.
Natalucci, F.M. and Federico Ravenna (2003), 'The road to adopting the Euro: monetary policies and exchange rate regimes in EU accession countries', mimeo, Washington, DC: The Federal Reserve Board – Division of International Finance.
Nuti, M.D. (2002), 'Costs and benefits of unilateral euroisation in Central Eastern Europe', *Economics of Transition*, **10** (3), 419–44.
Orlowski, L.T. (2000), 'Direct inflation targeting in Central Europe', *Post-Soviet Geography and Economics*, **41** (2), 134–54.
Orlowski, L.T. (2001a), 'Central European economies in the aftermath of the Russian payment crisis', in Lucjan T. Orlowski (ed.), *Transition and Growth in Post-communist Countries: The Ten-year Experience,* Cheltenham, UK and Northampton, MA, USA: Edward Elgar, pp. 148–65.
Orlowski, L.T. (2001b), 'From inflation targeting to the euro-peg: a model of monetary convergence for transition economies', *Economic Systems*, **25** (3), 233–51.
Orlowski, L.T. (2003), 'Monetary convergence and risk premiums in the EU accession countries', *Open Economies Review*, **14** (3), 251–67.
Orlowski, L.T. (2004a), 'Money rules for the eurozone candidate countries', *Journal of Policy Modelling*, **26** (7), 817–37.
Orlowski, L.T. (2004b), 'Exchange rate risk and convergence to the euro', University of Bonn-Centre for European Integration Studies (ZEI), Working Paper B25/2004.
Orlowski, L.T. (2005a), 'Monetary convergence of the EU accession countries to the eurozone: a theoretical framework and policy implications', *Journal of Banking and Finance*, **29** (1), 203–25.
Orlowski, L.T. (2005b), 'Targeting relative inflation forecast as monetary policy framework for adopting the euro', William Davidson Institute Working Paper No. 754, University of Michigan School of Business.
Republic of Poland (2004), *Convergence Program*, Warsaw: Council of Ministers, www.mofnet.gov.pl, April 30.

Rogoff, K.S., A.M. Husain, A. Mody, R. Brooks and N. Oomes (2003), 'Evolution and performance of exchange rate regimes', IMF Working Paper No. 03/243, Washington, DC: International Monetary Fund.

Sachs, J.D. (1993), *Poland's Jump to the Market Economy*, Cambridge, MA: MIT Press.

Schadler, S. (2004), 'European macroeconomic challenges and EU enlargement', Paper to the 17 Symposium Moneda y Credito, Madrid, November 18–19.

Svensson, L.E.O. (1999), 'Inflation targeting as a monetary policy rule', *Journal of Monetary Economics*, **43** (3), 607–54.

Us, V. (2004), 'Monetary transmission mechanism in Turkey under the Monetary Conditions Index: an alternative policy rule', *Applied Economics*, **36** (9), 967–76.

von Hagen, J., A. Hughes-Hallett and R. Strauch (2001), 'Budgetary consolidation in EMU', Economics Paper No. 148, Brussels: European Commission.

COMMENTS

Ali M. Kutan

Orlowski reviews Poland's monetary and fiscal policy since the beginning of reforms initiated in early 1990s. He covers macroeconomic stabilization policies and policy strategies for adopting the euro, which is officially planned for 2009, with a particular emphasis on the current inflation targeting regime. The chapter includes useful lessons for other transition economies, as well as those that are currently in the process of negotiations for full European Union (EU) membership, such as Turkey and Bulgaria. The key conclusions and recommendations of the paper can be summarized as follows:

(1) Disciplined and effective coordination of monetary and fiscal policies are critical for Poland's timely adoption of the euro.
(2) Polish fiscal authorities face many challenges, including tax reforms, reducing the amount of future social transfers and public administration expenses, and pressures on the budget associated with an ageing population. Without fiscal discipline and sustainability, it would be hard to tackle these challenges effectively.
(3) In terms of monetary policy, the existing direct inflation targeting regime needs to be relaxed by allowing a reduction in the exchange rate risk premium within the Exchange Rate Mechanism (ERM) II through foreign exchange market interventions. A relative inflation forecast targeting policy that is based on adjusting the differential between domestic and euro zone interest rates should instead be adopted. However, the central bank's main goal should still be low inflation.
(4) A stable political environment, such as single-party government, fight against corruption, and a minimum level of populist pressures, needs to be promoted for a smooth transition to the euro zone area.

I would like to start with some suggestions to further improve the clarity of the chapter. First, the available empirical evidence on real and nominal convergence in the literature is in line with the chapter's recommendations.[1] A brief description of the evidence from related studies would therefore further strengthen the conclusions here. Second, the discussion on future revenue implications of net EU transfers needs to be expanded. For example, some empirical studies suggest that such funds may not necessarily improve economic growth and hence increase future tax revenues. Third, it would be useful to explain how the National Bank of Poland (NBP) estimates forecasts of inflation. Fourth, discussing the short-run costs and long-run benefits of the EU accession, using the experience of previous members, would be important for the NBP to assure the general public that the accession may indeed be welfare-inducing in the long run. This issue is especially important in inflation targeting economies, because the regime requires credible and transparent policies. Finally, the section on equilibrium real exchange rates needs a discussion of the econometric issues in estimating the real exchange rates.[2]

My second suggestion to improve and further motivate this chapter is to further discuss issues as to whether an inflation targeting regime is suitable for transition economies, such as Poland. For instance, some observers have argued that forecasting inflation in transition economies is difficult because of ongoing structural changes, inflation inertia, Balassa–Samuelson effects, and a lack of good knowledge of monetary transmission mechanism. In addition, central banks may not simultaneously achieve both a desired inflation target and 15 per cent band during the ERMII. Moreover, some of the accession countries have been quite successful in reducing inflation using alternative exchange rate regimes. For example, the Baltic States have implemented different versions of the currency board regime and reduced inflation to single digits. Perhaps more important, unlike other accession countries, including Poland, they do not have to change their existing regime to be able adopt the euro in the near future. These considerations make the effectiveness of inflation targeting, especially when it requires a regime change, questionable. Perhaps, the chapter could emphasize that an inflation targeting regime can be best viewed as one of the many alternative regimes available to the new EU members or candidate EU members for adopting the euro. Given their specific economic conditions and institutions, countries may choose a regime that best suits their needs in preparation for entering the euro zone.

In reading the chapter and related literature, I have recognized that many research questions regarding inflation targeting regimes may deserve further investigation. The following lists some of the important research questions that are empirical in nature:

(1) Is there an optimal timing of inflation targeting?
(2) Do countries with an *implicit* inflation targeting regime perform better in reducing inflation than those with an *explicit* inflation targeting regime?
(3) Do countries with non-inflation targeting regimes perform better than those of inflation targeting regimes?
(4) Is the evidence on inflation performance in inflating targeting countries sensitive to the inclusion of data on emerging, developing or developed countries?

(5) What are the key economic and political characteristics of countries that adopt an inflation targeting regime?
(6) Given the growing number of countries adopting inflation targeting regimes, should the International Monetary Fund (IMF) follow a different approach in terms of its advice to these countries? For example, given the importance of credible and transparent policies for such regimes, the IMF might focus more on designing reforms in these areas.

Overall, the chapter is well written and offers many useful lessons for policymakers in EU candidate countries and those in transition economies. One can summarize the lessons for Turkey as follows. First, the Central Bank of Turkey needs to continue coordinating its monetary policy with fiscal authorities, as well as maintaining its commitment to low inflation. However, the bank should also consider real exchange rate developments in its policy formulation, because exports play a key role in the Turkish economy. In addition, in terms of political stability, the outcome of the elections in 2007 will be critical. The current single-party government is committed to full EU membership. A new multi-party government in 2007 might endanger the existing political stability in the country and hurt Turkey's chances of being in the Union in the near future by deferring necessary reforms that the current government has been undertaking.

Notes

1. See, among others, Brada et al. (2005), de Grauwe and Schnabl (2004), Kočenda (2001), Kočenda et al. (2006) and Kutan and Yiğit (2004 and 2005).
2. For a discussion of these issues, see Égert and Kutan (2005) who edited a special issue on equilibrium real exchange rates in transition economies.

References

Brada, J.C., A.M. Kutan and S. Zhou (2005), 'Real and monetary convergence between the European Union's core and recent member countries: a rolling cointegration approach', *Journal of Banking and Finance*, **29**, 249–70.
Égert, B. and A.M. Kutan (2005), 'Exchange-rate economics in transition countries', *Economic Systems*, **29** (2), June, 123–9.
De Grauwe, P. and G. Schnabl (2004), 'Nominal versus real convergence with respect to EMU accession: how to cope with the Balassa–Samuelson dilemma?', European University Institute Discussion Paper RSCAS No. 2004/20.
Kočenda, E. (2001), 'Macroeconomic convergence in transition economies', *Journal of Comparative Economics*, **29**, 1–23.
Kočenda, E., A.M. Kutan and T. Yiğit (2006), 'Pilgrims to the euro zone: how far, how fast?', *Economic Systems*, **30** (4), December, 311–27.

Kutan, A.M. and T. Yiğit (2004), 'Nominal and real stochastic convergence of transition economies', *Journal of Comparative Economics*, **32**, 23–36.

Kutan, A.M. and T. Yiğit (2005), 'Nominal and real stochastic convergence: are the new EU members ready to join the euro zone?', *Journal of Comparative Economics*, **33**, 387–400.

7. Preconditions for a successful euro adoption

Paul De Grauwe*

7.1 INTRODUCTION

The conditions for successful entry into a monetary union have been hotly debated by economists. In order to clarify the issues, it is useful to make a distinction between long-run and short-run success. Success in the long run can be defined as membership in the monetary union that is sustainable in the long run. This is a situation in which the member countries consider the benefits of the union to outweigh their costs so that there are no incentives to leave the union. In a way it can be said that the equilibrium reached by the member countries is a Nash equilibrium.

Success in the short run relates to the success that prospective countries have in mastering the obstacles that have been erected by the present members of the union. For example, the Treaty of Maastricht has specified a series of conditions that prospective members have to satisfy in order to be allowed into the union. As will be argued later, these conditions have little to do with long-run success. They can be considered as a rite of passage for new members before they enter the monetary club.

7.2 CONDITIONS FOR LONG-RUN SUCCESS

The conditions for the long-run success of entry into a monetary union were first analysed by Mundell in his celebrated article introducing the concept of optimal currency areas (Mundell, 1961). These are the conditions which determine whether a country will be in a position where the benefits of the union exceed its costs in which case member countries have no incentive to leave the union. They form an optimal currency area. Or, as observed above, they are in a Nash equilibrium.

The conditions that are needed to guarantee long-run success are well known from the literature on optimal currency areas (OCA).[1] They can be summarized by three concepts:

(1) Symmetry (of shocks)
(2) Flexibility
(3) Integration.

Countries which wish to join a monetary union should experience macroeconomic shocks that are sufficiently symmetric with those experienced in the rest of the union (*symmetry*). These countries should have sufficient *flexibility* in their labour markets to be able to adjust to asymmetric shocks once they are in the union. Finally they should have a sufficient degree of trade *integration* with the members of the union so as to generate benefits from using the same currency.

This theory can be summarized in graphical form. This is done in figures 7.1 and 7.2.

Figure 7.1 presents the minimal combinations of symmetry and flexibility that are needed to form an optimal currency area by the downward sloping OCA-line. Points on the OCA-line define combinations of symmetry and flexibility for which the costs and the benefits of a monetary union just balance. It is negatively sloped because a declining degree of symmetry (which raises the costs) necessitates an increasing flexibility. To the right of the OCA-line the degree of flexibility is sufficiently large given the degree of symmetry to ensure that the benefits of the union exceed the costs. To the left of the OCA-line there is insufficient flexibility for any given level of symmetry.

Figure 7.2 presents the minimal combinations of symmetry and integration that are needed to form an optimal currency area. The OCA-line

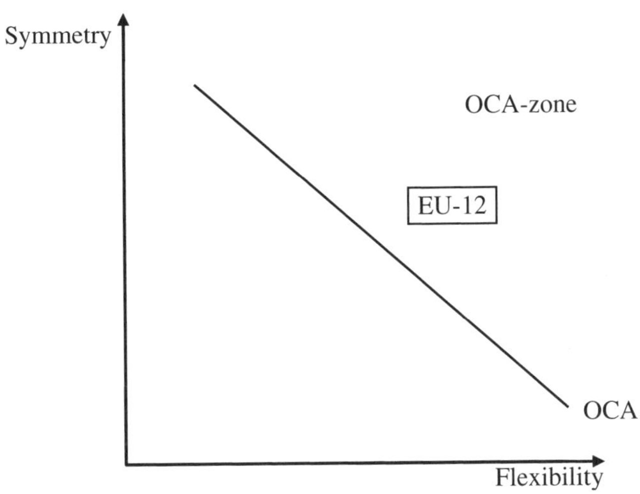

Figure 7.1 Symmetry and flexibility as OCA-criteria

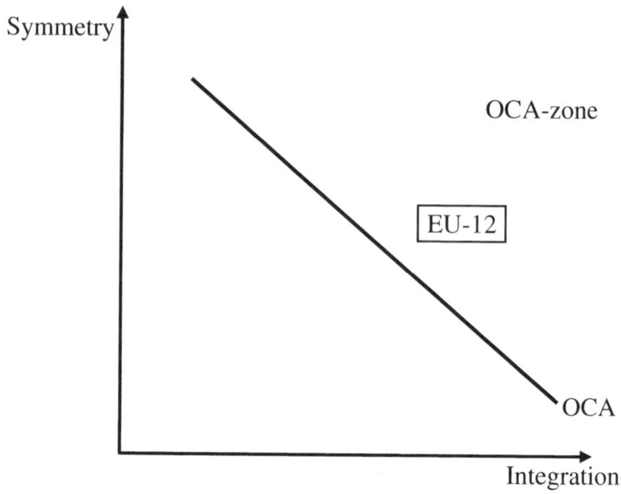

Figure 7.2 Symmetry and integration as OCA-criteria

represents the combinations of symmetry and integration among groups of countries for which the cost and benefits of a monetary union just balance. It is downward sloping because a decline in symmetry raises the costs of a monetary union. These costs are mainly macroeconomic in nature. Integration is a source of benefits to a monetary union, that is, the greater the degree of integration the more the member countries benefit from the efficiency gains of a monetary union. Thus, the additional (macroeconomic) costs produced by less symmetry can be compensated by the additional (microeconomic) benefits produced by more integration. Points to the right of the OCA-line represent groupings of countries for which the benefits of a monetary union exceed its costs.

We have put the present eurozone within the OCA-zone, taking the view that the eurozone is an optimal currency area. This implies that it is sustainable in the long run, that is, that its members have no incentive to depart from the monetary arrangement. We are not really sure this is the case. But we take an optimistic viewpoint here.

The position of the OCA-lines in figures 7.1 and 7.2 depend on a number of factors. Here we concentrate on one factor that has received relatively little attention in the economic literature. This is the degree of political integration among the member countries of the monetary union. We take the view that the degree of political integration affects the optimality of a monetary union in several ways. First, political union makes it possible to organize systems of fiscal transfers that provide some insurance against asymmetric shocks. Second, and more importantly, a political union reduces the risk of asymmetric shocks that have a political origin. To give some examples that are relevant for the eurozone. Today spending and taxation in the eurozone remain in the hands of national governments and parliaments. As a result, unilateral decisions to lower (or to raise) taxes create an asymmetric shock. Similarly, social security and wage policies are decided at the national level. Again this creates the scope for asymmetric shocks in the eurozone, as when France decided to lower the working week to 35 hours. It follows that political unification reduces the scope for such asymmetric shocks.

The way to represent the effect of political unification is by a downward shift in the OCA-lines in figures 7.1 and 7.2. As a result, political unification enlarges the OCA-zone and increases the long-term sustainability of monetary unions. Conversely a political disintegration shifts the OCA-lines upwards thereby shrinking the OCA-zone and creating the risk that the EU-12 ceases to be an optimal arrangement.[2]

What happens when other countries join the union (adopt the euro)? We concentrate on two possible effects. First, it is likely that the larger group of countries will face less symmetry of shocks than the original group. This is all the more likely as the prospective members of the eurozone have a very different level of development and a very different production structure (see Fidmruc, 2004, for empirical evidence). This creates more scope for asymmetric developments within the enlarged eurozone. We represent this case in Figure 7.3. The EU-12 is now merged into a larger group of countries which we call EU-25. This larger group experiences more asymmetric shocks than the smaller more homogeneous EU-12. As a result, the EU-25 is located below the EU-12. We have placed EU-25 low enough so that the enlarged eurozone is outside the OCA-zone, but this does not have to be the case. If it is, it implies that it will not sustainable in the long run. Put differently, euro adoption by the new member states will then not be successful in the long run. Note that the reason for the lack of success may be that the present members of the eurozone cease to perceive the enlarged monetary union as beneficial, while they saw the smaller eurozone as fitting their national interests. Thus enlargement changes the cost–benefit calculus of the existing members and can make the monetary union unsustainable. Whether or not this is the case is an empirical matter. Here we have assumed that the degree of asymmetry in the enlarged eurozone is so large as to make it a non-optimal monetary union. As stressed earlier, this does not have to be the case. In addition, as the theory of endogeneity of the OCA criteria has stressed, it is possible that while the enlarged eurozone may not be optimal at the start, it may become so over time if monetary unification speeds up the process of economic integration (Frankel and Rose, 1998).[3]

We stressed earlier that the dynamics of political integration is important in evaluating the optimality of a monetary union. In principle, enlargement

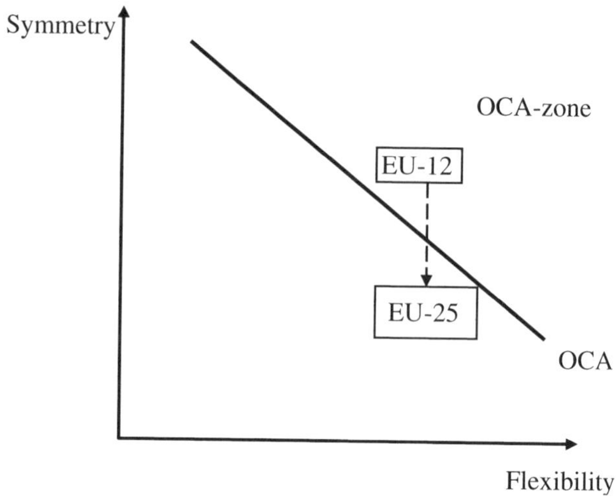

Figure 7.3 Effect of enlargement

should be neutral as far as the dynamics towards political union is concerned. Political reality, however, is likely to be different. Enlargement is increasingly seen as threatening in the old member states. This perception creates the danger of national retrenchment and soul searching. Instead of being neutral, enlargement may in fact reduce the degree of political integration achieved in the union. The implications for the long-run sustainability of the monetary union are important. In graphical terms it means that the OCA-line in Figure 7.3 shifts upwards, thereby making it less likely that the enlarged eurozone is an optimal arrangement.

If this analysis of the link between enlargement and political union is correct it has far-reaching implications for the long-run sustainability of an enlarged eurozone, for it leads to the conclusion that its enlargement will reduce its long-run sustainability. The long-run success of euro adoption by new member states would be very small.

7.3 MUNDELL I VERSUS MUNDELL II

The analysis above is very much based on the traditional theory of optimal currency areas, although this has come under pressure as a result of the monetarist critique of the traditional OCA theory. This criticism, perhaps surprisingly, was initiated by the same Robert Mundell, in a less well-known 1973 article (Mundell, 1973). This criticism can be formulated as follows.[4]

First, national monetary policies are poor and ineffective instruments to use when asymmetric shocks occur. In general the systematic use of national monetary policies to offset shocks or to stabilize output will lead to an inflation bias and macroeconomic instability.

Second, the existence of exchange rates and exchange markets in a financially globalized world is a sure recipe for attracting speculative disturbances that can destabilize the economy. Thus, instead of being a stabilizer against asymmetric shocks, exchange rates become major sources of asymmetric shocks.

Finally, in a monetary union financial market integration becomes a potent insurance mechanism against asymmetric shocks. In contrast when countries stay outside the monetary union, the exchange rate risk premia prevent financial markets from performing the role of providing for insurance against asymmetric shocks.

This is certainly a powerful criticism of the traditional OCA theory. It has also had much influence especially in countries with a history of monetary instability, where the main benefit of joining a monetary union has been seen as a means to import monetary and macroeconomic stability.[5]

Yet it would be a mistake to discard the traditional OCA theory. As we show in the next section the degree of asymmetry within the eurozone has remained surprisingly large, creating major problems for the conduct of monetary policies.

7.4 HOW IMPORTANT ARE ASYMMETRIC SHOCKS WITHIN THE EUROZONE AND WILL ENLARGEMENT CHANGE THIS?

Have asymmetric shocks been important in the operation of the euro system since 1999? We answer this question by first looking at the growth rates of output and the inflation rates in the 12 members of the euro system in 2002 and 2003 (see Figures 7.4 and 7.5). It is very striking to observe that there was a relatively wide range of experiences, especially in the growth rates of GDP. For example, while Greece experienced a growth rate of more than 4 per cent in 2003, Portugal and the Netherlands experienced negative growth rates.

In order to concentrate on temporary asymmetric shocks and the stabilization issue, we focus next on the output gaps. These measure deviations of output from its long-run growth path. Thus the output gap is a good measure of the business cycle position of countries. We use a measure of the output gap as computed by the OECD, and show the results for the year 2003 in Figure 7.6 (Similar results are obtained for other years). We observe

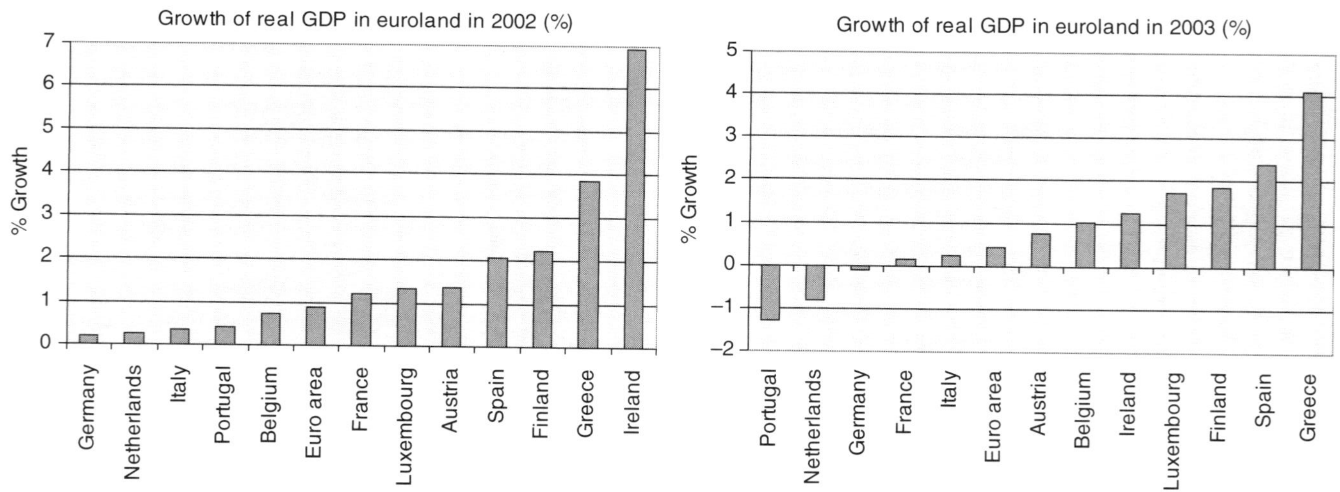

Source: European Commission, European Economy.

Figure 7.4 Growth of real GDP in euroland in 2002 and 2003

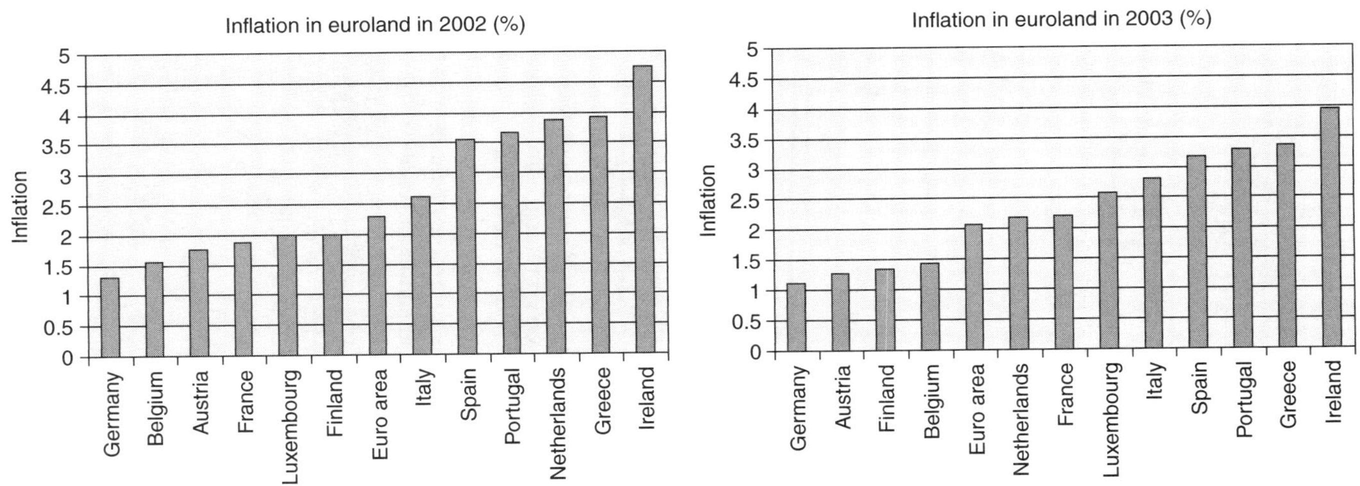

Source: European Commission, European Economy.

Figure 7.5 Inflation in euroland in 2002 and 2003

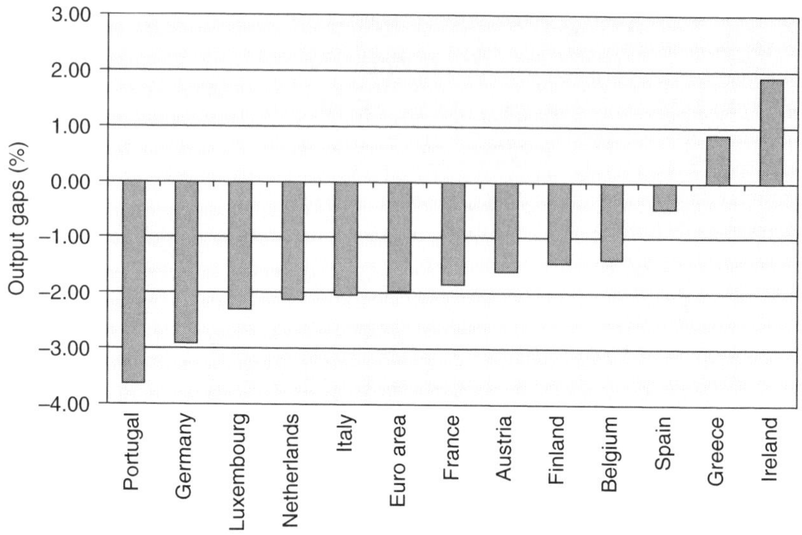

Source: European Commission, European Economy.

Figure 7.6 Output gaps in the eurozone in 2003

that there were large differences in the cyclical position of eurozone member countries during 2003. Some countries, such as Portugal, experienced severe slowdowns of their economies. Others, such as Ireland and Greece, experienced booms in economic activity. We conclude from Figure 7.6 that eurozone countries experienced very different short-term output movements during 2003 (and in fact also during other years). Together with very different inflation experiences these differences in economic conditions must have affected the views of the governors of the central banks of these countries about what the appropriate monetary policies should be.

Another way to look at the size of the asymmetries is to ask what the optimal interest rate would be for each country, given their rates of inflation and the output gaps observed. In order to compute these desired interest rates we used the Taylor rule and applied it to each individual country. We also assumed the same Taylor rule in each country. Thus, we compute the interest rate each country would have found optimal given its own domestic economic conditions (inflation and output gap). The results are shown in Table 7.1. We observe a wide range of desired interest rates, with Germany at one extreme with an interest rate of 1.2 per cent and Ireland at the other with 7.9 per cent.

These wide divergences in desired interest rates are also observed in other years. They help to explain the policy paralysis suffered by the ECB especially during 2002–03. Such a paralysis is not surprising. When

Table 7.1 Desired interest rate using the Taylor rule, 2003

Country	Desired interest rate
Germany	1.22
Austria	2.13
Finland	2.29
Belgium	2.48
Eurozone	3.12
Netherlands	3.24
France	3.40
Luxembourg	3.73
Portugal	4.13
Italy	4.20
Spain	5.51
Greece	6.48
Ireland	7.87

Sources: Inflation: European Commission, European Economy; Output gap: OECD Economic Outlook.

economic conditions differ so widely within the eurozone, taking action is likely to be difficult as it quickly leads to disagreement and conflict.

The divergences in economic conditions observed within the eurozone have come as a surprise. There are probably many factors responsible for these divergences. One has to do with the wide divergences in real interest rates which arise from the fact that inflation rates are very different while nominal rates are basically the same. We show the real interest rates in Figure 7.7. These strong differences in real interest rates have contributed to the large differences in business cycle developments. They are also responsible for the very wide differences in developments in the housing markets. This is shown in Figure 7.8 for a selected group of eurozone countries. We observe that in some countries (Spain, Ireland) house prices more than doubled since the start of EMU, while in Germany they actually declined. From Figure 7.9 we observe that there seems to be a strong correlation between real interest rates and house price increases.

Another important factor in understanding the wide divergences in economic conditions within the eurozone is formulated here as a hypothesis. The slowdown in a number of eurozone countries after 2001 has much to do with what Keynes called 'animal spirits'. These are movements of pessimism and optimism that affect consumers and investors, and that have self-fulfilling properties. In a fully integrated union these 'animal spirits' would be present at the level of the eurozone. Today, however, these 'animal spirits' remain largely national, mainly because of the overwhelming importance of

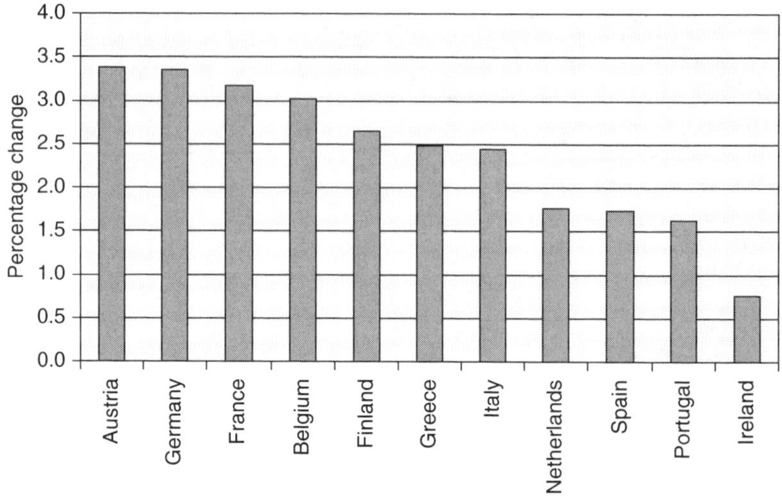

Source: European Commission, European Economy.

Figure 7.7 Average real interest rates in eurozone countries, 1997–2004

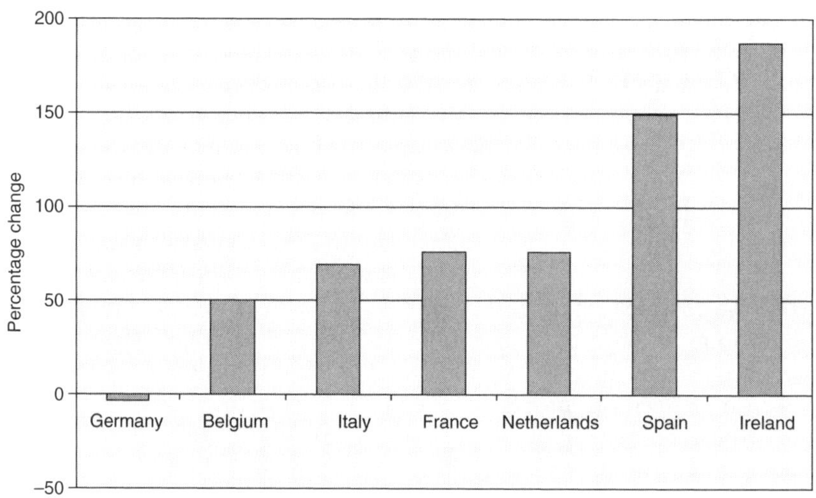

Source: *The Economist*, 11 December 2004.

Figure 7.8 House price indices (% change, 1997–2004)

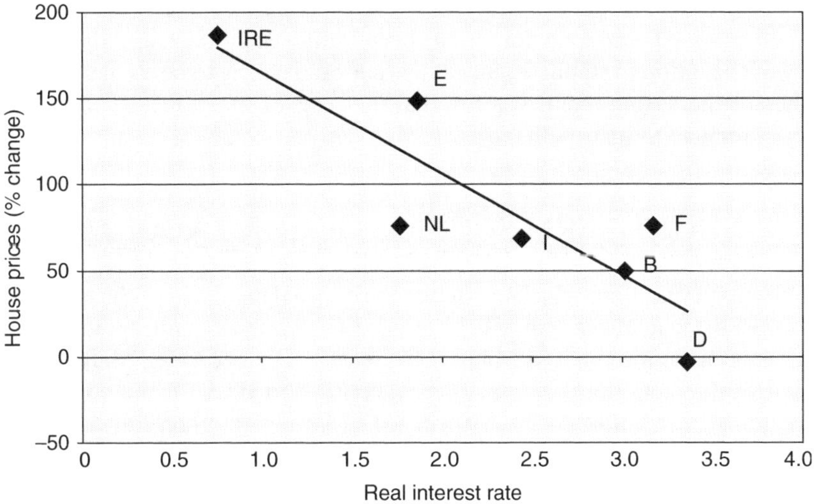

Source: EU Commission and *The Economist*.

Figure 7.9 Real interest rate and house prices 1998–2004 (% change)

the nation-states. This manifests itself not only in the fact that most instruments of economic policy are in the hands of national authorities, but also in the differences in national cultures and languages. The latter produce national debates and analyses about economic conditions that greatly affect how consumers and producers perceive the economic situation. Thus, in Germany and Italy there was a deep pessimism about the future during the early 2000s, which was fed by extremely pessimistic analyses by German and Italian economists and non-economists. These pessimistic analyses received widespread attention in the national media, and had the effect of making everybody pessimistic. In other countries, however, optimism prevailed at pretty much the same time. The result of this national segmentation of the 'discours économiques' was to create unsynchronized 'animal spirits' which in turn produced unsynchronized business cycles. Much more political integration will be necessary to overcome these national idiosyncrasies in psychological movements of optimism and pessimism.

How is the enlargement of the eurozone going to affect all this? The answer is straightforward: it is quite likely to aggravate this problem of asymmetric economic trends within the (enlarged) eurozone. As long as nation-states remain what they are, the national 'animal spirits' will continue to do their work of driving countries' economic conditions in different directions. Since there will be more of these nation-states in the enlarged eurozone, the problem is likely to be more intense.

As a result, the policy paralysis of the ECB is likely to be even stronger in an enlarged eurozone than it has been in the recent past, and the capacity of the union to stabilize output fluctuations is likely to be eroded further, thereby increasing the perception that the costs of the monetary union are large relative to its benefits.

7.5 SHORT-TERM SUCCESS OF EURO ADOPTION

The entry conditions which applied to the original members of the eurozone are the same as those that will be applied to the new member states. They have been defined in the Maastricht Treaty. The surprising thing about these entry conditions is that they have little to do with the conditions identified in traditional OCA theory. The latter are structural in nature, while the Maastricht entry conditions are macroeconomic convergence criteria (inflation and interest rate convergence, budget deficits and debts, and fixed exchange rates) that have no predictive power as far as the long-term sustainability of the union is concerned. In this sense, these entry conditions are not sufficient to guarantee the long-term success of the union.[6]

Another important difference between the long-term conditions for success (the OCA conditions) and the Maastricht convergence criteria, is that the latter are relatively easy to satisfy. They mainly involve the use of macroeconomic policies, in contrast to the structural policies that are needed to satisfy the OCA criteria. In addition, some of the Maastricht convergence criteria have a self-fulfilling dimension. For example, the interest rate convergence criterion will be automatically satisfied once the decision is taken that a country will join the union. At that moment arbitrage in the long-term bond market will ensure that the long-term interest rate converges to the long-term rate prevailing in the eurozone. This arbitrage worked quite forcefully prior to the start of the eurozone in 1999. It led to a dramatic decline in long-term interest rates in Italy and Spain. In the case of Italy this mechanism had the beneficial effect of drastically reducing the interest payments on the government debt. As a result, the budget deficit declined dramatically without the Italian government having to take major decisions to reduce the deficit.[7]

On the whole the new member states that are committed to join the eurozone should not experience major difficulties in satisfying the Maastricht convergence criteria. As argued earlier, this likely success, however, says nothing about the long-term success of their euro adoption.

In the rest of this section we concentrate on two issues that have been extensively analysed in the literature, that is, the Balassa–Samuelson problem,[8] and the setting of the conversion rates at the time of entry in the union.

7.5.1 Balassa–Samuelson and the Inflation Convergence Criterion

An issue that has arisen is the potential for conflict between the inflation criterion and the requirement for joining the exchange rate mechanism, ERM II.[9] The reason why such a conflict could arise is the following. Most new member states experience high productivity growth in their tradable sectors. This is part of their catch-up process with Western Europe. As a result, the well-known Balassa–Samuelson effect could be important and could lead to structurally higher inflation (measured by the consumption price index). There will be nothing to worry about when these countries are in the eurozone. They will simply show a higher inflation rate, which is part of their catching up process and that should be considered to be an equilibrating process. During the transition process, however, this could be a problem. This is because the Maastricht convergence process mandates these countries to maintain a rate of inflation that is close to the eurozone level[10] until entry into the monetary union. At the same time entry into the ERM II also reduces countries' scope to use the exchange rate as an instrument to lower the inflationary dynamics coming from high productivity growth. Let us use a simple model to illustrate this point. Let us call the low productivity growth country the eurozone (*E*) and the high productivity growth country the new member state (*N*). Inflation in the two 'countries' can then be defined as follows:

$$\dot{p}c_E = \alpha\dot{p}_E + (1-\alpha)\dot{w}_E \tag{7.1}$$

$$\dot{p}c_N = \alpha\dot{p}_N + (1-\alpha)\dot{w}_N \tag{7.2}$$

where $\dot{p}c_E$ and $\dot{p}c_N$ are the rates of change in the *consumption* price indices in the eurozone and the new member countries. These are a weighted average of the rates of price increases of tradables ($\dot{p}_E$ and $\dot{p}_N$), and non-tradables ($\dot{w}_E$ and $\dot{w}_N$) whereby the weights are given by α and $1-\alpha$, respectively. (We assume these weights to be the same in both countries.) For the sake of simplicity we assume that wage costs (w) are the only source of costs in the non-tradable sectors.

Since we describe the transition process during which the exchange rate of the new member state can change relative to the euro we introduce the purchasing power parity as follows:

$$\dot{e} = \dot{p}_E - \dot{p}_N \tag{7.3}$$

where $\dot{p}_E$ and $\dot{p}_N$ are the rates of price increases in the tradable sectors of the eurozone and the new member state respectively and $\dot{e}$ is the rate of depreciation of the euro relative to the currency of the new member state.

We now subtract (7.2) from (7.1) and use (7.3). This yields:

$$\dot{p}c_E - \dot{p}c_N = \alpha\dot{e} + (1-\alpha)(\dot{w}_E - \dot{w}_N) \quad (7.4)$$

or assuming that the wage increases arise form productivity growth ($\dot{q}$)

$$\dot{p}c_E - \dot{p}c_N = \alpha\dot{e} + (1-\alpha)(\dot{q}_E - \dot{q}_N) \quad (7.5)$$

which can be rewritten as:

$$\dot{p}c_E - \dot{p}c_N - \alpha\dot{e} = (1-\alpha)(\dot{q}_E - \dot{q}_N). \quad (7.6)$$

We can now illustrate the constraints imposed by the convergence criteria as follows. If productivity growth is faster in the new member countries than in the eurozone, that is $(\dot{q}_E - \dot{q}_N) < 0$, then the inflation convergence and the fixed exchange rate requirement cannot be kept at the same time. If the exchange rate is fixed ($\dot{e} = 0$) then $\dot{p}c_E - \dot{p}c_N < 0$, that is, inflation in the new member countries must exceed the eurozone inflation. Alternatively, if the inflation convergence is met, that is $\dot{p}c_E - \dot{p}c_N = 0$, then the new member country's currency must appreciate ($\dot{e} > 0$).

Empirical evidence on the likelihood of higher inflation in the new member states is provided in Table 7.2. The first line of Table 7.2 lists the 1994–2004 average of whole economy productivity gains for the new member states in comparison with Germany. Productivity in Central and Eastern European member states has been and can be expected to grow considerably faster.

The changes of consumer prices relative to wholesale prices (as a proxy for traded goods prices) can be used as an indicator of productivity driven inflation. Between 1994 and 2004 on average for all Central and Eastern European countries consumer prices have increased relative to producer prices considerably faster than in Germany. This trend is weaker for countries such as the Czech Republic and Poland which have (temporarily) allowed for considerable nominal appreciations of their currencies.

In the third line of Table 7.2 we use Germany as the reference country to compute the real appreciations against the euro and the German mark back to 1994. Negative values indicate real appreciations against the German mark (representing the euro starting in 1999).

It is evident from Table 7.2 that the currencies of all new member states were under real appreciation pressure, which is in line with the relative productivity gains vis-à-vis the euro area. Real appreciation is on average least for Cyprus, Malta and Slovenia which have reached the highest stage of economic development in terms of GDP per capita. The catch-up process of the new member states and therefore the rise of price levels can be expected

Table 7.2 Indicators for relative productivity changes, 1994–2004

	CY	CZ	EE	HU	LV	LT	MT	PL	SI	SK	DE
Productivity	2.7	4.6	7.0	2.8	1.7	6.2	6.8	4.2	4.2	3.5	1.0
CPI/WPI	0.6	1.9	2.8	2.6	4.2	3.6	n.a.	1.8	1.8	2.3	0.6
Real appreciation	−0.9	−4.5	−8.7	−3.2	−8.0	−11.6	−1.5	−2.7	−1.9	−5.2	–

Notes:
CY = Cyprus; CZ = Czech Republic; EE = Estonia; HU = Hungary; MT = Malta; LV = Latvia; LT = Lithuania; PL = Poland; SI = Slovenia; SK = Slovak Republic.
Productivity corresponds to yearly average productivity percentage changes in the whole economy (per cent).
CPI/WPI corresponds to yearly average percentage changes of consumer prices relative to wholesale prices between.
Real appreciation corresponds to yearly average CPI based real appreciation against the euro (German mark) (per cent).

Sources: Productivity: ECB; CPI/WPI: IMS, IFS; Real appreciation: IMF, IFS.

to continue for a considerable period of time. As shown in Figure 7.10 differences in terms of both GDP per capita and price levels are still significant. In many countries both indicators are still less than half of the EU-15. Given a robust relationship between real GDP per capita and the price level which is suggested by the Balassa–Samuelson effect and empirically shown by Kravis and Lipsey (1988) we would expect that both the economic catch-up process and the increases in price levels will continue for some time.

The inconsistency between the inflation convergence criterion and the requirement to join ERM II looks formidable. There are, however, several features of the convergence requirements that soften this inconsistency. First, the inflation convergence requirement allows for a margin of 1.5 per cent. That is, the inflation criterion requires the inflation differential $(\dot{p}c_E - \dot{p}c_N)$ to be less than 1.5 (in absolute value). This means that if the exchange rate is not allowed to change ($\dot{e} = 0$) the inflation criterion will be satisfied if the productivity growth differential $(\dot{q}_E - \dot{q}_N)$ is lower (in absolute value) than $1.5/(1 - \alpha)$ (see equation (7.6)). Assuming that the share of nontradables is 0.7, this implies that a productivity differential that is not larger than 2.1 would allow the inflation criteria to be met. The evidence of Table 7.2 suggests that productivity growth differentials have been larger than 2.1 per cent for most countries. Thus, additional flexibility is required.

Second, the requirement to join the ERM II does not prevent the exchange rate from moving somewhat within a given band of fluctuation. How large is this band? The Maastricht Treaty prescribes countries to join

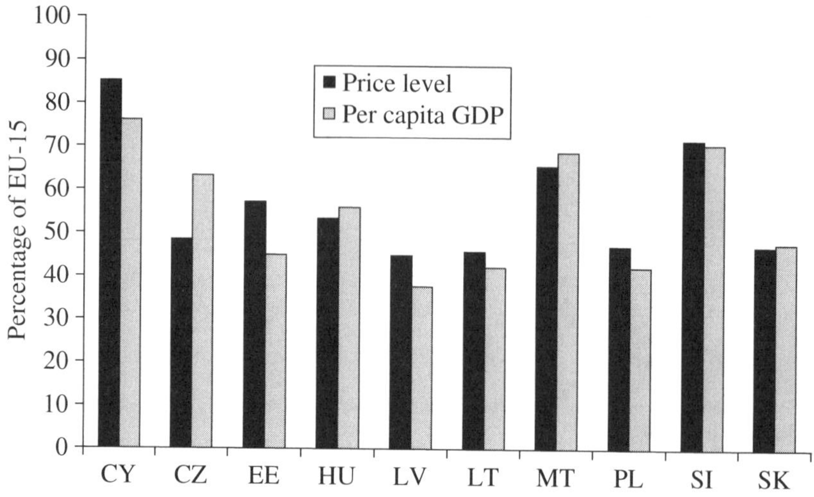

Source: Eurostat. GDP per capita is based on purchasing power parities.

Figure 7.10 Differences in price levels and GDP per capita (% of EU-15)

the exchange rate mechanism using the 'normal' band of fluctuation. Prior to 1993 when the ERM I collapsed the normal band of fluctuation was 4.5 per cent (2 × 2.25 per cent). Since 1993, countries joining the ERM have been allowed to enjoy a higher band of fluctuation, that is, 30 per cent (2 × 15 per cent). This was the regime that prevailed from 1993 until the run-up to EMU in 1999. Thus, it appears that the new definition of the 'normal' band should be 30 per cent. The argument for considering this to be the 'normal' band is based on equal treatment. Since the present members of the eurozone have been able to enjoy this wider band, equal treatment would suggest that this should also be the regime for the new member countries when they join ERM II. If this is the right interpretation, then the Balassa–Samuelson problem ceases to be a serious problem. For in that case the inflationary pressure coming from the productivity growth differential in equation (7.6) can easily be accommodated by movements of the exchange rate, in this case by appreciations of the currencies of the new member countries within the wide band. Appreciations of 2–3 per cent per year together with the 1.5 per cent additional inflation margin would accommodate these productivity differentials in most countries. If the transition period is not too long, the wide band of 30 per cent could easily take care of these appreciations.

Things are different if the interpretation of the 'normal' is the pre-1993 situation of 4.5 per cent. In that case, after two years this band may prove insufficient for the new member countries to accommodate for productivity differentials that are significantly higher than 2.1 per cent.

One important remark should be made here. The Treaty prescribes that candidate countries should join the ERM and that they should not have devalued during the two years prior to entry. They are, however, allowed to revalue their currency. This means that even if the narrow band is selected, countries would still have the option to revalue their currency. However, this option would be difficult to implement systematically because the knowledge that the authorities could revalue the currency could lead to speculative pressure and volatility in the market.

A narrow band would lead to other problems. The new member countries are committed to allowing the free flow of capital. Free capital mobility has the effect of making fixed exchange rates fragile and prone to speculative attacks.[11] The risk of speculative attacks can be reduced significantly if the band is wide enough. The experience of the ERM I illustrates this. When at the end of the 1980s countries such as France and Italy liberalized their capital flows, the ERM I (which used a small band of 4.5 per cent) quickly became subject to speculative attacks and collapsed in 1993. The subsequent enlargement of the band of fluctuations contributed to stabilizing the system.

We conclude that the Balassa–Samuelson phenomenon should not lead to serious problems of implementation of the Maastricht convergence requirements if the permissible band of fluctuations in the ERM II is set wide enough. In that case ERM II should provide for enough flexibility for the new member countries to safely land into the eurozone.

7.5.2 How to Set the Conversion Rates?

In order to analyse the nature of the problem we use a simple model of the determination of the exchange rate. Let us call the exchange rate that will be fixed at the moment of euro adoption the euro/zloty rate. We can write that exchange rate as follows:

$$S_t = Z_t + bE_t\Delta S_{t+1} \tag{7.7}$$

where S_t is the euro/zloty rate at time t, $E_t\Delta S_{t+1}$ is the expectation held at t about the change in the exchange rate at $t+1$; Z_t is a vector of fundamental variables at time t affecting the exchange rate at time t. These fundamentals can be the money stock, prices, current account, and so on.

We rewrite (7.7) as follows:

$$S_t = (1 - \beta)Z_t + \beta E_t S_{t+1} \tag{7.8}$$

where $\beta = b/(1+b)$ and $(1-\beta) = 1/(1+b)$.

This equation says that the current exchange rate is a weighted average of current fundamentals and the expected future level of the exchange rate.

One can now solve this equation assuming rational expectations as follows. Rational expectations imply that agents use all available information to forecast the future exchange rate. This means that they will use the same model as in (7.8). Thus:

$$E_t S_{t+1} = (1-\beta) E_t Z_{t+1} + \beta E_t S_{t+2} \tag{7.9}$$

Substituting (7.9) into (7.8) yields:

$$S_t = (1-\beta) Z_t + \beta[(1-\beta) E_t Z_{t+1} + \beta E_t S_{t+2}]. \tag{7.10}$$

When forecasting S_{t+2} rational agents will proceed in exactly the same way, that is, using (7.8). Continuing this process of forecasting future exchange rates yields:

$$\begin{aligned} S_t = (1-\beta)[Z_t + \beta E_t Z_{t+1} + \beta^2 E_t Z_{t+2} + \ldots \\ + \beta^{T-t-1} E_t Z_{T-1}] + \beta^{T-t} E_t S_T \end{aligned} \tag{7.11}$$

where T is the time of the euro adoption (conversion time). Thus the exchange rate at time t is a weighted average of the fundamental variables that agents forecast until the time of the euro adoption (at time T) and their forecast of the conversion rate that will be applied. As time moves forward more and more terms in the brackets drop out and so do the weights attached to the fundamentals. Note also that β can be considered as a discount factor, so that as we move closer and closer to T, β converges to 1. Thus, in the limit as we have moved arbitrarily close to T we obtain:

$$S_t = E_t S_T$$

which becomes $S_t = S_T$ when $t = T$.

This result illustrates the potential indeterminacy of the exchange rate at conversion time. Without a prior announcement of the conversion rate, the market will have to guess this rate. Any guess will do and drive the exchange rate to that guessed number. Any expectation that the market has about the conversion rate would be self-validating, creating a potential for turbulence if there is uncertainty about the value of the conversion rate.

In order to anchor the market's expectations it is necessary to announce in advance what the conversion rate would be. This is what the authorities did in May 1998 when they announced the fixed conversion rates for the prospective member countries. A similar announcement will have to be made before euro adoption. Let us call the announced euro/zloty rate S* (a fixed number). The market rate of the euro/zloty then becomes:

$$S_t = (1 - \beta)[Z_t + \beta E_t Z_{t+1} + \beta^2 E_t Z_{t+2} + \ldots + \beta^{T-t-1} E_t Z_{T-1}] + \beta^{T-t} S^* \quad (7.12)$$

As we move closer to T the exchange rate must smoothly converge towards the fixed number S*.

Note also that the variance of S_t can be written as the sum of the variances and covariances of the present and future fundamentals. As we move closer to T, more and more fundamentals between the brackets drop out and so do their variances and covariances. In addition the weight of the final conversion rate increases. Since the final conversion rate is a fixed number, its variance is zero. Thus, as we move closer to T the variance of S_t also converges to zero. All this, of course, assumes that the announced conversion rate S* is fully credible.

The prediction of this simple model came out beautifully in the case of the conversion of the currencies of the present eurozone member countries prior to the start of EMU. A smooth convergence towards the announced conversion rate occurred. In addition the variability declined as one moved towards conversion time (see De Grauwe et al., 1999) for evidence.

7.6 CONCLUSION

The success of a euro adoption can be evaluated in the short and in the long run. From our short-term analysis we conclude that new member countries which want to join the eurozone can do this without major difficulties. A strong political will to use macroeconomic instruments to guide the country towards the Maastricht mandated convergence criteria will be sufficient to obtain success.

We argued, however, that success in complying with the Maastricht convergence criteria has no predictive power for the long-run success of the euro adoption. This long-run success depends on the OCA criteria. If these criteria are not satisfied the incentive for some countries to leave the union in the future will be strong, undermining the sustainability of the eurozone.

The risk that we face today is that enlargement will lead to a weakening of the dynamics to political unification in the eurozone. We argued that this is likely to maintain large asymmetric developments within the eurozone. These could even increase if enlargement leads to a loosening of the political union.

There can be little doubt that the long-run success of the eurozone depends on the continuing process of political unification. There is, however, a strong 'integration fatigue' in the European Union today, making it unlikely that significant progress in political unification can be made. This will continue to make the eurozone a fragile regime, and increasingly so after enlargement.

NOTES

* I am grateful to Ali Hakan Kara and Jürgen von Hagen for comments and criticism.

1. McKinnon (1963), Kenen (1969).
2. For important additional insights into the link between monetary and political union see von Hagen (1996), where it is argued that political unification can also lead to increased tensions between member states. As a result, the link between monetary and political union is not a linear one.
3. For a survey of the literature see De Grauwe and Mongelli (2005). See also Fidrmuc (2004) for empirical evidence.
4. See also Tavlas (1993).
5. De Grauwe and Schnabl (2005) provide some empirical evidence sustaining the Mundell-II hypothesis. It is shown that on average central European countries that have pegged their exchange rates profited from more macroeconomic stability (less inflation) and more growth.
6. In addition, it can be argued that they are not necessary either. This argument is developed in De Grauwe (2004). See also Buiter and Grafe (2002).
7. Note that the Maastricht nominal deficit rule signalled an improvement in the Italian public finances while no improvement in fact occurred. See Buiter and Grafe (2002) on this.
8. Balassa (1964) and Samuelson (1964).
9. There is an extensive literature on this issue. See, for example, Halpern and Wyplosz (2001), Mihaljek and Klau (2003), Szápary (2000).
10. We assume here that common sense will prevail and that the reference value will not be the average rate of inflation of the three EU-member countries with the lowest inflation rate.
11. See Eichengreen (2001) and Begg et al. (2000) on issues relating to capital flows.

REFERENCES

Balassa, B. (1964), 'The purchasing-power parity doctrine: a reappraisal', *Journal of Political Economy*, **6**, 584–66.

Begg, D., B. Eichengreen, L. Halpern, J. von Hagen and C. Wyplosz (2001), 'Sustainable regimes of capital movements in accession countries', CEPR Policy Paper No. 10.

Buiter, W. and C. Grafe (2002), 'Anchor, float or abandon ship: exchange rate regimes for accession countries', *Banca Nazionale del Lavoro Quarterly Review*, **55**, 111–42.

De Grauwe, P. (2004), *The Economics of Monetary Union*, 5th edn, Oxford: Oxford University Press.

De Grauwe, P. and F. Mongelli (2005), 'Endogeneities of optimum currency areas: what brings countries sharing a single currency closer together?' ECB Discussion Paper.

De Grauwe, P. and G. Schnabl (2005), 'Exchange rate regime and macroeconomic stability in Central and Eastern Europe', in Susan Schadler (ed.), *Euro Adoption in Central and Eastern Europe: Opportunities and Challenges*, Washington, DC: International Monetary Fund.

De Grauwe, P., H. Dewachter and D. Veestraeten (1999), 'Explaining recent European exchange rate stability', *International Finance*, **2**, 1–31.

Eichengreen, B. (2001), 'Capital account liberalisation: what do the cross-country studies tell us?', mimeo, University of California, Berkeley, April.

European Central Bank (ECB) (2004), 'Convergence report 2004', Frankfurt am Main.

Fidrmuc, J. (2005), 'The endogeneity of the optimum currency area criteria and intra-industry trade: implications for EMU enlargement', in Paul De Grauwe and Jaques Melitz (eds), *Monetary Unions after EMU*, Cambridge, MA: MIT Press.

Frankel, J. and A. Rose (1998), 'The endogeneity of the optimum currency area criteria', *Economic Journal*, **108**, 1009–25.

Halpern, L. and C. Wyplosz (2001), 'Economic transformation and real exchange rate in the 2000s: the Balassa–Samuelson connection', mimeo, University of Geneva.

Kalemli-Özcan, Ş., B.E. Sorensen and O. Yosha (2003), 'Risk sharing and industrial specialization: regional and international evidence', *American Economic Review*, **93** (3), 903–18.

Kenen, P.B. (1969), 'The optimum currency area: an eclectic view', in R.A. Mundell and A.K. Swoboda (eds), *Monetary Problems of the International Economy*, Chicago: University of Chicago Press.

Kravis, I. and R. Lipsey (1988), 'National price levels and the prices of tradeables and nontradeables', *American Economic Review*, **78**, 474–8.

McKinnon, R. (1963), 'Optimum currency areas', *American Economic Review*, **52**, 712–25.

Mihaljek, D. and M. Klau (2003), 'The Balassa–Samuelson effect in Central Europe: a disaggregated analysis', BIS Working Paper 143.

Mundell, R. (1961), 'A theory of optimal currency areas', *American Economic Review*, **51**, 657–65.

Mundell, R. (1973), 'Uncommon arguments for common currencies', in H.G. Johnson and A.K. Swoboda (eds), *The Economics of Common Currencies*, Cambridge: Allen and Unwin, pp. 114–32.

Samuelson, P. (1964), 'Theoretical notes on trade problems', *Review of Economics and Statistics*, **64,** 145–54.

Szapáry, G. (2000), 'Maastricht and the choice of exchange rate regime in transition during the run-up to EMU', National Bank of Hungary Working Paper 2000/7.

Tavlas, G.S. (1993), 'The "new" theory of optimum currency areas', *The World Economy*, 663–85.

von Hagen, J. (1996), 'Währungsunion, fiskalunion, politische union', mimeo, Universität Mannheim.

Wyplosz, C. (1997), 'EMU: why and how it might happen', *Journal of Economic Perspectives*, **11** (4), Fall.

COMMENTS

Ali Hakan Kara

At the end of 2004, the European Council decided that Turkey should be a candidate country for membership of the European Union and that accession negotiations would start in late 2005. Needless to say, the start of accession negotiations is only the beginning of a rather lengthy process. A lot remains to be accomplished for Turkey to join the EU. That is why for some of us Professor De Grauwe's chapter may seem rather abstract. However, these ideas are by no means purely academic issues for Turkey. Although Turkey is still in the pre-EU membership phase of the process that leads to the eventual adoption of the euro, some of the challenges that have been set out in the chapter apply to Turkey even at this early stage. To name one, we may have been observing Balassa–Samuelson type effects in the recent period.

In my discussion, first I would like to summarize the challenges and preconditions that the new and future members are likely to face on the path to the euro, which, I believe is only briefly mentioned in the chapter, due to space limitations. The general policy prescriptions for progress towards monetary union and ERM participation in particular are now broadly accepted: countries should build a consistent set of credible economic policies aiming at stability and preserving competitiveness. Of course, these will require continued and demanding efforts to implement the appropriate macroeconomic policies and the necessary structural reforms. Three elements are of central importance for a successful euro adoption:

(1) First, fiscal deficits and rigidities from subsidies and formula driven social transfers must be low. Once the ability to conduct national monetary policy is relinquished, fiscal policy need to be able to respond quickly to smooth out demand shocks.
(2) Second, financial market supervision must be strong. Rapid growth of bank credit to the private sector is almost inevitable, regardless of the timing of euro adoption, as bank intermediation approaches European levels. Effective supervision, alongside fiscal restraints, will be key to containing any risks of asset price bubbles and overheating.
(3) Third, structural reforms enhancing market flexibility are important to ensure that current account positions and the central rate in ERM II remain sustainable, and to help pursue nominal convergence in parallel with real convergence.

These conditions, together with an appropriate choice of central parity rate in ERM II and final conversion rate will increase the chances of success in euro adoption. However, successfully entering the euro area (euro adoption) for a single country – as Professor De Grauwe wisely observes – does not necessarily mean that the future of the euro will be a success. I would like to put this issue aside for a moment and concentrate, first, on some of the crucial points regarding the euro adoption process by the new member states.

The path to euro adoption can be described in two phases. The first phase is the period after acceding to the EU and before joining the exchange rate mechanism II (ERM II) the second phase starts with entry into the ERM II and stretches all the way to the actual introduction of the euro, including a final period between the official EU council decision for a country to join the euro area and the actual adoption of the euro. Both of these phases will entail different challenges for monetary policy. Obviously, there is no single route to the euro. Diversity of economies in nominal, real and structural terms and differences in monetary and exchange rate regimes across countries call for an assessment on a case-by-case basis. However, there is one challenge which applies to almost all the candidate countries: countries in the process of real convergence will display higher productivities than the early members. This would lead to real exchange rate appreciation through the well-known Balassa–Samuelson effect.[1]

The literature on the B–S effect is now vast. The main argument is that under a fixed exchange rate arrangement, the Balassa–Samuelson effect might prevent compliance with the Maastricht inflation criterion (see for example Natalucci and Ravenna, 2002, for a demonstration of this idea using a DSGE framework). Given that the Maastricht criteria will be binding, in the presence of such an effect candidate countries face a trade-off between trend appreciation of the nominal exchange rate and high inflation rates. However, there is a solution – albeit an unpleasant one – to this problem: pursue a contractionary policy during the ERM II phase. After all, the Balassa–Samuelson effect is visible only when an economy is close to full employment. However, if the country enters the ERM II with a significant output gap, that is, when the economy is operating beneath its potential, there may be no upward pressure on wages in the tradable sector, let alone in nontradables. Indeed, this is exactly what has happened in Turkey between 2001–04 (in the final couple of quarters though, the B–S effect started pushing in).

Going back to the new members, it should not be too challenging to fulfil the Maastricht criteria by a particular year. After all, satisfying the Maastricht criteria is a macroeconomic problem. A country with a sufficient output gap, in the absence of large fluctuations in global liquidity conditions, should engineer a safe trip through the ERM II and fulfil the Maastricht criteria at the same time. However, pushing economic activity beneath its potential will increase the cost of managing the fixed exchange rate. As a consequence, the requirement of membership in the ERM II and the Maastricht inflation criterion constrain the policy choice, while providing no additional benefit. Professor De Grauwe's solution to this problem is very simple: just make the ERM II band wide enough. Let the nominal exchange rate adjust, rather than forcing a recession.

There is one more option to ensure that the B–S constraint is not binding. Changing the interpretation of the inflation criterion can help the new members to satisfy the Maastricht criteria without pursuing unnecessary contractionary policies. The Maastricht Treaty says that inflation should not exceed by more than 1.5 percentage points the average of the three 'best performing' member states. The meaning of the term 'best performing' is not explicit, however. If we interpret the phrase 'best performing' as meaning the lowest-inflation countries, this would put the ceiling (Finland, Nederland and Germany) at 2.9 per cent as of March 2005. However, if we interpret it according to the ECB definition – as close to but below 2 per cent – the best performing countries would include Ireland, France and Italy, which would give a ceiling of about 3.5 per cent, fairly close to the estimated structural inflation rates for the CEE countries (see the Czech Republic and Poland inflation reports). I believe that interpreting the rules flexibly, would be less costly than changing them. For once the 'rule box' is opened, it is likely that you will never be able to close it. Indeed this takes us to the infamous rules versus discretion debate, but I will not go further on this, which could be the topic of another study.

Nevertheless, managing the B–S effect during the euro adoption process does not mean that this debate will end. It is likely to continue to be a problem for a while, even after enlargement. For it will lead to high inflation and thus low real interest rates in the new member states, probably raising the average inflation in the euro area. This could lead to a higher common policy interest rate than would have been the case without EMU enlargement. Therefore, tighter than optimal monetary policy could be one more reason for the old EU members for not staying in the union.

I would like to focus on the future of EMU in the remainder of my discussion. Indeed, when I first saw the topic of this session, 'Preconditions for a successful euro adoption', my first impression was that we would be talking about the prerequisites for the new member states for joining the euro area, which is a rather short-term problem. However, the contribution turned out more complex than I expected. Professor De Grauwe approaches the topic from the perspective of the future of EMU. Although I have no problem with the content, I believe that the title could be misleading. I would like to suggest changing the title of the chapter: perhaps to 'Preconditions for a successful euro area enlargement', or may be a more fancy (and daring) topic such as 'Will EMU Survive?'

Should We Expect Business Cycles to be More Closely Synchronized after Euro Adoption?

Let me consider the main theme of the chapter.

Andrew Rose (2004) concludes that a currency union can increase trade between members by amounts ranging from 10 to 100 per cent. It is also often argued in the literature that monetary union will reduce the scope for asymmetric shocks, which will lead to greater alignment in business cycles among the member states.

If this were true, we would expect currency unions to be a robust variable in explaining the co-movement of business cycles. However, a recent study by Baxter and Kouparitsas (2005) argues that bilateral trade is the only variable that is robust in explaining the co-movement of business cycles. More interestingly, one variable that the literature has argued is important for business cycles – currency unions – are not robust. To put it another way, countries belonging to a currency union do not have significantly more correlated business cycles than countries that do not share a common currency.

A puzzling result emerges from Baxter and Kouparitras's study. If bilateral trade is a robust variable in explaining the co-movement of business cycles, why, then, is monetary union not a robust variable? Could it be that the monetary union itself is leading to the disparity between the cyclical movements?

As Professor De Grauwe writes, perhaps 'strong differences in real interest rates contribute to the large differences in business cycle developments'. It is evident that real convergence will lead to higher growth rates for the new members. In other words, they should exhibit higher potential growth rates. But countries with higher potential growth rates do tend to have higher natural rates of interest; and disparities between natural rates of interest can amplify the macroeconomic impact of asymmetric shocks under a unified monetary policy. It is not hard to picture an example: suppose an asymmetric adverse demand shock hits a single country. The agents in that country will be aware that monetary policy will not react to fully counteract the idiosyncratic demand shock. This may, in turn, bring consumer confidence further down, deepening the slowdown in the economy.

Indeed one can go one step further and argue that so long as the members of the currency union continue to have large differences in their natural rates of interest, even symmetric shocks can create asymmetric effects. For the optimal nominal interest rates path that would stabilize the economies would differ largely across countries. These arguments are already indicating the possibility that entering the currency union will not, in itself, ensure the synchronization of business cycles.

Having said that, this argument ceases to hold if the real convergence is close to completion, in which case, potential growth rates and the natural rate of interest of new entrants will be close to that of the early members. In such a circumstance, the benefits of increased economic integration may exceed the costs of enlargement for the old member states, even in the short run.

I thus conclude that, in so far as the EMU candidates complete real convergence, or if they are close to completion, the long-term prospects for the monetary union should not be too poor. If this is correct, we are left with a simple prescription. The statement that 'the enlargement of the eurozone will reduce its own long-run sustainability' will critically depend on the timing of enlargement. There is more chance for success if countries are allowed into the euro area conditional on substantial progress on real convergence. This would also alleviate the arousal of national retrenchment and soul searching on which Professor De Grauwe elaborates. In that sense, conditional on the timing of enlargement, I tend to be more optimistic about the future of EMU than is implied in this chapter.

All in all, I find this chapter very stimulating and insightful. It argues that the issue of preconditions for euro adoption should not just focus on the short-term concept of the ERM II mechanism, but should ask the question 'Will there be life in the euro area after enlargement?' Professor De Grauwe wisely asks the right question. I believe that his question and the way he addresses it will be discussed more and more in the future.

Note

1. Previous studies have concluded that productivity shocks have negligible effects on real exchange rate fluctuations. A recent empirical study by Alexius (2005) shows that when long-run equilibrium relations between real exchange rate levels and fundamental variables are taken into account, relative productivity shocks account for most of the long-run movements in the real exchange rates.

References

Alexius, A. (2005), 'Productivity shocks and real exchange rates', *Journal of Monetary Economics*, **52**, 555–66.

Baxter, M. and M. Kouparitsas (2005), 'Determinants of business cycle co-movement: a robust analysis', *Journal of Monetary Economics*, **52**, 113–57.

Natalucci, F. and F. Ravenna (2002), 'The road to adopting the euro: monetary policy and exchange rate regimes in EU candidate countries', Board of Governors of the Federal Reserve System International Finance Discussion Paper No. 741.

Rose, A.K. (2004), 'A meta-analysis of the effect of common currencies on international trade', NBER Working Paper 10373.

8. Managing capital inflows: Eastern Europe in an Asian mirror

Barry Eichengreen and Omar Choudhry

8.1 INTRODUCTION

The accession economies of Eastern Europe and the rapidly industrializing economies of East Asia are facing similar problems of managing capital inflows.[1] Both regions are attractive destinations for foreign investment by virtue of their relatively low labour costs – which makes them competitive export platforms – and their rapidly growing domestic markets. The magnitude of financial flows to the two regions is fairly similar: the Institute of International Finance forecasts for 2005 were for private financial flows of $122 billion to Emerging Europe and $134 billion to Emerging Asia.[2] Both regions maintain relatively stable exchange rates against their principal trading partners: Eastern Europe vis-à-vis the EU-15 and East Asia vis-à-vis the United States.[3] Both have capital market regimes that are substantially open to financial flows.

At the same time, outcomes in the two regions are visibly different. In Emerging Europe savings are insufficient to underwrite domestic investment; in most years the investment–savings gap translates into a current account deficit that is financed by capital inflows. (This was the case in 2003 and was again forecast to be the case in 2005, although Emerging Europe's current account was actually in modest surplus in 2004.) In Emerging Asia, in contrast, savings more than suffice to finance the region's investment. The result is a current account surplus, requiring private capital inflows to be more than absorbed into foreign reserves if they are not to produce unacceptable inflationary pressure.[4] Thus, in 2004 reserve accumulation in Emerging Asia was roughly twice the private capital inflow, whereas in Emerging Europe it was only half. In 2005 reserve accumulation in Emerging Asia was again forecast to be twice the private capital inflow whereas in Emerging Europe it is forecast to fall to less than a third (see Table 8.1).[5]

Understanding the problems associated with these outcomes and the policies that should be pursued in response requires first understanding the sources of these divergent patterns. The two regions differ in four relevant

Table 8.1 External financing (billions of dollars)

	Emerging Europe				Emerging Asia			
	2002	2003	2004e	2005f	2002	2003	2004e	2005f
Current account balance	8.2	−1.1	3.1	−6.7	73.6	100.7	120.4	113.1
External financing, net								
Private flows, net	45.6	65.6	97.4	101.1	60.5	116.3	146.3	125.6
Equity investment, net	22.3	5.7	27.9	30.4	59.5	91.1	100.5	105.0
Direct Investment, net	21.3	3.6	20.7	25.2	56.2	55.5	69.3	74.6
Portfolio investment, net	1.0	2.2	7.3	5.1	3.4	35.6	31.2	30.4
Private creditors, net	23.3	59.9	69.5	70.7	0.9	25.2	45.8	20.6
Commercial banks, net	5.5	23.1	29.3	33.9	−1.0	13.8	33.5	11.6
Nonbanks, net	17.8	36.8	40.2	36.8	2.0	11.4	12.3	9.0
Official flows, net	2.2	−4.3	−5.4	−17.5	−12.1	−14.4	−6.8	−4.1
IFIs	7.2	−0.3	−2.9	−4.7	−9.0	−9.7	−3.3	−1.7
Bilateral creditors	−5.0	−4.0	−2.4	−12.7	−3.1	−4.7	−3.5	−2.4
Resident lending/other, net[a]	−27.0	−24.4	−38.3	−41.5	−8.4	32.5	20.6	5.7
Reserves (− = increase)	−29.0	−35.9	−56.8	−35.4	−113.5	−235.1	−280.5	−240.3

Notes: e = estimate; f = IIF forecast; a. Including net lending, monetary gold and errors and omissions.

Source: Institute of International Finance (2005).

respects. First, compared to Emerging Europe, Emerging Asia, which is dominated by China, is even further behind the high-income countries and thus has even more scope for rapid growth. Fast-growing economies tend to be characterized by high private savings rates as residents attempt to capture the returns associated with the catch-up process.[6] Second, demographics have been conducive to higher savings rates in Emerging Asia – countries with higher old age dependency ratios such as those of Emerging Europe tending to save less – although this contrast should eventually disappear as a result of Asia's demographic transition (and China's one-child policy). Third, Emerging Asian economies (with some exceptions) have displayed greater fiscal discipline: high rates of public dissaving have not neutralized high private savings. Lastly, Emerging Asian countries, perceiving current account deficits as a source of vulnerability since the crisis of 1997–98, have been willing to accept less investment than they might otherwise have been able to sustain in order to limit their dependence on foreign capital, short-term foreign capital in particular.[7] Rightly or wrongly, the economies of Emerging Europe have been more confident about financing investment with foreign funds.

These policies and behavioural patterns have implications for relative prices. Eastern European countries have been running their economies under higher pressure of demand. Their current account deficits are telling us that domestic absorption exceeds domestic production. This relatively high level of demand creates a tendency for real exchange rates to appreciate. In Emerging Asia, in contrast, absorption falls short of production and the upward pressure on real rates is less. It is thus not surprising that discussion in Eastern Europe has centred on the question of whether real exchange rates are overvalued and current account deficits at current levels can be sustained, whereas in Emerging Asia the focus has been on whether real exchange rates are undervalued and there are limits to reserve accumulation.

Emerging Asia has been able to limit the impact of capital inflows on domestic demand and real exchange rates through low-cost sterilization. Because interest rates in the region, notably in China, are low, it has been able to sell domestic currency denominated government bonds and bills to mop up the monetary consequences of inflows without creating a burden for the fisc.[8] This low level of interest rates reflects the relatively depressed investment demand of the post-crisis period and the special financial circumstances prevailing in China. In Emerging Europe, in contrast, interest rates are higher than in the advanced countries that are the source of the capital inflows (which is the circumstance more typical of emerging markets). This renders sterilization costly, forcing central banks and governments to allow financial inflows to feed through into domestic demand

and real appreciation to a greater extent and to search for other expedients for coping with foreign capital.

This chapter develops these themes and their implications, mainly for the accession economies, including Turkey, but also implicitly for Asia. Section 8.2 first considers the extent to which real exchange rates in Emerging Europe and Emerging Asia can be interpreted in terms of the factors enumerated above. We extend a framework based on Kim and Korhonen (2002) relating the real exchange rate to productivity trends, the shares of investment and government consumption in GDP, trade openness and – in our implementation – capital account openness. This allows us to attribute observed real exchange rates to Balassa–Samuelson effects, investment ratios, government spending ratios and policies toward the external accounts.

Section 8.3 reviews the risks associated with large capital inflows and appreciating real exchange rates. We argue that these risks are at least as immediate for the economies of Emerging Europe as for many other parts of the world and more immediate than for the economies of Emerging Asia. This leads us in Section 8.4 to consider policies for managing capital movements and real exchange rates. The analysis there builds on evidence from a potential accession economy, Romania, which has already travelled a considerable way down the road that will eventually be followed by Turkey.

The basic message of this section is that although there exists a lengthy list of strategies that might be pursued in response to capital inflows, the only policy that is likely to be effective is fiscal consolidation. Unfortunately, there are political constraints to adjusting fiscal policy in response to the challenges of managing capital flows, although one can imagine some approaches to the design of fiscal mechanisms which might ameliorate this problem. This conclusion has implications for Emerging Asia as well: as financial conditions there, notably in China, continue to normalize, it will become more difficult for central banks and governments to sterilize inflows, creating the same challenges for fiscal policy.

Section 8.5 summarizes these points and reiterates their implications for current and future accession economies.

8.2 REAL EXCHANGE RATES

In this section we analyse the proximate determinants of real exchange rates in the accession economies. By now there is an immense literature on this subject (surveyed by Egert, 2004). Our goal is not to add to the catalogue of explanatory factors but to consider the extent to which the obvious policy and behavioural variables (investment ratios, government spending ratios, trade openness, capital account openness) can explain real exchange rate movements in Emerging Europe (and, by implication, the contrast with Emerging Asia).

We adapt a framework from Kim and Korhonen (2002) which permits a simple characterization of real exchange rates in the region. The model builds on the so-called Behavioural Real Exchange Rate literature (for example Clark and MacDonald, 1998). In this literature the long-run real exchange rate is related to a set of observable behavioural variables, such as relative per capita GDP (as a proxy for the Balassa-Samuelson effect), gross fixed investment as a share of GDP, government consumption as a share of GDP and trade openness (exports plus imports as a share of GDP). In our implementation we also consider proxies for the volume of capital inflows. Variable definitions and sources are given below.[9]

Panel unit root tests reject the null of stationarity, so the model is estimated in first differences. We treat the data as a panel, including country fixed effects. Like Kim and Korhonen, we also estimate the equation with lags of the independent variables, using the Akaike information criterion to choose the optimal number of lags.[10] We start with the sample of small and medium-sized countries (both developed and developing) considered by Kim and Korhonen (KK). The advantage of this is that the typical country in the sample is not radically different in size from the typical accession economy; the corresponding problem is that the resulting sample is something of a hodge-podge.[11] However, our sample period is different: whereas Kim and Korhonen consider the period 1975–99, our data continue through 2003. We define the real exchange rate as the product of the nominal exchange rate E and the foreign price level P^* divided by the domestic price level P. We use US consumer prices as a proxy for P^*.

Taking the natural logarithm of EP^*/P as the dependent variable, we obtain the results reported in the first column of Table 8.2 (including only the concurrent values of the independent variables) and Table 8.3 (including also lagged values). The results are consistent with those reported by Kim and Korhonen. Higher per capita incomes are associated with real appreciation, consistent with the operation of the Balassa–Samuelson effect.[12] Higher levels of fixed investment and government consumption are similarly associated with real appreciation; this makes sense in so far as higher levels of domestic demand tend to drive up the prices of domestic goods. The coefficient on trade openness does not have a consistent sign. In Table 8.2 a higher level of trade openness is associated with real depreciation, which is again intuitive, since a lower real exchange rate is necessary to encourage foreign demand for domestic goods (to ensure adequate domestic consumption). In Table 8.3 the estimated effect of trade openness is negative.

We then re-estimated the relationship on data for a sample of emerging markets. We chose middle-income countries, largely in East Asia and

Table 8.2 Fixed-effects estimates of determinants of real exchange rates

	Fixed effects (KK)	Fixed effects (EC)	Fixed effects (EC)	Fixed effects IV (EC)
GDP per capita	−0.10	0.04	0.02	0.05
	(0.05)	(0.06)	(0.06)	(0.06)
Fixed investment	−1.49	−0.53	−0.13	0.02
	(0.20)	(0.26)	(0.29)	(0.30)
Government cons.	−1.28	−1.54	−1.16	−1.61
	(0.44)	(0.38)	(0.39)	(0.39)
Trade openness	0.58	0.78	0.78	0.80
	(0.07)	(0.08)	(0.08)	(0.08)
Capital flows	–	–	−0.88	−3.02
			(0.22)	(0.63)
N	781	819	775	795
Adj. R^2	0.99	0.46	0.46	0.47

Notes: Standard errors appear in parentheses. KK denotes Kim–Korhonen sample. EC denotes Eichengreen–Choudhry sample.

Source: See text.

Table 8.3 Fixed-effects estimates of determinants of real exchange rates, with lags

	Static FE (KK)	Static FE (EC)	Static FE (EC)	Static FE IV (EC)
GDP per capita	−0.46	−0.72	−0.58	−0.65
	(0.03)	(0.03)	(0.03)	(0.03)
Fixed investment	−0.70	−0.72	−0.65	−0.65
	(0.04)	(0.04)	(0.03)	(0.03)
Government cons.	−0.49	−0.60	−0.53	−0.53
	(0.04)	(0.03)	(0.04)	(0.03)
Trade openness	−0.39	−0.26	−0.50	−0.45
	(0.04)	(0.04)	(0.03)	(0.04)
Capital flows	–	–	−0.45	−0.30
			(0.03)	(0.03)
N	812	868	868	868
Adj. R^2	0.23	0.25	0.29	0.44

Notes: Standard errors appear in parentheses. KK denotes Kim–Korhonen sample. EC denotes Eichengreen–Choudhry sample.

Source: See text.

Latin America, most comparable to Emerging Europe.[13] (We refer to this as the Eichengreen–Choudhry or EC sample.) The results in column 2 of tables 8.2 and 8.3 are broadly similar to before, the main difference being that our crude proxy for the Balassa–Samuelson effect no longer enters with a coefficient that differs significantly from zero at standard confidence levels when only the contemporaneous value is included, as in Table 8.2.[14]

Next we added capital inflows, measured as the net sum of the balance of direct investment, portfolio investment, and other investment transactions as a share of GDP, in order to capture their impact on the real exchange rate. In column 3 of tables 8.2 and 8.3 this variable enters with a negative sign, confirming that inflows lead to real appreciation.[15] A potential problem is simultaneity: real exchange rate movements affect capital inflows as well as the other way around. We therefore instrumented the capital inflows variable using measures of the age structure of the population (following Eichengreen and Fifer, 2002) and the quality of institutions (following Kalemli-Özcan et al., 2003). Our instruments are the percentage of the population between 15 and 64, the ratio of dependants to working-age population, the percentage of the population in urban areas, Freedom House's two-yearly scores of economic freedom and strength of property rights, polity scores of the strength of political institutions, and year and country fixed effects. The estimated effect of capital inflows, reported in the fourth column of the tables, is robust to this econometric treatment.[16]

We now use the coefficient estimates in column 3 of Table 8.2 and the values of the independent variables to compare actual exchange rates with their predicted levels. We show three series in Figures 8.1–8.11. The line interrupted by diamonds is the actual real exchange rate. (Recall that, as defined, a decline denotes a real appreciation.) The bold line is the level of the real exchange rate predicted by country-specific values of the independent variables. Finally, the light line is the value of the real exchange rate predicted by sample mean values of the independent variables for each year. The Czech Republic, Hungary, Slovakia and, to a lesser extent, Slovenia appear at least modestly overvalued. Poland appears to be fairly valued on the basis of our estimates. Turkey appears to have gained some relief from a modest overvaluation as a result of its 2001 devaluation but that problem seems to have re-emerged subsequently as a result of its relatively high inflation and relatively strong nominal rate.[17]

In contrast, most of the East Asian countries appear at least modestly undervalued in the post-financial crisis period, the devaluations of 1997–98 having led to large real depreciations and subsequent policies having kept their currencies competitively valued. Note, however, that Thailand is not

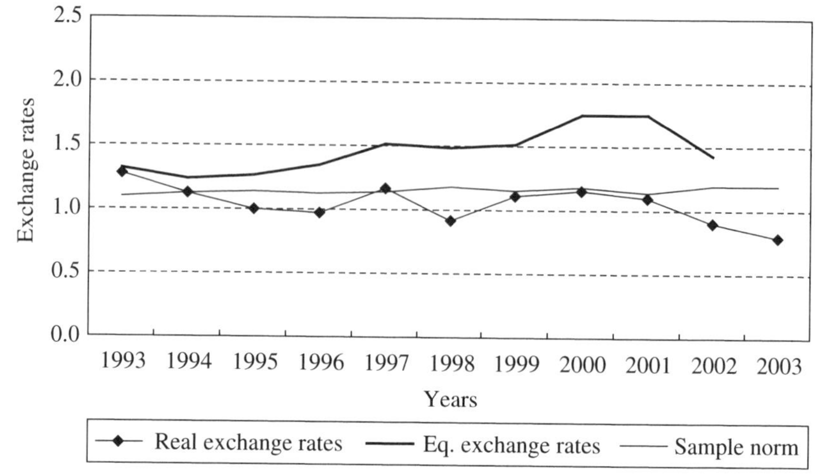

Figure 8.1 Real exchange rates for the Czech Republic

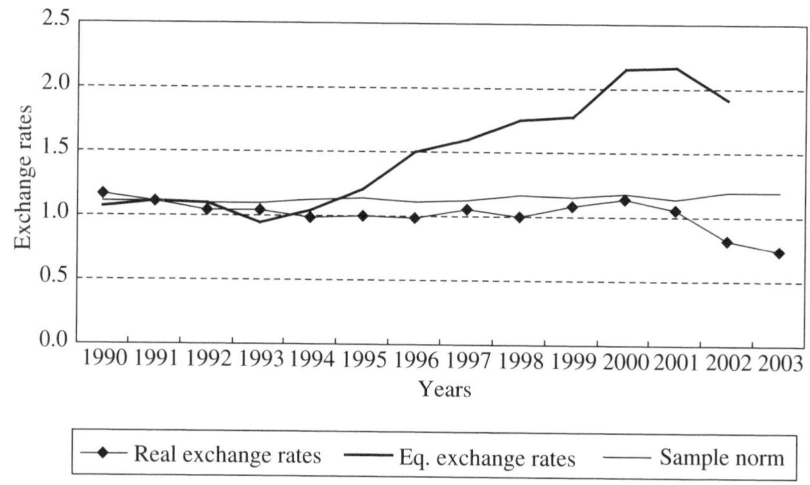

Figure 8.2 Real exchange rates for Hungary

obviously undervalued relative to the levels warranted by the country-specific values of the independent variables. And, by this measure, there is little evidence that China is significantly undervalued.[18]

The particularities of these country-specific results notwithstanding, our results broadly confirm that the Eastern European and East Asian countries have managed capital inflows in ways which have very different

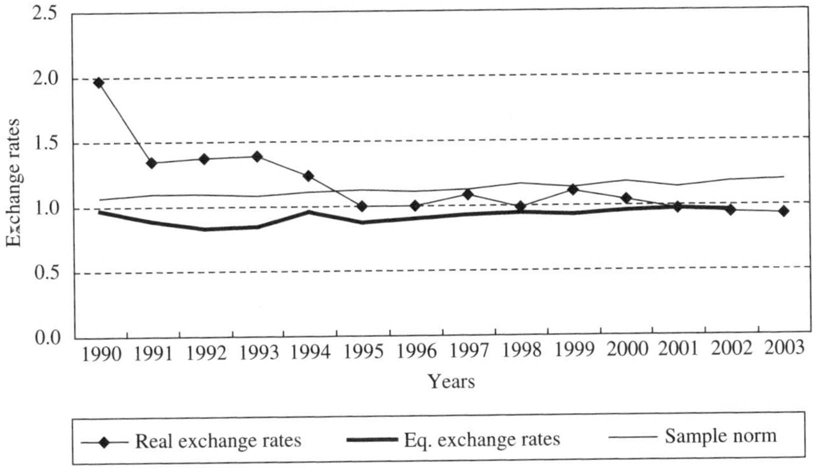

Figure 8.3 Real exchange rates for Poland

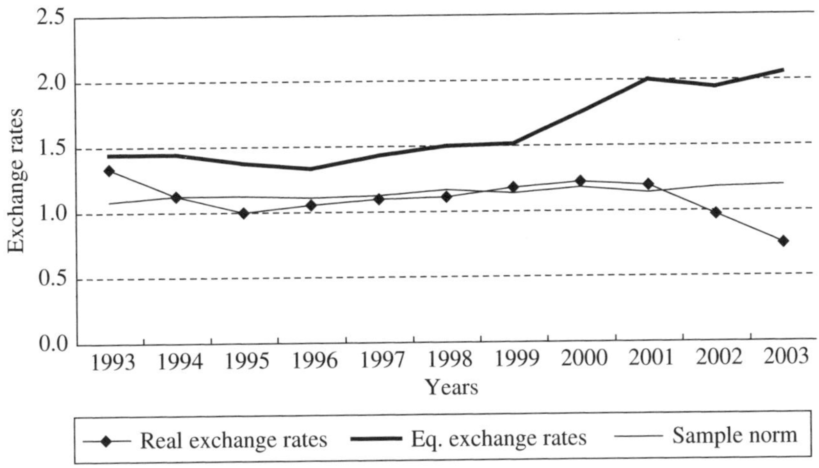

Figure 8.4 Real exchange rates for Slovakia

implications for the evolution of real exchange rates. Although capital inflows have important implications for the evolution of exchange rates, differences in their magnitude – and differences in the other determinants of real exchange rates analysed in Table 8.2 – cannot by themselves explain observed differences in real exchange rate outcomes. In addition there is evidently a role for the management of capital inflows of the sort pointed to in the introduction to this chapter.

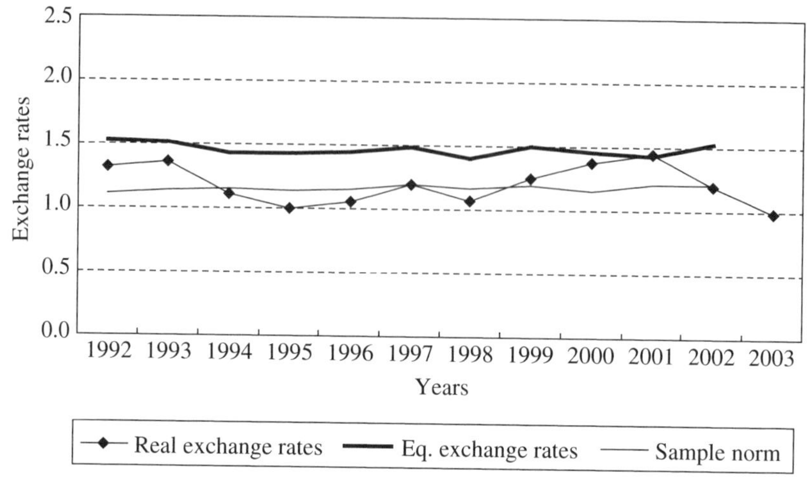

Figure 8.5 Real exchange rates for Slovenia

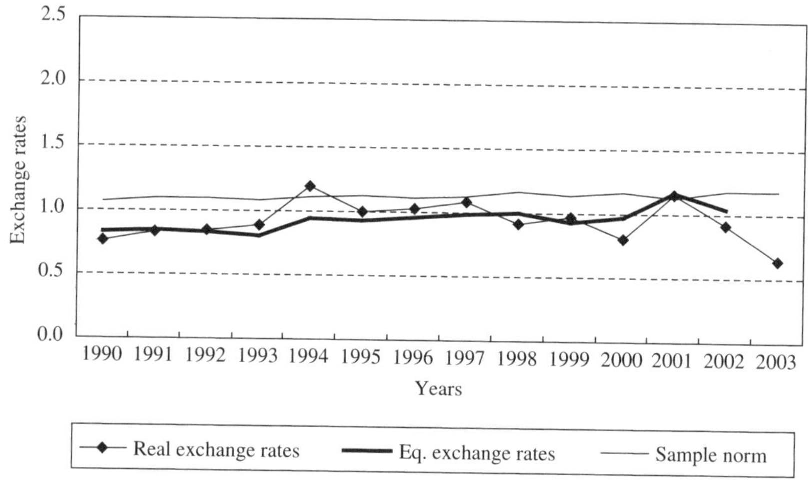

Figure 8.6 Real exchange rates for Turkey

8.3 REAL EXCHANGE RATE RISKS

The risk of allowing a current account deficit to develop and the real exchange rate to appreciate substantially in response to capital inflows is that those inflows can dry up abruptly, requiring sudden compression of the balance and a sharp shift in the real exchange rate. As observers

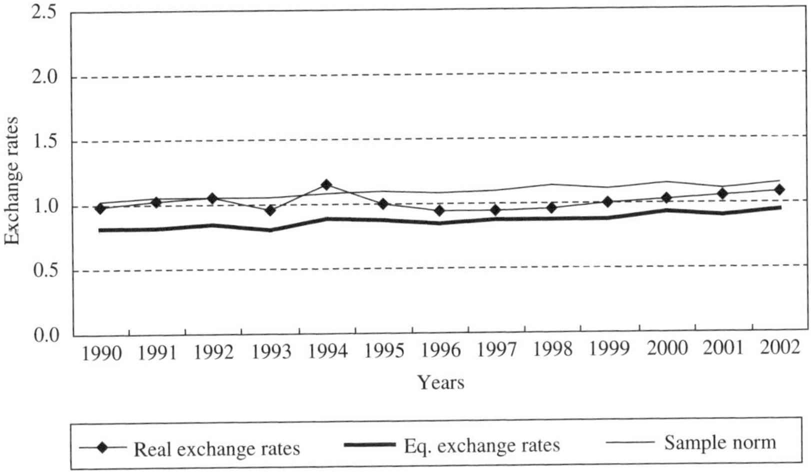

Figure 8.7 Real exchange rates for China

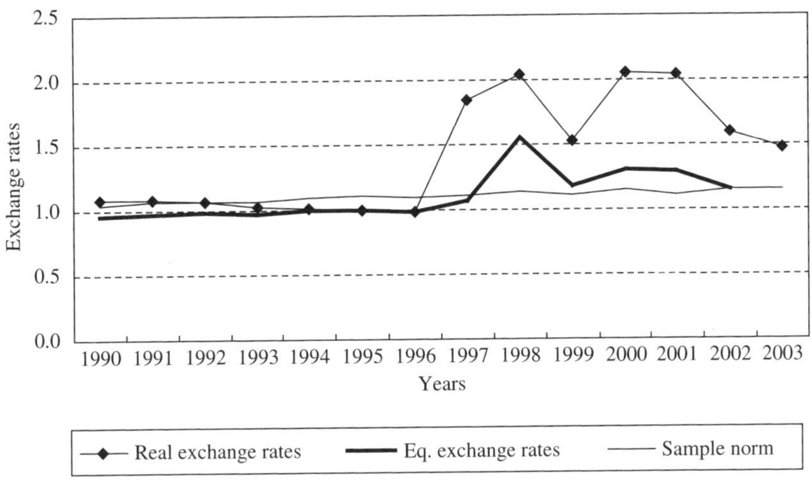

Figure 8.8 Real exchange rates for Indonesia

familiar with the experience of Emerging Asia will know, 'sharp compression of the balance' is an antiseptic phrase that disguises the painful nature of the fall in spending necessary for narrowing a current account deficit. In practical terms, the adjustment works as follows. As foreign capital stops flowing in, financial conditions tighten. The trigger has often been a rise in US interest rates, as higher yields make investing in the safe haven of US Treasury bonds more attractive. This possibility was much discussed,

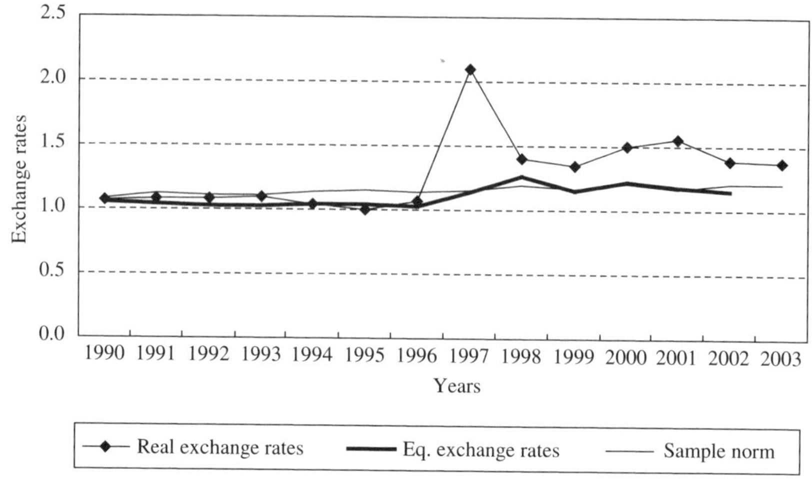

Figure 8.9 Real exchange rates for Korea

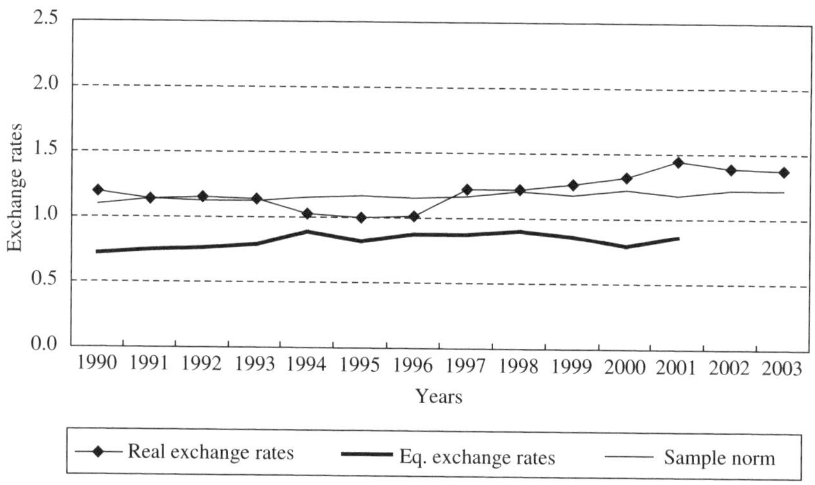

Figure 8.10 Real exchange rates for Singapore

of course, after the Fed issued a strong statement of concern about inflation in mid-March 2005. But one can equally imagine other factors, such as political uncertainty in the capital-importing country, capable of triggering a similar reaction. The resulting rise in interest rates facilitates adjustment to the declining availability of financial resources by reducing spending in general and investment spending in particular. As absorption falls,

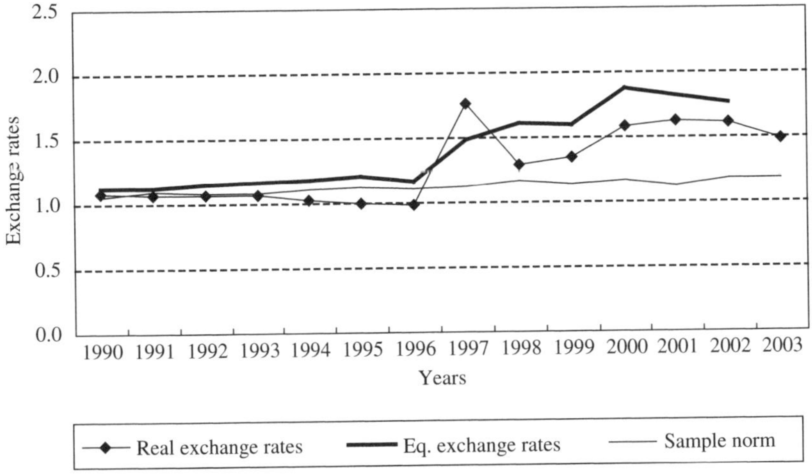

Figure 8.11 Real exchange rates for Thailand

resources are redeployed to the export sector. This reallocation is facilitated by a rise in the relative price of exports (depreciation of the real exchange rate), which is in turn achieved through a combination of lower domestic inflation, and more likely, a higher rate of currency depreciation.

In the industrial countries this adjustment has sometimes been completed without severe disruptions. The decline in the exchange rate is orderly. Exports are crowded in. The fall in the rate of growth is moderate.[19] In emerging markets, in contrast, the adjustment associated with sudden stops has frequently been disruptive.[20] Typically the size of the capital account reversal and the requisite change in domestic spending have been larger, requiring still larger changes in the relative price of traded goods. In addition, the financial system is more susceptible to destabilization by these events. The exchange rate depreciation brought on by the sudden stop has caused financial distress for banks and non-financial firms with currency mismatches on their balance sheets. The result has been a sharp fall in output, major declines in asset prices and a surge in bankruptcies. This is a simple way of characterizing what happened in Emerging Asia in 1997–98. The question is whether something similar could happen in Emerging Europe. A number of reasons are given for why policymakers in Emerging Europe can afford to be more sanguine. The Czech Republic, Slovakia, Slovenia, Hungary, Poland and the Baltics already possess the safety net of EU membership. Eventually – in most cases presumably by the end of the decade – they will also adopt the euro. The main advantage of EU membership in this context is that it minimizes the risk of destabilizing shifts in government policy that might precipitate a sudden reversal in the direction of flows. Both the strictures of the *acquis communautaire* and the widening web of commitments to their EU partners minimize the risk that some future populist government will nationalize foreign owned enterprises or otherwise expropriate foreign investments. Unfortunately, they do not also rule out the possibility that new doubts about fiscal sustainability or a major bank failure could precipitate the reversal of capital flows, especially in the period prior to adoption of the euro. In a period when the new member states are supposed to be demonstrating their readiness for adopting the euro, it seems unlikely that the incumbents will bail them out of their difficulties.

To be sure, once these countries are allowed to adopt the euro, one channel through which the destabilizing effects of such reversals are felt – the interaction of exchange rate depreciation with currency mismatches – will be eliminated. Since these countries will be borrowing mainly within the euro area, there will be neither exchange rate movements nor currency mismatches to exert destabilizing balance-sheet effects. The only problem is that the EU seems intent on consigning the new members (most of them at least) to an extended waiting period in the euro area's anteroom. All estimates of the dates by which the new members will be permitted to adopt the euro seem to be undergoing revision in the same direction, namely that of later adoption. In any case, just eliminating currency mismatches will not eliminate the other sources of financial fragility that may still cause capital flows to reverse abruptly.

Two other observations commonly offered to provide reassurance regarding Emerging Europe's position are that its current account deficits reflect imports of capital goods and intermediate inputs required for the production of exports and that its deficits are being fully financed by FDI inflows.[21] That imports have a high capital goods and intermediate-input component is perhaps more reassuring than the alternative.[22] But the argument that imports of investment goods are not a problem (and its cousin, the argument that current account deficits reflecting high investment are benign) has been discredited by the Asian crisis. High investment is not the same as efficient investment and inefficient investment is unlikely to deliver a significant increase in exports. Even if funds are allocated efficiently, there is still certain to be a considerable delay between the importation of capital goods and the subsequent increase in exports during which any number of things can go wrong.

Some economists (for example Taylor and Sarno, 1999) suggest that FDI is more stable than portfolio capital flows – that the permanent component of FDI is larger.[23] But if a shock causes FDI to fall off abruptly, the result can still be a sharp shift in the real exchange rate to which banks and firms find it painful to adjust. The saving grace, it is said, is that FDI is unlikely to reverse direction and flow out in large amounts. Foreign capital equipment, once installed, is effectively bolted to the floor. The limitation of this view is that foreign owned enterprises also hold local financial assets that they can and will sell if things go wrong, resulting in large outflows and an even larger shift in the real exchange rate.

All these are reasons to worry that the risks posed by large current account deficits and appreciated real exchange rates are no less in Emerging Europe than other regions. The question is then what governments and central banks should do when faced with a surge of capital inflows.

8.4 STRATEGIES AND TACTICS

What is the standard advice for dealing with these risks? The standard menu includes seven items: increasing exchange rate flexibility, maintaining capital account restrictions, strengthening prudential supervision, sterilizing inflows, loosening monetary policy, tightening fiscal policy and negotiating a programme with the IMF. The economies of Emerging Europe have experimented with most of these strategies. However, all but one of them have serious limitations. In practice most of the burden falls on tightening fiscal policy. And this is problematic since there are political constraints on fiscal adjustment.

In what follows we illustrate these points with evidence from the experience of Romania. We focus on this case because Romania is at the stage of the accession process that Turkey is likely to enter, say, five years from now, and also because Romania has attempted to deploy the entire range of policies commonly recommended for managing capital inflows. Romania is currently scheduled to join the EU in 2007, although the safeguard clause could conceivably be invoked, pushing back accession to 2008. The country is running a substantial current account deficit on the order of 7.5 per cent of GDP, although most of this is being financed by FDI, given Romania's attractiveness as one of the next wave of accession economies and restrictions on other forms of foreign investment. According to the agreement negotiated with the EU, all restrictions on financial flows will have to be eliminated by 2007 at the latest. In fact, the government is moving even faster. It allowed non-residents to start opening leu-denominated deposit accounts on 11 April 2005 and at last report it was planning to substantially open the capital account by the end of June 2005.[24]

The danger is that the country will then be identified as the next convergence play if it hasn't been already.[25] Large amounts of portfolio capital could flow in, creating inflationary pressures and leading to real appreciation in the short run and the risk of a disruptive reversal subsequently. The IMF worries that real appreciation could erode the competitiveness of the textile and furniture sectors into which much of the FDI inflow is currently going, causing this relatively stable source of financing to dry up. If doubts then develop about the sustainability of the current account, the inevitability of convergence could be called into question and financial capital flows might reverse direction with devastating consequences.

Standard advice for discouraging hot money inflows is to introduce greater exchange rate uncertainty (Goldstein, 2002). In the presence of two-way bets, speculators are less likely to take large unhedged bets on trend appreciation. In late 2004 the National Bank of Romania (NBR) therefore announced that it intended to limit foreign exchange market intervention and stop announcing indicative real appreciation targets for the leu. Both measures are designed to render the path of the exchange rate less predictable.[26] The effectiveness of this measure can be questioned, however, since there has been only a limited increase in currency volatility.[27] Expectations of secular appreciation remain strong, forcing the NBR to lean against the wind, damping volatility. In addition, once Romania actually enters the EU, it will come under pressure to enter the Exchange Rate Mechanism of the European Monetary System, whose bands will further limit the scope for exchange rate variability and the central bank's ability to introduce a modicum of exchange rate uncertainty.

The Romanian National Bank is reportedly considering a package of measures to limit short-term inflows, including a minimum reserve requirement on financial investment by non-residents and/or a tax on investments under one year (Deutsche Bank, 2005b).[28] The experience of other countries, Chile for example, suggests that such measures can help to limit the volume of portfolio capital inflows or at least lengthen their average maturity. In addition the evidence suggests that the effectiveness of such restrictions tends to decline over time, as market participants find a growing number of ways of circumventing them. The fact that Romania has closed the chapter of the *acquis* concerned with the free movement of capital suggests in any case that these measures have to be regarded as temporary, since Brussels is unlikely to permit their retention once the country joins the EU. Whether it will object to them even before membership is an accomplished fact remains unclear. One hopes not, for such measures can play a useful role in limiting the extent of maturity mismatches.

This way of framing the regulation of short-term capital inflows encourages one to think of such measures as prudential policy. In turn, this suggests buttressing these transitory measures with permanent prudential regulations. Strengthening the prudential supervision of the banks is a way of reducing the risks to the financial system from large capital inflows and the possibility of their reversal.[29] Raising capital and liquidity requirements above internationally mandated minimum standards and limiting permissible currency mismatches are the standard recommendations in this connection.[30] At the same time, the case of Argentina, where exceptionally ambitious capital and liquidity requirements were in fact adopted, suggests that these policies have limits; the banks will still suffer severely if the firms and households to which they have passed on that currency exposure find themselves unable to repay when capital flows reverse direction and the currency depreciates. In the corporate sector, excessive dependence on foreign currency funding can be discouraged by strengthening corporate governance (requiring firms to disclose more financial information and strengthening the legal rights of outside shareholders). Unfortunately, such fundamental institutional reforms are difficult for emerging markets; even under the best of circumstances they take time to complete.

The other obvious way of attempting to neutralize the impact of imported capital on real and financial conditions is by sterilizing inflows. The central bank sells domestic currency denominated bonds in exchange for the foreign currency finance that has flowed in, mopping up the additional liquidity and adding foreign bonds to its asset portfolio. The problem for a country like Romania is that sterilization is costly: the interest rates on the additional domestic currency denominated bonds that the authorities must now service exceeds the yield on the foreign bonds that they add to their portfolio. Injecting additional domestic currency denominated bonds into the market drives up interest rates, which further increases the costs of sterilization, while at the same time heightening the incentive for foreign investors to shift more financial capital toward the country. This makes large-scale sterilization costly for the fisc and potentially problematic.

In contrast, many Asian countries, enjoying low interest rates, have not encountered this problem when sterilizing inflows, at least not yet. In China, for example, sterilization is economical because the interest rate on domestic government securities remains less than that on US Treasury bonds. Over time, however, Chinese interest rates will rise, rendering this strategy more problematic.

Another alternative sometimes recommended for dealing with capital inflows is to cut interest rates. Lower rates will moderate the inflow-induced appreciation of the currency, limiting the erosion of competitiveness, and make interest arbitrage less attractive. This strategy avoids the problems with sterilization reviewed above. Thus, the first half of March 2005 saw a number of Central and Eastern European central banks cut interest rates with this goal in mind. But cutting interest rates when inflation and demand are accelerating is perverse and potentially damaging to credibility. It is undesirable to the extent that it simply substitutes one source of excess liquidity and inflationary pressure for another. In so far as the cut in interest rates is inappropriate given domestic conditions, expectations will develop that it will probably be reversed anyway, minimizing its impact.[31]

This leaves fiscal policy. Consolidated budget deficits in the four big Central and Eastern European countries are averaging about 4 per cent of GDP. In Romania the deficit is 2 per cent. In Turkey it is 6 per cent.[32] In all these countries experiencing capital inflows there is room for fiscal tightening. Tightening fiscal policy will offset some of the expansionary impact of capital inflows on domestic demand, thereby limiting inflation and real appreciation. It will put downward pressure on interest rates, limiting the incentive for capital inflows.

For Romania the IMF has duly recommended cuts in public spending and/or increases in taxes. The difficulty is that its call comes in the wake of an electoral campaign in which the victorious party promised tax reductions. It flies in the face of the additional fiscal costs of readying the country for EU membership. Romania will receive transfers from the EU for public investment in the amount of 4 per cent of GDP over the next 3 to 4 years, and these require domestic co-financing through the budget. Pension reform in preparation for EU membership will also have substantial short-run fiscal costs.[33] In the hope of remaining an attractive destination for FDI, Romania has matched Slovakia's move to a flat 16 per cent tax (replacing a corporate profits tax of 25 per cent and personal income taxes ranging from 18 to 40 per cent); this too is likely to have some short-run revenue cost. The IMF recommends an offsetting increase in VAT tax rates (to 21 per cent), the problem being that this would be highly visible to consumers.

Not infrequently one observes reluctance on the part of the authorities to pursue fiscal consolidation. This is not surprising when one recalls that the measures in question operate by increasing the cost of funding to the private sector and reducing effective demand and growth. Fiscal consolidation will tend to reduce demand and growth assuming that the standard Keynesian effects dominate. This means that growth will decelerate in the short run, other things equal.[34] The argument for nonetheless pursuing these measures is that growth at this now slightly slower rate is more likely to be sustainable. It is less vulnerable to sudden interruption by the disruptive reversal of capital flows. Unfortunately, in new democracies it is often difficult for governments to incur these short-term costs in return for long-term benefits.

The same difficulty also arises for the other measures recommended for managing capital inflows. Requiring banks to hold more liquid balances or preventing them from funding themselves in foreign currency when they lack foreign currency denominated assets increases lending and borrowing costs. A higher cost of capital slows investment and growth. Lower investment and growth are precisely what strengthen the current account. They are what produce a balance of payments equilibrium consistent with the now lower level of portfolio capital inflows. But they are not easy for governments to justify and defend in the face of electoral pressure.

An IMF programme is often recommended as a way of coping with these difficulties. Romania (like Turkey) has a programme that requires the government to commit to specific fiscal actions. Fiscal consolidation may be easier for the government to sell to the public when the authorities can point to the availability of IMF resources as one of the benefits. In addition investor confidence may be strengthened by the presence of a Fund programme, rendering a country less susceptible to sudden capital flow reversals. Unfortunately, the record of compliance of programme countries with the Fund's fiscal conditions is at best chequered.[35] We are unaware of research showing that programme countries are less susceptible to sudden stops.[36] The financial insurance provided by a Fund programme is very limited compared to the size of the potential reversal, while changes in disbursals are unlikely to occur at the same speed as changes in capital flows.

At the time of writing, we see these problems visibly in Hungary. The Hungarian government is running budget deficits on the order of 4 per cent of GDP (5 per cent if payments associated with reform of the pension system are included). This combines with large capital inflows to create strong demand pressure, which is pushing up the real exchange rate and fuelling a current account deficit currently running at 8 per cent of GDP. The removal of restrictions on capital flows, as required by the country's accession to the EU, has enabled financial institutions to fund themselves abroad, in foreign currency, and make euro and Swiss franc denominated loans to households and firms. (Sixty per cent of new mortgages are now foreign currency denominated. Mortgage loans and consumer loans, notably for financing purchases of motor vehicles, were the best selling bank products in 2004.)[37] The result is the creation of growing currency mismatches threatening to create serious financial problems and the collapse of consumer confidence if and when a shock to confidence causes the exchange rate to weaken.

The obvious treatment is to reduce the budget deficit and thereby moderate demand pressure, limit the appreciation of the real exchange rate, lower domestic interest rates and stem capital inflows. Unfortunately, in a new democracy this is easier said than done. The Hungarian government has a history of setting ambitious fiscal targets and missing them. Whether it does better this time may turn out to be critical for financial stability.

8.5 CONCLUSION

This chapter has considered the challenges of managing capital flows in Emerging European countries aspiring to membership in the European Union. It has shown that policies leading to dependence on capital inflows can have important implications for relative prices and macroeconomic conditions. For a variety of reasons the countries of Emerging Europe have run larger current account deficits and relied on foreign finance for a larger share of their investment than the economies of Emerging Asia. This explains, at least in part, the different evolution of their real exchange rates. It also renders them more vulnerable to real and financial disruptions if capital inflows are interrupted.

We then considered a variety of policies that have been suggested for addressing these problems: increasing exchange rate flexibility, maintaining capital account restrictions, strengthening prudential supervision, attempting to sterilize inflows, loosening monetary policy, tightening fiscal policy and negotiating a programme with the IMF. The experiences and arguments here suggest that only fiscal policy adjustments are likely to contribute significantly to a solution. The other strategies tend to have either a marginal impact or counterproductive side effects. Although Asia has had an easy way out of this dilemma as a result of special financial circumstances causing interest rates in the region to be even lower than those prevailing in the rest of the world, this is not likely to remain the case indefinitely. Sooner or later, the burden on and need for adjustments in fiscal policy will become greater.

These dilemmas are already evident in Turkey, which has adopted most of the standard treatments for coping with large capital inflows. The country has already moved to a managed float: central bank intervention in the foreign exchange market is limited to preventing excessive volatility without attempting to target a trend level.[38] Subject to these constraints it has sought to sterilize inflows, purchasing foreign exchange through market friendly auctions. It has negotiated a new three-year programme with the IMF. It has strengthened supervision and regulation of the banking and financial system. It has tightened fiscal policy, aiming for a primary surplus of at least 6.5 per cent of GDP. The modest impact of these measures on the volume of capital inflows is a visible demonstration of the limited efficacy of the standard measures.

What more, then, can the authorities do? Clearly, there are political limits to further adjusting fiscal policy in a new democracy. One additional measure that the Turkish authorities might contemplate is imposing holding-period taxes and/or deposit requirements on portfolio capital inflows in an effort to skew these in the direction of longer maturities, such as the taxes and deposit requirements used for a time by Chile and currently under consideration by Romania. Another is to redesign the country's fiscal institutions so that they do some of the necessary adjustments automatically. A fiscal system that taxes nontraded goods as extensively as traded goods will raise additional revenues when capital inflows cause the real exchange rate to appreciate and shift additional resources into the nontradables sector. Recent efforts at tax simplication, by seeking to bring the underground economy to the surface, may have some effect in these terms. Special taxes on real estate transactions may provide automatic stabilization, given that the property market tends to be disproportionately stimulated by capital inflows.[39]

Unfortunately, none of this guarantees the country insulation from the ebb and flow of international capital movements. Such is the unavoidable fate of a country committed to globalization and to accession to the European Union.

NOTES

1. Because this chapter was finalized in 2005, it refers to Bulgaria and Romania as potential rather than actual accession economies, neither country actually having acceded to the EU at that time. In the case of Emerging Asia, we include China as well as the Newly Industrializing Economies and the principal ASEAN countries.
2. See Institute of International Finance (2005). Given the magnitude of the respective regional economies, this means that private inflows scaled by regional GDP are greater in Emerging Europe.
3. And the associated dollar zone.
4. As we will see in Section 8.2, the reality is somewhat more complex, although the preceding is still a useful way of characterizing the contrast. In addition, there is the question of what elements of the preceding account are fundamentally exogenous. The paragraph essentially characterizes the current account and the capital flow as exogenous and the reserve accumulation as the endogenous balancing item. At some level, of course, all three elements are endogenous and depend on deeper structural and behavioural characteristics like those about to be described.
5. Where the forecasts again are those of the Institute of International Finance (2005).
6. The association of income growth with savings rates is theoretically ambiguous, since the income and substitution effects work in opposite directions. Empirically, the evidence is strongly supportive of the view that the two variables are positively correlated.
7. Another way of saying this is that they have been intent on accumulating large foreign reserves. This reaction is evident in the swing into current account surplus of Emerging Asia ex. China starting in 1998. The fall in investment rates is particularly evident in the ASEAN 4, led by Indonesia.
8. Japan, one of the region's large accumulators of reserves, has not attempted to sterilize the impact on the domestic money supply of its large reserve accumulation, despite also possessing very low interest rates. But it, clearly, is a special case.
9. Most data are obtained from the World Bank's *World Development Indicators* (*WDI*) and the International Monetary Fund's *International Financial Statistics* (*IFS*). Data on exchange rates, price levels and capital inflows come from *IFS*. Macroeconomic data on

GDP, per capita GDP, gross fixed capital formation, government final consumption expenditure, imports and exports are obtained from *WDI*.

Freedom House scores for political rights and civil liberties are available at http://www.freedomhouse.org. Polity scores for regime type can be found at the website for the Polity IV Project, http://www.cidcm.umd.edu/inscr/polity. Variables on the age structure of the population, the percentage of the population that is urban, and political risk are obtained from *WDI*.

10. We also experimented with the Pooled Mean Group estimator proposed by Pesaran et al. (1999), which allows for dynamics by introducing lags and allowing the coefficients to differ across countries in the short run while constraining them to equality in the long run. The joint Hausmann test statistic constructed by Pesaran et al. confirms that we can constrain the long-run coefficients to be equal across countries. While the results using this more general specification are broadly consistent with those obtained using fixed effects where the coefficients are constrained to be equal across countries in the short run as well as the long run, they are sensitive to the composition of the sample. Dropping out an individual country can alter both the sign and significance levels of a number of the common long-run coefficients. We experimented as well with the Mean Group estimator that allows the coefficients to differ by country in both the short run and the long run, but the large number of parameters estimated in this case meant that few coefficients were significantly different from zero.
11. Kim and Korhonen's (2002) sample consists of Algeria, Chile, Colombia, Guatemala, the Republic of Korea, Malaysia, Mexico, Morocco, the Philippines, South Africa, Thailand, Turkey, Venezuela, Australia, Austria, Belgium, Canada, Cyprus, France, Greece, Hong Kong, Iceland, Ireland, Italy, Japan, Norway, Portugal, Sweden and Switzerland.
12. Note that since we are including country fixed effects, we are picking up here the impact of secular income growth on changes in real exchange rates over time, not of cross-country variations in incomes and productivity.
13. The countries in our sample are Argentina, Bolivia, Brazil, Chile, China, Colombia, Costa Rica, Dominica, the Dominican Republic, Ecuador, El Salvador, Guatemala, Guyana, Honduras, Indonesia, Israel, the Republic of Korea, Malaysia, Mexico, Nicaragua, Panama, Papua New Guinea, Paraguay, Peru, the Philippines, Singapore, Thailand, Trinidad and Tobago, Turkey, Uruguay and Venezuela. Note that the accession economies are themselves omitted from this sample, given the problems for estimation created by rapid structural change over the sample period. Thus, the forecasts of real exchange rates for the accession economies we provide below can be regarded as out-of-sample forecasts.
14. Fixing this would presumably require constructing a measure of productivity growth that distinguished traded and nontraded goods sectors.
15. The other effects are basically unchanged.
16. The point estimate in Table 8.2 may be implausibly large: it suggests that a capital inflow in the amount of 4 per cent of GDP leads to a 12 per cent real appreciation, other things equal. That in Table 8.3 suggests instead an effect an order of magnitude smaller.
17. That the predicted value of the real rate depreciates over time in most of these countries is counterintuitive, given the tendency toward real appreciation generally evident in transition economies. Here it reflects the strong estimated effect of greater trade openness (which leads to real depreciation, other things equal) in combination with the weak estimated effect of real GDP (the absence of a strong estimated Balassa–Samuelson effect working in the other direction). Thus, we would not make too much of the predictions generated by these equations, except in so far as they confirm the tendency for capital inflows to cause real appreciation.
18. The progressively greater openness of the Chinese economy translates into real depreciation according to our estimates. This is offset by growing capital inflows and a rising investment rate, both of which make for real appreciation. Be this as it may, this controversial finding clearly warrants further analysis.

19. See Croke et al. (2005) for a study that reaches these conclusions but also Edwards (2005) for a dissenting view where it is argued that even in the industrial countries the output effects are more likely to be negative.
20. Often but not always: see Milesi-Ferretti and Razin (1997) and Edwards (2004).
21. Not in all cases, however; in Hungary, for example, FDI inflows cover only about half of the current account deficit. The remainder is largely accounted for by portfolio capital flows, substantially in the form of non-resident purchases of government bonds.
22. In Turkey, capital and intermediate goods account for more than 80 per cent of total imports.
23. Although not all studies reach the same conclusion.
24. As an early step in that direction, it allowed non-residents to open leu-denominated accounts beginning in June 2005.
25. For evidence of this see Deutsche Bank (2005a).
26. They are also seen as preconditions for the central bank's eventual move to inflation targeting, an exchange rate centred policy strategy being seen as incompatible with this approach to monetary management.
27. The date of the NBR's announcement was 2 November 2004. Before this time, the standard deviation of daily changes in the leu was about 180 leu per dollar. After the announcement, the standard deviation as of mid-April 2005 increased to 430 leu per dollar. The standard deviation of the daily percentage changes was 5 per cent before the announcement and 1.5 per cent afterwards.
28. In part this is an effort to respond to the growing ability of investors to get around more selective regulations through, inter alia, the use of special purpose vehicles.
29. The greater internationalization of their banking systems may be an area where Emerging Europe has an advantage over Emerging Asia, in so far as the foreign banks that have penetrated the region have tighter internal controls and tighter prudential standards. To be sure, the extent of banking system internationalization varies considerably within the region (see Valintinyi, 2003). This is an area where Turkey, for example, can go considerably further.
30. See for example Goldstein and Turner (2004).
31. A related strategy is to intervene in the foreign exchange market to limit the currency's appreciation (as for example Slovakia did starting in March 2005). But this approach is limited by the costs of sterilization and by the incompatibility of the measure with the desire to introduce greater exchange rate uncertainty (see above).
32. As estimated by Morgan Stanley for 2005.
33. As recognized in the recent revision of the Stability and Growth Pact.
34. Non-Keynesian effects may be felt in circumstances where the public debt is clearly on an unsustainable path, in which case early fiscal consolidation may in fact inspire confidence and therefore prove expansionary. But when the fiscal consolidation is temporary rather than permanent and undertaken for other reasons, such as to limit the inflationary effects of capital inflows, this case is more difficult to make.
35. See Schadler, Bennett and Carsovik (1995) for an early review of the literature and Dreher and Vaubel (2003) for a more recent analysis.
36. Studies of this question would have to confront the intrinsic difficulty of identifying the effects of IMF programmes which bedevil previous such analyses. Among other things, they would have to address the very non-random assignment of IMF programmes.
37. See Barcza (2005).
38. It plans to move to an explicit inflation targeting strategy in 2006, at which point a still greater degree of exchange rate volatility will presumably be permitted.
39. On the other hand, the kind of flat taxes that are increasingly popular in the region may be counterproductive from this point of view since they make it less likely that the increased incomes and activity produced by capital inflows will push taxpayers into higher brackets.

REFERENCES

Barcza, G. (2005), 'Hungary: domestic FX borrowing supports HUF', *ING Emerging Markets Biweekly Report* (4 February), 16–18.

Clark, P.B. and R. MacDonald (1998), 'Exchange rates and economic fundamentals: a methodological comparison of BEERs and FEERs', IMF Working paper no. 98/67, Washington, DC: IMF (May).

Croke, H., S.B. Kamin and S. Leduc (2005), 'Financial market developments and economic activity during current account adjustments in industrial countries', International Finance Discussion Paper 827, International Finance Division, Board of Governors of the Federal Reserve System, Washington, DC (February).

Deutsche Bank (2005a), 'Could Romania be the next Slovakia?', Global Markets Research/Emerging Markets (13 April).

Deutsche Bank (2005b), 'Romania: notes from our recent visit', Global Markets Research/Emerging Markets (23 March).

Dreher, A. and R. Vaubel (2003), 'The causes and consequences of IMF conditionality', unpublished manuscript, University of Mannheim.

Edwards, S. (2004), 'Thirty years of current account imbalances, current account reversals and sudden stops', NBER Working Paper No. 10276 (February).

Edwards, S. (2005), 'Is the US current account deficit sustainable, and if not how costly is adjustment likely to be?', unpublished manuscript, UCLA (March).

Egert, B. (2004), 'Assessing equilibrium exchange rates in CEE acceding countries: can we have DEER with BEER without FEER?', Institute for Economics in Transition Discussion Paper No. 1, Helsinki: Bank of Finland.

Eichengreen, B. and M. Fifer (2002), 'The implications of aging for the balance of payments between north and south', in Horst Siebert (ed.), *The Economics of Aging Societies*, Kiel: Kiel Institute for World Economics.

Goldstein, M. (2002), *Managed Floating Plus*, Policy Analysis in International Economics No. 66, Washington, DC: Institute for International Economics.

Goldstein, M. and P. Turner (2004), *Controlling Currency Mismatches in Emerging Markets*, Washington, DC: Institute for International Economics.

Institute of International Finance (2005), 'Capital flows to emerging market economies', Washington, DC: Institute for International Economics (19 January).

Kalemli-Özcan, S., L. Alfaro and V. Volosovych (2003), 'Why doesn't capital flow from rich to poor countries? An empirical investigation', Working Paper No. 2003–1, Department of Economics, University of Houston (December).

Kim, B.Y. and I. Korhonen (2002), 'Equilibrium exchange rates in transition economies: evidence from dynamic heterogeneous panel models', Institute for Economics in Transition Discussion Paper No. 15, Helsinki: Bank of Finland.

Milesi-Ferretti, G.M. and A. Razin (1997), 'Sharp reductions in current account deficits: an empirical investigation', NBER Working Paper No. 6310.

OECD (2004), *Economic Survey of Hungary*, Paris: OECD.

Pesaran, H. and R. Smith (1995), 'Estimating long-run relationships from dynamic heterogeneous panels', *Journal of Econometrics*, **68**, 79–113.

Pesaran, H., Y. Shin and R. Smith (1999), 'Pooled mean group estimation of dynamic heterogeneous panels', *Journal of the American Statistical Association*, **94**, 621–54.

Schadler, S., A. Bennett and M. Carsovik (1995), 'IMF conditionality: experience under stand-by and extended arrangements', IMF Occasional Papers Nos 128 and 129.

Taylor, M. and L. Sarno (1999), 'Hot money, accounting labels, and the permanence of capital flows to developing countries: an empirical investigation', *Journal of Development Economics*, **59**, 337–64.
Valintinyi, K. (2003), 'The role of foreign banks in five central and Eastern European economies', Working Paper 2003/10, Budapest: National Bank of Hungary.

COMMENTS

Fatma Taşkın

Eichengreen and Choudhry address the important issue of how to manage large capital flows to avoid crisis in emerging economies. The chapter focuses on two groups of emerging economies, namely Central and East European (CEE) and East Asian countries, and reviews the risk of large inflows of capital and appreciation of exchange rates for these countries. After evaluating alternative strategies for the management of the inflows and the exchange rate regimes the authors arrive at the conclusion that fiscal management is the most effective strategy.

Eichengreen and Choudhry state that CEE and East Asian countries are similar in many aspects, such as large private inflows of capital and stable exchange rate policies with their trading partners. However, they differ significantly in their savings and investment balance and the repercussions of this imbalance for the equilibrium in the rest of the economy. The challenge in devising policies for the management of large capital inflows originates from these differences. They stress that the East Asian countries, with more growth to catch up and favourable demographic conditions have higher saving rates. With better fiscal discipline, which exerts less of a burden on the private savings and prudent selection of investments, following the financial crisis of 1997–98 the countries have a surplus in their domestic investment–savings balance. The surplus in the savings–investment balance in these countries translates to current account surplus and reserve accumulation. The authors emphasizes that CEE countries present a contrasting picture with large current account deficits and large deficiency of savings relative to investment which may be attributed to large investment projects financed mainly with foreign capital.

After presenting a careful summary of macroeconomic conditions in these countries, the chapter elaborates on the impact of these differences on relative prices and real exchange rates. In the CEE countries, large current account deficits coupled with capital inflows that are not sterilized due to high interest costs result in high domestic demand which in turn, has led to the appreciation of the real exchange rate. The low cost of sterilization in East Asia in conjunction with careful policies conducted to dampen the effect of the large capital inflows on prices led to less of an appreciation of the domestic currency. The chapter adopts the Behavioural Real Exchange Rate model and re-estimates Kim and Korhonen's (2002) model and an extension augmented with a capital flow variable, using the original sample and an alternative sample including an extended set of developing countries. The exchange rates for these two sets of countries are evaluated by comparing the actual exchange rates and the predicted values obtained from these models. The results of this comparison reveal that most of the CEE countries have overvalued exchange rates whereas the East Asian countries either have slightly overvalued or undervalued exchange rates, especially when one considers the correction that took place after the 1997 98 crisis. This difference in exchange rates was interpreted by the authors as another indicator that the two groups of countries have managed the large capital inflows with significantly different strategies.

Eichengreen and Choudhry list exchange rate flexibility, maintaining capital account restrictions, strengthening prudential supervision, sterilizing inflows, loosening monetary policy and tightening fiscal policy and probably negotiating a programme with the IMF as the set of policies to be utilized to manage the capital flows in emerging countries. The paper examines some of these issues for the case of Romania and claims that the stage of the accession in Romania today will be what Turkey can expect in about five years time. We would like to present a comparative evaluation of the Romanian and Turkish economies in terms of the sustainability of their external positions and international capital flows.

Romania and Turkey are quite different, both in terms of their present economic structure and their economic history. Romania is a transition country, which was originally centrally planned and has had little more than decade of market economy experience. Its population is 22 million and the country's Gross Domestic Product (GDP) is $56.95 billion.[1] It is scheduled to join the EU in 2007, although there is a possibility that this will be postponed for a few years. The Turkish economy, with a population of 71 million and a GDP of $240.38 billion, is three to four times as large as that of Romania. Its market economy, after three decades of import substitution development policy, underwent extensive liberalization policies in international trade, capital flows and exchange rate regimes during the 1980s and early 1990s. The accession talks to join the EU began in the second half of 2004.

Despite these differences, at the present time there are large similarities in their current economic conditions. Both countries experience high real growth rates accompanied with large current account deficits. In the case of Romania, following the large contractions in the second half of 1990s the economy has experienced high growth rates and falling but relatively high inflation rates, improved external stability and rising international reserves.[2] Since then, output growth has been above 5 per cent a year. As reported in Table 8C.1, between 1995–2004 the current account deficit of Romania was, on average, 5.47 per cent of its GDP, with little variation across the years. Turkey showed a more erratic performance, where high growth rates were interrupted by periods of financial crisis and large drops

Table 8C.1 Economic indicators for Romania and Turkey, 1995–2004

Years		1995	1996	1997	1998	1999	2000	2001	2002	2003	2004	1995–2004 Average
Real GDP growth rate (%)	Romania	7.14	3.95	−6.05	−4.82	−1.15	2.15	5.75	5.12	5.16	8.29	2.55
	Turkey	7.19	7.00	7.53	3.09	−4.71	7.15	−7.32	7.79	5.95	8.93	4.26
Current account balance/GDP	Romania	−5.00	−7.28	−5.96	−6.93	−3.64	−3.66	−5.55	−3.33	−5.81	−7.50	−5.47
	Turkey	−1.38	−1.35	−1.39	0.99	−0.73	−4.93	2.33	−0.83	−3.29	−5.12	−1.57
Gross domestic savings /GDP	Romania	18.68	17.43	13.56	9.72	11.25	13.84	14.82	17.32	15.31	15.80	14.77
	Turkey	21.01	18.60	19.30	20.62	19.70	17.02	19.18	19.84	19.68	15.62	19.06
Gross fixed capital formation/GDP	Romania	21.38	22.95	21.17	18.17	17.71	18.90	20.47	21.14	22.53	22.11	20.65
	Turkey	23.84	25.09	26.42	24.58	21.87	22.35	18.17	16.59	15.46	–	21.60
S-I balance (nongovernment)[a]	Romania	−1.00	−3.20	−2.80	−4.10	0.20	0.00	−2.40	−0.90	−3.90	–	−2.01
S-I balance (government)		−2.60	−3.80	−3.30	−3.00	−1.80	−4.00	−3.20	−2.70	−2.30	–	−2.97
S-I balance (nongovernment)[a]	Turkey	0.67	2.2	1.72	7.63	10.83	5.56	16.68	9.88	5.91	1.29	6.24
S-I balance (government)		−3.89	−7.02	−5.52	−8.69	−13.33	−12.19	−15.35	−12.53	−10.1	−6.67	−9.53
FDI/GDP	Romania	1.19	0.74	3.47	4.84	2.97	2.83	2.92	2.54	3.31	0.00	2.79
Portfolio investment/ GDP		0.11	0.71	1.69	0.38	−2.39	0.33	1.56	0.84	0.99	0.00	0.42
Other investment/GDP		1.30	3.82	2.22	−0.37	1.29	3.07	3.22	5.68	3.45	0.00	2.37
FDI/GDP	Turkey	0.52	0.40	0.43	0.47	0.43	0.49	2.25	0.56	0.65	0.53	0.56

Portfolio investment/GDP		0.18	0.42	1.17	−4.04	2.40	0.55	−3.67	−0.35	1.00	2.51	0.02
Other investment/GDP		2.79	3.14	3.41	3.19	0.99	4.03	−10.48	0.63	1.29	2.19	1.12
Real exchange rates (% change)[b]	Romania	11.00	11.28	−48.71	−19.13	19.04	−2.07	−15.53	−17.34	−22.23	−26.67	−13.48
	Turkey	−33.35	2.83	9.23	−22.73	16.61	−25.81	60.82	−30.17	−38.06	−13.95	−4.58
Nominal exchange rates (% change)	Romania	45.90	56.52	98.84	36.50	66.70	42.02	21.87	6.02	−2.70	−10.82	34.99
	Turkey	53.30	80.68	90.77	52.95	72.17	24.38	115.35	13.35	−15.03	−4.09	47.84
GDP deflator (% change)	Romania	34.90	45.24	147.54	55.63	47.66	44.09	37.40	23.36	19.53	15.84	48.48
	Turkey	87.20	77.84	81.54	75.68	55.56	50.19	54.53	43.51	23.03	9.85	52.41
Export growth (% change)	Romania	17.02	2.03	11.41	−4.59	10.46	23.44	11.12	16.93	8.21	6.91	10.29
	Turkey	7.98	21.96	19.12	12.00	−7.04	19.18	7.40	11.14	15.98	6.84	11.46
Foreign currency liabilities/foreign currency assets (%)	Romania	56.97	76.23	67.99	59.03	48.72	32.84	41.00	84.32	204.07	276.90	–
	Turkey	53.19	85.80	108.42	125.78	121.16	134.33	81.05	76.37	100.05	96.22	–
Total debt service/total exports (%)	Romania	10.51	46.89	32.71	24.75	37.08	19.69	18.83	19.08	17.32	–	–
	Turkey	27.66	21.56	20.50	23.97	35.41	35.41	39.96	46.50	38.47	–	–
Short-term debt/total debt (%)	Romania	19.07	13.44	9.52	5.69	4.07	3.52	3.46	3.13	6.42	–	–
	Turkey	21.28	21.73	21.22	21.84	22.96	24.64	14.42	12.52	15.80	–	–

Notes:
a. Savings–investment balances are computed as percentages of GNP. For savings–investment (SI) balances: SPO for Turkey, IMF Country Reports for Romania.
b. Real exchange rates changes are computed for both countries as the difference between the percentage change in nominal exchange rates and the percentage change in the GDP deflator.

Sources: Cross-country comparable data used in computations are obtained from International Financial Statistics, IMF.

in output. In this case, the average current account to GDP ratio is 1.57 per cent for the period but shows high year to year volatility, usually reaching its highest levels at times of financial crisis or prior to them. For Turkey, a current account to GDP ratio of 5 per cent is typically considered as a threshold level above which either the external balance or the capital inflow financing the deficit will not be sustainable. In 1994 and in 2001 financial crisis occurred under similar conditions. To evaluate the risks involved with these current account deficits and the capital flows financing these deficits one has to take a closer look at the economic balances behind the current account deficit, its sources and how it is financed.

In terms of economic theory, the current account deficit is the reflection that the country is living beyond its means and the same imbalance can be observed in the national savings and national investment equilibrium. An increase in national investment or a decline in national savings – that is, the sum of public and private savings – might be the source of the current account deficit. In both Romania and Turkey, as in many other fast growing countries, total investments are higher than total savings. That is to say that the national investment spending is more than the resources available through domestic savings in these countries. During 1995–2004, in Romania the average gross domestic savings to GDP ratio was 16.6 per cent. During the same period investment measured by gross capital formation to GDP was higher, with a period average of 20.6 per cent. During the turbulent economic conditions of the second half of the 1990s both savings and investment declined but the current account deficit widened when saving rates declined faster than investment. During the economic upswing, the faster recovery of savings led to a brief narrowing of the gap. But with improving economic conditions, investment expenditures were quick to catch up, which led to a further widening of the savings–investment gap and current account deficit. When one looks at the role of the private and public sectors in this economic imbalance both private and public sector investment was greater than their savings. Even though the government sectors' contribution to the savings–investment deficiency has been steady, the private sectors' gap narrowed considerably in the periods of economic contraction. With the fast growing private investment in Romania the savings–investment gap of the private sector has been growing in recent years and the public sector savings and investment gap has been declining.

In Turkey, as in Romania, investment has always been higher than savings with the exception of the crisis year of 2001. The average investment to GDP ratio is 21.6 per cent during the period under consideration whereas the savings to GDP average is 19 per cent for the same period. The volatility in investment has been larger compared to the fluctuations in savings especially in the second half of the period, and the sharp decline in investments following the financial crisis led to a temporary positive current account and investment–savings balance. However, the share of the private and public sector in the investment–savings balance presents quite a different picture in Turkey to that in Romania. Public sector saving has been negative for almost all of the period and the private sectors' savings surplus over private sector investment has been used to finance the deficiency in the public sectors' savings–investment gap. The public sector savings gap reached its largest value of 15 per cent of GNP during the crisis of 2001. With fiscal policy reform and more prudent fiscal spending, the public sector gap has declined considerably in recent years but as of 2004 the savings surplus of the private sector was not sufficient to finance the public sector deficit which contributes to the growing current account imbalance balance.[3]

This savings deficiency over investment or the current account deficit in these growing countries has to be financed by the flow of foreign savings. This foreign flow can take many alternative forms ranging from long-term direct investment to short-term portfolio flows or external borrowing. The exact form of this flow will have considerable impact on the sustainability of the current account deficits and its repercussions for the domestic economy.

The willingness of foreign investors to finance this current account deficit or investment and savings gap is crucial for the sustainability of the deficit. One source of finance is direct foreign investment in long-term projects. The shares of foreign direct investment in Romania and Turkey are quite different. Romania, with larger current account deficit to GDP ratios also has the opportunity to finance a significant share, that is more than 60 per cent, of these deficits through direct foreign investment. In Turkey, on the other hand, this source of finance is relatively smaller and only 20 per cent on the average of the current account deficit is financed by foreign direct investment. Since foreign direct investment is usually considered to be more long term and stable this feature by itself creates an important difference in the sustainability of the external deficit in both countries and the degree of vulnerability of the domestic economy in face of large capital flows. The part of the deficits not financed by foreign direct investment needs to be financed either through portfolio investment or through borrowing.

The share of portfolio investment relative to foreign direct investment in financing the current account deficit is more important in Turkey. In Turkey the average net portfolio inflow was 1.17 per cent of GDP in the last decade, with the exception of crisis years where there are net portfolio outflows. As for the details of the portfolio investment, debt securities rather than equity securities play a significant role both in the liabilities and assets of capital flow items. This indicates that perhaps more short-term assets or assets which can be resold easily represent the form of the capital flow into Turkey. In Romania the share of portfolio investment relative to foreign direct investment is significantly less, and the average net portfolio inflow for Romania is only 0.42 per cent of GDP. In Romania the difference in the share of debt securities and equity securities is less pronounced and most of the portfolio assets are in equity securities. This is in parallel to more foreign direct investment in the Romanian economy.

The most important impact of the large capital flows is observed on the exchange rates, especially real exchange rates of the countries. The examination of the real exchange rates show that there has been a more or less steady appreciation of the real exchange rates in both countries. In 2003–04 years the Romanian lei experienced a real appreciation of above 20 per cent annually and in Turkey the real value of the lira appreciated by close to 39 per cent in 2003 and 14 per cent in 2004. The reasons behind this change in the value of domestic currency are the slowing down of inflation rates and the declining rate of nominal depreciation and eventual appreciation of the nominal exchange rates, which can be attributed mostly to large capital flows in both countries. The average rate of annual depreciation of the nominal exchange rate is 35 per cent in Romania and 48 per cent in Turkey. The average increase in the GDP deflator over the same period is 48.5 per cent in Romania and 52.4 per cent in Turkey. For Romania, with the exception of 1995 and 1998, there is a steady real appreciation of the domestic currency and the rate of appreciation has been increasing in the last five years. In Turkey with the exception of financial crisis years the appreciation of the real exchange rates is a common phenomenon in the last decade. The disinflation programmes which led to inflation falling to single digits for the first time in several decades, and the nominal appreciation of the domestic currency (Turkish lira) in the last two years, in the face of large inflows of capital, are again the main reasons for this real appreciation.

The most important destabilizing factor in both countries, which are facing large capital flows and real exchange rate appreciation, is the loss of competitiveness and consequently loss of export revenues. With average growth rates of exports at 10.3 per cent in Romania and 11.5 per cent in Turkey, both countries in the decade to 2004 have comparable growth rates for their exports. Usually, rapid export growth follows large real depreciations. The continued real appreciation of the exchange rates has significant effect in slowing down the growth rate of exports. In Romania the largest growth in exports, 23.4 per cent, occurred in 2000, which was the year with the smallest real appreciation of the domestic currency. In 2004, when real output growth reached its highest rate of the decade, the growth rate of exports dropped to 6.9 per cent. In Turkey, export growth slowed down in the years with large real appreciation especially prior to financial crises and picked up after the large depreciations that occurred following the crisis periods. The country experienced large real depreciations in 1999 and 2001 and export growth had been close to 20 per cent in 2000 and was 11 and 16 per cent following the major currency depreciation after the financial crisis of 2001. In both countries, export growth has slowed down in the last couple of years, making them more vulnerable to capital inflow reversals and leading to unsustainability in the current account deficits.

A further impact of capital flows will be on the level of financial intermediation, which creates further consequences for the economy, and more specifically for the banking sector and balance sheets of the banks. Typically large capital inflows and easy access to foreign financing leads to a mismatch of assets and liabilities in all sectors of the economy but especially in the banking sector, which in turn leads to vulnerability of the financial sector. This phenomenon is evident in both Romania and Turkey when one compares foreign currency liabilities with foreign currency assets of the deposit money banks. In Romania, the balance of the foreign currency liabilities and assets became critical in the last two years, with the ratio of foreign currency liabilities and assets of deposit banks reaching 204 per cent in 2003 and 277 per cent in 2004. This mismatch of assets and liabilities makes the banks in question and the banking system extremely sensitive to changes in the exchange rate and to changes in the flow of foreign capital. With the financial crisis of 2001, the Turkish banking sector has demonstrated how crucial this imbalance can be. The ratio of foreign currency liability to foreign currency assets in the banking sector increased steadily, to 134 per cent when the financial crisis occurred. After the adjustment following the crisis, foreign currency assets were maintained at a level that would be sufficient to finance the foreign currency liabilities, with the liabilities to assets ratio well below the critical value of 100 per cent. However, there is evidence that foreign liabilities of deposit banks have been increasing recently.

The depth of the financial sector is another crucial factor in making the economy less vulnerable to reversals in foreign capital flows. Romania, like many other transition countries, has relatively less developed stock and bond markets. With only a short history as a market economy and the adversely affected corporate profitability following the collapse of previous economic regimes, the stock market has not developed to levels comparable to EU countries. Furthermore, readily available foreign direct investment to finance investment decreases the need of developing the means of domestic financing. Domestic capital markets – both stock and bond markets – are small and insignificant and incapable of being an alternative source of finance if a reversal occurs in the inflow of foreign capital. In the Turkish case, even though there is a longer history as a market economy, stock market liberalization only dates back to 1989 and the depth of the stock market has not reached the level of mature markets. Looking at the measure of stock market size and its importance by comparing the stock market capitalization to GDP ratio for the two countries, in 2004 for Romania the ratio is only 1.4 per cent while for Turkey it is 41 per cent. Since EU-area capitalization is on average 72 per cent of GDP, it is not possible to say whether the domestic capital markets will be able to prevent or dampen the effects of a reversal of capital inflows by relying on alternative domestic financing.

Another indicator of sustainability can be seen on the external debt accumulated by the emerging country. Large external debt stocks will increase the vulnerability of the country to changes in worldwide interest rates and exchange rate volatility. The long-term debt indicators such as total debt service to exports and short-term debt to total debt ratios indicate that even though both emerging economies have important external debt liabilities, Turkey has a larger external debt burden which increases its vulnerability to changes in the world economy. Romania increased its external liability in the late 1990s with the economic crisis and since then both the total debt service to export ratio and the share of short-term debt in the total debt has been steadily declining. Debt service to exports dropped to 17.32 per cent in 2003 and only 6.42 per cent of the total debt is short-term debt. For Turkey the external liability continues to be a point of concern. The debt service to exports reached close to 50 per cent and the share of short-term debt, which had declined following the financial crisis of 2001, started to increase more recently. The increase in the external liabilities of an emerging country is clearly an indicator of increasing vulnerability to world economic conditions, such as changes in world interest rates and depreciation of the domestic currency.

Emerging countries have to establish an economic environment and a set of policies to manage their inflow of foreign capital and to decrease the vulnerability of the economy to possible reversals of this inflow. However countries usually have a wide variety of economic and political histories and economic relationships. A standard policy mix may not produce the same outcome in all countries, which may look similar at first sight but possess quite different characteristics. The conditions and the sensitivities present in each emerging country have to be evaluated individually, then a decision has to be made on which aspect of the set of policies mentioned by Eichengreen and Choudhry needs to be emphasized when managing the external balance and inflow of foreign capital.

Notes

1. GDP figures of 2003, measured in terms of current US dollars are obtained from the IMF World Development Indicators database.
2. International Monetary Fund Country Report, No. 04/220, Romania, July 2004.
3. The public and private sector decomposition of the savings and investment balance is conducted with savings/GNP and investment/GNP ratios obtained from the State Planning Office of Turkey.

9. Current account sustainability: the case of Turkey

Sübidey Togan and Hasan Ersel*

During the last three decades Turkey has experienced three balance of payments crises. The first crisis occurred in late 1970s, the second in 1994 and the third in 2001. These crises highlighted the danger of having too large current account deficits when coupled with other weaknesses in the economy. The crises occurred when Turkey was facing large fiscal deficits and high inflation rates, and when the current account deficits during the periods prior to the crises were largely financed by short-term foreign borrowing. During the 1990s the unhealthy structure of the financial sector contributed to the worsening economic situation.[1] Currency and maturity mismatches on the balance sheets of the banks had left the public authorities little leeway for using either interest rate or exchange rate adjustments to restore the external balance without undermining the stability of the banking sector. Furthermore Turkey lacked competent supervisory authorities and a regulatory framework in the banking sector. Finally, prior to the 2001 crisis Turkey had accumulated huge debts. Thus Turkey before the 2001 crisis had neither resolved its fiscal problems, nor attained price stability, and it did not have a sound banking sector. There were also major problems with governance in general.

The past few years have witnessed three major attempts at addressing underlying weaknesses. The first was during 2000 under the three-year stand-by agreement with the IMF initiated in December 1999, following a significant drop in output as a result of mostly external factors, including the earthquake. Despite some notable achievements, a worsening current account and a fragile banking system led in late 2000 to a liquidity crisis which turned into full-blown banking crisis in February 2001. The government decided to abandon the crawling peg regime and floated the currency. In May 2001 the IMF increased its assistance under a new stand-by arrangement. Just as the revised programme was beginning to show results, the events of September 11 triggered the re-emergence of serious financing problems. In February 2002 the IMF approved a new three-year stand-by credit for Turkey to support the government's economic programme. In

August 2004 Turkey approached the IMF in hopes of achieving a final three-year stand-by agreement as an exit programme from instability and excessive debt. The new stand-by agreement was approved in May 2005.

Actions to stabilize the economy through IMF stabilization programmes proved successful at combating inflation, measured by the annual average percentage change in the CPI, which fell from 54.9 per cent during 2000 to 10.6 per cent in 2004 as a result of maintaining fiscal and monetary discipline. The fiscal deficit decreased from 20.9 per cent in 2001 to 9.8 per cent of GNP in 2003, and further to 6.2 per cent in 2004. The primary balance amounted to 6.2 per cent of GNP in 2003, and 6.9 per cent in 2004. After contracting by 9.5 per cent in 2001, real GNP expanded by 7.9 per cent in 2002, 5.9 per cent in 2003 and by 9.9 per cent in 2004. The unemployment rate, which reached 12.3 per cent in the first quarter of 2002, fell to 10.3 per cent in 2004, and the average interest rate on government debt declined from 96.2 per cent in 2001 to 25.7 per cent in 2004. Net public debt to GNP ratios are still high but have been falling, from 90.5 per cent of GNP in 2001 to 70.4 per cent in 2003, and to 63.5 per cent in 2004, as a result of significant income growth, attainment of sizeable primary surpluses over the last three years, and appreciation of the real exchange rate (RER).[2]

In 2004 the annual current account deficit amounted to about $15.5 billion, and the current account deficit to GDP ratio was 5.1 per cent. The deficit is funded mainly by short-term funds, and foreign direct investment inflows remain weak. Total foreign debt in Turkey in 2004 reached $161.7 billion or 53.4 per cent of GDP, which reflects a significantly higher level of indebtedness than in other emerging countries.[3]

The purpose of this chapter is to study issues related to the sustainability of the current account in Turkey. While Section 9.1 summarizes macroeconomic developments during the last two and half decades, Section 9.2 analyses issues related with sustainability of the current account. Section 9.3 discusses policies for attaining current account sustainability. Section 9.4 concludes.

9.1 CURRENT ACCOUNT, REAL EXCHANGE RATE AND COMPETITIVENESS

Figure 9.1 shows the developments in the current account to GDP ratio over the period 1975–2004. Turkey faced balance of payments crisis in the late 1970s, 1994 and 2001. The figure indicates that the probability of a balance of payments crisis increases in Turkey as the current account deficit to GDP ratio increases above a critical level of 5 per cent. Figure 9.2 shows the time path of the RER over the last two decades.[4] The figure reveals four

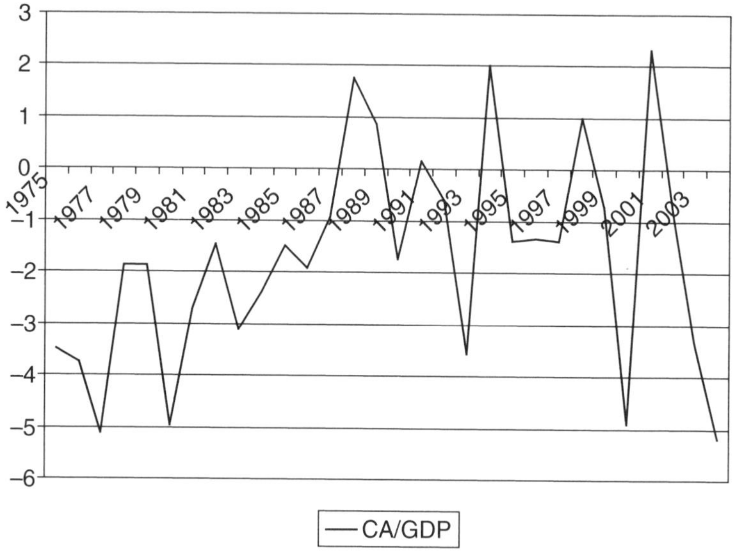

Source: Central Bank of Turkey.

Figure 9.1 Current account (CA) to GDP ratio, 1975–2004

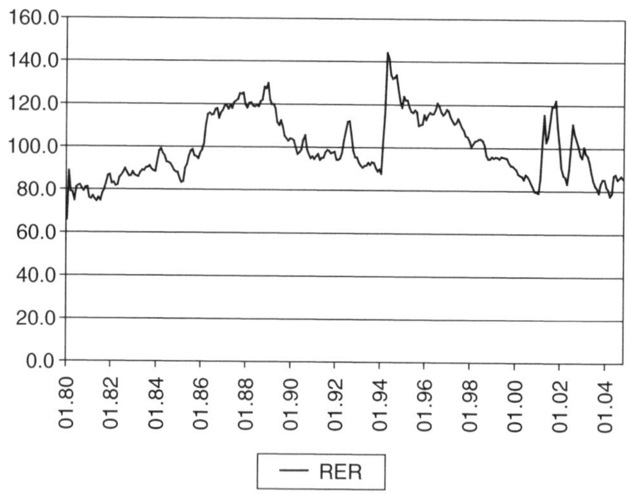

Note: An increase in RER indicates depreciation of the RER.

Figure 9.2 Real exchange rate, 1980–2004

episodes of RER developments. After the foreign exchange crisis of the late 1970s, the government pursued a policy of RER depreciation.[5] That policy continued until 1988.

In 1989 foreign exchange operations and international capital movements were liberalized.[6] During the 1990s, Turkey's public finances deteriorated considerably.[7] Large public sector deficits were financed by borrowing from the market at very high real interest rates.[8] Significant amounts of capital flowed into the country because it was offering not only high real interest rates but also the prospect of steady real appreciation of the exchange rate. Thus the government's implicit commitment to RER appreciation insured the private sector, domestic and foreign, against currency risk. The appreciation of the RER carried on under various coalition governments until 1994 when the country was faced with another currency crisis. The RER again depreciated sharply in April 1994, but thereafter it started to appreciate again. The appreciation of the RER carried on until February 2001, when the country faced yet another currency crisis. After the sharp depreciation of the RER from February to April 2001, the RER again began to appreciate, particularly after October 2001. It has appreciated from October 2001 to October 2004 by about 30 per cent in parallel with a strong economic recovery.

To study the factors determining the developments in the RER, we define the RER as $(p^* E/p)$, where p stands for the price level of the home country under consideration, p^* the price level in rest of the world, and E the exchange rate defined as domestic currency units per foreign currency unit. Concentrating on the manufacturing sector we write the nominal value added in the manufacturing sector as the sum of labour and capital income, that is, $p\,y = w\,L + r\,K$ where p stands for manufacturing sector value added deflator, y for real manufacturing value added, w for the nominal wage rate in the manufacturing sector, L for total employment in the manufacturing sector, r for the return on capital and K for the stock of capital in the manufacturing sector. Expressing capital income as $rK = \lambda(wL)$, where λ stands for the mark-up rate in the manufacturing sector, the RER can be written as:

$$\frac{Ep^*}{p} = \frac{\left(\frac{y}{L}\right) Ew^*(1+\lambda^*)}{\left(\frac{y^*}{L^*}\right)(1+\lambda)\,w} = \frac{\rho Ew^*(1+\lambda^*)}{\rho^* w(1+\lambda)},$$

where the variables with a star denote the corresponding variables in the foreign country, and ρ labour productivity in the home country's manufacturing sector. We note from the above relation that developments in the

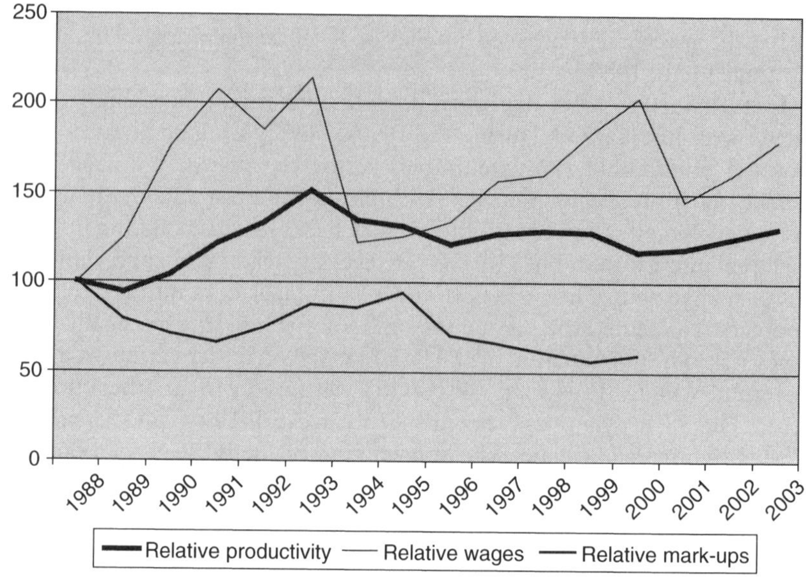

Figure 9.3 *Factors affecting the real exchange rate, 1988–2003*

RER depend on developments in the productivity ratio ρ/ρ^*, the relative wage ratio Ew^*/w, and the relative mark-up ratio $(1 + \lambda^*)/(1 + \lambda)$. Thus, the competitiveness of the country as measured by the RER increases with a rise in the productivity ratio ρ/ρ^*, with a fall in the relative wage ratio w/Ew^* and with a fall in the relative mark-up ratio $(1 + \lambda)/(1 + \lambda^*)$. Figure 9.3 shows the developments in relative wages w/Ew^* relative productivities ρ/ρ^*, and relative mark-up ratio $(1 + \lambda)/(1 + \lambda^*)$ over the period 1988–2003.[9] The figure reveals that there is an increase in relative productivity levels and a decline in relative mark-up ratios where both factors have improved the competitiveness of the country. The results may largely be due to the opening of the economy to intense competition from abroad.

As we have seen the RER depreciated considerably during the period 1980–88. A drawback of the RER depreciation policy pursued during the 1980s was the decline in real wages. By the second half of the 1980s, popular support for the government had begun to fall off. In the local elections of March 1989, the governing party suffered heavy losses. To increase political support, the government conceded substantial pay increases during collective bargaining in the public sector. Pressure then built up in the private sector to arrive at similarly high wage settlements, real wages began to increase and the RER started to appreciate. As a result of these developments, relative wages w/Ew^* increased considerably after 1988 leading to a substantial decline in competitiveness. Since the increase in relative wages surpassed the positive effects of developments in relative productivities and mark-up rates on competitiveness, the RER appreciated. In 1994 when the country was faced with a balance of payments crisis, relative wages declined as the RER depreciated, but after 1994 the relative wage ratio w/Ew^* started to increase again, surpassing the positive effects of changes in relative productivities and relative mark-up rates on the competitiveness of Turkish products. In 2001, relative wages declined again with the sharp depreciation of the currency, but started to increase thereafter.

9.2 SUSTAINABILITY OF THE CURRENT ACCOUNT

The causes of the three balance of payments crises during late 1970s, 1994 and 2001 were different.[10] Whatever the causes of the crises, we note that a widening of the current account deficit always occurred before an exchange rate crisis. The large current account deficits led to an accumulation of foreign debt that eventually became unsustainable and led to a currency crisis. Hence a major factor causing the crises was the unsustainability of the current account.

Table 9.1 shows the developments in ratios of GNP of savings, investment and current account from 1990–2004. Saving–investment gaps prior to both the 1994 and 2001 crises were considerable. During 1992–93 the average public savings–investment gap to GNP ratio amounted to −8.78 per cent, and the average private savings–investment surplus to GNP ratio to 5.35 per cent. Similarly, the average public savings–investment gap to GNP ratio during 1999–2000 amounted to −12.76 per cent, and the average private savings–investment gap to GNP ratio to 8.2 per cent. With the stabilization measures in place, the gap between public savings–investment to GNP ratio declined to −4.73 per cent in 1994, but there was no similar decline after the 2001 crisis. During 2001 most of the adjustment was achieved by improvement in the private savings–investment surplus to GNP ratio. While private saving ratio did not change very much during 2001 there was a considerable decline in the private investment ratio.

The importance of current account imbalances and hence the excess of investments over savings as a warning signal of currency crisis has been emphasized by various authors including Corsetti et al. (1999), Radelet and Sachs (2000) and Edwards (2004). Among these authors Edwards shows that the probability of experiencing an abrupt current accounts reversal is linked to the size of the current account deficit and the level of external debt.

Table 9.1 *Saving, investment and current account to GNP ratio, 1990–2004 (%)*

	1990	1991	1992	1993	1994	1995	1996	1997	1998	1999	2000	2001	2002	2003	2004
Investment/GNP ratio	25.23	23.45	23.55	27.59	21.60	25.32	24.64	25.14	23.74	23.70	24.82	16.08	21.66	23.46	27.48
Public investment to GNP ratio	8.63	7.61	6.76	7.29	3.64	3.81	5.32	6.35	6.80	6.59	6.99	5.46	6.30	4.78	4.76
Private investment to GNP ratio	16.60	15.85	16.79	20.31	17.96	21.50	19.32	18.79	16.94	17.11	17.84	10.62	15.37	18.68	22.71
Savings/GNP ratio	22.03	21.35	21.58	22.74	23.07	22.09	19.82	21.34	22.68	21.20	18.20	17.42	19.02	19.28	22.09
Public savings to GNP ratio	3.43	0.72	−0.82	−2.68	−1.10	−0.08	−1.70	0.83	−1.89	−6.74	−5.20	−9.89	−6.23	−5.32	−1.91
Private savings to GNP ratio	18.60	20.64	22.37	25.43	24.17	22.17	21.52	20.51	24.57	27.94	23.40	27.31	25.25	24.59	24.00
Current account to GNP ratio	−3.20	−2.10	−2.00	−4.85	1.47	−3.23	−4.82	−3.80	−1.06	−2.51	−6.62	1.34	−2.64	−4.18	−5.38
Public savings–investment gap to GNP ratio	−5.20	−6.89	−7.58	−9.97	−4.73	−3.90	−7.03	−5.52	−8.69	−13.33	−12.18	−15.35	−12.53	−10.09	−6.67
Private savings–investment gap to GNP ratio	2.00	4.79	5.58	5.12	6.21	0.67	2.20	1.72	7.63	10.83	5.56	16.69	9.88	5.91	1.29

Notes: Figures for 2004 are preliminary.

Source: State Planning Organization.

A simple definition of current account sustainability is the following: a current account position is sustainable as long as foreign investors are willing to finance it. But in light of the recent crises in Turkey as well as abroad it should be mentioned that the short-term debt poses special problems for the maintenance of financial stability. Serious problems occur when capital suddenly flows out of the country in the form of debt, portfolio equity and even direct investment. But the macroeconomic consequences are most disruptive when they involve debt, especially sovereign debt and debt within the banking and financial systems. Although defaults by individual enterprises on foreign currency debts are not generally a problem, large-scale defaults by much of the corporate sector can be very disruptive, especially in so far as they threaten the stability of the banking system. If investors suddenly lose confidence in the creditworthiness of a country, they may refuse to roll-over its stock of short-term debt, and the country will be forced to finance its debt service out of reserves or current account proceeds. If reserves and current account proceeds prove to be inadequate, a sharp current account reversal takes place. Inasmuch as domestic banks and corporations are rendered illiquid, the reversal can take place only through a severe and costly contraction of output. Thus, a high percentage of short-term debt increases the probability of sudden capital outflows leading to a crisis.

In the following we consider the simple accounting methodology developed by Milesi-Ferretti and Razin (1996) and make use of the balance of payments relation written as $TB_t^{\$} - i^*D_{t-1} + FDI_t + D_t - D_{t-1} = \Delta R_t$ where $TB^{\$}$ denotes the noninterest current account, i^* the foreign rate of interest, D the stock of foreign debt, FDI the net foreign direct investment, R the foreign exchange reserves of the country, and ΔR_t the change in reserves. Also $(TB_t^{\$} - i^*D_{t-1}) = Current\,Account_t$ and $(FDI_t + D_t - D_{t-1}) = Capital\,Account_t$. All variables are measured in terms of foreign currency. If $d_t = E_tD_t/p_ty_t$ is the foreign debt to GDP ratio, $tb_t = E_tTB_t^{\$}/p_ty_t$ the noninterest current account to GDP ratio, $fdi_t = FDI_tE_t/p_ty_t$ the FDI to GDP ratio, and $\Delta r_t = (\Delta R_t)E_t/p_ty_t$ the change in reserves to GDP ratio, the equation determining the time path of d_t can be written as:

$$d_t = -tb_t + \frac{(1+r^*)(1+\eta)}{(1+g)}d_{t-1} - fdi_t + \Delta r_t \tag{9.1}$$

where r^* denotes the foreign real rate of interest and η the rate of depreciation of the RER. The equation reveals that the external debt to GDP ratio decreases with increases in the noninterest current account to GDP ratio tb, the FDI to GDP ratio fdi, and the growth rate of GDP g. By contrast, the debt to GDP ratio increases with increases in the foreign real interest rate r^*, rate of depreciation of the RER η, and changes in the reserves to GDP ratio Δr.

Following the approach of von Hagen and Harden (1994), we solve the difference equation determining the time path of d_t forward for n periods and obtain:

$$d_t = \Gamma_t \delta_{t,n} d_{t+n} + \Gamma_t \sum_{i=1}^{n} \delta_{t,i} A_{t+i} \tag{9.2}$$

$$\text{where } \delta_{t,k} = \prod_{i=1}^{k} \frac{1 + g_i}{(1 + r_i^*)(1 + \eta_i)}$$

and $A_t = tb_t + fdi_t - \Delta r_t$. Here, $\delta_{t,k}$ can be interpreted as the 'k-periods ahead' discount factor used to calculate the present value of assets and liabilities in period $t+k$ for period t. $\Gamma_t x_{t+k}$ denotes the period t expectation of the variable x in period $t+k$. The equation shows that current debt to GDP ratio equals the expected discounted present value of foreign debt outstanding in period $t+n$ relative to GDP, plus the sum of all discounted A_t's between period t and period $t+n$.

To translate the intertemporal budget constraint into a practically more relevant requirement we consider the budget constraint for a limited period of time n^* and add the sustainability condition that the discounted debt/GDP ratio at the end of period $t+n^*$, discounted d_{t+n^*}, should not exceed the debt/GDP ratio at time t, d_t. We say current account is not sustainable if:

$$S(n^*) = d_t - \Gamma_t \delta_{t,n} d_{t+n} = \Gamma_t \sum_{i=1}^{n} \delta_{t,i} A_{t+i} < 0. \tag{9.3}$$

But this sustainability condition, while useful, is not easy to assess in practice. Even under initial negative A_t values over the next few years the current account can be said to be sustainable if during the latter periods large positive noninterest current account to GDP and FDI to GDP and thus A_{t+i} values are assumed. Consider the year 2004. During that year we had the following values for the variables under consideration: $d_{2004} = 53.45$ per cent, $tb_{2004} = -3.54$ per cent, $fdi_{2004} = 0.62$ per cent, $\Delta r_{2004} = 1.44$ per cent, $A_{2004} = -4.35$ per cent, $g_{2004} = 8.9$ per cent, $\eta_{2004} = -6.45$ per cent and $r^*_{2004} = 5.2$ per cent. If the value of A_{2004+i} over the next few years, say three years, were to remain negative the present value $\Gamma_t \Sigma_{i=1}^{n} \delta_{t,i} A_{t+i}$ could turn out to be positive if one were to assume sufficiently large positive future noninterest current account to GDP and FDI to GDP values over the latter periods, namely from 2008 onwards. Current account will then turn out to be sustainable. The analysis thus depends on the assumptions one makes about the evolution of A_{2004+i} over time.

In the following we assume the continuation of the present policies into the future. In particular we introduce the following assumptions. We assume that $n^* = 10$, and that the government, private sector, and rest of the world will not change the policies they pursue in period 2004 over the time period 2005 to 2014. In addition we assume that there will be no accumulation/decumulation of international reserves and that the country will neither depreciate nor appreciate the RER over the next ten years so that $\Delta r_{t+i} = 0$ and $\eta_{t+i} = 0$ for $i = 1, \ldots, 10$. We suppose that the values of tb_{t+i} and fdi_{t+i} for $i = 1, \ldots, 10$ will remain unchanged at their initial values of tb_{2004} and fdi_{2004}. Furthermore we assume that real GDP will grow at the average rate of 4.1 per cent annually and that foreign real interest rate equals 6.86 per cent over the next 10 years.[11] Finally, we assume that $\Delta r_{2004} = 0$ so that $A_{2004} = -2.92$ per cent rather than the actual value of $A_{2004} = -4.36$ per cent. We then calculate the value of debt to GDP ratio in 2014 using the difference equation (9.1) and then the value of the sustainability measure (9.3).

When over the next 10 years A_{2004+i} stays constant at -2.92 per cent, current account in 2004 turns out to be unsustainable in the sense that the actual debt to GDP ratio in 2004 falls short of the expected discounted present value of foreign debt outstanding in period 2014 by 25.31 per cent. The sustainability of the current account requires that the value of the sustainability measure be increased so that it becomes positive. This goal can be achieved either through an increase in the noninterest current account to GDP ratio tb_t or through an increase in the FDI to GDP ratio fdi_t during the period 2005–14 or through a combination of increases in both the noninterest current account to GDP and FDI to GDP ratios. For Turkey to achieve the minimal condition for external sustainability, the value of A_t during each time period of the interval 2005–14 would have to be 0 per cent. Thus Turkey has to increase the sum of its noninterest current account to GDP ratio and its FDI to GDP ratio during each period of the interval 2005–14 by at least 2.92 per cent.

Suppose first that fdi_t during the time period 2005–14 remains constant at its 2004 level of 0.62 per cent. Economic theory tells us that the noninterest current account to GDP ratio can be increased by decreasing aggregate demand for domestic goods and services and/or by depreciating the RER. Decreasing the aggregate demand for goods and services requires that the country uses contractionary policies. But Turkey, as of the beginning of 2005, was already in the midst of a determined campaign to turn around decades of weak performance due to pervasive structural rigidities and weak public finances. Aiming for more ambitious fiscal objective than the constant primary surplus of 6.5 per cent of GNP will be very painful after so many failed stabilization attempts. The alternative is to depreciate the RER and keep the RER around its 'long-run equilibrium level' over time. To determine the extent of depreciation in the RER required for achieving current account sustainability we consider the elasticity of the ratio of noninterest current account to GDP with respect to the RER,

$$\theta = \left(\frac{dNICA/GDP}{dRER}\frac{RER}{NICA/GDP}\right)$$

Then starting from initial trade balance we derive that:

$$\theta = (\eta_{im} + \eta_{exp} - 1),$$

where η_{im} and η_{exp} denote the import and export elasticities with respect to the RER. Estimates based on estimated Turkish import and export equations range quite widely. Here we consider the estimates of Tansel and Togan (1987) who determine the export price elasticity as 0.933 and import price elasticity as 0.472. Thus, $\theta = 0.405$. Considering the ratio of exports to GDP of 19.6 per cent, the parameter values imply that a reduction of the ratio of noninterest current account to GDP of 1 per cent requires a depreciation of the RER by 12.6 per cent. Thus sustainability of the current account requires that the RER be depreciated by 36.8 per cent.

Note that the above results were derived under the condition that $A_{2004+i} = 0$ for $i = 1, \ldots, 10$. Solving the difference equation (9.1) for the value of debt to GDP ratio in 2014 with the values of $tb_{2004+i} = -0.62$ per cent, $fdi_{2004+i} = 0.62$ per cent, $\Delta r_{2004+i} = 0$ per cent, $g_{2004+i} = 4.1$ per cent, $r^*_{2004+i} = 6.86$ per cent and $\eta_{2004+\mathrm{i}} = 0$ per cent we note that the debt to GDP ratio increases from its value of 53.45 per cent in 2004 to 69.43 per cent in 2014. The increase in debt to GDP ratio is thus perfectly compatible with the sustainability condition specified above.

An alternative specification of the sustainability condition requires that the ratio of the stock of foreign liabilities to GDP stay constant over time at its initial value in time period 2004. In that case, the equation determining the time path of the debt to GDP ratio d can be solved for the equilibrium value of the sum of tb and fdi, under the assumption that $\Delta r = 0$, as:

$$(tb + fdi) = -\left[\frac{(g - r^* - \eta - r^*\eta)}{(1 + g)}\right]d$$

where η denotes the rate of depreciation of the RER, g the growth rate of real GDP and r^* the foreign real interest rate. Considering the same parameter values as before, the equilibrium value of $(tb+fdi)$ is determined to be 1.42 per cent.[12] Because in 2004 the actual value of (tb_t+fdi_t) equalled −2.92 per cent, Turkey needs to increase the sum of its noninterest current account to GDP and FDI to GDP ratios over time by 4.34 per cent. Suppose again that fdi_t over time stays constant at its 2004 level of 0.62 per cent. Then the increase in tb_t, and thus in A_t over time, can be achieved by depreciating the RER by 54.7 per cent.

Finally, following the suggestion of Reinhart et al. (2003), we consider a case in which the country tries to decrease its ratio of stock of foreign liabilities to GDP from its initial value of 53.45 per cent to 40 per cent over a period of 10 years. In that case, Turkey has to increase the sum of its noninterest current account to GDP ratio and its FDI to GDP ratio over time by 5.53 per cent. This change, under the assumption that fdi_t over time stays constant at its 2004 level, requires that the RER be depreciated by 69.7 per cent.

Once Turkey is able to attract higher levels of FDI into the country, it does not need to depreciate its currency by as much as 36.8 or 69.7 per cent in order to attain sustainability in its current account.[13] With increases in the FDI to GDP ratios, the depreciation rate of the RER required to attain sustainability in the current account decreases. When the FDI to GDP ratio increases to 3 per cent of GDP, then the system becomes sustainable under the approach of von Hagen and Harden (1994) when the RER is depreciated by 6.7 per cent. On the other hand when the ratio of the stock of foreign liabilities to GDP stays constant over time at its initial value in time period 2004, the system becomes sustainable when the RER is depreciated by 24.7 per cent. Finally, to reduce the debt to GDP ratio to 40 per cent over a period of 10 years, the RER needs to be depreciated by 39.7 per cent.

Finally, in order to determine the robustness of the analysis we consider pessimistic and optimistic scenarios. Under the pessimistic scenario we assume that $g=0.031$ and $r^*=0.0786$ and under the optimistic scenario we have $g=0.051$ and $r^*=0.0586$. Under pessimistic (optimistic) scenario when the FDI to GDP ratio stays constant at 0.62 per cent of GDP over the period 2005–14, the system becomes sustainable under the approach of von Hagen and Harden (1994) when the RER is depreciated as before by 36.8 per cent. On the other hand when the ratio of the stock of foreign liabilities to GDP stays constant over time at its initial value in time period 2004, the system becomes sustainable when the RER is depreciated by 67.9 (41.6) per cent. Finally, to reduce the debt to GDP ratio to 40 per cent over a period of 10 years, the RER needs to be depreciated by 81.6 (58.1) per cent. When the FDI to GDP ratio increases over time from its value of 0.62 per cent, the required rate of depreciation of the RER in order to attain sustainability in the current account decreases with increases in the FDI to GDP ratio.

9.3 POLICIES FOR ATTAINING CURRENT ACCOUNT SUSTAINABILITY

The sustainability analysis in Section 9.2 reveals that the exchange rate as of the beginning of 2005 was overvalued. According to Eichengreen and Choudhry in Chapter 8 of this book the standard advice in such a situation would be: (i) increasing exchange rate flexibility, (ii) maintaining capital account restrictions, (iii) strengthening prudential supervision, (iv) sterilizing inflows, (v) loosening monetary policy, (vi) tightening fiscal policy and (vii) negotiating a programme with the IMF. Currently, the Turkish exchange rate regime is an independent float. The Central Bank of Turkey (CBT) intervenes in the foreign exchange market in a strictly limited fashion to prevent excessive volatility without targeting a certain trend level. Regarding the second point we note that Turkey is committed not to impose any restrictions on capital account transactions. Regarding the third point it should be stressed that the soundness of the banking system is considered by Turkey as an important element for attaining a sustainable regime for capital movements. The country has been trying to develop effective systems of supervision and, in particular, the necessary administrative capacity to enforce the rules since the 2001 financial crisis. It realizes that both domestic and international banks operating in the country should be sound and stable institutions.[14] Regarding the fourth point we note that the CBT has purchased foreign exchange through market-friendly auctions: the mechanism through which the CBT purchased foreign exchange and how much it was going to purchase daily were set in advance and announced. Whenever the reverse dollarization process and capital inflows stopped, the CBT also stopped opening purchase auctions. In other words, it has not been aggressive in reserve accumulation. Through foreign exchange purchase auctions, the CBT purchased (as mentioned by Özatay, in Chapter 5 of this book) \$0.8 billion in 2002, \$5.7 billion in 2003, and \$4.1 billion in 2004. CBT did not open purchase auctions in 9 months in 2002, 6 months in 2003 and 7 months in 2004. During 2005 CBT intended to have daily auctions where it will buy foreign exchange between minimum and maximum amounts. These pre-announced amounts have been set as \$15 million and \$45 million daily. Regarding the fifth point it should be emphasized that Turkey is following an implicit inflation targeting policy and will introduce inflation targeting explicitly in 2006. Monetary policy will be used for attaining the inflation target. Regarding the sixth point we note that Turkey is following tight fiscal policy. It is committed to keeping the primary surplus at 6.5 per cent of GDP over the next three years. Aiming for a more ambitious fiscal objective than the constant primary surplus of 6.5 per cent of GDP will be very painful. Finally, Turkey has recently negotiated another 3-year stand-by arrangement with the IMF. Thus Turkey has been trying to follow the policies under (i), (iii), (vi), (vii) and also partially (iv).

If Turkey intends to reverse the appreciation of the RER and attain sustainability in the current account there seem to be, in principle, three feasible policy alternatives: (1) taking measures to increase FDI inflow into Turkey, (2) changing the exchange rate regime from independent float to crawling bands or managed float and (3) imposing restrictions on capital account transactions.

9.3.1 Foreign Direct Investment Policies

One of the main culprits behind the failure of Turkey to attract large FDI inflows was the uncertain macroeconomic environment, which, along with the uncertainties stemming from domestic politics and the ensuing high real interest rates, produced a very erratic growth performance. Infrastructure-related factors were in play as well. Although the quantity and quality of Turkey's broadly defined infrastructure, including its geographic and demographic endowments and its physical and financial infrastructure, help to position Turkey as a potentially powerful magnet for FDI inflows, these factors were ineffective in Turkey's effort to increase those flows. According to the Foreign Investment Advisory Service (2001a, 2001b) seven major problems impeded the operations of FDI enterprises up until the early 2000s: (i) political instability, (ii) government hassle, (iii) a weak judicial system, (iv) heavy taxation, (v) corruption, (vi) deficient infrastructure and (vii) competition from the informal economy.

On the other hand, according to Dutz et al. (2005) the main bottlenecks seemed to have been insufficient respect for the rule of law and weak competition in local markets, reinforced by an uneven application of bureaucratic red tape. Finally, OECD (2004) maintains that Turkey, in addition to the factors mentioned above, needs to eliminate unfair competition from the informal economy.[15] Thus, Turkey, in order to attract higher levels of FDI flows in the future, has to improve its political stability and its macroeconomic environment, increase respect for the rule of law, re-evaluate the legal framework governing the privatization programmes, create a clear understanding with employee unions on the labour relations framework, increase competition in local markets, reduce bureaucratic red tape, and take measures to reduce the informal sector.[16]

The above considerations reveal that Turkey could attain sustainability in the current account by taking appropriate measures to increase the inflow of FDI inflow over time.[17]

9.3.2 Exchange Rate Policy

The sustainability analysis in Section 9.2 reveals that the currency needs to be depreciated. But any depreciation of the currency will result in offsetting forces, deflationary and expansionary. First, home produced goods will become more competitive, both in the domestic market against imports and in foreign markets where exports gain a competitive edge. This effect will be expansionary. Second, devaluation will cause an increase in the domestic price level and this will reduce the real value of the money supply, which is contractionary. Third, since the country has taken loans denominated in a foreign currency, devaluation will increase the value of debts in terms of domestic currency. Unless these loans were contracted by agents with export income there will be no corresponding increase in the ability to service debt. Furthermore, where a relatively high percentage of public debt is denominated in foreign currency, devaluation will result in increases in debt to GDP ratio of the public sector as well as in increases of foreign debt to GDP ratio for the whole economy. Thus, this effect will be contractionary. Fourth, there may be indirect contractionary effects of this, in reducing the value of stocks (equities) and, if the solvency of the financial sector is threatened, deterring domestic lending. Fifth, the country will have to contract foreign loans in order to cover any current account deficit that remains and in order to roll-over maturing loans. This will occur in an environment where foreign confidence in the worth of the government's word has just been undermined by a devaluation undertaken in defiance of its previous commitments. This may require some combination of high interest rates, which will be contractionary.

Turning to the question of which exchange rate regime the country should choose in order to attain sustainability in the current account, the situation as of the beginning of 2005 suggested that Turkey should avoid adopting a fixed exchange rate regime since the country still faced fiscal problems, inflation was higher than in competitor countries, the country had not completely resolved its problems in the banking sector and the current account was unsustainable. A fixed exchange rate regime would make the situation worse. Thus, exchange rate regimes with no separate legal tender – including regimes with another currency as legal tender (formal dollarization or euroization) and currency unions, currency board, and conventional fixed pegs – should not be alternatives for Turkey during the pre-accession period until the conditions improve.[18] The country should also not use horizontal bands since the inflation rate is still high relative to the inflation rates in major partner countries. On the other hand an independent float in the case of Turkey has led to the problems of sustainability of the current account. Since during the pre-accession period Turkey will further liberalize capital transactions, achieving sustainability in the current account will become more and more important as time passes. Hence, an independent float should also not be an alternative for Turkey. Among the intermediate regimes Turkey could in principle choose between crawling pegs, managed float or crawling band regimes. But a crawling peg regime should also be not an alternative.[19] Last time Turkey adopted the crawling peg with a foreign exchange regime close to currency board, the system failed in 2001, as Turkey had neither a sound fiscal framework nor a sound banking sector and had not attained price stability. In addition the exchange rate at the beginning of the stabilization period was not set at the competitive equilibrium exchange rate, and the country did not depreciate the exchange rate fast enough to attain its long-run equilibrium level. Furthermore, since the determination of the competitive equilibrium exchange rate is not easy, and it can be determined at best with an error margin, a crawling peg would not be an appropriate exchange regime for Turkey. Thus, in principle, Turkey could choose between crawling band and managed float regimes.

The crawling band system consists of a rule on the determination of the peg, the choice of parity, a rule for changing the parity, and a band around the parity within which the rate floats.

Choice of peg and intervention currency Under a crawling peg regime the country needs to decide whether to peg to a single foreign currency or to a currency basket. In the case of Turkey it would be sensible to use a basket of currencies as a peg. Such a basket could contain the currencies of major competitors of Turkey in world markets as well as of major suppliers of imported commodities. The countries could consist, as in the determination of the RER, of various countries in Western Europe, of different countries in America, of various countries in Central and Eastern European and the Commonwealth of Independent States, of different countries in Asia, and of some of the countries in Middle Eastern and North African countries. The weights of different countries could be determined using the approach of Zanello and Desruelle (1997). Since the operation of the crawling band also requires the choice of a currency in which to intervene when necessary, Turkey could use either the US dollar or the euro as the intervention currency.

The choice of parity The choice of parity is a perennial source of tension between those who want a strong exchange rate to serve as a nominal anchor in curbing inflation and those who want a more competitive rate in the interest of promoting exports and strengthening the balance of payments. It is our contention that the parity should be determined from considerations of competitive equilibrium exchange rate as explained above in Section 9.2 on sustainability of the current account.

Choice of rate of crawl Experience suggests the changes in parity will have to be small and very frequent. The rate of crawl could be determined from the formula:

$$\frac{\dot{E}}{E} = \textit{Inflation target} - \textit{expected foreign inflation rate}$$

when the country is interested in keeping the RER constant over time. In that case we deduct from the inflation target the expected foreign inflation rate and obtain the rate of change of the central parity. Alternatively, one could use the formula:

$$\frac{\dot{E}}{E} = \textit{Inflation target} - \textit{expected foreign inflation rate} - \textit{estimated productivity growth differential}$$

In this case we deduct from the inflation target the expected foreign inflation and the difference between productivity growths in the home and foreign countries. By determining the rate of change of the central rate by this formula the country tries to keep the relative wages w/Ew^* constant over time.

Choice of band width The fourth parameter to be considered is the choice of band width. A wide band allows a capital inflow to push the exchange rate a considerable way before reaching the bottom of the band. Williamson (1996), who has studied the crawling band experiences of Chile, Colombia and Israel, notes that Chile has widened its band in a series of steps, from 0.5 to 2 to 3 to 5 to 10 per cent on either side of the parity. Similarly, Israel in January 1989 chose a band width of +/−3 per cent. In March 1990 the band was widened to +/−5 per cent, and to +/−7 per cent in May 1995. Similarly, Turkey could choose a relatively wide band width. The reason for the choice of the wide band lies in the fact that it is impossible to know exactly the equilibrium exchange rate. Countries need scope to discourage unwelcome capital inflows without jeopardizing their monetary policy. Therefore a crawling band width of +/−7 to +/−10 per cent seems to be the preferred band width for Turkey.

Under the crawling band, Israel since the late 1980s and 1990s and Poland since the mid-1990s, pledged to intervene when the exchange rate hit pre-announced margins on either side of central parity. In both cases the rate of crawl has been pre-announced for up to a year in advance, with the objective of influencing expectations and price-setting behaviour. Experience shows that crawling bands function best when there is also readiness to adjust the central parity and rate of crawl in a timely manner in response to changing economic fundaments. On the other hand, it is sometimes stressed that even if there is no commitment by the central bank to maintain the limits, statements by the central bank offering guidance to the reasonable limits of the exchange rate, taking fundamentals into account, will affect market behaviour. But such procedures would come under the headings of managed floating.

A country can use a wide range of instruments, including sterilized and unsterilized interventions, to defend its exchange rate band. In Israel, sterilized interventions have been directed to defending an inner band. Authorities intervened within the inner band to reduce volatility, and thereby discouraged the rate from approaching the edge of the band. Outside the inner band interventions were used more progressively to push the rate back towards the middle of the band. Countries have also used unsterilized interventions to defend the band. Furthermore countries could use interest rate policy and also change the reserve requirements to which commercial banks are subject in order to defend the band.

On the other hand the managed float, also known as a dirty float, is defined as a readiness to intervene in the foreign exchange market, without defending any particular parity. There is no commitment to an exchange rate. Most intervention is intended to lean against the wind – buying the currency when it is rising and selling when it is falling. A managed floater responds to a 1 per cent change in demand for its currency by partial accommodation – changing the supply of currency by say α per cent and letting the rest of the change in demand show up in the price. When α is close to 1, the exchange rate is fixed; when it is close to 0, the rate is floating. The aim under managed float as emphasized by Corden (2002) is to stabilize exchange rate movements occasionally, or at least moderate fluctuations, and avoid extreme movements. Since there is no explicit commitment by the central bank, there is never a danger of losing credibility. This property gives policymakers discretion in exchange rate policy. They might have an informal target concept such as the crawling band in mind, but the limits of the band are not made public. Thus, the country can pursue an implicit rather than a formal or announced target zone. This kind of regime would be attractive for Turkey because of the discretion it will allow governments.

The above considerations reveal that Turkey could attain sustainability in the current account and thus the long-run equilibrium level of the RER by discontinuing the regime of an independent float and adopting either a crawling band or managed float regime. In 2005 the Turkish Central Bank was focusing its primary attention on reducing the inflation rate, and was in the process of formally adopting the 2006 inflation targeting regime. But the Central Bank, besides targeting the inflation rate must also have the objective of maintaining a sustainable current account deficit, and hence targeting the RER.

9.3.3 Policy on Capital Account Transactions

A major instrument which countries have used to attain sustainability in the current account and then to sustain it over time is the use of capital controls, which has taken a variety of forms. An interesting experiment is that of Chile. During 1990–97 Chile was the recipient of massive capital inflows. In order to avoid large appreciation of the currency the authorities implemented capital controls on inflows and liberalized outflows. In 1991 Chile introduced the Unremunerated Deposit Requirement (UDR). The UDR applied to almost all foreign borrowing except foreign direct investment inflows and trade credit. It applied to both short-term and long-term loans and to portfolio investment, such as purchases of stocks. At first 20 per cent of the relevant foreign borrowing had to be deposited in non-interest bearing deposits with the central bank for a period of 3 to 12 months, depending on the maturity and nature of the credit. The implicit tax would fall the lengthier the maturity of the loan, which reflected the objective that short-term inflows should be reduced more than long-term inflows. In 1992 the proportion was raised to 30 per cent and the period was set at 12 months regardless of the term of the credit. Later UDR was reduced and finally in 1998 it was brought down to zero. Eichengreen et al. (1998) maintain that the evidence on the effectiveness of the controls in reducing the short-term external debt is somewhat ambiguous. On the other hand Edwards (1998) and Cowan and De Gregorio (2005) emphasize that the introduction of UDR had the desired effect of reducing the share of short-term capital inflows.

Eichengreen (2003a) points out that in most of the developing countries monetary and fiscal institutions lack credibility, the regulators lack administrative capacity, the financial markets are shallow, and they cannot borrow abroad in domestic currency. So long as these conditions are present, there are arguments for capital controls to limit the risks to the financial system. Capital flows should not be freed before progress has been made in liberalizing domestic financial markets and strengthening prudential supervision. This in turn means, according to Eichengreen (2003b), liberalizing, first, foreign direct investment, second, access to stock and bond markets, and finally, offshore bank funding. As developing countries take necessary measures to strengthen their financial systems, rationalize prudential supervision, achieve sound and stable fiscal policy and attain price stability they should remove capital controls. Thereafter capital account liberalization will help more than it hurts.

Table 9.2 shows the controls prevailing in 2003 on different types of capital transactions in Central and Eastern European countries and Turkey. The table reveals that Hungary has the most liberal capital transactions regime, and that Poland and Turkey the most restrictive among the countries under consideration. In Poland and Turkey there were eight types of capital transactions subject to controls, with a restrictiveness value of 73 per cent. Hungary has a restrictiveness value of only 9 per cent. Here we should note that Turkey liberalized international capital movements in 1989, and accepted the obligations of Article VIII of the Agreement of the IMF on 22 March 1990. In Turkey a number of sectors, such as broadcasting, aviation, marine transport, port and financial services are subject to FDI restrictions. Recently Turkey has opened up the broadcasting sector to foreign competition and has also removed restrictions on the acquisition of real estate.

Regarding the policy on capital controls we note that in order to attain sustainability on the current account, Turkey could, in principle, introduce holding-period taxes as in Chile as a form of prudential supervision, until banks' risk management practices and regulatory oversight have been upgraded.[20]

9.4 CONCLUSION

Under perfect capital mobility there will be the unavoidable risk of attacks on the currency unless the country resolves its fiscal problems, attains price stability, achieves a sound banking sector, and the RER does not deviate considerably from its long-run equilibrium value. During the last few years Turkey has been trying hard to resolve its fiscal problems, attain price stability and achieve a sound banking sector. The remaining issue concerns the attainment of sustainability in the current account. Turkey could achieve this objective by adopting measures that will increase FDI inflows into the country, changing the exchange rate regime from independent float to either a managed float or crawling band regime, and by introducing restrictions on capital movements.

Table 9.2 Restrictions on capital transactions in Central and Eastern European countries and Turkey, 2003

	Bulgaria	Czech Republic	Estonia	Hungary	Latvia	Lithuania	Poland	Romania	Slovakia	Slovenia	Turkey
Capital market securities		X					X	X	+		X
Money market instruments							X	X	+		X
Collective investment securities									X	X	X
Derivatives and other instruments								X		X	
Commercial credits							X		+		X
Financial credits	X						X		+		X
Guarantees, sureties and financial backup facilities	X						X		+		
Direct investments	X	X			X	X	X			X	X
Liquidation of direct investment									+	X	
Real estate transactions	X	X	X	X	X	X	X	X	X	X	X
Personal capital transactions	X		X			X	X		+		X
Restrictiveness index	45	27	18	9	18	27	73	36		45	73

Notes: X denotes that there are restrictions, and + indicates that the specific practice is not regulated. Higher values of restrictiveness index indicates more restrictions on capital transactions.

Source: Exchange Rate Arrangements and Restrictions (IMF).

NOTES

* The authors gratefully acknowledge the comments of Jürgen von Hagen and Emin Öztürk. We are particularly in debt to Manfred Neumann, whose comments helped us to correct several errors in an earlier draft. However, the views expressed in this paper are the authors' sole responsibility.

1. There were huge distortions created by the state banks, which had substantial shares in the banking sector's total assets. These banks faced unrecovered costs from duties carried out on behalf of the government and they covered their financing needs from markets by borrowing at high interest rates and short maturities. In addition some banks started to borrow funds from abroad with which they bought government bonds and treasury bills which yielded high real interest returns.
2. Fiscal deficit, primary balance and debt figures are obtained from IMF (2005), and all other data from the web sites of State Planning Organization (www.dpt.gov.tr) and Undersecretariat of the Treasury (www.hazine.gov.tr).
3. Foreign debt to GDP ratio amounted to 71.4 per cent in 2002 and 61 per cent in 2003. The large decrease in debt to GDP ratio is mainly due to real exchange rate (RER) appreciation.
4. When constructing real exchange rate indices one is faced with four decisions: choice of the price index, choice of the currency basket, choice of weights and choice of mathematical formula. In the formulation of the real exchange rate we use CPI, as CPI data are available on a monthly basis for a large number of countries. Choice of currency basket is composed of countries which are major competitors of Turkey in world markets as well as major suppliers of imported commodities to Turkey. The countries considered consist in Western Europe of Belgium, France, Germany, Greece, Italy, the Netherlands, Portugal, Spain, Switzerland and the UK; in America of Brazil, Canada, Mexico and the USA; in Central and Eastern European countries and the Commonwealth of Independent States of the Czech Republic, Hungary, Poland and Russia; in Asia of China, Indonesia, Japan, Korea, Malaysia, Taiwan and Thailand; and in Middle Eastern and North African countries of Egypt, Tunisia and Morocco. For weights assigned to different countries and formula used for estimation of RER we use the approach developed by Zanello and Desruelle (1997).
5. Until the end of the 1970s, Turkey followed a fixed and multiple exchange rate policy while experiencing relatively high inflation rates. The policy led to a loss of competitiveness and eventually to the foreign exchange crisis of the late 1970s. GNP shrank by 0.5 per cent in 1979 and by 2.8 per cent in 1980. With the stabilization measures of 1980, Turkey devalued its lira by 100 per cent and eliminated the multiple exchange rate system. After May 1981, the exchange rate was adjusted daily against major currencies to maintain the competitiveness of Turkish exports. Multiple currency practices were phased out during the first two years of the 1980 stabilization programme, and the government pursued a policy of depreciating the RER – on average by about 6 per cent annually over the period 1980–88.
6. Turkey opened the capital account in 1989 before it had taken measures to upgrade banking and financial market supervision and regulation, adopt international auditing and accounting standards, strengthen corporate governance and shareholder rights and modernize bankruptcy and insolvency procedures.
7. The average budget deficit measured by the public sector borrowing requirements to GNP ratio amounted to 9.6 per cent during 1990–2000.
8. The real interest rate is defined as

$$r_t = \left[\left\{ \frac{1 + \left(\frac{i_t}{100} \right)}{1 + \left(\frac{\pi_t}{100} \right)} \right\} - 1 \right] * 100,$$

where i_t denotes the annual rate of interest on government bonds and treasury bills, attained as the weighted average rate in auctions during the month t weighted by total sales during the month, and π_t denotes the expected annual rate of inflation at time t over the period t to $t+12$. In the calculations of the real interest rate, we set the expected annual rate of inflation at time t over the period t to $t+12$ equal to the actual annual rate of inflation over the period t to $t+12$. The average level of real interest rates over the period January 1991 to March 1993 amounted to 9 per cent, and between February 1994 and October 2003 to 25.5 per cent.

9. The data for wage rates have been obtained from AMECO, the European Commission Annual Macroeconomic Database, http://europa.eu.int/comm/economy_finance/indicators/annual_macro_economic_database/ameco_en.htm.

   The foreign wage has been determined as the weighted average of the wage rates in Belgium, Canada, Germany, Italy, Japan, Korea, the Netherlands, the United Kingdom and the United States. On the other hand the data for labour productivity have been obtained from US Department of Labor, Bureau of Labor Statistics Database, http://www.bls.gov/fls/home.htm. Foreign productivity has been determined as the weighted average of the productivity of the above countries.
10. Eichengreen (2004) summarizes the factors leading to financial crises under the headings of unsustainable macroeconomic policies, fragile financial systems, institutional weaknesses, and flaws in the structure of international financial markets. Thus, countries suffer currency crises because they run inconsistent and unsustainable macroeconomic policies. Fragile financial systems indicate that balance sheet vulnerabilities put banks, non-bank financial institutions, corporations and other borrowers at risk when confidence erodes and capital begins to haemorrhage out of the financial system. Institutional weaknesses refer to weak corporate and public sector governance issues, which allow excessive risk-taking, resulting in vulnerable financial structures. Finally, flaws in the structure of international financial markets refer to sudden stops and capital flow reversals that can cause crises independently of conditions in the afflicted economies. In Turkey the crises of late 1970 and of 1994 occurred mainly because of unsustainable macroeconomic policies. In the case of the 2001 crisis the main factors causing the crisis were unsustainable macroeconomic policies, fragile financial systems, and institutional weaknesses.
11. A look at Turkey's annual GDP growth rate over the period 1980–2004 reveals that the average growth rate of GDP amounted to 4.1 per cent during 1980–89 and again 4.1 per cent during 1990–2004. Hence, for the growth rate of GDP over the time period 2004 to 2014 we take the figure of 4.1 per cent. On the other hand, we determine the foreign interest rate from Eurobond issues of the Turkish Treasury. The average rate of return on Turkish US$ Eurobonds during the time of issue was 10.13 per cent in 1998, 12.08 per cent during 1999, 11.61 per cent in 2000, 11.35 in 2001, 10.66 per cent in 2002, 10.08 in 2003 and 8.06 per cent in 2004. By deflating the nominal return figures by US CPI inflation rates observed during the following period we obtain, as the average figure for the time period 1998–2004, 7.84 per cent, and for the time period 2002–04, 6.86 per cent. In the calculations we set the value of foreign real interest rate as 6.86 per cent. We would like to thank Tekin Çotuk of the Undersecretariat of the Treasury for providing the data on Turkish Eurobonds.
12. We assume as before that $\eta = 0$ and set the values of the parameters as $g = 0.041$, $r^* = 0.0686$, and $d_{2004} = 0.5345$ for the year 2004.
13. The formulation of the sustainability problem through equation (9.1) assumes that FDI is a surer and safer form of external financing. Thus the analysis in the chapter assumes that current account deficits financed mainly by FDI inflows do not lead to problems of sustainability of the current account. But if FDI takes the form of purchases of stocks and if these shares can be liquidated easily in domestic markets, then it is possible to take the money out of the country as in other forms of investment. In those cases FDI makes no difference and there is no reason to separate FDI flows in equation (9.1). Under these conditions, sustainability of the current account will require higher rates of depreciation of the RER than those obtained above.

14. However, the country still faces problems in the real sector. There is a need to strengthen corporate governance, and there is also a large informal sector in the economy, where accounting practices need to be improved.
15. Foreign-owned firms usually comply strictly with the formal regulatory and tax rules, possibly more completely than most domestic firms, in order to avoid any friction with the government authorities. They therefore do not enjoy the flexibility of incomplete enforcement.
16. In Turkey foreign-owned firms had long been subject to special authorizations and sectoral limitations. In 2001 the Turkish government requested the Foreign Investment Advisory Service of the World Bank to conduct a study on the business environment affecting foreign direct investment (FDI) firms in Turkey. On the basis of this work, a new Law on FDI and important amendments in various laws (Commercial Law and in the laws concerning the Employment of Foreigners, the Registry of Title Deeds and Public Procurement) were adopted by the parliament in 2003. The new legislation removed the screening and pre-approval procedures for FDI projects, redesigned the company registration process on an equal footing for domestic and foreign firms, facilitated the hiring of foreign employees, included FDI firms in the definition of 'domestic tenderer' in public procurement, and authorized foreign persons and companies to acquire real estate in Turkey. Thus the new law guarantees national treatment and investor rights. According to the law a company can be 100 per cent foreign owned in almost all sectors of the economy. Acquisitions of more than 30 hectares by foreigners are subject to permission from the Council of Ministers, and establishments in the financial, petroleum and mining sectors require special permission, according to appropriate laws.
17. Here we assume that FDI does not take the form of purchases of stocks and that these shares can not be liquidated easily in domestic markets.
18. Williamson (1991) recommends a fixed exchange rate regime for a country that satisfies all of the following four conditions: (i) The economy is small and open, so that it satisfies the conditions for being absorbed in a larger currency area according to the traditional literature on optimum currency areas; (ii) the bulk of its trade is undertaken with the trading partner(s) to whose currency (or whose mutually-pegged currencies) it plans to peg; (iii) the country pursues a macroeconomic policy that will result in an inflation rate consistent with that in the country (or countries) to whose currency (or currencies) it plans to peg; and (iv) the country is prepared to adopt institutional arrangements that will assure continued credibility of the fixed rate commitment.
19. Under a crawling peg regime the adjustments are pre-announced, and in high inflation countries, the peg can be regularly reset in a series of mini devaluations, as often as weekly.
20. Edwards (1998) maintains that restrictions on capital inflows in Chile have not been effective in affecting the RER behaviour. According to Edwards the impact of increasing capital restrictions on RER is limited and short lived. Furthermore, we note that accession countries during the pre-accession period have to complete the orderly liberalization of capital movements.

REFERENCES

Corden, W.M. (2002), *Too Sensational: On the Choice of Exchange Rate Regimes*, Cambridge, MA: The MIT Press.

Corsetti, G., P. Pesenti and N. Roubini (1999), 'Paper tigers? A model of the Asian crisis', *European Economic Review*, **43**, 1211–36.

Cowan, K. and J. De Gregorio (2005), 'International borrowing, capital controls and the exchange rate: lessons from Chile', in S. Edwards (ed.), *Capital Controls*

and Capital Flows in Emerging Economies: Policies, Practices and Consequences, Chicago: University of Chicago Press (forthcoming).
Dutz, M., M. Us and K. Yılmaz (2005), 'Foreign direct investment challenges: competition, the rule of law and EU accession', in B. Hoekman and S. Togan (eds), *Turkey: Economic Reform and Accession to the European Union*, co-publication of the the World Bank and Centre for Economic Policy Research (CEPR), pp. 261–93.
Edwards, S. (1998), 'Capital flows, real exchange rates and capital controls: some Latin American experiences', NBER Working Paper No. 6800.
Edwards, S. (2004), 'Thirty years of current account imbalances, current account reversals and sudden stops', NBER Working Paper No. 10276.
Eichengreen, B. (2003a), 'Capital controls: capital idea or capital folly?', in B. Eichengreen (ed.), *Capital Flows and Crises*, Cambridge, MA: MIT Press.
Eichengreen, B. (2003b), 'Taming capital flows', in B. Eichengreen (ed.), *Capital Flows and Crises*, Cambridge, MA: MIT Press, pp. 289–306.
Eichengreen, B. (2004), 'Financial instability', in B. Lomborg (ed.), *Global Crises, Global Solutions*, Cambridge: Cambridge University Press, pp. 251–80.
Eichengreen, B. and O. Choudhry (2005), 'Managing capital inflows: Eastern Europe in an Asian mirror', paper presented at the Turkish Central Bank Conference on Macroeconomic Policies for EU Accession, Ankara, 6–7 May.
Eichengreen, B., M. Mussa, G. Dell'Ariccia, E. Detragiache, G.M. Milesi-Ferretti and A. Tweedie (1998), 'Capital account liberalization: theoretical and practical aspects', Occasional Paper 172, Washington, DC: IMF.
Foreign Investment Advisory Service (2001a), *Turkey: A Diagnostic Study of the Foreign Direct Investment Environment*, Ankara: World Bank and the Treasury of Turkey.
Foreign Investment Advisory Service (2001b), *Turkey: Administrative Barriers to Investment*, Ankara: World Bank and the Treasury of Turkey.
International Monetary Fund (2003), *Annual Report on Exchange Arrangements and Exchange Restrictions*, Washington, DC: International Monetary Fund.
International Monetary Fund (2005), 'IMF executive board approves US$10 billion stand-by arrangement for Turkey', Press Release No. 05/104, May 11, Washington, DC: International Monetary Fund.
Milesi-Ferretti, G. and A. Razin (1996), 'Sustainability of persistent current account deficits', NBER Working Paper No. 5467.
Organization for Economic Co-operation and Development (2004), *OECD Economic Surveys: Turkey*, Paris: OECD.
Özatay, F. (2005), 'Monetary policy challenges for Turkey in European Union accession process', paper presented at the Turkish Central Bank Conference on Macroeconomic Policies for EU Accession, Ankara, 6–7 May.
Radelet, S. and J. Sachs (2000), 'The onset of the East Asian financial crisis', in P. Krugman (ed.), *Currency Crises*, Chicago: NBER and Chicago University Press, pp. 105–62.
Reinhart, C., K. Rogoff and M. Savastano (2003), 'Debt intolerance', *Brookings Papers on Economic Activity*, **1**, 1–74.
Tansel, A. and S. Togan (1987), 'Price and income effects in Turkish foreign trade', *Weltwirtschaftliches Archiv*, **123**, 521–34.
von Hagen, J. and I.J. Harden (1994), 'National budget process and fiscal performance', *European Economy Reports and Studies 3*, Towards Greater Fiscal Discipline, European Commission, Directorate-General for Economic and financial Affairs, Belgium, pp. 311–93.

Williamson, J. (1991), 'Advice on the choice of exchange rate policy', in E. Claassen (ed.), *Exchange Rate Policies in Developing and Post-Socialist Countries*, San Francisco: ICS Press, pp. 395–403.

Williamson, J. (1996), *The Crawling Band as an Exchange Rate System: Lessons from Chile, Colombia and Israel*, Washington, DC: Institute for International Economics.

Zanello, A. and D. Desruelle (1997), 'A primer on the IMF's information notice system', IMF Working Paper WA/97/71, Washington, DC: IMF.

COMMENTS

Manfred J.M. Neumann

Sübidey Togan and Hasan Ersel are to be complimented for providing us with a very informative study of Turkey's balance of payments problems and the implications of an attempt at reducing the current account deficit by devaluing the Turkish lira. The authors show that Turkey's current account has deteriorated during recent years while the lira has appreciated in real terms. They argue that the present state of the current account is not sustainable but needs correction. Consequently, they propose to devalue the lira by a sizeable margin and to this end to abandon the current system of an independent float in favour of a managed float or alternatively a crawling exchange rate band. To be sure, this is a strong policy message that requires careful evaluation.

In this comment I will first use a few economic indicators in order to characterize the macroeconomic developments of the 1990s and the current state of affairs; next I will discuss the authors' analysis of current account sustainability and the issue of the controllability of the real exchange rate; and finally I will draw a few policy conclusions. On my reading of the data, I am not convinced that a major change of exchange rate policy is advisable.

9C.1 Macroeconomic Assessment

The main macroeconomic characteristics of the Turkish economy can be read from Table 9C.1 where the first column summarizes the average performance of the 1990s up to 1998 and the additional columns provide more detailed information on the developments since then. To judge from the average performance over the past fifteen years, Turkey is a high-inflation, twin-deficit country. During the early and mid-1990s the country suffered from high inflation of 78 per cent on average, accompanied by an average rate of real growth of about 4.8 per cent. Growth performance during the 1990s was not particularly impressive for an emerging market economy and less than what it used to be during the 1960s and 1970s. As a rule, the current account has been in deficit, 0.8 per cent of GNP on average since 1990, and this has gone along with a rather large budget deficit, 6.6 per cent of GNP on average. The deficit was financed by selling debt to the central bank, the banks at large and to international investors. Apparently in response to a recession in 1999 the budget deficit was doubled in 1999/2000, up to 12.7 per cent of GNP, and this unleashed a currency and banking crisis in 2000–01 that enforced another recession. As a result, Turkey

Table 9C.1 Selected indicators of the Turkish economy (%)

	Annual averages				
	1990–98	1999–2000	2001	2002–2003	2004
Inflation	78.4	59.9	54.4	35.1	10.7
Real GDP growth	4.8	1.2	−7.3	6.9	8.9
Current account (% GNP)	−0.8	−2.8	2.3	−2.1	−5.2
Appreciation of Turkish lira					
Nominal	−56.8	−35.8	−57.3	−21.8	−3.1
Real	1.2	8.2	−22.2	9.3	5.0
Budget surplus (% GNP)	−6.6	−12.7	−19.6	−11.3	−7.1
Overnight money	75.9	65.1	92.0	42.8	21.6

Sources: IFS-statistics, Nominal effective exchange rate: OECD. Real effective exchange rate: Chapter 9.

switched from a crawling peg to float and the lira was devalued by about 60 per cent. To stem further devaluation the central bank pushed up the money market rate from 65 to 92 per cent in nominal terms, from 5 to 38 per cent in real terms.

The crisis of 2001 was severe enough to set the stage for a remarkable turnaround of policies supported by stand-by arrangements with the IMF. The visible results are impressive. Inflation was brought down to about 10 per cent in 2004 and this has not gone at the expense of real growth. On the contrary real growth has recovered strongly, from 7 per cent in 2001 to about 9 per cent in 2004, the highest rate of growth since 1990. This favourable performance has helped to reduce the budget deficit from its record high of 20 per cent of GNP in 2001 to 7 per cent in 2004. It seems that Turkey's government is prepared to hold on to the new path of fiscal consolidation, as summarized by the primary surplus target of 6.5 per cent of GNP and that the Central Bank is longing for a further decline of the inflation rate. Thus, overall prospects seem bright for the Turkish economy even though the labour market appears to be sticky. However, as Togan and Ersel rightly note the current account is deteriorating. Accompanied by a strong real appreciation of the lira the current account deficit widened to 3.4 per cent of GNP in 2003 and even further, to 5.2 per cent in 2004.

9C.2 On the Sustainability of the Current Account Deficit

The authors believe that Turkey's current account deficit is not sustainable and to underpin this belief they compute measures of current account sustainability. The measures are derived from the following balance of payments equation, expressed in foreign currency:

$$(TB_t^{\$} - i_t^* D_{t-1}^{\$}) + (FDI_t^{\$} + \Delta D_t^{\$}) = \Delta R_t^{\$}, \tag{9C.1}$$

where the first bracketed expression on the left-hand side describes the current account (non-interest current account minus debt service on the stock of external net debt), the second expression specifies the capital account (net inflow of foreign direct investment plus change in the stock of net debt) and the sum of both equals the transactions change in the central bank's net foreign reserves on the right-hand side of the equation. Multiplying through by the current exchange rate, dividing by nominal GNP, and assuming a clean float, that is, the central bank keeps net reserves unchanged, yields after rearranging:

$$(tb + fdi)_t + d_t = \frac{(1 + r_t^*)\,(1 + \eta_t)}{1 + g_t}\, d_{t-1}, \tag{9C.2}$$

where *tb*, *fdi* and *d* denote the ratios of the non-interest current account balance, the net inflow of foreign direct investment and the stock of external net debt to GNP; *g* is the economy's real rate of growth, r^* the foreign real rate of interest, and η the rate of real depreciation of the Turkish lira. Solving forward equation (9C.2) yields:

$$E_t \sum_{i=1}^{n} \delta_{t,i} (tb + fdi)_{t+i} = d_t - E_t \delta_{t,n} d_{t+n}, \tag{9C.3}$$

where the discount factor δ is defined as:

$$\delta_{t,i} = \prod_{i=1}^{k} \frac{1 + g_i}{(1 + r_i^*)\,(1 + \eta_i)}. \tag{9C.4}$$

Accordingly, the current state of the balance of payments, as summarized by the ratios of the non-interest current account plus the net inflow of foreign direct investment, may be called to be sustainable if the discounted value of the future net debt ratio, expected for period $t+n$, does not exceed the current net debt ratio:

$$E_t \delta_{t,n} d_{t+n} \leq d_t \tag{9C.5}$$

or, equivalently,

$$E_t \sum_{i=1}^{n} \delta_{t,i} (tb + fdi)_{t+1} \geq 0 \qquad (9C.6)$$

if the present value of the summed future balance of payments deficits is expected to be non-negative.

To provide content to this analysis the authors assume that (i) the Turkish economy will grow at a trend rate of 4 per cent, (ii) it will be able to borrow in the international capital market at a permanent real interest rate of 8 per cent and (iii) the real effective exchange rate will stay put:

$$g_{t+i} = g_t = 0.04, \quad r^*_{t+i} = r^*_t = 0.08, \quad \eta_{t+i} = \eta_t = 0,$$
$$\textit{and} \quad (tb + fdi)_{t+i} = (tb + fdi)_t$$
$$\textit{for} \quad i = 1,\ldots\ldots,10 \quad 1,\ldots\ldots,20 \quad \textit{and} \quad 1,\ldots\ldots,25.$$

Using equation (9C.6) these assumptions permit the authors to compute for each balance of payments observation the following three forward-looking sustainability measures $S(n)$ (see Table 9.2):

$$S(10)_t = 8.17 \times (tb + fdi)_t; \quad S(20)_t = 13.78 \times (tb + fdi)_t;$$
$$S(25)_t = 15.88 \times (tb + fdi)_t.$$

As the definitions indicate, the sustainability measures are constant multiples of the actual current account indicator, $tb + fdi$. Hence they carry the same sign as the indicator but rise in numerical size with the number of periods looked ahead because any additional period adds more of the same.

The question is what can we learn from the measures as regards the prospects of the country's international indebtedness? Let us compare for illustration the values of the sustainability measure $S(10)$ computed for the crisis years 2000 and 2001:

$$(tb + fdi)_{2000} = -3.0; \quad S(10)_{2000} = -24.76;$$
$$(tb + fdi)_{2001} = 7.2; \quad S(10)_{2001} = 58.92.$$

The negative $S(10)$ value computed for 2000 carries the following information: if the current account remained for another nine years at its level of 2000, the present value of Turkey's net indebtedness to foreign countries to be expected for the year 2010 is 24.8 per cent of GNP *higher than* the actual indebtedness of 2000. Hence the sustainability condition (9C.5) is violated, and the analysis yields the verdict that Turkey's current account of 2000 was not sustainable. From 2000 to 2001 the current account indicator changed from –3.0 to + 7.2 per cent of GNP. Accordingly, the sustainability measure

S(10) switches sign and more than doubles numerically to almost 59 per cent. This yields a radically different interpretation: the present value of Turkey's net indebtedness to foreign countries to be expected for the year 2011 is *not higher but* about 59 per cent of GNP *lower than* the actual indebtedness observed for 2001. It follows that the current account of 2001 was sustainable.

While it is useful to illustrate what will happen if a given state of the current account is extrapolated into the future, the example demonstrates the narrow limits of the exercise. Within a year an evaluation may quickly reverse if the current account turns around. Moreover, given that the sustainability measures are computed as constant multiples of the actual current account figures, they do not yield any additional insight into the question of whether a particular deficit is a serious one. The very essence of sustainability is expectations as regards long-run trends. As long as international investors have reason to believe that a given current account deficit will reverse or at least shrink in the not too distant future, they will hardly withdraw.

9C.3 Enforce Real Devaluation?

The authors conclude that the lira is overvalued and needs to be devalued by a large margin in order to induce a correction of the current account. They employ estimated price elasticities of export and import demand to compute the likely size of the required exchange rate adjustment. If the estimates of the elasticities are robust, it seems that the required real depreciation is in the range of 40 to 80 per cent. These are large numbers. It goes without saying that the required exchange rate adjustment will be much smaller, provided the permanent inflow of foreign direct investment can be expected to be higher in the future. On the other hand, it needs to be taken into account that the authors' focus is on *real* depreciation. This means that the size of *nominal* depreciation would have to be higher. More importantly, a nominal devaluation can serve to achieve a real devaluation in the short run but it cannot anchor the real exchange rate at the desired lower level because the domestic price level will start rising. Matters are different if the nominal exchange rate has been driven up by a bubble but the authors do not make that claim and in fact, evidence is lacking.

Now suppose the authorities drive down the external value of the lira by a large margin in one stroke (managed float) or in a pre-announced more gradual fashion (crawling exchange rate band). In both cases this can only be achieved by permitting the money supply growth to rise. As a result, the rate of inflation will turn around and the current perspective of disinflation is likely to be destroyed. Moreover, the government's current drive for fiscal consolidation will also be endangered because the devaluation will step up the cost of servicing foreign debt. This is not to be taken lightly given that the government's foreign indebtedness exceeds 20 per cent of GNP. The authors are aware of the potentially huge cost of a large devaluation and point to the negative experience of 2001. They nevertheless hold that the exchange rate is overvalued by too large a margin to be neglected.

But note that it is not obvious that the conjecture of overvaluation is justified. While it is true that the current account has deteriorated since 2002, it need not imply that this has happened because Turkish exporters have lost competitiveness. In fact, the export of consumption goods, measured in dollars, has almost doubled in comparison to late 2002. This observation does not suggest a serious loss of competitiveness. Closer inspection of the structure of imports reveals that the deterioration of the trade account is due to booming imports, and the dominant factor is not the import of consumption goods but of capital and intermediate goods. The import of the latter has risen from $45.9 billion in 2002 to $84.8 billion in 2004. This suggests that Turkey experienced a boom in private fixed capital formation. It fits that, according to data published by the State Planning Organization, the private investment to GNP ratio has risen since 2001 from 10.6 to 22.7 per cent in 2004; see Table 9.1. Even though we cannot rule out the possibility that some of this investment is inefficient, the strong rise in private investment is a positive development. The real capital stock of the country is rising and this is likely to generate a permanent increase in exports and real growth. Hence, it seems that the recent deterioration of Turkey's current account is less dangerous than may appear at first sight.

The role of private investment may be highlighted by constructing an indicator of the current account to GNP ratio that adjusts the actual ratio by the contribution of unusually high imports for private investment purposes. The underlying idea is that imports required for building the capital stock bear fruit in the future, hence must not be hindered by economic policy. Such an indicator can be defined in different ways. For example, one might augment the current account balance by adding the difference between the actual imports of capital and intermediate goods and their normal trend value. The procedure amounts to not counting as part of the current account balance the excess (or shortfall) of such imports relative to normal. Alternatively, we might add to the actual current account ratio the difference between the actual private investment to GNP ratio and its normal trend rate. This is done in Figure 9C.1 where the normal trend rate has been approximated by the average private investment ratio of the period 1990–2004.[1] The figure is to be interpreted as follows: when the adjusted current account ratio, represented by the dashed curve, lies above (below) the unadjusted ratio, unusually high (depressed) private investment

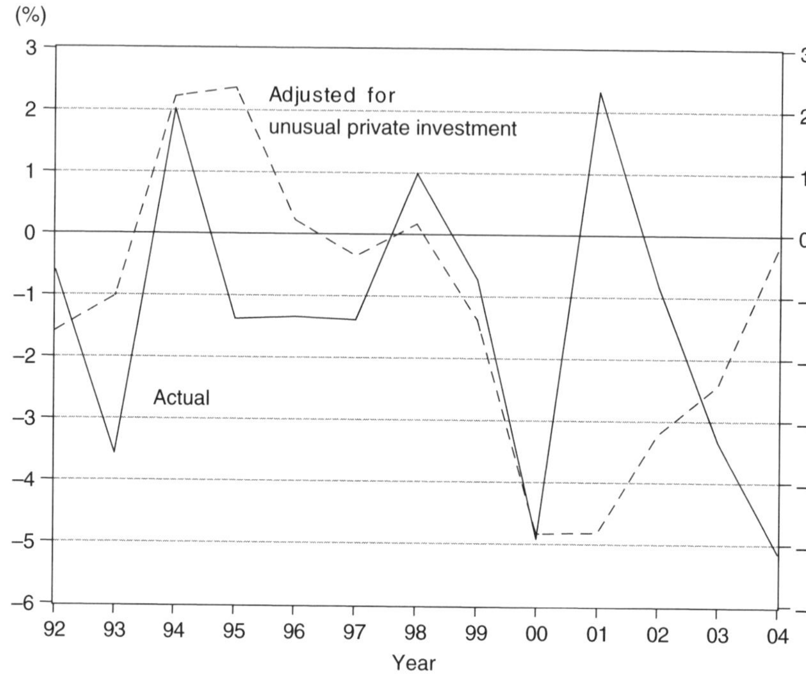

Figure 9C.1 Turkey's current account ratio (% GDP)

is a major source of the observed actual stance of the current account. For example, in 2000 the private investment ratio was equal to its average value of 17.8 per cent of GNP. Therefore, the adjusted current account ratio for that year does not differ from the actual ratio and this signals that the high current account deficit of 2000 was caused by other factors, namely by an exploding budget deficit. In the following year, 2001, the currency crisis induced the private investment ratio to fall drastically to a low of 10.6 per cent, and this negative development permitted the current account to improve. If we inspect 2004, the dashed curve in Figure 9C.1 sends the information that the actual current account deficit of about 5 per cent has been caused to a large extent by the rapid rise of the private investment ratio above normal. When private fixed capital formation returns to a more normal level, the current account deficit is likely to shrink in response.

9C.4 Concluding Remark

Turkey has experienced a remarkably strong recovery from the crisis of 2000–01. Inflation has come down from double digits and economic growth has doubled. These are the fruits of internal reform, notably from a switch to a more disciplined fiscal policy stance that makes it easier for the central bank to keep the money supply on a credible track. Looking at Turkey from the outside, it appears advisable to continue the path of institution-building. A major change in exchange rate policy, away from the current float, puts the macroeconomic achievements at risk. Political stability, continued fiscal consolidation and independent monetary policymaking appear to be key to stronger real growth and stability. At the same time they add to the credibility of Turkey's currency, thus reducing the danger of another large currency crisis.

Note

1. Given that there is no one-to-one relationship between the levels of private investment and of imports of capital and intermediate goods, the adjustment factor might be multiplied by a weight of smaller unity.

10. Macro policy challenges for Turkey: some comments

Marco Buti, Max Watson, Pierre van der Haegen and Ricardo Hausmann

10.1 GROWTH AND STABILITY DURING CONVERGENCE: EXPERIENCES OF EU MEMBER STATES

Marco Buti and Max Watson*

1. Introduction

Enlargement is already bringing new sources of dynamism to the EU economy and the accession of Turkey holds great potential for extending this process into the future. The challenge for the EU is to put in place policies that realize the full benefit of this and especially to accelerate economic growth. For Turkey, a different challenge lies ahead: to prolong the phase of strong growth of 2004 and 2005 and make it truly sustainable.

The experience of Turkey in recent years underscores the role of sound macroeconomic policies in this respect. Over the medium term, stability and growth go hand-in-hand and nowhere is this clearer than in economies that are dependent on external flows and have a high public debt. In the short run, though, policymakers can face major tensions in designing policies to assure both stability and growth, not least at times of major transformation in the economy (see Table 10.1.1).

How far do earlier EU experiences offer guideposts in this regard, especially during periods of accession and economic convergence? Turkey is grappling with some challenges that have parallels with the experiences of a number of EU member states. It is embarked on a major transformation of the economy and adoption of the *acquis communautaire*. Like some, it has shifted from a fixed to a flexible exchange rate in pressing through disinflation. It faces market discipline as it rolls over debt maturities, but also (as in earlier convergence cases) has the scope for a virtuous circle as real interest rates continue to decline. Turkey, too, has embarked on banking reform after a serious financial crisis in 2001. Credit, as in a majority of

Table 10.1.1 Selected economic indicators

Countries	GDP per capita (% of euro area, PPS) 2004	GDP growth (%) (annual average) 1997–2004	STD st. deviation of growth 1997–2004	Unemployment 2004	HICP inflation (annual % change) 2004	Current account balance (% GDP) 2004	Openness[b] Exports+ Imports (% GDP) 2004
TR	27.1	3.2	6.1	10.3	8.6	−5.1	63.9
EU-10	51.0	3.7	2.0[a]	14.1	4.1	−4.4	112.6
Baltics	44.6[a]	6.1[a]	2.8[a]	9.9[a]	3.5[a]	−11.2[a]	128.4[a]
EE	47.7	6.0	3.0	9.2	3.0	−12.9	169.3
LV	41.1	6.7	1.8	9.8	6.2	−12.5	103.7
LT	45.1	5.7	3.4	10.8	1.1	−8.3	112.1
CE	58.6[a]	3.5[a]	1.4[a]	11.4[a]	4.8[a]	−4.0[a]	126.7[a]
CZ	65.7	1.9	2.0	8.3	2.6	−5.2	143.0
HU	58.0	4.1	0.7	5.9	6.8	-9.0	133.6
PL	44.6	3.9	1.9	18.8	3.6	−1.3	80.0
SI	73.8	3.9	1.1	6.0	3.6	−0.9	120.4
SK	50.8	3.8	1.4	18.0	7.4	−3.4	156.3
Islands	71.9[a]	3.0[a]	2.1[a]	6.2[a]	2.3[a]	−7.9[a]	127.5[a]
CY	76.0	3.6	1.3	5.0	1.9	−5.7	97.0
MT	67.9	2.3	3.0	7.3	2.7	−10.0	158.1
Euro area	100.0	2.1	1.5[a]	8.8	2.1	0.6	71.3

Notes:
a. Unweighted average.
b. Goods and services.

Source: AMECO.

recently acceded member states, is still low relative to GDP, especially as regards credit to the private sector; but, again, lending to households and firms has recently grown rapidly.

But there are major differences. Turkey was not a centrally planned economy. The challenge is to modernize institutions, not to reinvent them. In banking, private and specifically foreign ownership is lower, even though changes are now under way. Trade and investment integration with the EU is lower, despite a decade of customs union. And external financing patterns have been different – with current account deficits covered to a much greater extent by debt-creating flows.

Against the background of these parallels and contrasts, this discussion highlights three aspects of experience in EU member states that may be relevant to Turkey in the period ahead: the links between macroeconomic and structural reform, the contribution of different branches of policy in safeguarding stability and challenges in reconciling key priorities for fiscal policy.

2. The structural underpinning of macroeconomic goals

The policy success of member states in the Baltics and Central Europe during their accession period is striking, especially when measured against the scale of transition challenges. It is clear, moreover, that they did not follow a 'cookie-cutter' approach. Poland embarked on macroeconomic shock therapy, restructured its debt and took time to privatize, including in banking. Hungary's sequencing and debt strategy were essentially the reverse. Estonia achieved success through a rigid rules-based strategy, a currency board and balanced budget; and this, in combination with foreign ownership in banking, has allowed the smooth financing of very large external deficits.

Across this diversity, though, there is an unmistakable family resemblance in their reform strategies. It lies in the deep complementarities of macroeconomic and structural reforms, even though sequencing varied greatly. By the late 1990s all of these former transition economies had in place strengthened institutions as well as good macroeconomic policies. It is probably this feature that marks them out more than anything else from many economies of comparable income levels.

The complementarities of institutional reforms and favourable macroeconomic policies helped to allocate resources more efficiently and imparted deeper resilience to their economies. Of course, they experienced crises en route; and in some areas, such as the public finances, institutional reform is unfinished business. But four examples will serve to make the point:

(1) Tax codes and expenditure management were transformed in ways essential to underpin fiscal and monetary stability. Slovakia's recent

steps to streamline spending and adopt a flat tax in a revenue-neutral package are examples of a continuing process.

(2) A radical opening to foreign direct investment injected badly needed equity finance and management skills into industry while also facilitating the stable financing of current accounts. Estonia and Hungary were two front runners in this respect and in both cases the strengthening of regulatory frameworks and governance standards undoubtedly was one of the factors helping to catalyse investment inflows.

(3) Bank reform was a cornerstone in allocating resources efficiently and safeguarding stability as credit to the private sector expands from levels (as in Turkey) low relative to GDP (see Table 10.1.2). Privatization, in many cases to foreign owners, helped improve efficiency and underpin funding. The share of foreign owned banks is some 80 per cent or higher in the Czech Republic, Estonia, Lithuania, Slovakia and Hungary. Public banks now have a significant share only in Poland and Slovenia (some 25 per cent of assets).

Table 10.1.2 Financial intermediation

Countries	M2 2004 (% GDP)	Domestic bank claims to private sector 2003 (% of GDP)	Domestic bank claims to private sector (% change Dec.03/Dec. 02)
TR	44.6	15.5	44.6
EU-10	57.1[a,b]	49.8[a]	22.2[a]
Baltics	38.3[a]	29.4[a]	45.6[a]
EE	42.2	33.1	32.6
LV	39.8	34.6	45.3
LT	32.8	20.4	58.9
CE	54.8[a]	35.2[a]	15.6[a]
CZ	70.0	30.7	8.6
HU	48.1	43.0	33.3
PL	42.1	29.0	6.7
SI	54.1	41.5	15.4
SK	59.7	31.6	13.9
Islands	125.3[a,b]	117.1[a]	3.7[a]
CY	125.3	119.4	5.1
MT	n/a	114.7	2.3
Euro area	94.2	112.1	5.5

Notes:
a. Unweighted average.
b. Excluding Malta.

Source: IMF IFS.

(4) In part as a result of these reforms, hard budget constraints were imposed on state enterprises and quasi-fiscal deficits were eliminated, although in some cases slowly.

Domestic policymakers deserve great credit for these achievements. In the process, though, it worth noting that they made skilled use of the *acquis communautaire* and the Copenhagen criteria as a fulcrum for reform.

This, in essence, is the opportunity that Turkey can now seize. The economic aspects of the Copenhagen criteria – the competitive capacity of the economy and its functioning along market lines – are centrally relevant to the goals of macroeconomic policy. Through a deepening of institutional structures, the *acquis communautaire* can embed stability and foster sustained growth. This in turn will depend crucially on continuing structural change – better mobilization of production factors, stronger investment in physical and human capital, faster absorption of know-how and accelerated productivity growth. But experience also suggests that these benefits are not guaranteed – they are contingent on the quality of the policy framework and the reform momentum.

In addressing policy challenges ahead and benefiting from the experience of others with the *acquis communautaire*, two words of nuance are in order.

The first issue concerns the different nature of the structural challenges to be addressed. Many recent accession countries faced a daunting task of transformation, since institutions had to be created from scratch. Turkey faces a different challenge, which is more analogous to the experience of earlier Mediterranean candidates. It is of adapting existing institutions. This means overcoming inertia, facing down well-established interest groups and substituting market-based incentives in areas where rent-seeking has been a problem. Where transition economies had to address such challenges (for example, in soft lending to state enterprises or in ending dependency on subsidized energy), they faced some of their toughest challenges. These will be important issues in implementing the *acquis communautaire* in the Turkish context. But addressing them has the potential to unlock major gains in terms of efficiency and innovation in the private sector. A key lies in the efficient functioning of markets – including the labour market, where improved performance will be most important.

The second issue concerns the EU framework as a reference point for fiscal policy. Turkey has benefited from IMF programmes as an anchor and their continuing value is evidenced by the further stand-by arrangement initialled in April 2005. Policymakers should not look to EU frameworks such as the Maastricht criteria and the Stability and Growth Pact as a fiscal commitment mechanism tailored to Turkish circumstances in the sense of a well-designed IMF programme even though the revised SGP embodies more differentiation. Among EU members, Belgium's experience is relevant here. Over an extended period it pursued a tough fiscal policy based on a very high primary surplus. This anchor helped trigger a virtuous circle of debt reduction in a strategy to restore stability and growth. This experience with a country-specific choice of fiscal anchor is relevant for Turkey; and Belgium's perseverance in holding to it contrasts with the erosion of policy effort in Italy where a primary surplus of some 7 per cent of GDP in 1997 collapsed to 2 per cent in 2004, and virtually disappeared by 2005. Again, a public debt ceiling of 60 per cent is clearly too high for an economy undergoing rapid transformation and subject to real and financial volatility. These are important qualifiers to the 'policy fulcrum' argument. National fiscal policies need to address squarely the specific stability challenges in each economy.

3. Addressing the stability challenge

The most obvious risks to stability in emerging market countries arise from real or financial shocks. Policymakers in the accession countries became all too familiar with these challenges. Economies that are open and where credit to the private sector is developing rapidly show a dependency on external flows – typically including foreign currency borrowing – that brings risks as well as heightened opportunities. In Turkey, given the level and maturity of the public debt, still high real interest rates and external challenges, the economy remains vulnerable to shocks and changes in market sentiment (see Table 10.1.3). Policy progress during accession will reduce vulnerability. But there will be factors that heighten the risks in policy setbacks, including strong and potentially reversible capital flows to the private sector.

When comparing Turkey with earlier candidates, one needs to bear in mind also that policy challenges can surface at different stages in the accession process. Rapid growth in credit to the private sector – though from a low base – could be such a case. This is fundamentally a highly positive development, of course, and central to rapid convergence. But it can also be a watch point for stability. This issue began to attract attention, in a preventive sense, at late stages of accession in some member states, as their financial systems embarked on a phase of rapid expansion. In Turkey, it may move to centre stage at an earlier point, as in the other current candidate countries.

The process of financial catching-up entails inherent hazards in addition to those arising from external or policy shocks. Financial market risk premia face particular challenges in steadying the pace of credit growth in a setting of high returns to capital and potentially low real base interest rates (Lipschitz et al., 2002). In a benign scenario, high investment and

Table 10.1.3 Selected fiscal indicators

Countries	GG deficit (% of GDP) 2004	GG gross debt (% of GDP) 2004
TR	3.9[a]	80.8
EU-10	3.9	45.4
Baltics	0.5[b]	13.0[b]
EE	−1.8	4.9
LV	0.8	14.4
LT	2.5	19.7
CE	3.5[b]	42.3[b]
CZ	3.0	37.4
HU	4.5	57.6
PL	4.8	43.6
SI	1.9	29.4
SK	3.3	43.6
Islands	4.7[b]	73.5[b]
CY	4.2	71.9
MT	5.2	75.0
Euro area	2.7	71.3

Notes:
a. Fiscal notification Spring 2005.
b. Unweighted average.

Source: IMF IFS.

consumption-smoothing result in wider but stably financed external deficits. Risks are perceived 'correctly' by banks and foreign investors – keeping credit growth, capital accumulation and consumption on a sustainable path.

There are, however, clear risks to this scenario. Familiar market imperfections (asymmetric information, moral hazard and other risk premia distortions) could trigger credit growth above an equilibrium path, in a setting of strong capital inflows – risking a misallocation of credit towards property and consumption, asset price bubbles and growing exposure to unhedged borrowing (Borio, 2001; Borio and White, 2003). At the economic level, the counterparts to this market 'exuberance' would be unproductive investment and excessive consumption, which could drive the external current account into unsustainable territory. If this cycle reverses sharply, this could inflict serious and lasting damage. Boom–bust phenomena may be more likely, as a result, in financially developing economies (Aghion et al., 2004).

A lesson from, for example, the Baltic states is that the tell-tale signs of emerging risk can be hard to disentangle in a convergence setting. How can one distinguish them from equilibrium features of growing credit, rising asset prices and productivity-driven real appreciation? This calls for deeper analysis of financial stability – including the extent of threats to the real economy. Strong policies are in part an insurance against risk and it makes a difference to know how deep and enduring these risks could be in terms of economic growth.

The analytical agenda, in other words, is complex. Firstly, financial stability is a property of the economic system, not just of its parts. This means probing the strengths of economic sectors but also the linkages between them. Banks' exposure to the public sector and indirectly, to the exchange rate through lending to unhedged firms and households are prime examples. Secondly, the impact of crises on growth will depend on whether the prevailing exchange regime directs stress initially to financial or real sector markets and how flexible and resilient are those markets. Financial stability reports represent a useful diagnostic tool in these respects; and indeed these are now prepared in all the central European member states as well as by many other EU members and the ECB.

Safeguarding stability has opportunity costs. The trade-offs for policy in this regard can be improved by designing frameworks that help to pre-empt instability and which complement each other in a well-designed policy mix. All the macroeconomic and financial regimes (fiscal, monetary, prudential) have long-run goals, such as price stability, that are highly congruent with financial stability. But policy regimes also have secondary features that influence risk behaviour in the private sector and can help buttress stability. Fiscal stabilizers help to cushion the economy against shocks and dampen fluctuations in the external current account. Supervisory approaches that use stress tests to assess compound risks and internalize risks in asset classes (for example, property lending) help pre-empt a systemic build-up of risk. And floating exchange rates that are truly variable offer a 'two-way bet' and thus help discourage unhedged exposure to currency risks among firms and households.

Trade-offs for growth will improve where the burden of safeguarding stability does not fall on one policy only. In this respect internal policy coordination is crucial. For example, tight money and easy fiscal policy may trigger volatile capital inflows and impair resource allocation by causing unwarranted real appreciation. Hungary's experience with internal policy coordination late in the accession process is an example of such challenges, with tensions between fiscal and monetary policy in early 2003, and again in summer 2006, contributing to sharp shifts in the exchange market and speculative pressures. Again, Poland's varied experience has underscored how credible fiscal discipline and greater budgetary predictability would improve the policy mix.[1] This is an important issue for Turkey. Effective fiscal management is key in combining a disinflationary monetary policy with financial stability. And fiscal policy, monetary policy and financial sector reform are tightly interlinked, given the outstanding stock of public debt.

In sum, well-designed and well-balanced policy frameworks can help safeguard stability – not just by avoiding errors that jeopardize confidence, but by helping to shape a stabilizing environment for private sector risk behaviour. Looking forward, this may be an aspect of accession experience that is very relevant in Turkey. Much will hang on the role of policies in setting a clear framework for the dynamism of the private sector including through clear regimes for collateral enforcement and a transparent legal framework. Nowhere, though, are these considerations more relevant than in managing the public finances.

4. Challenges for fiscal policy

Fiscal policy can make a key contribution to sustainable growth both through efficient tax and expenditure policies and through its stabilizing role. Over the long run, these two channels of influence are complementary. Strong growth enhances the economy's debt-carrying capacity, while stability is crucial for private investment and sustainable catching up. But in the short run, recent experience in converging EU economies – and not only that of the recent joiners – underscores that policymakers can potentially face difficult choices in this regard.

To support rapid economic catching-up, the public sector typically needs to shift resources towards priority areas such as infrastructure investment, education and vocational training programmes that develop the skills required in an evolving market economy. Making up gaps in educational levels is critical in assuring rapid convergence – accelerating absorption of know-how, and participation in high value added cross-border production networks. Financing for such programmes can be at odds with the priority of ensuring that deficits and debt do not jeopardize stability. Hence commentators have raised questions whether growth would be enhanced by tolerating wider deficits (for example, Buiter and Grafe, 2003).

At the same time, a second element in fiscal support for growth lies in the incentive effects and signals to the private sector that result from the structural features of policy. These are elements that can enhance the setting for investment and job creation including the avoidance of excessive non-wage labour costs. Taxation needs to be broad-based and to avoid as far as possible distorting economic activity, and progress here is consistent with efforts to shift more activity into the formal sector, where productivity is also much higher. Marginal rates of taxation and benefit withdrawal need to avoid profiles that discourage employment. Pension reforms can improve employment incentives and the profile of the public finances. Well-targeted benefits, moreover, can facilitate restructuring by easing adjustment strains. Transfers to firms that distort resource allocation need to be phased out. Wage structures in the public sector are also an important part of the labour market context: here the cost of the public payroll in Turkey is high compared to the number of employees, suggesting scope for restructuring. A number of such approaches can increase savings in the short or medium term.

In other words, the cost of priority measures may be offset by restructuring existing programmes in ways favourable for growth, such as cutting subsides and streamlining administration. So one should not jump prematurely to equate growth-oriented reforms, mechanically, with a net widening of deficits. Indeed, preliminary analysis suggests significant scope for expenditure restructuring in those new member states with deficit challenges. In Turkey, a key priority now is indeed to undertake expenditure-based reforms. Of course, in candidate economies and converging member states, the EU also makes a significant contribution to the public finances through its financial support. In some cases, for example Ireland and Spain, these funds were used to very good effect in the context of administrative reforms in the public sector.

This is not to suggest that policymakers in the converging EU member states faced an easy task in managing their fiscal positions during accession. In streamlining costs, much of the low-hanging fruit was gathered early. What remained typically were important but challenging structural reforms in the public sector which require careful design and preparation and in some cases may take time to accomplish. These are still under way.

There appear to be strong analogies in Turkey as regards, for example, the opportunities for improving expenditure composition and enhancing the tax base and the need to found such changes in well-designed structural reform programmes, thus ensuring that fiscal savings do not have to be made at some point among priorities such as infrastructure investment.

An important question is whether the environment of economic catching-up implies that fiscal policy should be more risk-averse than in other cases. On the favourable side in converging economies is the potential for higher growth, which will enhance debt-carrying capacity. On the other hand, some central European economies, unlike the Baltic states for example, have actually or potentially quite high public debt ratios. Moreover, economies undergoing structural transformation may experience volatility and hit creditworthiness constraints. In this setting, policies to assure credible debt dynamics move to centre stage.

When we think of these trade-offs in Turkey, the case seems clear-cut. In fostering both stability and growth, Turkey's present situation places a very high priority on reducing the public debt. Unlike the recent accession countries, Turkey is exposed to a high interest burden and the gains available from embedding market credibility make earlier adjustment successes in Belgium or Italy more relevant than the accession experience. This is, moreover, a setting where Ricardian effects may be strong. The relatively short maturity of the public debt and the high foreign currency component, reinforce these considerations.

There are other factors that underscore the need for prudence in formulating fiscal goals in the EU's catching-up economies and three appear particularly relevant to Turkey:

(1) The EU members that were formerly command economies have completed many of the most sweeping challenges of transition but may continue to experience greater volatility in their public finances including as financial sectors undergo rapid expansion. Shocks to output, interest rates and exchange rates can substantially affect debt dynamics and call for wider fiscal safety margins than in economies that are not undergoing rapid structural change and which are less exposed to financial shocks. Safety margins, here, relate not just to SGP ceilings but also to keeping a margin for manoeuvre in terms of market access and funding strategy. This is relevant to Turkey.

(2) During credit and asset price booms, it will be particularly important not to overestimate potential growth and also to allow for temporary boosts to revenue that may inflate fiscal revenues during credit and asset price booms. There are significant risks that the underlying strength of the public finances may be overestimated, curtailing the scope for stabilizers – and hence the resilience of the economy – during an ensuing downturn (Jaeger and Schuknecht, 2004). This is an issue to watch carefully in Turkey, ensuring that the structural primary surplus is assessed after allowing for transient gains (over and beyond conventional business cycle effects).

(3) Third, in high debt countries it is critical to guard against risks that sizeable domestic and external financing requirements could trigger a rise in risk premia that threatens capital market access. Particularly when domestic financial systems are relatively small and undiversified, the economy is heavily dependent on external financing. Tapping foreign savings is a major advantage for rapid catching-up, but it also exposes the economy to shocks and to cycles of feast and famine in international capital markets. The international yield environment, prevailing in the years 2003–06 with strongly compressed spreads, makes this concern timely. The signalling role of fiscal policy as well as its direct impact on the saving–investment balance, can be critical. Indeed, where there are risks to confidence and constraints on the resources available to the private sector, this may outweigh the case for

allowing free play of stabilizers during a downturn.[2] The structure and maturity of Turkey's debt, while in process of strengthening, still underscore the crucial relevance of these considerations.

Among EU members, convergence experience in earlier accession countries such as Portugal and Spain illustrates contrasting approaches to managing the public finances. In some cases, such as Spain, fiscal policy helped keep the economy stable by allowing strong booms to swing the budget towards smaller deficits or a surplus and using periods of strong growth to speed up consolidation. This helped to stabilize longer-run cycles in credit and the real exchange rate and provided a cushion when growth slowed down because of external shocks or when households and firms came to feel overextended. Fiscal policy thus complemented and balanced strong private sector expansion. In other cases, such as Portugal, fiscal positions had to be tightened just when a strong and credit-fuelled domestic boom was ending, amplifying contractionary forces in the economy. Maintaining a strong fiscal stance during such periods will also help to moderate pressures for unwarranted real appreciation, but without generating the potentially sizeable fiscal costs of major sterilization operations.

A further lesson of fiscal experience in the converging EU economies lies in a challenge they are still confronting. This is that the institutional setting of policy can influence expectations favourably through sound governance, transparency, credibility and time-consistency, thus enhancing stability. For many of the member states that joined the EU in 2004, a key challenge is indeed to build credibility with markets that they can hold firm to budgetary commitments, overcoming the 'common pool problem'. Fiscal institutions can be designed in ways that help limit expenditure bias – a topic examined in depth in the European Commission Public Finance Report for 2005 (European Commission, 2005).

There are different approaches to achieving this. One is to delegate formation, monitoring and implementation of the budget to a single body, for instance, a finance minister with a leading role in the budgetary process. A further approach is to address fragmentation of the process by increased coordination among spending ministers and different levels of government through formalized rules and procedures. Most of the member states that joined the EU in 2004 have embarked on reforms in their fiscal institutions that embody elements of the latter approach. In recent years, most have introduced multi-year budgetary frameworks to internalize medium-term consequences of decisions on spending programmes and improve ex post monitoring. Many had already moved to integrate the activities of extra-budgetary funds in the budget process and to increase coordination of spending decisions across levels of government (Gleich, 2003; Ylaoutinen,

2004). It is important also not to create new sources of public debt outside the budget through a failure to control tightly the incurring of contingent liabilities through public-private partnerships.

Nonetheless, there is still room to strengthen fiscal governance in these countries, particularly in light of the 'reform fatigue' which (as in the Czech Republic, Hungary and Poland, for example) can easily set in after periods of strong adjustment effort. For example, agreement on how to use better than expected budgetary outcomes in 'good times' will be helpful to avoid loosening the stance of fiscal policy during periods of strong growth. Such a rule might be to dedicate all over-budget revenues to deficit and debt reduction, thus building a buffer during good times. Future reforms could also contribute to reducing the high share of expenditures that to be changed require additional legislation on top of the budget law, improving flexibility.

Strengthened practices for evaluating expenditure (for example, via cost–benefit analysis techniques in the selection of projects, periodic reviews of programmes, establishment of selected output-based indicators) could also contribute to increasing the effectiveness of expenditure and to achieving cost savings. A crucial element of all such approaches is sound and transparent fiscal data, following ESA 95 principles, which provide policymakers and markets with a reliable basis for assessment. Effective fiscal management will need to rely on a range of indicators, not just a few headline numbers; and it will need to incorporate key consistency checks in accounting areas such as stock-flow adjustments – as well as economic areas such as the compatibility of projections for sector balances in the economy.

As well as strengthening institutions, an approach that may improve trade-offs for fiscal policy lies its microeconomic aspects as these influence stability. A priority is to avoid distortions that can amplify cycles in the private sector (such as interest rate deductibility for mortgages, or other tax subsidies such as the now-discontinued car purchase scheme in Turkey). The design of funding programmes for the public debt can also help limit vulnerability to market shocks. A further structural issue relates to fiscal decentralization, which poses challenges in this regard among others. An overriding concern is that decentralization should not weaken expenditure control and the design of such mechanisms may inhibit stabilizers – a challenge in designing fiscal rules for lower levels of government (Daban et al., 2003).

The framework of the Pre-Accession Economic Programmes is an instrument that Turkey can use to its advantage in integrating these challenges for fiscal policy. In particular, this can help impart a more medium-term orientation to policy. The experience of recent candidates in using the PEP instrument has been mixed. These programmes should be seen not as simple projections but as vehicles for articulating medium-term strategy, defining supporting policies, including expenditure management priorities, and exploring risk scenarios. Strengthening the institutional underpinning of policy in such ways can enhance support for both growth and stabilization, improving potential trade-offs during the convergence process.

5. Final remarks

This comment on experience in accession countries and converging EU member states has been highly selective. It suggests a number of potential lessons in fostering the twin priorities of stability and growth. The experience is, of course, far richer than the present contribution might suggest. One of its leitmotifs is worth reiterating. It is that candidate countries have been able to use the accession process as a strong support in achieving reforms that were valuable in their own right. In terms of growth and stability, this included improving market mechanisms, strengthening institutions and reducing vulnerability to shocks.

In this regard, the challenges are interlinked. A strong medium-term macroeconomic framework can ensure debt sustainability and strengthen confidence, while also improving the quality of fiscal consolidation so as to make room for the financing of key public services. At the same time structural reforms can help energize private investment and improve productivity, so unlocking the country's growth potential. Some of these challenges are long term in nature, but because the reform agenda is complex, the efforts have to begin early on. Experience with strengthening markets and institutions in other candidate countries confirms that meeting these challenges will depend to a large extent on success in aligning frameworks with the *acquis communautaire*.

Experience, of course, never translates one-to-one across cases. A prudent insight would be broader: that the accession process and EU membership offer valuable access to a shared learning process in policy reform. This is not truly a lesson. It is an invitation to find, in ways closely tailored to Turkey's needs, a key route to benefit from the accession process, following in the steps of other strongly performing economies.

Notes

* The authors gratefully acknowledge contributions from Peter Grasmann, Siegfried Steinlein and Dirk Verbeken. The views expressed are the responsibility of the authors alone, and do not purport to represent views of the Directorate General for Economic and Financial Affairs or the European Commission.

1. On the policy mix tensions in Hungary and Poland, see Darnaut and Kutos (2005) and Kovacs and Moulin (2004).
2. For a discussion, see for example Caballero (2000) and Saint-Paul (1994).

References

Aghion, P., P. Bachetta and A. Banerjee (2004), 'Financial development and the instability of open economies', *Journal of Monetary Economics*, **51**, 1077–106.
Borio, C. and W. White (2003), 'Whither monetary and financial stability? The implications of evolving policy regimes', BIS.
Borio, C., C. Furfine and P. Lowe (2001), 'Procyclicality of the financial system and financial stability: issues and policy options', BIS.
Buiter, W. and C. Grafe (2003), 'Reforming EMU's fiscal policy rules: suggestions for enhancing fiscal sustainability and macroeconomic stability in the enlarged European Union', in M. Buti (ed.) *Monetary and Fiscal Policies in EMU – Interactions and Coordination*, Cambridge: Cambridge University Press, pp. 92ff.
Caballero, R.J. (2000), 'Macroeconomic volatility in Latin America: a view and three case studies', NBER Working Paper No. 7782.
Daban, T., E. Detragiache, G. Di Bella, G. Milesi-Ferretti and S. Symansky (2003), 'Rules-based fiscal policy in France, Germany, Italy and Spain', IMF Occasional Paper, 225.
Darnaut, N. and P. Kutos (2005), 'Poland's policy mix: fiscal or monetary leadership?', European Commission, Country Focus, **2** (1), http://europa.eu.int/comm/economy_finance/publications/countryfocus_en.htm.
European Commission (2005), *Public Finances in EMU – 2005*, European Economy.
Gleich, H. (2003), 'Budget institutions and fiscal performance in Central and Eastern European countries', European Central Bank, Working Paper Series, 215.
Jaeger, A. and L. Schuknecht (2004), 'Boom-bust phases in asset prices and fiscal policy behaviour', IMF Working Paper WP/04/54.
Kovacs, V. and L. Moulin (2004), 'Hungary's policy mix: from stabilisation to crisis to . . .?', European Commission, Country Focus, **1** (9), http://europa.eu.int/comm/economy_finance/publications/countryfocus_en.htm.
Lipschitz, L., T. Lane and A. Mourmouras (2002), 'Capital flows to transition economies – master or servant?', IMF Working Paper WP/02/11.
Saint-Paul, G. (1994), 'Monetary policy in economic transition: lessons from the French Post-War experience', *European Economic Review*, **38**, 891–8.
Ylaoutinen, S. (2004), 'Fiscal frameworks in Central and Eastern European countries', mimeo, Ministry of Finance of Finland.

10.2 MACROECONOMIC CHALLENGES FOR EU ACCESSION: THE CASE OF TURKEY

Pierre van der Haegen

It is a great honour to participate in this high level conference and to be given the opportunity to comment from an ECB perspective on some macroeconomic issues arising on Turkey's path to the EU. I accepted this invitation with all the more pleasure as being in Ankara today is a kind of anniversary for me: I came to Turkey for the first time exactly 40 years ago, in 1965, as a young student still in secondary school. I was not yet interested in economics, let alone in central banking, but I was struck by what I saw. The country was bursting with energy, with a youthful population, and thereby an enormous potential for growth and development. The still vivid memories I have of this first encounter have prompted me today to take a long-term perspective on developments in Turkey. I will therefore start my remarks by briefly reviewing Turkey's starting point in terms of macroeconomic stability. Second, I will analyse where the country currently stands. And I will conclude by outlining the major macroeconomic challenges Turkey is likely to face on the road to EU accession. As you can expect of a central banker, I will focus my contribution on monetary policy, inflation and the role of the central bank.

1. Where is Turkey coming from?

That striking impression of great energy and vast potential I got forty years ago still holds true today. As Ricardo Hausmann eloquently put it: 'this country is richly endowed with entrepreneurial spirits'. At the same time, when looking at the four decades between my first visit to Turkey and today, from an economic point of view, the results appear rather mixed. While progress in improving living standards, infrastructure and institutions is indisputable, over this period Turkey has, in fact, enjoyed a less impressive growth performance than some other emerging market economies with similar starting points. It has, until very recently, not been able to exploit its formidable growth potential to the full.

This is underpinned by casting a quick glance at some figures comparing Turkey with emerging Asian market economies such as South Korea, Thailand and Malaysia and also, for example, with Chile in Latin America. From the mid-1960s to the beginning of the new millennium (1968–2002) Turkish GDP per capita has increased by around 180 per cent. In the same period South Korea's GDP per capita grew by 740 per cent, Thailand's by 445 per cent, and Malaysia's by 370 per cent, while Chile's GDP per capita increased by 234 per cent.

These noticeable differences call for an explanation. I think it is widely agreed that a history of macroeconomic instability is one of the key factors explaining why the country has not been able to exploit its enormous growth potential over this period. The country has been characterized for decades by high inflation and high fiscal deficits, banking sector problems and financial crises, all of which point to great weaknesses in macroeconomic management. Inflation is one striking indicator of this macroeconomic instability. Turkey's annual average inflation rate over the last four decades was 40 per cent, while for instance in South Korea it was 9 per cent, in Thailand 5 per cent and in Malaysia 4 per cent.

The contrast in terms of macroeconomic stability between Turkey and some of the more successful emerging markets becomes even more pronounced when looking at the last 15 years. Indeed, Turkey was one of the few emerging market economies that was not able to bring down inflation during the 1990s, a period when most such economies made significant progress in terms of macroeconomic stabilization. Actually, at 62 per cent (1990–2004) Turkey's annual average inflation rate was even higher than in the decades before, while inflation rates in the countries mentioned above declined. Moreover, Central European transition economies such as Poland, Hungary and the Czech Republic, now member states of the EU, entered the global economic stage in the early 1990s. After an initial transition-related burst, these countries were also able to bring down inflation and subsequently increase GDP per capita somewhat faster than Turkey. In this period, the lack of fiscal discipline also stands out as another indicator of macroeconomic mismanagement as, on average, budget deficits exceeded 10 per cent of GDP.

In terms of unrealized growth potential, the price this country had to pay as a result of macroeconomic instability is also strikingly reflected in the numbers for FDI inflows. In many emerging markets FDI has been a key factor in enhancing growth. In Turkey, over the last 15 years annual FDI flows were less than 1 per cent of GDP on average. This compares with 6.5 per cent for Hungary, 6 per cent for the Czech Republic, 3 per cent for Poland, 5 per cent for Chile and Malaysia and 2.5 per cent for Thailand. Today, China attracts FDI flows of around 4 per cent of GDP per year. This list of illustrations could easily be lengthened. The rather poor figures for FDI inflows to Turkey are reflected in those for the FDI stock, which amounts to only around \$250 per capita in Turkey (2002). This compares with \$2100 for the eight Central and Eastern European states that joined the EU in 2004, to give just one example.

Accordingly, at a time when FDI flows were multiplying on the global scale, Turkey remained extremely weak in attracting FDI in spite of the size of its domestic market and its close integration with the EU (a customs union was established in 1995), features that made the country a potentially very attractive destination for FDI flows. However as international investors increasingly faced a choice between alternative FDI destinations with a stable macroeconomic environment, the high inflation rate became a negative trademark of Turkey, in particular during the 1990s. Even putting aside all the other well known negative effects of high inflation, this 'negative trademark' effect of high inflation in an environment of increasing stability is a compelling reason for bringing down inflation to the low levels prevailing in those destinations competing with Turkey for FDI, mainly countries in the region which is often referred to as 'emerging Europe'.

2. Where does Turkey stand?

I have taken a few moments to highlight these past developments because they allow me to highlight the magnitude of the transformation process on which the country has embarked since 2001 and to stress the key requirements for success in the longer-term perspective. Macroeconomic developments over the last four years, since the 2001 crisis, have indeed been impressive, with strong growth and a fast pace of disinflation, supported by enhanced fiscal discipline and progress in structural reforms. In particular, the progress in disinflation has been remarkable, given the high and persistent levels of inflation in the past. The key question that arises in this context is whether the recent developments represent a structural break with the past or whether they are just another short-lived boom in an economy that, for a long time, faced boom and bust cycles and policy reversals.

A break with the past . . . If I turn to the area of central banking and monetary policy, I find good arguments to support the notion of a structural break with the past. The key development here is the greatly enhanced independence of the Central Bank of the Republic of Turkey (CBRT) as a result of the Central Bank Law enacted in May 2001. This law grants the CBRT a high degree of instrument independence, sets price stability as its primary objective and forbids lending to the government. Even if further amendments have to be made at a later stage to bring the Central Bank Law fully into line with the *acquis communautaire*, the law of 2001 constitutes a significant rapprochement to the *acquis*. It marks a break with past central bank legislation and practice in Turkey. Enhanced central bank independence has been a key ingredient in Turkey's macroeconomic stabilization during the last four years. That being said, it is an asset that needs not only to be enshrined in law, but also lived up to and respected in practice. Experience reveals that the latter may at times be difficult, when central bank independence is a relatively new concept that does not have deep roots in the political culture of a country. I sincerely hope that this great institutional achievement of enhanced central bank independence in Turkey is irreversible and I would welcome any further steps bringing Turkey even closer to and finally fully into line with the *acquis* in this area.

The success achieved by the CBRT on the basis of the new institutional framework can hardly be overemphasized. The CBRT has met or undershot its end-year inflation objectives in three consecutive years – 2002, 2003 and 2004. It brought inflation down to single-digit levels in the course of last year. Inflation expectations have for some time now been in line with the year-end inflation objectives and that is also the case for this year's objective of 8 per cent. This is a striking achievement, as breaking inflation inertia is a formidable challenge in a country with Turkey's track record, all the more so as fiscal dominance of monetary policy has receded only gradually. The smooth introduction of the new Turkish lira by the beginning of 2005 was another very encouraging step, which was made possible by the successful disinflation process and may also support a further reduction in inflation rates by instilling public confidence in the domestic currency. Disinflation, inflation expectations in line with objectives, the introduction of the new Turkish lira and the beginning of reverse currency substitution all point to the credibility that the CBRT has gained since 2001 as an independent central bank. This success is, of course, not only the result of the new institutional framework. In its 2004 Article IV report on Turkey the IMF states 'The CBRT's skilful use of monetary policy has been central to this success'. I have nothing to add to this assessment from an ECB perspective. It clearly points out that, over the last four years, the CBRT has made wise use of its newly gained independence, and done so with remarkable professionalism. I should probably add that, key to its success, monetary policy has been assisted by a remarkable turnaround in fiscal policy, about which I will say a few more words later on.

. . . but a difficult legacy Of course, notwithstanding the impressive achievements in terms of macroeconomic stabilization over the last four years, the legacy of the past still places a heavy burden on the country. This is reflected not least in high real interest rates which, despite a significant decline, remain among the highest in the world. In combination with the still high level of public debt, they result in high interest payments, which put the budget and the economy under considerable strain. Bond spreads also point to the difficult legacy. While Turkish bond spreads have fallen significantly, from around 1000 basis points back in 2002 to around 300 basis points now, they still remain three times as high as those of the other EU candidate countries (Bulgaria, Croatia and Romania). They also

sometimes tend to react quite strongly to reversals in market sentiment vis-à-vis emerging markets, as experienced in April–May 2004, and to regional and domestic political disturbances.

The fact that Turkey and the IMF have recently agreed a new three-year stand-by arrangement to follow the one that expired in February 2005 is another reflection of these continued vulnerabilities that are a legacy of the past. While it may have been tempting to argue that in view of the macro-economic stabilization achieved in the last four years, now would be the right time for Turkey to graduate from long-standing IMF support, as Brazil recently decided to do, the legacy of the last four decades is still too heavy to be ignored. In any event, the IMF has, alongside the perspective of accession to the EU, been a crucial external anchor to Turkey over the last four years and has significantly contributed to the remarkable economic performance of the country since 2001. In this context I would like to stress that Turkey's EU accession process and the continuation and further strengthening of policies under the new IMF programme should be seen as complementary and mutually reinforcing in order to anchor policy discipline and foster market confidence.

3. Key macroeconomic challenges on the road to EU accession

It goes without saying that the road to Turkey's ultimate objective, accession to the EU, is a long one and that the challenges lying ahead are considerable. The key challenge for Turkey over the next decade will be to further advance and entrench macroeconomic stability. What does this mean in concrete terms?

In the area of monetary and exchange rate policy, advancing disinflation further is key. The experience of other former high inflation countries shows that reducing inflation from high double-digit levels to high single-digit levels may sometimes prove to be easier than moving on from high single-digit levels to a reasonable degree of price stability. Completing the disinflation process and achieving low and stable inflation rates would enable Turkey to further reduce the still high interest rates and risk premia, thereby significantly alleviating the burden on the budget. Dealing with capital inflows, which can be expected both to increase and to be substantial in the course of the EU accession process, is another issue that Turkish policymakers will have to face up to, and this has already been extensively discussed during previous sessions in this conference.

Fortunately, the CBRT can build on its achievements of the past four years for advancing disinflation further and dealing with forthcoming challenges. The exchange rate regime, a free float with discretionary foreign exchange interventions limited to smoothing volatility, has served the country well since 2001. This new regime, established after the failed attempt back in 2001 at exchange rate-based stabilization, necessitated the search for a new, domestic anchor for monetary policy. This led to the CBRT's strategy of implicit inflation targeting, which combines end-year inflation objectives with monetary targets set under the IMF programmes. The strategy has so far been successful, as reflected by disinflation. The CBRT has announced the transition to a formal inflation-targeting regime by 2006. Some steps have already been taken in 2005 to enhance the transparency of monetary policy decision-making with a view to this transition in 2006. These steps, such as the strengthened role for the Monetary Policy Committee and greater clarity on the timing of interest rate decisions, are very much to be welcomed.

Besides completing the necessary technical preparations, such as developing inflation forecasting capabilities and a solid understanding of the monetary transmission mechanism, the key precondition for the success of inflation targeting is policy credibility. In my view, the CBRT has been well advised in being cautious as regards the timing of the transition to a formal inflation targeting regime. It was indeed wise to avoid a premature introduction of the new framework. First, inflation rates were still high compared with other emerging market economies that had moved to inflation targeting. Second, fiscal discipline is the key to credibility and fiscal dominance has dissipated only gradually. Accordingly, the conditions for a successful implementation of formal inflation targeting were not yet fully in place. However, the prospects are good for a successful start of the new framework in 2006, if fiscal discipline is fully adhered to.

This brings me to the subject of fiscal policy. While fiscal dominance of monetary policy has receded, continued fiscal discipline is crucial for further entrenching macroeconomic stability in Turkey. Continued fiscal discipline – as reflected in ambitious primary surplus targets – needs to be complemented by an improvement in the quality of fiscal consolidation. This is not only important to the continuation of the disinflation process, it is also the key to ensuring debt sustainability, as despite recent improvements both the level and the structure of Turkish public debt continue to be a major source of vulnerability and as any relaxation of fiscal policy would immediately translate into higher interest rates. Some might object, saying that continuing with high primary surpluses would be detrimental to economic growth. However, Turkey's record over the last four years is an example par excellence of how rapid disinflation and tight fiscal policies can go hand in hand with buoyant economic growth.

Another challenge is the high current account deficit, which has emerged as an issue against the background of the otherwise satisfactory macroeconomic performance during recent years. While it can be debated whether the level as such (around 5 per cent of GDP in 2004) is a source of concern or whether, for instance, it primarily reflects the growth differential between Turkey and its main trading partners, the quality of financing is an issue that needs to be addressed. In the absence of significant FDI inflows, Turkey has so far mainly relied on short-term financing. This reliance on short-term capital inflows has created a vulnerability to shifts in market sentiment, as experienced for instance in April–May 2004, when expectations about a tightening of monetary conditions in the United States led to a general weakening of emerging market sentiment. It could be argued that with a floating exchange rate regime a depreciation of the currency would be the natural channel to address a high current account deficit. While this is obviously true, it has to be kept in mind that in Turkey both debt dynamics and the disinflation process could be negatively affected by a sharp depreciation of the exchange rate, implying that the floating exchange rate regime needs to be supported by appropriate monetary and fiscal policies.

Furthermore, as in other countries with a similar long-term track record, the continuation of the structural reform process in Turkey is crucial to underpinning macroeconomic stabilization. This applies, for example, to social security, where it is striking that a country with a favourable demographic structure like Turkey's produces a deficit of above 4 per cent of GDP (2004) in its social security system. It also holds true for the banking sector. A sound and functioning banking sector is key to both enhancing financial intermediation and thereby realizing growth potential and to an effective monetary policy. Much has been achieved since 2001 in Turkey with regard to reforming the banking sector, whose problems were at the root of the 2001 crisis. Now it is important to complete this reform process, for example by bringing the supervisory framework further into line with international best practice and by privatizing state banks. The hitherto very low level of foreign participation in the Turkish banking sector compared with that in the new EU member states and EU candidate countries is another aspect of the general weakness in attracting FDI and the particular problems of the banking sector in Turkey in the past. However very recently there have been some encouraging signs that this might be about to change, with some euro area banks showing interest in buying Turkish banks.

Overarching these issues is the challenge to maintain the momentum for structural reforms and macroeconomic stabilization. Reform fatigue combined with complacency and overconfidence might become a risk on the road to EU accession, in particular as the process is expected to span around a decade. A lasting commitment to stability-oriented macro policies and a continuation of the structural reform process are indispensable to keeping Turkey on a sustainable track and to achieving the ultimate objectives of macroeconomic stability and economic structures that are both comparable and compatible with the EU. While Turkey's EU accession process will probably resemble a marathon rather than a sprint, increasing macroeconomic and institutional convergence with the EU will be highly beneficial for the country even prior to full membership. The process as such will allow Turkey to reap the benefits of the already existing high degree of integration with the EU. A firm membership perspective would reassure investors that economic policies will remain on track, lead to an upfront reduction of risk premia, and position Turkey as an increasingly attractive destination for FDI flows. In this respect, the experience of the new EU member states should encourage Turkey.

Let me conclude by summarizing my key messages:

(1) First, Turkey has made remarkable progress in terms of macroeconomic stabilization and structural reforms in a surprisingly short time. This is in stark contrast to past economic and policy performance, the legacy of which still places a heavy burden on the country. Disinflation, the independence of the CBRT and its skilful steering of monetary policy have been the key factors in this success. Greater fiscal discipline has been the other indispensable ingredient.

(2) Second, Turkey's achievements so far have been very encouraging, but overconfidence, complacency and reform fatigue may pose risks. If they are avoided, the country will have demonstrated that the past four years have not been just another short-lived boom in an environment of policy volatility.

(3) Third, the country is in an excellent position to reap great rewards from a lasting commitment to macroeconomic stability. It will also be able to gain substantially from closer integration with the EU, irrespective of when the ultimate goal of full membership is attained.

10.3 MACRO POLICY CHALLENGES FOR TURKEY: SOME COMMENTS

Ricardo Hausmann

Back in the late 1980s and early 1990s an approach to economic policy emerged that became known as the Washington Consensus. That approach implied achieving macroeconomic stability, undertaking an expanding list of structural reforms and promoting education in the context of an improved political regime. Many countries took this agenda to heart and put in place many of the agreed reforms. Inflation was brought under control, the economy was opened, the public sector was scaled back through privatization, financial systems were restructured and educational systems were expanded. However, in many cases, as in much of Latin America or South Africa, growth was disappointing. This has lead to a rethinking of growth strategies.

In this brief comment, I would like to present a framework on how to improve on the way we diagnose countries and to apply it to Turkey to see what view emerges.

Consider the following proposition. The amount of income a society can expect to make depends on three elements. First, the amount of physical and human assets it can deploy, the productivity with which it can use those assets and the appropriability of the returns that those assets will generate. Hence, we can write:

$$\text{Income} = \text{accumulated assets} \times \text{productivity} \times \text{appropriability}$$

To accelerate growth, countries are advised to work on all three fronts.

(1) First, to accelerate the accumulation of assets by increasing savings (through greater public savings, social security reform and financial reform), education and health.
(2) Second, to increase the productivity of those assets by opening up the economy, privatizing state-owned enterprises, improving competition policy, increasing flexibility of labour and other markets, and so on.
(3) Third, to improve appropriability by maintaining low and predictable taxes, by lowering the risk of macroeconomic crises by maintaining prudent fiscal, monetary and banking policies, by reducing corruption, red tape and crime and by improving contract enforcement and the rule of law.

Hence, in the pursuit of these strategies, countries are usually given a long laundry list of necessary reforms. Countries are told to reform what they can as much as they can, with no sense of priority. This advice rests on the following assumptions: (i) any reform is good; (ii) the more areas reformed, the better; and (iii) the deeper the reform in any area, the better. But the problem is that economic theory provides no reason to think any of these assumptions are true. In fact, the theorem of the second-best clearly shows that when there is more than one distortion in the economy, a reform designed to reduce that distortion is not guaranteed to have positive effects. The problem is that there is an interaction between distortions and hence the effect of partial reform on growth and welfare can be big, small or even negative. For example, a reform to lower distortionary taxes, to privatize social security or to lower trade tariffs may raise the fiscal deficit and worsen macro stability. So when there are a large number of distortions, eliminating one distortion is not necessarily welfare enhancing.

We are in need of an alternative method which would focus attention on those reforms that are more likely to have net positive effects. As argued in Hausmann et al. (2004) one way of doing it is by focusing on the most binding constraint. Instead of offering an un-prioritized laundry list, this approach would focus on relaxing the constraint that would offer the biggest growth pay-off. Such a diagnostic approach would allow governments to invest political capital in those reforms that will bring the largest real effects.

Growth diagnostics

Consider the following proposition: output is a function of physical capital, human capital, infrastructure, institutions, and so on. Moreover, these factors are all complements (rather than substitutes), meaning that the more you have of one, the better it is to get more of the others. We know that this is a sensible assumption because rich countries have more of all those elements than poor countries. Suppose now that output is particularly constrained by one of those factors, say infrastructure. This would imply that the marginal return of that factor will be particularly large. However, because infrastructure is in such short supply, it will drive down the returns to all other factors: it will be hard to invest private capital or to effectively use labour because of the infrastructure constraint. Hence, the binding constraint will have a high actual or shadow price while the non-binding constraints will exhibit low prices.

To identify what that most binding constraint is, we must become attuned to diagnostic signals. Shadow prices and the dynamic effects of changes in the constraint are often the best form of direct evidence. If low education is a serious problem, the return to education should be high and unemployment of educated people should be low. If investment is savings constrained, interest rates should be high and growth should respond vigorously to changes in available savings (for example inflows of foreign resources). If poor transport links are a serious constraint, we should observe bottlenecks and high private costs for transport.

As measurable relevant shadow prices cannot be identified for every potential constraint, we can also consider indirect evidence. Thoughtful observation of the current state can signal what constraints are binding. If you have trouble figuring out why there are so few animals in the Sahara, you may actually benefit from noting that the few animals there are, tend to be camels rather than hippopotami. This might tell you something about the role of water as a potential explanation, since camels are so efficient at using it. Analogously, when economic constraints bind, they result in activities designed to get around them. For example, high taxes lead to high informality, poor legal institutions lead to a high demand for informal mechanisms of conflict resolution and contract enforcement and poor financial intermediation leads to the internalization of finance in large business groups. The key with indirect evidence is that more than one hypothesized constraint may be consistent with what is observed, so the diagnostic process requires the systematic exclusion of other causes of observed states of nature.

The result is a systematic approach to diagnosing the binding constraints to growth, illustrated in Figure 10.3.1.

The idea is to start from the top and to ask: what is limiting investment and entrepreneurship. Is it lack of finance or low returns to investment? And if it is the former, is it caused by domestic or international sources of finance? And if domestic, is it because of low savings or because those savings cannot be adequately mobilized.

Alternatively, if people do not invest because the perceived returns are low, is it because the returns are really low, or is it because they fear that those returns will not be appropriable? And so on.

What is the binding constraint in Turkey?

Let us apply this framework to Turkey. Here is a country where we observe very high real interest rates. Yet, despite this high cost of borrowing, investment exceeds savings by 5 per cent of GDP, that is, by a sum equal to the rather hefty current account deficit. This suggests that there are ample returns available in the economy. Furthermore, changes in financing constraints apparently have large effects on output. For example, the increase in foreign savings in 2004 was translated into 9.9 per cent growth. Based on this evidence, I conclude that the savings rate is the binding constraint on growth in Turkey.

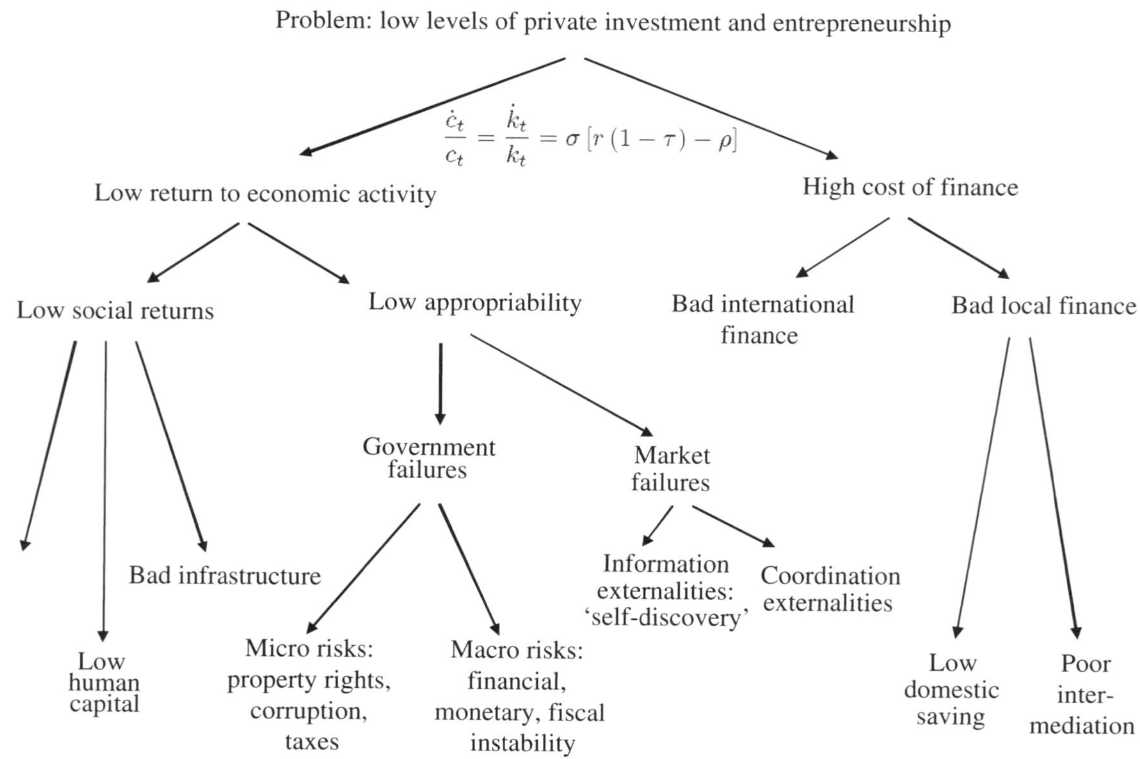

Figure 10.3.1 A decision tree for growth diagnostics

The next question is what causes the low savings rates in Turkey. The cause is probably fiscal. The government has had to appropriate a very large chunk of national income in order to pay the obligations it has assumed over time, including a very large stock of debt. Moreover, in spite of a very large primary surplus, the overall position of the government is still in deficit so that in net terms, the government does not contribute to national savings. This leaves the private sector with a rather diminished after-tax income with which to provide all the national savings, and these happen to be highly insufficient given the large number of investment ideas that Turkish entrepreneurs have. Hence, the country has been overly reliant on external savings and these have run against borrowing limits, causing the country to have recurrent balance of payments crises. In the end, foreign savings cannot be a permanent source of financing as the external debt needs to be paid back. Hence, in the final analysis the country is restricted by its paltry domestic savings.

How to 'loosen' the binding constraint?

By following the evidence, this diagnostic exercise has revealed where Turkey lies on the decision tree: low domestic savings. As a result, it reveals how the response can be prioritized to generate the biggest pay-off on growth.

The priority for the government is to improve public savings by maintaining a large primary surplus and pursuing social security reform. Equally important is what this diagnostic shows is *not* a priority for growth. Improving the investment climate is not a priority at this point because despite its defects, investment exceeds savings. In fact, improving the investment climate further would force the central bank to raise interest rates in order to bring investment back in balance with available savings, but the increased interest rate would worsen the debt dynamics and do potential harm to macroeconomic stability. In addition, lowering taxes in an attempt to avoid microeconomic distortions or improve business climate would also be ineffectual, as it would most likely cause a reduction in government savings and hence would worsen the binding constraint, while not causing much increase in investment as there would not be additional savings to fund it.

Monetary policy

Regarding monetary policy, long-run economic growth in Turkey will depend on the growth of exports. But discovering new opportunities abroad for export is difficult and involves many market failures (Hausmann and Rodrik, 2003). A competitive and stable real exchange rate is very helpful to this process. The level of the real exchange rate affects the profitability of exports and the incentives to experiment and explore in new areas. The volatility of the real exchange rate increases the relative risk of investing in tradables vis-à-vis nontradables, causing the economy to become less open and dynamic (Hausmann and Rigobon, 2003). The dual of the real exchange rate is the current account deficit. Unsustainably large current account deficits often lead to currency collapses that complicate the achievement of the central bank's inflation target as well as other macro objectives.

Most models of inflation targeting assume that the central bank has a loss function that includes deviations of inflation from its target and deviations of output from full employment. There are no provisions for deviations of the real exchange rate from what is perceived as equilibrium levels or deviations of the current account from what seems prudent and reasonable. In practice, central banks do think about these issues, but lack the formal framework for incorporating these considerations and communicating them to the market.

Hence, I would propose amending the central bank's loss function with either a term for the deviation of the real exchange rate from its equilibrium or the current account from a sustainable position. This will mean that the market should expect the policies of the central bank to react to perceived deviations from the equilibrium real exchange rate. The central bank should be very clear in communicating its views as to where it believes the equilibrium real exchange rate is, but tolerate significant deviation from this level without explicit bands. Furthermore, the credible pursuit of both a stable real exchange rate and inflation rate means that the central bank should commit to acting with more than one instrument, as discussed below.

Can the central bank know where the equilibrium real exchange rate lies? One context in which to think about it is the Salter–Swan model. Consider Figure 10.3.2, where we place the real exchange rate in the y-axis and the level of aggregate domestic spending on the x-axis. The real exchange rate is defined in such a way that a higher value implies a more depreciated exchange rate. We present two curves. The upward slopping BB curve represents external balance. It is upward sloping because, starting from equilibrium, an increase in aggregate demand would cause an external deficit. To return to equilibrium, a real depreciation is needed. The downward sloping NN curve represents full employment. It slopes down because starting from equilibrium, a real appreciation would cause unemployment. To return to full employment, domestic demand would need to increase. Above (below) the BB curve the balance of payments is in surplus (deficit). Above (below) the NN curve the labour market is in overheating (unemployment).

Where is Turkey? Clearly the country still has significant unemployment and a rather large external deficit. This suggests that the achievement of both external and internal balance would require a more depreciated real exchange rate.

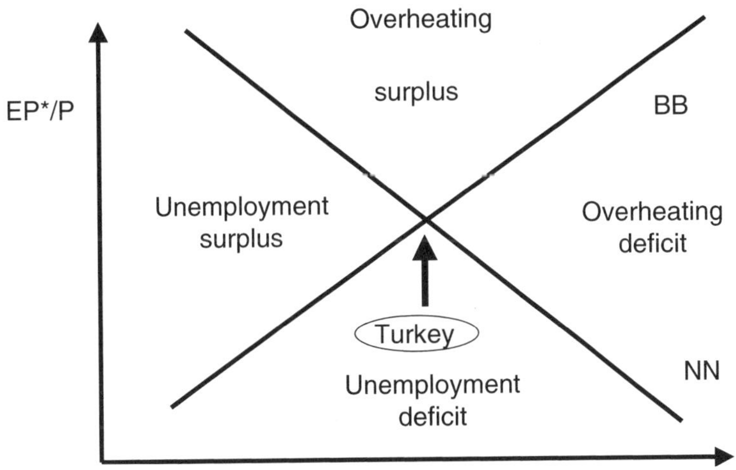

Figure 10.3.2 *Real exchange rate, domestic demand and the conditions for external and internal balance*

Influencing the real exchange rate

There are a variety of instruments at Turkey's disposal to influence the exchange rate. First, obviously, is the policy interest rate, which could respond not only to deviations of inflation from its target, but also to deviations of the real exchange rate from its target. But it is ideal to have more instruments to optimize the trade-off between the policy goals. An additional instrument is foreign exchange intervention. After all, the interest rate determines the demand for base money, but the central bank is free to supply it with either net foreign assets or net domestic credit. If these two types of assets are not perfect substitutes, then the composition of the central bank's balance sheet is an instrument of policy. On the same lines, the composition of the public debt between lira and foreign currency assets is an additional instrument. Financial policy can be used by changing either reserve requirements or capital adequacy requirements to affect credit expansion for any given interest rate. In the domain of the capital account, the government can introduce unremunerated reserve requirements or other restrictions on capital inflows. And as always, fiscal policy is a possibility.

One potential strategy is to have three elements: first, a clear commitment to the inflation and the real exchange rate targets; second, to back that commitment with a sufficiently large arsenal of instruments capable of achieving the goals; third, to adopt an imprecise reaction function in order to create 'constructive ambiguity' and stimulate stabilizing speculation.

Clearly, the pursuit of a real depreciation to stimulate growth suggests that Turkey should not commit to Article VIII of the International Monetary

Fund Articles of Agreement. Capital account convertibility is not a priority for the country. It will not attract the kind of foreign savings that are needed. Foreign greenfield investors will be more positively impacted by the commitment to real exchange rate stability than to the openness of the capital account. The experience of China in this respect is fairly conclusive.

In addition, the goal of maintaining a stable real exchange rate suggests that Turkey should not commit to predictable foreign exchange interventions. There is nothing to be gained by eliminating the volatility of the level of reserves if that involves dumping that volatility in the exchange rate. If the demand for lira assets is volatile, let that volatility be expressed in the supply of money and the level of reserves rather than in the price of money.

More generally, in a volatile and unpredictable world, explicit rules are too rigid. The challenge is to develop effective monetary institutions that instead of rules are able to manage discretion without abusing it, and that are open to new information and learning.

Concluding remarks

I am optimistic about Turkey. The country has the investment ideas and the entrepreneurs to make the economy grow. Because of a difficult fiscal legacy, it lacks the savings to finance those investment ideas. A sustained tight fiscal policy in the context of an expanding economy will diminish the tightness of this constraint and allow for more growth. The central bank has done a remarkable job in bringing inflation down. It needs now to move to a policy stance that can assure the sustainability of the balance of payments and an adequate level and stability of the real exchange rate. Compared to the recent policy achievements, this seems a feasible task. This makes me even more optimistic.

References

Hausmann, R. and R. Rigobon (2003), 'An alternative interpretation of the "resource curse": theory and policy implications', in J.M. Davis, R. Ossowski and A. Fedelino (eds), *Fiscal Policy Formulation and Implementation in Oil-producing Countries*, Washington, DC: IMF Press.

Hausmann, R. and D. Rodrik (2003), 'Economic development as self-discovery', *Journal of Development Economics*, **72** (2), December, 603–33.

Hausmann, R., D. Rodrik and A. Velasco (2004), 'Growth diagnostics', mimeo, Harvard University.

Index

Abbreviations used in the index include:
CBT – Central Bank of Turkey
ECB – European Central Bank